T0326204

small arms survey 2008

risk and resilience

THE GRADUATE INSTITUTE | GENEVA

INSTITUT DE HAUTES ÉTUDES
INTERNATIONALES ET DU DÉVELOPPEMENT

GRADUATE INSTITUTE OF INTERNATIONAL
AND DEVELOPMENT STUDIES

CAMBRIDGE
UNIVERSITY PRESS

Shaftesbury Road, Cambridge CB2 8EA, United Kingdom

One Liberty Plaza, 20th Floor, New York, NY 10006, USA

477 Williamstown Road, Port Melbourne, VIC 3207, Australia

314–321, 3rd Floor, Plot 3, Splendor Forum, Jasola District Centre, New Delhi – 110025, India

103 Penang Road, #05–06/07, Visioncrest Commercial, Singapore 238467

Cambridge University Press is part of Cambridge University Press & Assessment,
a department of the University of Cambridge.

We share the University's mission to contribute to society through the pursuit of
education, learning and research at the highest international levels of excellence.

www.cambridge.org
Information on this title: www.cambridge.org/9780521706551

First published 2008

A catalogue record for this publication is available from the British Library

ISBN   978-0-521-88040-4   Hardback
ISBN   978-0-521-70655-1   Paperback

FOREWORD

In many parts of the world, armed violence is a daily occurrence. Whether because of repressive regimes, civil war, or widespread criminality, the health and security needs of many people go tragically unmet in war-torn regions such as Sudan's Darfur—as well as in places at peace, such as Rio de Janeiro, Port-au-Prince, and Nairobi.

I have fought hard for the international community to recognize its collective obligation to assist populations in danger, and to intervene to alleviate acute suffering due to violence. Over the past 40 years, the principle of humanitarian intervention has helped motivate relief efforts in the Democratic Republic of the Congo, Chad, Cambodia, Somalia, Haiti, and elsewhere. But intervention is not always possible, and when it is, access to health care for violence-affected populations often disappears after aid workers depart.

It is therefore essential that we also focus on ways to improve the long-term health of communities at risk of armed violence. This is not only a matter of health promotion, but of security provision, good governance, and sustainable development. It is a complex, delicate project that requires the expertise of many disciplines and collaboration of many sectors. It means working at the macro-level, to understand the political, social, and other factors that give rise to violence, as well as at the micro-level, where specific local conditions may influence an individual's decision to use violence. When we look at violence in these ways, we readily recognize patterns that can be used to inform our responses.

The *Small Arms Survey 2008: Risk and Resilience* provides compelling evidence for expanding our approach to armed violence reduction from one focused on treating symptoms to one that also aims at prevention. This volume shines a light on public health-based efforts to identify risk and resilience factors of armed violence as well as a number of recent interventions. The 2008 *Survey* is a vital resource for policy-makers at all levels in our continuing collective work to protect populations at risk.

—**Bernard Kouchner**
French Minister of Foreign
and European Affairs

CONTENTS

Chapter 5. Who's Buying? End-user Certification

Chapter 6. The Meaning of Loss: Firearms Diversion in South Africa

Comic Strip. Adventures of a Would-be Arms Dealer

Chapter 7. Reducing Armed Violence: The Public Health Approach

Chapter 8. Risk and Resilience: Understanding the Potential for Violence

Chapter 9. Targeting Armed Violence: Public Health Interventions

Index

ABOUT THE SMALL ARMS SURVEY

The Small Arms Survey is an independent research project located at the Graduate Institute of International and Development Studies in Geneva, Switzerland. Established in 1999, the project is supported by the Swiss Federal Department of Foreign Affairs and by sustained contributions from the Governments of Belgium, Canada, Finland, the Netherlands, Norway, Sweden, and the United Kingdom. The Survey is also grateful for past and current project support received from the Governments of Australia, Denmark, France, Germany, New Zealand, and the United States, as well as from different United Nations agencies, programmes, and institutes.

The objectives of the Small Arms Survey are: to be the principal source of public information on all aspects of small arms and armed violence; to serve as a resource centre for governments, policy-makers, researchers, and activists; to monitor national and international initiatives (governmental and non-governmental) on small arms; to support efforts to address the effects of small arms proliferation and misuse; and to act as a clearinghouse for the sharing of information and the dissemination of best practices. The Survey also sponsors field research and information-gathering efforts, especially in affected states and regions. The project has an international staff with expertise in security studies, political science, law, economics, development studies, and sociology, and collaborates with a network of researchers, partner institutions, non-governmental organizations, and governments in more than 50 countries.

NOTES TO READERS

Abbreviations: Lists of abbreviations can be found at the end of each chapter.

Chapter cross-referencing: Chapter cross-references appear capitalized in brackets throughout the text. For example, in Chapter 8 on Risk and Resilience: 'This instrument can be a knife, a stick, a broken bottle, a firearm, or any item used to intentionally inflict harm on another individual or oneself (PUBLIC HEALTH APPROACH).'

Exchange rates: All monetary values are expressed in current US dollars (USD). When other currencies are also cited, unless otherwise indicated, they are converted to USD using the 365-day average exchange rate for the period 1 September 2006 to 31 August 2007.

Small Arms Survey: The plain text—Small Arms Survey—is used to indicate the overall project and its activities, while the italicized version—*Small Arms Survey*—refers to the publication. The *Survey,* appearing italicized, refers generally to past and future editions.

Web site: For more detailed information and current developments on small arms issues, readers are invited to visit the Small Arms Survey Web site at www.smallarmssurvey.org.

Small Arms Survey

Graduate Institute of International and Development Studies

47 Avenue Blanc, 1202 Geneva, Switzerland

t +41 22 908 5777

f +41 22 732 2738

e sas@smallarmssurvey.org

w www.smallarmssurvey.org

ACKNOWLEDGEMENTS

This is the eighth edition of the *Small Arms Survey*. Like previous editions, it is a collective product of the staff of the Small Arms Survey project, based at the Graduate Institute of International and Development Studies in Geneva, Switzerland, with support from partners. Numerous researchers in Geneva and around the world have contributed to this volume, and it has benefited from the input and advice of government officials, advocates, experts, and colleagues from the small arms research community and beyond.

The principal chapter authors were assisted by in-house and external contributors who are acknowledged in the relevant chapters. In addition, detailed reviews of the chapters were provided by: Philip Alpers, Neil Arya, Michael Ashkenazi, Ian Biddle, Todd Clear, Emperatriz Crespin, Peter Danssaert, Andrew Ebbens, Anne-Kathrin Glatz, Chandre Gould, Hugh Griffiths, Stephen Hargarten, David Hemenway, Richard Jones, Adèle Kirsten, Herbert Krauss, Guy Lamb, Gary Littlejohn, Jim Mercy, Maxim Piadushkin, Daniël Prins, Matt Schroeder, Camilla Waszink, and Adrian Wilkinson.

Eric G. Berman, Keith Krause, Emile LeBrun, and Glenn McDonald were responsible for the overall planning and organization of this edition. Tania Inowlocki managed the editing and production of the *Survey* with the help of Annette Ezekiel. Alex Potter and Michael James copy-edited the book; Jillie Luff

Small Arms Survey 2008

Editors
Eric G. Berman, Keith Krause, Emile LeBrun, and Glenn McDonald

Publications Manager
Tania Inowlocki

Designer
Richard Jones, Exile: Design & Editorial Services

Cartographer
Jillie Luff, MAP*grafix*

Copy-editors
Michael James and Alex Potter

Proofreader
Donald Strachan

Principal chapter authors

Introduction	Emile LeBrun
Chapter 1	Eric G. Berman and Jonah Leff
Chapter 2	James Bevan
Chapter 3	Aaron Karp
Chapter 4	Matt Schroeder, Helen Close, and Chris Stevenson
Chapter 5	Glenn McDonald
Chapter 6	Gregory Mthembu-Salter and Guy Lamb
Chapter 7	Jennifer M. Hazen
Chapter 8	Jennifer M. Hazen
Chapter 9	Jennifer M. Hazen and Chris Stevenson

produced the maps; Richard Jones provided the layout and design; Donald Strachan proofread the *Survey*; and Margaret Binns compiled the index. Ceri Thomas of Daly Design created the illustrations in Chapter 1 and Robert Butler of Constructive Lines produced the comic strip on pages 202–09 based on investigative work carried out by Brian Johnson-Thomas. John Haslam, Carrie Cheek, and Alison Powell of Cambridge University Press provided support throughout the production of the *Survey*. Katherine Aguirre Tobón, Sarah Hoban, Ben King, Jasna Lazarevic, Sarah Parker, Chris Stevenson, and Savannah de Tessières assisted with fact-checking. David Olivier, Benjamin Pougnier, and Carole Touraine provided administrative support.

The project also benefited from the support of the Graduate Institute of International and Development Studies, in particular Philippe Burrin, Oliver Jütersonke, and Monique Nathoo.

We are extremely grateful to the Swiss government—especially the Department for Foreign Affairs and the Swiss Development Cooperation—for its generous financial and overall support of the Small Arms Survey project, in particular Erwin Bollinger, Jean-François Cuénod, Thomas Greminger, Anna Ifkovits Horner, Cristina Hoyos, Roman Hunger, Peter Maurer, Kurt Raëz, Jean-Daniel Ruch, Jürg Streuli, Anton Thalmann, Reto Wollenmann, and Othmar Wyss. Financial support for the project was also provided by the Governments of Belgium, Canada, Denmark, Finland, Germany, the Netherlands, Norway, Sweden, the United Kingdom, and the United States.

In addition, during 2007 the Survey received financial support for various projects from within the framework of the European Cooperation in the field of Scientific and Technical Research (COST), the Francophonie, the Organisation for Economic Co-operation and Development, the UN Development Programme, and the UN Institute for Disarmament Research. The project further benefits from the support of international agencies, including the International Committee of the Red Cross, the UN Office for Disarmament Affairs, the UN High Commissioner for Refugees, the UN Office on Drugs and Crime, and the World Health Organization.

In Geneva, the project has received support and expert advice from: David Atwood, Megan Bastick, Peter Batchelor, Robin Coupland, Paul Eavis, Nicolas Florquin, Gillian Frost, Richard Garfield, Karin Grimm, Magnus Hellgren, Kari Kahiluoto, Judit Kiss, Patricia Lewis, Patrick Mc Carthy, Jennifer Milliken, and Marc-Antoine Morel.

Beyond Geneva, we also received support from a number of colleagues. In addition to those mentioned above, and in specific chapters, we would like to thank: Michael Cassandra, Pablo Dreyfus, Debarati Guha-Sapir, Yeshua Moser-Puangsuwan, Josh Sugarmann, and Alex Vines.

Our sincere thanks go out to many other individuals (who remain unnamed) for their continuing support of the project. Our apologies to anyone we have failed to mention.

—Keith Krause, Programme Director
Eric G. Berman, Managing Director

On a rooftop in Medellín, Colombia, teenage members of the '29' gang show off their arsenal. © Sam Faulkner/NB Pictures

Introduction

Armed violence is a complex phenomenon that is usefully viewed from a number of different perspectives. When examining large-scale armed conflict or criminality, it is common to take political, social, and economic approaches. These perspectives often lead us to identify systemic problems at the root of violence, such as drastic income disparity, long-term marginalization of minorities, or the lack of sustainable livelihoods. These factors, in turn, may suggest the need for profound changes, including institutional reforms, ethnic reconciliation, and increased development assistance.

The public health model represents a complement to these broad social science perspectives. Steeped in analytic methods that have helped reduce and sometimes eliminate the incidence of disease, the public health approach views armed violence as a phenomenon with identifiable patterns within particular populations. It is thus able to focus on small groups and to design targeted interventions at the local level. Another advantage is its use of health data, which—while sometimes difficult to collect—is less subject to changeability than social or political identifiers, such as group affiliation and political goals.

In previous editions of the *Small Arms Survey*, we have highlighted topics that bear on the theme of public health, including direct and indirect mortality arising from small arms and light weapons in armed conflict (2005), and the medical, economic, and social costs of violent acts perpetrated with firearms (2006). In addition, our country case studies invariably review the health effects of armed violence.

In the *Small Arms Survey 2008: Risk and Resilience* we take both a broader and more detailed look at the public health approach to armed violence. This approach involves far more than measuring health impacts. At its core is a set of conceptual tools and methods to identify risk and protective factors among victims and perpetrators of armed violence. Its aim is to generate evidence-based programming by unpacking those factors in order to design preventive interventions for target groups.

While public health research and related advocacy on armed violence prevention has been under way in a small number of countries—most notably the United States—for more than 25 years, the public health approach has been slow to penetrate international policy-making. That is now changing. The last five years have witnessed the emergence of a number of global initiatives that incorporate public health perspectives to address armed violence.

In 2002, the World Health Organization (WHO) launched its *World Report on Violence and Health*, which, while not exclusively focused on armed violence, laid the groundwork by presenting the first comprehensive health-based review of the problem of violence around the world. The following year, UN Member States adopted a World Health Assembly resolution calling for the support of evidence-based approaches for the prevention of violence and the evaluation of model violence prevention programmes. In 2005, WHO and the UN Development Programme (UNDP) established the Armed Violence Prevention Programme (AVPP). Now in its second phase, the AVPP is developing an armed violence prevention policy framework for applying public health tools to identify the causes, nature, and impact of armed violence.

More recently, public health concepts are at the core of the increasing convergence of armed violence prevention and human development assistance and planning. The signatories of the Geneva Declaration on Armed Violence and Development (2006), which seeks to integrate armed violence programming into sustainable development frameworks, have agreed to focus prevention efforts on specific risk factors and groups. These initiatives suggest that the international community is increasingly absorbing the public health model into its approach to armed violence.

Chapter highlights

In keeping with previous editions, the *Small Arms Survey 2008* is divided into two sections. The first comprises chapters that update or extend our knowledge on the production, transfer, stockpiles, and holdings of weapons, and measures to regulate them. The conceptual link tying this section together is the problem of diversion from legal to illicit users. The stockpiles and transfers chapters provide frameworks for understanding diversion in either context, while underscoring steps to prevent it from occurring. Similarly, the measures chapter examines the extent to which states are complying with their commitments regarding end-user certification—an important tool for preventing transfer diversions—while the South Africa chapter focuses on the diversion of firearms from civilians, private security firms, and public institutions. This section also includes a comic strip illustrating the potential ease by which someone with access to forged documentation can make arrangements to ship munitions virtually anywhere in the world.

The thematic section this year consists of three chapters that collectively introduce and explore the public health approach to armed violence. We examine the historical roots of the approach and the concepts that have been valuable in addressing disease and injuries in other contexts; the methods for identifying the multi-dimensional risk and resilience factors that affect the likelihood of violence; and the many challenges of addressing these factors through preventive programming. This section includes an overview of the global and regional burden of armed violence, and two detailed case studies of armed violence in El Salvador and the United States—focusing on specific initiatives to control violence in both countries. The thematic section concludes with a discussion of public health-oriented interventions, a review of lessons learnt from this approach over the last 20 years, and considerations for future work in this area.

Update and diversion chapters

Chapter 1 (Light weapons): This year's production chapter focuses on light weapons, highlighting their portability, lethality, availability, and potential for proliferation and technology transfer to non-state armed groups. At least 51 countries currently produce light weapons and a number of non-state armed groups manufacture and possess these weapons illegally.

This chapter generally follows the 1997 UN Panel of Governmental Experts categorization of light weapons to include: man-portable air defence systems (MANPADS), anti-tank guided weapons (ATGWs), heavy machine guns (including anti-aircraft guns), anti-materiel rifles, recoilless rifles and guns, hand-held, under-barrel, and automatic grenade launchers, unguided 'anti-tank' rocket launchers, and mortars.

Chapter 2 (Stockpile diversion): Diversion from the stocks of civilian users and state security forces lies at the heart of illicit arms proliferation. In some regions, this unauthorized transfer of arms and ammunition comprises 40 per cent of the illicit market. Across the world, diversion of arms and ammunition sustains the activities of non-state armed groups, terrorist organizations, and armed criminals. This chapter provides a timely and focused review of trends in diversion, encompassing both civilian-owned weapons and ammunition and military stockpiles.

The chapter observes that diversion stems from negligence on the part of states, militaries, and civilians. In most instances, states can address the problem through relatively low-cost improvements to accounting, monitoring, and the physical security of arms and ammunition. Many states fail to implement these measures, however. Weak regulatory frameworks governing the storage of civilian weapons, combined with inadequate management of security force stockpiles, leave states and societies prone to armed violence fuelled by diversion.

Chapter 3 (Surplus destruction): Dozens of small arms, light weapons, and ammunition destruction projects are currently under way, the largest systematic destruction of excess small arms and light weapons since the end of the Second World War. On average, about 430,000 surplus military small arms have been destroyed each year since 1991.

This chapter reviews the challenges of small arms and ammunition destruction projects. It finds that of some 200 million military firearms worldwide, at least 76 million can be considered surplus. The world also harbours 100–140 million tons of military ammunition, of which 20–30 million tons are for military small arms, much of it surplus. The most systematic progress in surplus destruction involves MANPADS.

The UN *Programme of Action* and other international instruments create a predisposition to eliminate surpluses through destruction, but in practice exports often are preferred. Two mechanisms that greatly increase short-term willingness to destroy surpluses are the promise of membership in regional organizations and security sector reform.

Chapter 4 (Transfer diversion): Arms transfer diversion takes many forms—from the illicit online sale of individual AR-15 rifles to massive, multi-ton shipments of machine guns, rocket launchers, and shoulder-fired missiles arranged by major international arms brokers and their associates. Diversion schemes are responsible for some of the largest documented illicit transfers of small arms and light weapons, sometimes rivalling—in quantity and quality—the national inventories of legitimate governments.

This chapter assesses the strategies employed by traffickers in several actual cases of diversion, and the various transfer controls adopted by governments to detect and prevent these schemes. This assessment reveals that diver-

Definition of small arms and light weapons

The Small Arms Survey uses the term 'small arms and light weapons' broadly to cover both military-style small arms and light weapons as well as commercial firearms (handguns and long guns). It largely follows the definition used in the United Nations' Report of the Panel of Governmental Experts on Small Arms (United Nations, 1997):

Small arms: revolvers and self-loading pistols, rifles and carbines, assault rifles, sub-machine guns, and light machine guns.

Light weapons: heavy machine guns, hand-held under-barrel and mounted grenade launchers, portable anti-tank and anti-aircraft guns, recoilless rifles, portable launchers of anti-tank and anti-aircraft missile systems, and mortars of less than 100 mm calibre.

The Survey uses the terms 'firearm' and 'gun' to mean hand-held weapons that fire a projectile through a tube by explosive charge. The terms 'small arms' and 'light weapons' are used more comprehensively to refer to all hand-held, man-portable, explosively or chemically propelled or detonated devices. Unless the context dictates otherwise, no distinction is intended between commercial firearms (such as hunting rifles) and small arms and light weapons designed for military use (such as assault rifles).

The UN definition was agreed through consensus by government officials. It was negotiated, in other words, to serve practical political goals that differ from the needs of research and analysis. While the UN definition is used in the *Survey* as a baseline, the analysis in this and subsequent chapters is broader, allowing consideration of weapons such as home-made (craft) firearms that might be overlooked using the UN definition. The term small arm is used in this chapter to refer to both small arms and light weapons (i.e. the small arms industry) unless otherwise stated, whereas light weapon refers specifically to light weapons.

sion occurs throughout the transfer chain and that all states—even if they do not produce or export small arms—are vulnerable to diversion. Yet the cases profiled in this chapter also show that, in many instances, the governments involved in the diverted transfer could have detected and prevented the diversion had they implemented the right combination of transfer controls.

The chapter also lists the top importers and exporters of small arms and light weapons, and includes the annual update of the Small Arms Transparency Barometer.

Chapter 5 (End-user certification): This year's measures chapter considers whether and how states are fulfilling their commitments to ensure 'effective control' over small arms transfers, by focusing on end-user documentation and systems. End-user certificates and other kinds of end-user documentation constitute a key line of defence against the diversion of authorized small arms transfers to unauthorized—often illicit—end users and end uses. Yet these documents are effective only in the context of a broader system that includes a thorough consideration of diversion risks at the licensing stage, the verification of end-user documentation, and complementary post-shipment controls.

Research conducted for the chapter indicates that, while the basic components of effective transfer control (diversion prevention) systems appear to be in place in leading exporting states, they leave much to the discretion of individual licensing officials, allowing them to decide when to increase or decrease the level of scrutiny in specific cases. It is unclear, in particular, how thoroughly diversion risks are being assessed at the licensing stage and how systematically end-user documentation is being verified. It is quite clear, however, that post-shipment controls are neglected. Many governments require that the delivery of weapons at destination be verified, but this is not uniform practice. With rare exceptions, verification stops at the time of delivery. As a rule, governments do not monitor the end-use of exported weapons, not even selectively. They do not know, in other words, whether their decision to export weapons to a specific end-user was wise.

Chapter 6 (South Africa): This chapter reviews what is known about the diversion of firearms in South Africa in the wake of recent sweeping domestic firearm legislation. It describes the provisions of the Firearm Control Act of 2000 (which came into effect in late 2004) that aimed to prevent diversion from civilians, private security firms, the South African Police Service, the South African National Defence Force, and other government agencies.

By reviewing available data on the number of firearms lost, stolen, and recovered from crimes, it maps out the sources of diverted firearms. The chapter finds that civilian-sourced firearms account for the significant majority of diverted firearms in South Africa. It also finds that diversion continues to occur from official institutions despite improvements in administrative controls.

Adventures of a Would-be Arms Dealer (Comic strip): This year's foray into the graphic arts illustrates the making of an illicit arms deal in comic strip form. What does diversion involve? A Survey researcher, employing well-established operating techniques, shows that with the right connections and modest 'start-up funds', one can buy a blank end-user certificate and use it to arrange the supply and transport of munitions to the destination of one's choice (e.g. Somalia). Although, in this case, no ammunition or weapons were purchased or transported, the real-world implications are clear. The risks remain manageable, the profits handsome.

Public health section
Chapter 7 (Public health approach): The public health approach to understanding and reducing armed violence emphasizes the preventable nature of violence. It also acknowledges the complexity of violence, the multi-dimensional

factors that contribute to it, and the need to design collaborative and multi-faceted interventions. The basis of the public health approach is a scientific model for research, evaluation, and the design of targeted interventions through the systematic collection of data.

This chapter provides an overview of the global and regional burden of armed violence. It then describes the public health approach and how it works in practice. A special focus on the community level reveals how community factors influence the risk as well as the impact of violence and the likelihood of future violence.

Chapter 8 (Risk and resilience): Preventing violence requires an understanding of why it occurs, who commits violent acts, and who is at risk of victimization. At the centre of this approach is the identification of risk and resilience factors—those factors that contribute to individuals engaging in violent acts and those that aid individuals in risky circumstances to overcome adversity and avoid violence. These factors paint a picture of perpetrators, victims, means, and types of violence in a community, which in turn enables communities to design interventions to target those committing violence and to protect those who are most vulnerable.

The chapter discusses how risk and resilience factors can be identified in practice, and provides an overview of key findings about risk and resilience. It also explains how risk and resilience factors can be used to develop violence reduction programmes, various possible types of interventions, and means to design more effective interventions in the future.

Chapter 9 (Interventions): Public health interventions include any programme, strategy, or policy designed to prevent violence, reduce the harmful effects of violence, or improve community perceptions about violence.

The chapter provides an overview of the range of available interventions developed to counter armed violence. It then offers detailed studies of such interventions undertaken in the United States and El Salvador. These case studies provide an overview of armed violence in each country, the countries' responses to the problems, and the programming put in place to reduce armed violence. The chapter concludes by highlighting a number of lessons learnt from various studies of violence reduction initiatives over the past two decades.

Conclusion

The core mission of the *Small Arms Survey*—to make reliable data and analysis of small arms and armed violence widely available—is wedded to the expectation that such work can help prevent human suffering. In this spirit, the 2008 edition of the *Survey* reviews a set of tools and concepts built on the understanding that interpersonal armed violence is in many contexts a preventable phenomenon.

While policy-makers at the international level have yet to fully embrace the public health approach, its appearance is already evident in a number of multilateral and national initiatives. This approach does face major challenges, which we explore in this volume, but it will continue to make valuable contributions to our collective work in the years ahead.

Future editions of the *Survey* will focus on post-conflict disarmament, demobilization, and reintegration (DDR); the intersection of gangs, armed groups, and guns; and our emerging understanding of the significance of security sector reform (SSR) for armed violence reduction. As in previous years, future editions will build on collaborative relationships with our many institutional partners around the world, and will seek to expand the knowledge base to support efforts to reduce and prevent armed violence.

—Emile LeBrun
Co-editor

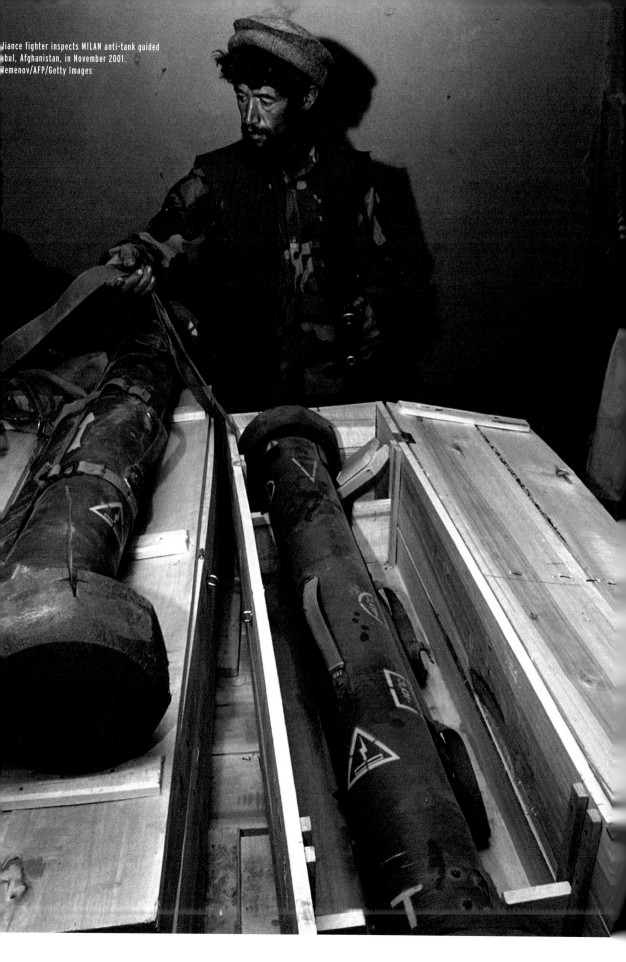

Light Weapons
PRODUCTS, PRODUCERS, AND PROLIFERATION

INTRODUCTION

Light weapons pose serious threats to human security. A shoulder-launched surface-to-air missile—commonly known as a man-portable air-defence system (MANPADS)—can be used to shoot down a civilian airliner with hundreds of passengers on board. A lone gunman can kill a head of state with a 12.7 mm sniper rifle from a distance of a kilometre or more. Lethal combinations of explosive power, technological sophistication, and range distinguish light weapons from small arms, and justify public concern over their illicit proliferation.

Yet, despite their lethality, most of the literature on 'small arms and light weapons' has focused on the first half of the equation: small arms, such as assault rifles and pistols. With the exception of a burgeoning international debate centred on MANPADS, international scrutiny has largely overlooked the illicit proliferation of light weapons.

This chapter addresses this imbalance and sheds light on the characteristics, development, and production of light weapons. It also looks at how they have been defined to date—specifically in the influential 1997 UN Panel of Governmental Experts report (UNGA, 1997). The chapter suggests additions to the Panel's list of light weapons, based on practical considerations related to their portability and to their use in armed violence.

The chapter distinguishes two categories of light weapons—guided and unguided weapons—in recognition of their important technological differences. Within each of these categories, the chapter profiles a range of specific weapons systems. It notes their producers, development, and important technological changes—whether indigenous or generated through licensing. It also presents available information on price, as well as marketing and worldwide distribution and proliferation. It pays special attention to craft production of light weapons, as well as the possession by non-state actors—including terrorist groups—of guided light weapons.

The chapter's main findings are as follows:

- At least 51 countries currently produce light weapons.
- Forty-five countries manufacture complete guided light weapons, while an additional five states manufacture components or upgrades for these systems.
- At least 31 countries produce light weapons under licence, but 26 additional countries produce weapons of foreign design without any licence, with an expired licence, or in an unclear licensing situation, underscoring the proliferation of risks inherent in intended and unintended technology transfer.
- Light weapons are becoming more lethal, more portable, easier to transport, less expensive, and longer lasting, increasing the prospect of their proliferation, especially to non-state armed groups.
- Armed groups have obtained numerous guided weapons and produce unguided weapons of increasing sophistication including rocket-propelled grenades, mortars, grenade launchers, explosively formed projectiles, and man-portable rockets.

- Some light weapons—principally anti-materiel rifles—are legally sold to civilians in several countries, including Switzerland, the United Kingdom, and the United States.
- We estimate that the average value of the annual production of anti-tank guided weapons (just one of the eight types of light weapons described by the UN) from 2001 to 2005 was USD 1.1 billion.

LIGHT WEAPONS: WHAT THEY ARE AND WHY THEY MATTER

Although there is some disagreement about the precise definition of 'light weapons', the threat such weapons pose to human security continues to come into greater focus. The first part of this section reviews efforts to define small arms and light weapons, focusing mostly on the list contained in the 1997 UN Panel report. It does not offer a new definition but does suggest some additional items to be included based on the criterion of portability. It also notes some developments in non-factory manufactured or 'craft' produced light weapons and ammunition. The second part discusses these weapons' importance and is divided into two subsections. The first notes trends in their operational capability and examines their effect even when they fail to work as intended or their use is only threatened. The second explores light weapons' proliferation—especially to armed groups—and highlights the use of improvised explosive devices as well as developments within craft production.

A working definition of light weapons

Governments have yet to agree on a universal definition of small arms and light weapons.[1] Differences of opinion have centred on civilian versus military classifications, and on whether certain weapons such as shotguns or hunting rifles should be included. Moreover, the distinction between what constitutes a 'small arm' and what qualifies as a 'light weapon' can vary from document to document.

Until the establishment, in 1996, of a Panel of Governmental Experts on Small Arms, the UN had not significantly addressed small arms and light weapons. Rather, the focus had been on weapons of mass destruction as well as conventional arms. Former UN Secretary-General Boutros Boutros-Ghali's much heralded 1992 'Agenda for Peace' did not even mention small arms or light weapons (UNGA, 1992). Three years later, in a 'Supplement to an Agenda for Peace', Boutros-Ghali did broach the subject. He spoke of the need for 'micro-disarmament' and used the terms 'small arms' and 'light weapons'. These terms were not clearly defined, however (UNGA, 1995, paras. 62–64). The UN Experts Panel filled this gap in its influential 1997 report. It roughly categorized certain varieties of small arms and light weapons, as well as their ammunition and explosives. The Panel classified 'small arms' as consisting of revolvers and self-loading pistols; rifles and carbines; sub-machine guns; assault rifles; and light machine guns. It included the following weapons within its light-weapons category:

- heavy machine guns;
- hand-held under-barrel and mounted grenade launchers;
- portable anti-aircraft guns;
- portable anti-tank guns;
- recoilless rifles;
- portable launchers of anti-tank missile and rocket systems;

s-Ghali's
led 1992
r Peace'
not even
all arms
weapons.

- portable launchers of anti-aircraft missile systems; and

- mortars of calibres of less than 100 mm.

In addition, the Panel listed: ammunition and explosives, which includes cartridges (rounds) for small arms; shells and missiles for light weapons; mobile containers with missiles or shells for single-action anti-aircraft and anti-tank systems; anti-personnel and anti-tank hand grenades; landmines; and explosives (UNGA, 1997, para. 26).

The Panel provided additional clarity for some terms, obfuscated others, and chose not to address anti-personnel landmines. Notably, it used the concept of portability to delimit and distinguish small arms and light weapons from each other and from larger conventional weapons. According to the Panel, the defining characteristic of small arms was that they could be carried 'by one person'. By contrast, light weapons necessitated transportation 'by two or more people, a pack animal or a light vehicle' (UNGA, 1997, para. 27). The Panel indicated that anti-personnel landmines came under its mandate, but decided not to include them in its deliberations as the international community was dealing with the issue in other forums (UNGA, 1997, para. 31).[2]

The portability distinction was not, however, uniformly applicable to the weapons in the two categories. Some light weapons in the Panel's list, such as rocket-propelled grenade launchers, can be carried and operated[3] by a single person, while some small arms, such as light (as opposed to heavy) machine guns, may need to be transported and operated by a small team of people (particularly when large volumes of ammunition are involved).

For the purposes of this chapter, the Survey largely accepts the categorization for light weapons that the 1997 UN Panel of Governmental Experts used. Like the Panel, we have chosen not to address mines. We believe, however, that this subject merits greater examination as other forums address only anti-personnel landmines and these weapons are attractive for armed groups (see Box 1.1).

The Panel did not define or provide an example of a light vehicle (or of a pack animal for that matter). For our purposes, a light vehicle is not heavily armoured, has four-wheel drive, and is designed for off-road use. There are many such vehicles, with varying capabilities. For our standard 'light vehicle', we chose one that was of low-to-moderate performance, the Russian UAZ-3151. This vehicle can transport up to 800 kg (1,760 lbs) on its chassis.[4] We estimate that four people, their kit, and fuel account for 500 kg (1,100 lbs). This leaves a maximum of 300 kg (660 lbs) for a light weapon, mounted on the vehicle chassis, and requisite ammunition. The maximum towing capacity of a trailer without brakes is 600 kg (1,323 lbs) (Jane's, 2000, pp. 308–09). If one accepts that a trailer and its accou-

Box 1.1 Mines: products and proliferation concerns

The Ottawa Convention has made considerable progress in reducing the number of producers and global stockpiles of anti-personnel landmines. For example, according to the Landmine Monitor, whereas more than 50 states are known to have manufactured these weapons, as of 2007 fully 38 had ceased to do so (LM, 2007, p. 13).[5] The convention is also believed to have brought a virtual if not total halt in the trade of this weapon, even among states not party to the treaty. Other types of man-portable mines, however, continue to be produced and developed. Anti-vehicle mines[6] have also attracted considerable attention, in large part because they continue to have a humanitarian and post-war impact by impeding reconstruction and development aid. Man-portable anti-ship and anti-helicopter mines, however, have generated less interest. While the numbers of these weapons in circulation are comparatively small, each weapon's destructive power is considerably greater. Two limpet mines (so named because like a mollusc they are small and can attach easily to a vessel's hull) were used to sink the *Rainbow Warrior* in 1985 (*Guardian*, 2007). Multiple limpet mines weighing only 10–20 kg (22–44 lbs) each could sink a cruise ship or a ferry, and would be difficult to protect against (Bonomo et al., 2007, pp. xvii, 8, 58-60).

trements can weigh up to 200 kg, then that leaves a maximum weight of 400 kg (882 lbs) for a light weapon designed to be towed. We assume no pack animal can transport more than a light vehicle, either on or off a road.

We have, therefore, slightly amended the Panel's list of mortars, using the Panel's own defining characteristic of portability. Mortars more than 100 mm in calibre are included in our analysis if they are designed to be transported by people, on a pack animal, or by a light vehicle. Argentina, for example, previously manufactured a 120 mm mortar that three infantrymen could disassemble and transport on their backs.[7] Moreover, many 120 mm mortars can be towed and sufficient ammunition carried on the same vehicle to be considered as light weapons. Mortars of 155 mm and 160 mm, on the other hand, weigh much more than 1,000 kg (2,205 lbs) with their requisite trailer, rendering them too heavy for inclusion according to the criteria we have established. While some of these systems could be towed by more robust and capable light vehicles, such carriers could not transport sufficient ammunition for the weapon to be operated as intended. The same emphasis on design explains why we do not necessarily consider the Minigun to be a light weapon (see Box 1.2).

With respect to grenade launchers, our working definition includes *both* hand-held *and* under-barrel models as they are distinct weapon systems. We also refer to 'automatic' grenade launchers rather than 'mounted' as many mounted models are also designed to function on tripods. As elsewhere, the defining feature of all these grenade launchers is their portability.

Some weapons omitted from the Panel's list altogether have been added. Rockets that are man-portable and launched on rails, not through tubes, are included. There are many examples of such weapons being produced and used in today's armed conflicts. All of them are craft manufactured.

Our analysis, however, does not include medium machine guns or general-purpose machine guns (GPMGs). The Panel distinguishes between 'light' and 'heavy' machine guns in name only and provides no reference to the size of the cartridges fired. We have defined heavy machine guns as fully automatic weapons that fire small-calibre cartridges exceeding 10 mm, but less than 20 mm, in calibre. (Indeed, with the exception of some pistols and revolvers,[8] we generally define firearms in the light weapons category as those chambered for 10 mm calibre rounds and larger.[9]) We slot medium machine guns and GPMGs into the 'light' UN category as they fire cartridges smaller than 10 mm (usually 7.62 mm) and are mounted or equipped with a bipod. We acknowledge, however, that such 'light' machine guns on a coaxial mount can fulfil a similar function to a heavy machine gun, though with a reduced range.

For the most part, this chapter does not focus on light weapons ammunition and explosives.[10] We have, however, profiled improvised explosive devices (IEDs), including explosively formed projectiles (EFPs, also known as explosively formed *penetrators*).

Box 1.2 The 5.56 mm and 7.62 mm Miniguns: light weapons?

The electrically fired 7.62 mm Minigun and 5.56 mm 'Mini-Minigun', both multi-barrelled machine guns developed in the 1960s that fire several thousand rounds of ammunition per minute, are clearly not 'small arms' as described by the Panel, but are they light weapons? The weapons themselves are relatively light, weighing less than 40 kg, but the requisite ammunition needed to allow the weapon to function as intended is very heavy due to the rate of fire. The UAZ-3151 that we have chosen to represent light vehicles could carry enough ammunition for it to function at continuous fire for a couple of minutes or so at most. (The external power supply would not be an issue as the gun could be run off the vehicle's battery or Power Take Off (PTO) unit.) The many tens of thousands of rounds of ammunition that these guns fire to operate as designed explain why helicopters and tracked vehicles serve as the weapons' platform.

Finally, we have chosen not to include examples of historic conventional arms, including live-firing replicas, which some people would consider to be light weapons. Thus, for example, a small-scale replica of the 19th-century Gatling gun with four barrels and a 720-round magazine is not covered.[11] Nor are replicas or refurbished models of machine guns from the late 19th and early 20th centuries such as the Maxim, Vickers, or Lewis, which normally fired a .303 in. (7.7 mm) cartridge and therefore do not qualify as a light weapon for the purposes of this study.[12]

Importance of light weapons

Light weapons are important because of each weapon's lethality, the growing number of producers, and their proliferation in the hands of non-state armed groups. States have begun to recognize the threats they pose to human security and the global economy (principally in respect of threats to civilian aviation). Many states have contributed tens of millions of dollars to destroy surplus light weapons, especially MANPADS, and improve stockpile security. There has also been a noticeable trend since the late 1990s for confidence-building and technology-control measures originally designed for conventional weapon systems to be modified to apply to some light weapons (Small Arms Survey, 2005, ch. 5). Such initiatives underscore the importance the international community attaches to controlling certain light weapons—and for good reason.

Lethality of light weapons

A single light weapon can be extremely lethal, notwithstanding its small size. A 60–120 mm mortar can cause casualties within a 15–35 m (49–115 ft) radius from point of impact (Jane's, 2004, pp. 677–751).[13] Lofted into heavily populated environments, these inexpensive and unsophisticated weapons can kill scores of people. This is exactly what happened in 2003 when Guinea-backed Liberians United for Reconciliation and Democracy (LURD) rebels laid

Bosnian soldiers and a bystander carry away the body of a casualty of a mortar shell attack on Sarajevo's main downtown marketplace in February 1994. © Laurent Rebours/AP Photo

siege to Monrovia. Hundreds of civilians were killed and thousands injured when mortar rounds rained down on the Liberian capital (HRW, 2003). Almost a decade earlier the 1994 Sarajevo market massacre that claimed more than 60 lives and injured more than 200 was the result of a single 120 mm mortar shell (Smith, 1994).

A heavy machine gun can saturate an area with bullets one kilometre and further from the weapon. In the Eastern Equatoria state of southern Sudan, a pastoralist group reportedly used a 12.7 mm machine gun (along with other small arms and light weapons) in an ambush that killed more than 50 civilians from another tribe in May 2007 (Small Arms Survey, 2007b, p. 2).

A rocket launcher firing a shaped charge warhead can penetrate armour plating on the most advanced tanks or reinforced bunkers, not to mention most domiciles. For example, a PG-7L shaped charge warhead for the ubiquitous RPG-7 is capable of penetrating 600 mm (23.62 in.) of armour, 1.3 m (4.27 ft) of reinforced concrete, and more than 2.5 m (8.2 ft) of logs and earth (Jane's, 2007c, p. 477). Shaped charges can be used in a variety of ways, which do not always necessitate the use of factory-manufactured weapons. One example is the use of explosively formed projectiles where a shaped charge or explosive can be used on its own as an improvised explosive device. Such an EFP, weighing no more than a few kilograms (several pounds), can accelerate to speeds of 2,000 m per second— more than twice as fast as a 12.7 mm machine-gun cartridge when fired (Atkinson, 2007b). This force permits the weapon to penetrate a substantial amount of armour plating on armoured vehicles or 762 mm (30 in.) of concrete (Blair, 2007). EFPs have claimed a much higher percentage of US casualties than their limited use would suggest (Gordon, 2007; Atkinson, 2007d).[14]

The potential effectiveness of MANPADS is well known (Small Arms Survey, 2004, pp. 77–97), if perhaps over-stated. Long-haul aircraft typically transport two hundred or more passengers, making them attractive targets for a group intent on causing many casualties. Since the late 1970s almost one civilian aircraft per year on average has been reportedly fired upon with such weapons, resulting in hundreds of casualties (USDoS, 2005) (see Table 1.1). Yet most of these attacks have occurred in war zones, and some regions remain largely unaffected; not a single civilian aircraft has been hit by a MANPADS in North America or western Europe, for example. Moreover, many missiles miss their targets and those that strike do not necessarily achieve their aim. (Attacks on military targets with MANPADS have been more frequent, and especially effective against helicopters.)[15]

The ancillary effects of an attack can be severe even if the missile misses its target or is believed to exist but has not been fired. The attack on an Israeli aircraft departing Mombasa for Tel Aviv in November 2002 resulted in two Strela SA-7 missiles missing their target and the plane landing safely in Tel Aviv as scheduled. But the ramifications for the Kenyan economy were severe.[16] The November 2002 attack, coupled with Britain's decision to halt British Airways flights to Nairobi for a short period in 2003 because of fears of an attack on its aircraft (which did not mate-rialize), resulted in what Kenyan tourism officials described as the worst crisis to hit the country since its independence (BBC News, 2003).[17] A 2005 RAND Corporation study of MANPADS threats to the civil aviation industry concludes that airline cancellations and downturns in tourism arising from such threats would have significant repercussions on the global economy (Chow et al., 2005).

Availability of light weapons

Light weapons, like small arms, are widely produced and readily available. As enumerated in greater detail in fol-lowing sections of this chapter, more than 50 countries produce light weapons. The reason more do not do so is not technological barriers to the production of certain systems, but rather the fact that the markets are so open that their needs are met easily through commercial transactions. The technology required to make many light weapons rests

Sarajevo massacre result of 120 mm tar shell.

Table 1.1 Selected incidents of reported MANPADS attacks on civilian aircraft

Date	Location	Target	Fatalities	Description
03.09.78	Zimbabwe	Air Rhodesia Vickers 782D Viscount	38	An SA-7 missile hit the passenger plane's right wing shortly after take-off from Kariba. The plane crash-landed. Zimbabwe People's Revolutionary Army (ZIPRA) rebels, responsible for the shooting, subsequently killed many of the plane's survivors.
12.02.79	Zimbabwe	Air Rhodesia Vickers 748D Viscount	59	ZIPRA fired on the aircraft with an SA-7 after it left Kariba, hitting the left engine, killing all aboard.
08.11.83	Angola	Angola Airlines Boeing 737-2M2	130	Immediately after taking off from Lubango, the plane crashed. National Union for the Total Independence of Angola (UNITA) rebels claimed credit for downing the plane with a missile. The Angolan government blamed the crash on a technical malfunction.
04.09.85	Afghanistan	Bakhtar Afghan Antonov AN-26	52	The plane was shot down with a surface-to-air missile shortly after take-off from Kandahar.
16.08.86	Sudan	Sudan Airways Fokker F-27	60	The Sudan People's Liberation Army (SPLA) firing an SA-7 brought down the aircraft shortly after take-off from Malakal.
11.06.87	Afghanistan	Bakhtar Alwatana Antonov AN-26	53	The plane was shot down near Khost on its way from Kandahar to Kabul.
08.12.88	Western Sahara	Two T&G Aviation Douglas DC-7CF	5	Two aircraft on the way from Senegal to Morocco were hit (in an engine) with SA-7s while flying at 3,352 m (11,000 ft) over Western Sahara. One crashed, killing all five aboard. The other managed to land safely in Morocco.
06.04.94	Rwanda	Rwandan govern-ment Dassault Falcon 50	12	The plane, carrying the presidents of Burundi and Rwanda from peace talks in Tanzania, was shot down on approach to Kigali.
10.10.98	Democratic Republic of the Congo	Lignes Aeriennes Congolaises Boeing 727-30	41	The plane was shot down with an SA-7 missile shortly after take-off from Kindu.
02.01.99	Angola	Transafrik Lockheed L-100-30 Hercules	9	UNITA shot down the plane some 20 minutes after take-off from Huambo on the way to Luanda. (A Hercules aircraft had suffered a similar fate upon departing Huambo a week earlier, in which 14 people perished.)
28.11.02	Kenya	Arkia Boeing 757-3E7	0	Two SA-7 missiles missed the plane carrying 271 people shortly after take-off from Mombasa.
22.11.03	Iraq	European Air Transport Airbus A300B4-203F	0	An SA-7 missile hit the cargo plane's wing as it climbed past 2,438 m (8,000 ft). The heavily damaged plane returned to Baghdad safely.
23.03.07	Somalia	Transaviaexport IL-76TD	11	The plane crashed after one of two SA-18 missiles fired by Hizbul Shabaab hit the plane shortly after take-off from Mogadishu.
13.08.07	Iraq	Nordic Airways MD-83	0	Pilots of the passenger jet said two missiles were fired at their plane after take-off from Sulaimaniya.

Sources: ASN (2007); Chivers (2007); USDoS (2005); UNSC (2007, para. 39)

on know-how that was widely acquired before the Second World War (WWII) or has been produced under licence for more than 25 years. Their portability and concealability in transit increase the ease of such transfers.

Like small arms, most light weapons have a shelf life that outlives the time span of one generation (10–15 years) of weapon technology. This allows states to transfer—often at a steep discount or for free—older generation models. Many of the recipients lack adequate safeguards for their weapons stockpiles or are engaged in hostilities with non-state actors in which the latter seize materiel in combat. Once in the hands of non-state actors, unguided light weapons in particular require relatively little maintenance and are able to withstand harsh conditions. Guided weapons, on the other hand, such as MANPADS (discussed in detail below), that have sophisticated battery-powered guidance systems and require significant training and practice for effective use may present certain challenges to non-state actors.

Improvised explosive devices are understandably attracting considerable attention because of their use in Iraq (see Box 1.3), but their significance is much broader than their use and effectiveness in that conflict. During 2006

Box 1.3   A 'new' light weapon: improvised explosive devices in Iraq

Improvised explosive devices (IEDs) are not unique to Iraq, but never before have they been deployed in such numbers and used with such deadly effect. The *Washington Post*'s Rick Atkinson, for example, reports that the US military encountered these devices in Afghanistan, but there were fewer than 25 in 2002. Most were unsophisticated, many set off by tripwires. In Iraq crude time-delayed IEDs have given way to pressure-plate triggers and increasingly sophisticated radio-controlled weapons that can be activated at distances that measure in kilometres. In some four years in Iraq, insurgents have employed more than 80,000 IEDs. The following account reflects the US experience in combating IEDs in Iraq.

Insurgents are believed to possess an almost limitless production capability and have exhibited planning and resource-fulness. The stockpiles of munitions throughout Iraq when Saddam Hussein's regime was overthrown have been estimated to number at least 650,000 tons (589,676 metric tonnes) of explosives, reportedly less than half of which had been secured more than a year after the invasion. Moreover, insurgents pilfered huge quantities of bomb-making materials that had been 'secured'. Less than 10 kg of explosives (about what a 155 mm artillery round can deliver) properly placed can destroy the heaviest armoured vehicle in service with US forces. In some cases insurgents have configured more than 20 artillery shells to explode simultaneously. Insurgents who, US government analysts believe, once took days to conduct surveillance of a site and bury the device in advance of the ambush are thought now to often successfully complete such preparations in two hours or less. Moreover, the number of bomb-makers in Iraq has grown (although the United States is undertaking concerted efforts to reduce their number). The United States has compiled information on 169 bomb-making networks representing numerous ethnic groups and political objectives. Each cell is believed to consist of five to ten members (not all of them bomb-makers). They do not believe this number to be comprehensive.

Countermeasures have been only partially effective. Passive measures include body armour for soldiers and additional armour protection for motorized vehicles, as the majority of vehicles operating in Iraq with US forces were not armoured–and as noted above, even the largest tanks can succumb to IEDs. Both of these measures are palliatives.

Active measures to disable the IED are numerous, but many have fallen far short of objectives. They include what might be described as traditional devices to jam frequencies used to cause an explosion, or manually rendering the weapon inoper-ative. The electronic countermeasures have shown themselves to be effective in certain instances, but they have created unintentional problems of electro-magnetic compatibility, such as interfering with communications as well as command-and-control equipment. Newer approaches include aerial and video reconnaissance to monitor and detect insurgent activity and the emplacement of the devices. Natural phenomena such as sandstorms and man-made 'countermeasures' such as strewn trash degraded the efficacy of these technical innovations. The US programme was discontinued after it was deemed that a concerted three-month effort in 2004 to fully employ such resources was unsuccessful.

Recently, electronic countermeasures have proven more effective against IEDs, but this has not slowed their use. Rather, Iraqi insurgents are now favouring devices that are detonated in ways other than by radio control. In 2003 the number of IEDs used reached 100 a month. In 2004 the number reached 100 a week. By 2007 the number had approached 100 a day. As of 2007, the United States had suffered more than 20,000 casualties in Afghanistan and Iraq from IEDs.

Sources: Atkinson (2007a; 2007b; 2007c; 2007d)

and 2007 more than 20 non-state armed groups in 19 countries and territories were reported to have employed IEDs. They have been made out of landmines (of both the anti-personnel and the anti-vehicle varieties), rockets, artillery shells, and other munitions (Moser-Puangsuwan, 2007). While many of these devices come from materiel (various kinds of munitions), some are fashioned from commercial civilian materials.

Non-state armed actors are producing light weapons other than just IEDs. They produce rockets, mortars, and grenade launchers. They also produce the munitions for these weapons (see Box 1.4).

Box 1.4 Craft production of light weapons

Non-state armed groups—and some territories outside state control—produce numerous light weapons of various levels of sophistication. Weapons produced include man-portable rockets and launchers, mortars and their munitions, as well as grenade launchers. Successful production depends on the skill level among members or supporters of the armed group, their access to appropriate resources, and the group's ability to take and hold territory in which production facilities can be maintained. The groups and weapons listed here are representative and not exhaustive.

Various Palestinian armed groups produce light weapons. The Ezzedine Al-Qassam Brigade of Hamas, for example, manufactures the Al-Qassam rocket.[18] The Al-Qassam, first introduced in 2001, has subsequently seen improvements in its payload

An Al-Qassam 2 rocket rests on a tripod in Gaza, 2002.
© Adrian Wilkinson

and range. According to initial reports there were at least three variants with different ranges (about 3-10 km), warheads (0.5-20 kg), and weights (5-90 kg). More recent reports have the rocket's range expanding to 12-14 km with distances up to 20 km expected. The one constant appears to be the weapon's imprecision and a relatively short-lived propellant that makes stockpiling the rocket impractical. It is foreseen, however, that improvements to the propellant will eventually allow the weapon to be stored for extended periods. This would permit the weapon to be fired en masse after numerous rockets have been produced. More than 4,000 Al-Qassam rockets have been fired into Israel, with over 1,000 Al-Qassams fired from Gaza in 2006 alone. The Al-Aqsa Martyrs Brigade of Fatah, the Al-Nasser Salah Al-Din Brigade of the Islamic Resistance Committees, and the Al-Quds Brigade of Islamic Jihad all produce their own rockets. The Quds 4 two-stage rocket of Islamic Jihad is reported to have a greater range than any Al-Qassam (Richardson, 2002; Blanche, 2003; Richardson, 2004a; Ben-David, 2006; Jane's, 2007a; Richardson, 2007).

Man-portable rockets reportedly are also being produced by rebels in Iraq. The United States claims to have recovered home-made rockets and rocket launchers in various parts of the country (Jane's, 2006b; USDoD, 2007).

The Revolutionary Armed Forces of Colombia (or FARC, for Fuerzas Armadas Revolucionarias de Colombia) also produce a range of light weapons. According to field research conducted by Pablo Dreyfus, the FARC have created War-Front Workshops (or TFGs for Talleres de Frente de Guerra) with help from co-opted technicians of the state-owned factories producing defence equipment for the Colombian government, known as INDUMIL (for Industria Militar). TFGs began operations in 1995. Materiel produced includes 60 mm, 81 mm, and 120 mm mortars, although it took some five years for all the kinks to be worked out in the serial production of these weapons and munitions. These workshops manufacture other light weapons such as grenade launchers as well as munitions for light weapons including rifle grenades and mortars (Dreyfus, 2005).[19]

In South-east Asia, numerous non-state armed groups have been reported to produce light weapons. The Liberation Tigers of Tamil Eelam (LTTE), for example, have produced a rocket—the Pasilan 2000[20]—with a 25 kg warhead (Chalk, 1999, pp. 6, 12), an RPG known as the Arul 89 (*India Today*, 1997), and mortars (Jane's, 2005). Elsewhere in the region, groups in Myanmar are said to produce 60-107 mm mortars, and at least one group, the Moro Islamic Liberation Front in the Philippines, has fabricated replicas of US and Soviet 40 mm RPGs (Davis, 2003; Koorey, 2007).

Some territories that have effectively seceded and are not under effective control of the 'former' capital also reportedly produce light weapons. There are numerous—albeit not always substantiated—reports that describe events in the self-declared Republic of Transdniester. According to a UN study, law-enforcement officials confiscated 53 handcrafted 40 mm multi-shot grenade launchers that were fabricated in that territory (SEESAC, 2006, p. 113, n. 156). Moreover, advertisements circulating in Transdniester in 2003 promoted the production and sale of homemade 'Kryzhovnik' mortars (IA, 2005, p. 2).

It is easier to record with a high degree of confidence what non-state armed groups produce than to document what they procure from others. The proliferation of MANPADS is fairly well established and it is clear that many non-state groups have used these weapons (see Table 1.1). But, as the incident of so-called 'Steyrgate' underscores, *reports* of diversion or illicit transfer do not always reflect reality. In this case, a report that Austrian 12.7 mm calibre anti-materiel rifles, sold to Iran, were recovered from rebels in Iraq was subsequently discredited (Wezeman, 2007). Annexe 1.1 presents information on guided light weapons in the possession of non-state armed groups. It includes unconfirmed as well as confirmed reports of holdings. Even established 'sightings' must be treated with caution given political agendas as well as poor journalism and research. Nevertheless, the compilation of reports provides a basis for discussing the nature and cause of the proliferation of these weapons. This can in turn lead to the development of policies and programmes designed to address this challenge.

GUIDED LIGHT WEAPONS

Guided light weapons are shoulder-launched or pedestal-mounted, and fire a missile that can be directed towards the target after launch. First introduced in the mid-1950s, these systems differ from unguided light weapons because once the projectile is released its trajectory can be altered in flight either by the operator or by an automated guidance control system. Early models require that soldiers manually steer missiles until they reach (or miss) their intended target. The drawback of this, however, is that soldiers are vulnerable to counterattack while controlling the missile in flight. Improvements in weapon technology in the last few decades have reduced the threat of counterattack. New-generation missiles travel greater distances, and engage targets autonomously with homing devices that enable the gunner to take cover, relocate, or reload immediately after firing.

Man-portable air defence systems (MANPADS)

Man-portable air defence systems are short-range surface-to-air missile systems[21] intended for attacking and defending against low-flying aircraft. Some are crew-served (known sometimes as CREWPADS, although we use MANPADS generically), but most are easily handled by a single individual and are shoulder-launched. MANPADS are generally categorized into three types of guidance system: passive infrared (IR) seekers, laser and radio command to line-of-sight (CLOS), and laser-beam riders.[22] Initial models could engage a target at altitudes of around 2,000–3,000 m and from slant ranges[23] of about 4,000 m (Jane's, 2006a, pp. 3–50; 1985, pp. 132–7). They were often inaccurate and susceptible to basic countermeasures. Moreover, they could engage aircraft only from behind. Today's most advanced systems can effectively engage aircraft at ranges of up to 8,000 m from multiple directions. Their effectiveness against large fixed-wing turbojet aircraft (as seen in Table 1.1) should not be exaggerated, however.[24]

Initial development of MANPADS began in the 1950s. Anti-aircraft guns from WWII were of limited use, and consumed vast quantities of ammunition against increasingly fast jet aircraft. The United States developed the Redeye—which got its name from the infrared homing device in its nose—over the better part of a decade, and it entered into production in the mid-1960s (Parsch, 2002). The Soviets countered in 1968 with the Strela-2 (also known as the SA-7, which is used here, or Grail).[25] Both were 'tail-chase' systems (their guidance was provided by an

IR-seeking homing head so they had to be fired from behind the target to home in on the engines' exhaust). By the end of the 1960s only these two countries produced MANPADS, although Sweden and the United Kingdom had undertaken research and development of indigenous weapons.

The 1970s saw significant changes to the industry. The United States began development of the Stinger missile system in 1972 (Parsch, 2002) and production began in 1979 (Jane's, 2006a, p. 43). Work on the Soviet Strela-3 (SA-14 Gremlin) began in 1968, and it entered service six years later in 1974 (Jane's, 2006a, p. 30). Like their predecessors, these systems used IR devices, but they had been improved to engage targets from all directions (not just from behind). Second-generation IR systems also achieved a greater range and accuracy. The British Blowpipe system was based on radio CLOS technology, but the Swedish RBS-70 differed in that it used a laser beam-riding tracking system that was more resistant to countermeasures (Jane's, 1985, pp. 133–44).

Whereas the first 25 years of MANPADS research and development had resulted in just four countries producing weapons, the next 25 years saw this number rise considerably—only partially because of formal licensing agreements. By 2007, 31 countries had manufactured an entire system, had produced important components, or had created systems that upgraded certain aspects of an existing system such as enhancing target acquisition (see Annexe 1.2).

Licensed production and reverse engineering (unauthorized copying of existing systems) of mostly early Soviet models largely explain this increase in states' production of MANPADS. The issue of licensing is sensitive and contentious for the Russian Federation and many former Warsaw Pact countries. Moscow claims that current MANPADS systems are being produced illegally in some of these countries. Those accused retort, however, either that no such licence exists or that the models being produced are their own missiles after years of indigenous improvements (Small Arms Survey, 2007a, pp. 20–21). For some producers there is no pretence of any licence having existed. In the late 1970s, for example, the Egyptians produced a reverse-engineered copy of the SA-7, called the Ayn-al-Saqr. In 1974 the Egyptian government allegedly supplied Beijing and Pyongyang with examples of this SA-7 in appreciation of their support during the 1973 Yom Kippur War. Subsequently, both China and North Korea produced their own versions of the weapon (Jane's, 2006a, p. 10). There are also reports that the US Stinger has been produced under licence and illegally copied, albeit not as widely as Soviet models.[26]

Improvements to later generation IR MANPADS include greater range and accuracy, and better resistance to IR countermeasures (Jane's, 2006a). Many systems also have larger warheads, with proximity, delay, or grazing fuses, which increase the missiles' lethality, hit probability, and, in some cases, the types of targets that can be engaged. The Bolide is a new High Velocity Missile, which is compatible with the RBS-70 launcher. By one account it reportedly has a range of 10,000 m and is effective against both ground and sea targets (FI, 2007c).

Newer models are not just more capable but considerably more expensive. Older IR systems such as the SA-7 and Stinger used to cost an estimated USD 25,000–40,000. Newer generation models like the laser-beam riding RBS-70 and British Starstreak, however, sell today for about USD 220,000 (FI, 2007c; TGC, 2007).

More than 100 countries—and non-state actors—possess these weapons. MANPADS have been transferred to at least 125 countries (FI, 2007b). Of the 500,000–750,000 MANPADS believed to be in circulation, some 99 per cent are estimated to be in state inventories. But many governments and regional organizations deem the stockpile management procedures for tens of thousands of these weapons to be wanting (see, for example, Schroeder, 2007). The United States alone has destroyed more than 20,000 MANPADS since 2002 in some two dozen countries (USFNS, 2007). Many non-state armed groups possess MANPADS (see Annexe 1.1), the result of deliberate government policy,

The US h
more tha
MANPAD
2002 in
dozen cc

seizure, corruption, lax export controls, and stockpile mismanagement. Batteries can last 20 years and more (Eagle Picher, 2003), making older systems still attractive on the secondary market.

Fourth-generation missile systems currently under development are incorporating more advanced guidance and sensor systems for improving accuracy at greater altitudes and ranges (CRS, 2006). Raytheon, for instance, is completing development on an upgrade to the US Stinger that enables the gunner with better cueing and target-acquisition capabilities. This variant is expected to provide a separate helmet with rangefinder that communicates with the missile via an Enhanced Position Location Reporting System (EPLRS) radio (Richardson, 2004b).

Other recent advances include the introduction of automated command-and-control systems. Belarus and Israel in particular have developed the Shlem and Red Sky, respectively. These are integrated multiple launch systems that rely on global positioning and infrared technology to reach targets with greater accuracy. One added benefit is that the launch unit is equipped so that the operator can send cues to the launcher from a distance via computer (Gyürösi, 2003; Jane's, 2006c).

Anti-tank guided weapons (ATGWs)

An anti-tank guided weapon is a launcher, accompanied by a missile fitted with a warhead that the operator manually, automatically, or semi-automatically steers to its target. These weapons are primarily designed to knock out armoured vehicles and frequently possess a useful secondary effect against hardened or reinforced targets such as bunkers. They were created when advances in armour made traditional direct-fire anti-tank guns less effective. Moreover, ATGWs offer soldiers the ability to engage targets from greater distances with increased accuracy than is possible with unguided anti-tank light weapons. These weapons have an effective range of up to 8,000 m, and armour penetration nearing 1,000 mm (Jane's, 1985, pp. 49–69; 2007b, pp. 445–509). However, each generation of weapon varies greatly in terms of its guidance, lethality, and portability.

Initially produced in the 1950s, there have been three distinct 'generations' within the weapon system's development, all of which primarily concern the guidance of the weapon. Besides changes to these systems' navigation, there have been improvements in each generation's range and payload.

First-generation ATGWs were guided to the target after launch by a wire in the rear of the missile which was connected to the firing unit. The operator often used a joystick to manually control the direction of the projectile. Early launchers were as simple as a disposable transport box that was either placed on the ground or mounted on a vehicle. This system was known as 'MCLOS' for manual command to line-of-sight. They achieved effective ranges between 1,500 and 3,000 m, and delivered a maximum penetration of 500 mm (Jane's, 2007b, pp. 445–509). During WWII the Germans employed the X-7, the first MCLOS system (Gander, 2000, pp. 136–52). The French SS-10 and German Cobra, both modelled after the X-7, were the first ATGWs available for export, although they remained in production for only a short time (Jane's, 1975, p. 743; 1985, p. 51). In 1964, the 9M14 Malyutka, also known as the AT-3 Sagger (North Atlantic Treaty Organization (NATO) designation), became the first Soviet ATGW. A drawback of first-generation models, independent of their relative effectiveness, was that the gunner had to remain in the same position while the warhead was in flight. If the target was not effectively neutralized, or if there were other forces within range of attack, the ATGW operator was quite vulnerable.

Second-generation systems, known as SACLOS (semi-automatic command to line-of-sight), saw significant improvements in performance. After the missile is launched, the operator keeps the sight on the target, whereby automatic guidance commands are sent to the missile via wire, radio, or laser-beam-riding technology. The United States introduced the tube-launched, optically tracked, wire-guided missile (TOW) in 1968. Although many countries are now shopping elsewhere for ATGWs, by 2000 more than 600,000 TOW missiles and 15,000 launchers had been procured, making the system the most widely deployed of all ATGWs (Gander, 2000, p. 140). France and Germany jointly began producing the Missile d'Infanterie léger antichar (MILAN, infantry light anti-tank missile) shortly thereafter. SACLOS missiles outperform first-generation systems with accuracy rates exceeding 90 per cent. Moreover, SACLOS missiles reach effective ranges between 2,500 and 5,500 m with warhead armour penetration of up to 900 mm, almost twice the range and payload of first-generation models (Jane's, 2007b, pp. 445–509).

Despite advances made in SACLOS models, operators were still vulnerable to counterattack due to their immobility. Third-generation guidance systems ameliorated this threat by having IR lasers installed on the nose of the missile to lock on and reach the target automatically. Unlike wire-guided and laser-beam-riding missiles, IR technology enables the operator to reposition or reload immediately. First developed in the 1980s, these 'fire and forget' (FaF) guidance systems allow the operator to retreat immediately after firing. The most notable of these weapons is Israel's Spike, which moved beyond 'fire and forget' to 'fire and correct', whereby the operator can change the target during missile flight (TGC, 2007). Other IR ATGWs include the Indian Nag and the US Javelin. Maximum range varies considerably. Whereas maximum ranges are typically between 4,000 and 8,000 m (Jane's, 2007b, pp. 445–509), some models have shorter firing ranges to suit current environments of combat (FI, 2007b). Moreover, IR models tend to be lighter and collapsible for transportability. These developments allow soldiers increased versatility in urban spaces. For example, these systems have been employed in Afghanistan and Iraq, where manoeuvrability is limited in comparison to prior military engagements in Vietnam and Latin America.

The costs of ATGWs vary considerably. The basic TOW and MILAN as well as other SACLOS missiles are priced at around USD 10,000 a piece. Third-generation systems that use IR guidance missiles cost considerably more—starting at between five and ten times the price of SACLOS missiles (FI, 2007c).

More than 30 countries have fully or partially produced ATGWs, but currently only six are fully manufacturing ATGWs with fire-and-forget guidance systems. Many of the countries that produced MCLOS systems have chosen to cease production for a variety of reasons: an obsolete design with low hit probability; gunner vulnerability; a limited ability to penetrate modern armour; and sufficient stockpiles to satisfy demand.[27] Roughly half of the systems produced are essentially copies of another country's design such as the Malyutka (Sagger), TOW, and Spike. Currently, roughly 14 countries produce ATGWs with technology acquired from six technology-owning countries, either with or without a formal licence. Most licensing agreements include offsets which are supplementary arrangements to compensate the purchaser in some fashion—either directly in terms of the item in question, or indirectly involving some other good or service (Small Arms Survey, 2007a, p. 12; see also Box 1.5).

Unlike with MANPADS, however, the international community has expended comparatively little energy to destroy excess stockpiles of ATGWs. As with MANPADS, ATGWs are to be found in the stocks of a great number of

Box 1.5   Licensing agreements and offsets: the case of the Spike in Poland

Israel has exported Rafael's Spike anti-tank guided weapon to several countries since Singapore first purchased the system in 1999. Subsequent orders have come from Finland, the Netherlands, Poland, and Spain. Several of these purchases have included licensed production and offset agreements.

The December 2003 deal between Poland and Israel for PLN 1.487 billion (USD 512 million) covered the sale of 2,675 missiles and 264 launchers with substantial local manufacture involved. Initial materials for the missile were provided by the Israeli manufacturer, with the Polish company ZM Mesko and Polish partners responsible for producing numerous components. Up to ten companies are to be involved, and hundreds of jobs created. The missiles' warheads, rocket engines (launch booster and sustainer), and launch tubes are among the parts to be made in Poland. All told, fully 70 per cent of the missile is to be manufactured in Poland. Rafael will supply the thermal imager, firing post, tripod, and simulators. Under the offset agreements, ZM Mesko will deliver 2,000 warheads and motors to Rafael. ZM Mesko will also be able to use some technologies received from Rafael to improve or develop other indigenous projects.

Sources: Holdanowicz (2004; 2007); Jane's (2005)

states. By one account, more than 100 countries have such weapons in their inventories (FI, 2007b). However, more than half of these states' arsenals are believed to possess mostly the less sophisticated and less able MCLOS systems. Non-state armed groups also possess ATGWs. Hezbollah, for instance, reportedly received hundreds of anti-tank guided missiles through state transfers from Iran and Syria (Wezeman et al., 2007, p. 410). But according to published reports fewer of these groups own ATGWs than possess MANPADS (see Annexe 1.1).

Recent developments of ATGWs have been aimed at designing more versatile weapons for use against varying ground targets. Rather than utilizing ATGWs solely in an anti-tank capacity, reports from Iraq demonstrate that these weapons are more likely to be used against 'low-value' targets, such as passageways and concrete walls.[28] With nearly 1,000 missiles fired in Iraq by 2005, the US Javelin has filled this role. The Javelin missile, however, is expensive for use against low-value targets. In response, the United States has begun research on the Spike (not to be confused with Israel's ATGW), a new lightweight fire-and-forget missile. It is expected to carry an average unit price of USD 4,000, and to be effective against stationary or moving ground targets and low- and slow-flying helicopters (FI, 2007c).

UNGUIDED LIGHT WEAPONS

Traditionally, unguided light weapons differ from their guided weapon counterparts in that the system operator cannot change the missile's course after it is fired. This does not mean unguided weapons are less accurate than guided weapons—they just cannot be directed while in flight (although technological developments are allowing the trajectories of some new mortars to be manipulated). Unguided weapons reach their intended targets through both direct and indirect fire. With direct-fire weapons, the target is seen directly, through a sight, in contrast to indirect-fire weapons, which have no direct line of sight to the target. Training and improved fire-control mechanisms permit even indirect weapons such as mortars to be extremely accurate at distances exceeding the most advanced man-portable air-defence systems. Recent technological progress has blurred the distinction between these two types of weapons, however. The development of 'smart' mortar bombs that can hit their intended targets with higher probabilities than traditional systems relying only on ballistics could have grave consequences should this technology proliferate to terrorist groups.

This section is organized into two parts: the first reviews systems that fire cartridge-based ammunition; the second covers weapons that launch rockets, mortars, and grenades.

Weapons firing cartridge-based ammunition

Heavy machine guns (including anti-aircraft guns)

Heavy machine guns are those capable of firing 12.7 mm (.50 calibre) ammunition to calibres of up to 20 mm, where it is generally accepted that cannon ammunition starts. They are man-portable, but are typically mounted on vehicles or ground mounts as an anti-personnel and anti-aircraft weapon. They are effective against personnel, light armoured vehicles, low- and slow-flying aircraft, and small boats. Modern heavy machine guns are belt-fed, recoil-operated, air-cooled, and have an effective range of up to 2,000 m (Jane's, 2007c, pp. 353–415). For all intents and purposes any heavy machine gun can serve in an anti-aircraft role. The distinction between heavy machine guns' ability to fire on land and air targets rests largely on the placement of the firer and the type of weapon mounting and sights.

Heavy machine guns date back to the late 1800s. However, most modern models fashion themselves after the US Browning .50 Calibre M-series Heavy Machine Gun, first designed in 1918. Extended firing of this calibre weapon generated very high temperatures, rendering the gun barrel a potential hazard for shooters. During the First World War (WWI) weapons such as the Browning M1921 used a water-cooling system to reduce the barrel's heat. To overcome the inconvenience associated with water-cooling, the 1928 Browning M2HB (Heavy Barrel) replaced this system, and addressed barrel heat with a thicker barrel construction which acted as a heat-sink and allowed higher volumes of fire to be obtained. The Soviets responded to the Browning in 1938 with the DShK, which featured similar capabilities to those of the Browning M2. The Soviets and later the Russians replaced the DShK with newer models, such as the NSV (1971) and Kord (1998). Improvements in weight, reliability, and production capability made these weapons superior to their predecessor (Jane's, 2007c, pp. 381–91). In contrast to developing new models, the United States continued to produce improved variants of the Browning M2 for the better part of the 20th century.

These two systems remained the global norm until 1986, when the M2HB-QCB (quick-change barrel), developed by FN Herstal of Belgium, introduced significant changes to the original model. The QCB variant reduced the risk of ammunition jamming (Hogg, 1999, p. 216).

More than 20 countries worldwide have produced heavy machine guns. Currently, nearly half of them have ceased production, primarily of the 14.5 mm heavy machine gun. With the exception of the Chinese, who have developed one new model each decade since the 1950s, most countries produce copies or variants (either licensed or unlicensed) of the Russian DShK and the US Browning M2 (Jane's, 2007b, pp. 353–415). Pakistan, for example, produces its 12.7 mm Type 54 anti-aircraft gun under an official licence from China, which itself acquired the DShK technology without formal licence from the Russian Federation (Small Arms Survey, 2007a, p. 19).

As noted earlier, heavy machine guns have made their way into the arsenals of non-state armed groups. It is not clear which avenues are most commonly used for illicit procurement, but what remains uncontested is the impact of these weapons when they are misused (see above).

Despite few technological changes over the past century, developments are under way to equip armies with more powerful and versatile heavy machine guns. The XM312 .50 calibre machine gun, under development by the US firm

General Dynamics Armament and Technical Products (GDATP), is claimed to be nine times more accurate than the Browning M2. It has reduced recoil, enabling the shooter to keep focused on the target. Moreover, it can be quickly converted to the XM307, a 25 mm grenade launcher system. Nearly half the weight of the M2, it is expected to be one of the lightest 12.7 mm machine guns on the market when it enters service (General Dynamics, 2007).

Anti-materiel rifles

Anti-materiel rifles are designed primarily to engage and neutralize a variety of targets at distances well beyond a kilometre. Specialized ammunition enables the weapon to pierce light armour and (parked) aircraft, but the rifle can be, and has been, used for anti-personnel purposes. Most of the weapons in this class are chambered for 12.7 mm (.50 calibre) ammunition, but some fire cartridges of up to 20 mm. The effective range for 12.7 mm and 14.5 mm anti-materiel rifles is 1,000–2,000 m (at the upper threshold, at least three times the effective range of a 7.62 mm assault rifle), but use of a mount can extend the range and its ability to engage the target.[29] A 20 mm anti-materiel rifle typically has an effective range of around 2,000 m (Jane's, 2007b, pp. 287–96).

Anti-materiel rifles have found favour among many countries' militaries as well as law-enforcement bodies, and are being widely produced. Rifles firing ammunition larger than 10 mm date back to WWI and were further developed during WWII. These weapons, which served ostensibly in an anti-tank capacity, were generally too heavy for a single soldier to transport. Other types of light weapons were developed to meet the same need, and rifles calibrated to fire large ammunition went out of favour. This changed dramatically in 1982 with the production of the Barrett M82. Although not designed to engage tanks, advances in ballistics, improvements in the weapons' design to reduce recoil and weight, and more destructive bullets resulted in a much more portable weapon that could engage a variety of targets. Today, 14 countries produce anti-materiel rifles that fire 12.7 mm, 14.5 mm, and 20 mm ammunition. The US manufacturer Barrett attempted to develop a weapon based on the M82 (and its successor the M107) that fired a 25 mm round, but this initiative was halted for technological reasons (Jane's, 2007b, p. 299).

The 12.7 mm rifle is popular with civilians in several countries, and numerous non-military versions are being produced to meet this demand. The civilian versions are generally heavier, less robust, and equipped with fewer optical and other electronic devices (although many of these items can be obtained commercially and fitted to most 'civilian' models) than the weapons designed to military specifications. In the United States alone, more than 20

Table 1.2 **Examples of 12.7 mm (.50 calibre) anti-materiel rifle prices from US companies (USD)***					
Company	**Prices**	**Company**	**Prices**	**Company**	**Prices**
A.L.S.	1,900	Christensen Arms	5,500	Robar	7,000
Armalite Inc.	3,000	East Ridge Gun Company Inc.	1,900–3,600	Safety Harbor Firearms Inc.	1,850–2,450
Barrett	3,000–8,050	E.D.M. Arms	2,250–8,500	Serbu Firearms	2,200–2,450
Bluegrass Armory	3,100	Ferret 50	3,300–4,000	Watson Weapons	2,150

*Prices are rounded to nearest USD 50.
Source: Leff (2007)

companies manufacture 12.7 mm calibre rifles (Boatman, 2004, pp. 51–52, 56, 58, 61; see Table 1.2 for a sampling of producers and prices). Interest in this type of firearm arises in part because it is legal for civilians in the United States to possess this weapon and because using these rifles has become a recognized sport not just in the United States but also in Switzerland and the United Kingdom.[30]

Non-state armed groups have also shown an interest in acquiring this weapon and in at least two cases have succeeded in obtaining some from civilian customers in the United States who have transferred them (illegally). Known instances are the Irish Republican Army (Vobejda and Ottaway, 1999) and the Kosovo Liberation Army (Sullivan, 2004).

Recoilless rifles and guns

Recoilless rifles and guns fire projectiles that achieve a depth of penetration that would normally require a much heavier conventional recoiling weapon. They are light, but are able to fire large calibre ammunition (57–105 mm). Their basic design is based on a lightweight rifled barrel and a locked breech that is vented rearward. Upon firing, the projectile is launched in one direction, and a precisely balanced flow of propellant gases or a counter-mass is vented in the opposite direction. These competing forces balance out to eliminate the recoil forces encountered with conventional weapons. Some versions can be shoulder-fired, others such as the 105 mm version are mounted on a light vehicle, but most are mounted on tripods. The gun barrel, tripod, optical sight, and ammunition are typically carried separately by a four-person team. Recoilless rifles and guns have maximum firing ranges superior to most other light weapons (2,000–8,000 m depending on the calibre of the weapon), but their effective range is significantly less (Jane's, 2007c, pp. 445–504).

Traditionally classified as an anti-tank weapon, recoilless rifles and guns were developed first by Commander Cleland Davis, an US naval officer, prior to WWI (NYT, 1912). The Davis Gun was restricted to use as an aircraft weapon, and was later scrapped due to its impracticality.[31] The Soviets began trials in the early 1930s for an anti-tank recoilless weapon, known as the RK system, intended for infantry use. The gun remained in service only for less than a decade because it was too dangerous to handle. Finally, in 1946 the Swedish defence industry introduced the Carl Gustaf, a shoulder-fired recoilless weapon (Gander, 2000, pp. 124–26). With more than 90,000 produced since WWII (FI, 2007a), the Carl Gustaf M2 is the most popular shoulder-fired recoilless rifle. Despite advances in ammunition, the design of the original launcher has not changed much over time.

At least 25 countries have produced recoilless rifles and guns. Of these, only about one-third continue to produce them. The US M40 105 mm, otherwise known as the 106, is the most widely produced and distributed recoilless rifle, with exports to more than 30 countries and production of both licensed and unlicensed copies in Austria, China, India, Iran, Pakistan, South Korea, and Spain. The 106 is typically mounted to a vehicle, but can be transported short distances by a crew (Jane's, 2007c, p. 504). Since the late 1990s, however, armies have begun to phase out large calibre recoilless rifles, opting for smaller systems with shorter engagement ranges that are effective in urban combat and against bunkers.

Recoilless rifles and guns themselves have not changed dramatically over time. But they have expanded their utility to accommodate various types of ammunition, including high-explosive fragmentation rounds, close-defence shrapnel-type ammunition, smoke, illumination, and several other types of warheads (Jane's, 2007c, pp. 445–504).

Hand-held, under-barrel, and automatic grenade launchers

There are three types of grenade launchers—hand-held, under-barrel, and automatic. They fire numerous types of grenades, including those filled with high explosives, lachrymatory agents (such as tear gas), bright burning compounds for illumination, and incendiary material.

Most launchers fire NATO 40 mm or ex-Warsaw Pact 30 mm ammunition. Hand-held and under-barrel grenade launchers are effective against point targets at less than 500 m, and are most commonly used in military operations. Police forces occasionally use them to launch rubber or tear gas projectiles for crowd and riot control. Automatic grenade launchers, on the other hand, have a maximum effective range against point targets of 150–1,500 m and against area targets of up to 2,200 m (Jane's, 2007b, pp. 417–32).

In the post-WWII period, countries began developing 'hand-held' single-shot grenade launchers to replace the rifle grenade launcher. The most common of these was the US M79, which was widely used during the Vietnam War. In order to increase firing versatility, countries developed under-barrel grenade launchers. This is a complete weapon with its own barrel, trigger, and sights. It is attached under the barrel of the rifle to allow for either rifle or grenade fire from the same platform.

In 1967, The US began producing the MK 19—the first automatic grenade launcher to be used during the Vietnam War. The Soviets followed suit with the introduction of the AGS-17 in the mid-1970s. These weapons are light and compact, enabling them to be used in close to medium range battle (Jane's, 2007c, pp. 423–24, 431–32). Automatic grenade launchers are mounted on a tripod or vehicle, and are capable of firing 40–480 rounds per minute up to ranges of 1,700 m. The production status of the Russian AGS-17 is currently dormant, as it has been replaced with a newer model. It is in service with many countries throughout the world, and is produced under licence by China and Serbia (Jane's, 2007c, pp. 423–24).

The 1980s and 1990s saw the development of stand-alone rapid firing six-shot multiple grenade launchers. Their effective range does not differ from low-velocity single-shot grenade launchers, but their ability to fire up to six grenades within seconds constitutes an important difference. These have been used in urban warfare and small-scale conflicts. Examples of six-shot grenade launchers include the Russian 6G30 and South African MGL Mark 1 (Jane's, 2007b, pp. 332–33, 339).

At least 25 countries currently produce one type or a combination of hand-held, under-barrel, and automatic grenade launchers. Manufactured in 17 countries, under-barrel grenade launchers are the most widely produced version. The US M203 replaced the M79 in 1969, and is now the most broadly produced and traded grenade launcher in the world. Canada, Egypt, South Korea, and Taiwan all produce launchers that are directly licensed from or closely resemble the M203. Out of about 20 countries that have produced automatic grenade launchers, a little more than half continue to do so.

Current advances in grenade launchers afford users lighter systems with greater accuracy. The German XM320 is under development to replace the US M203. Operators benefit from a lighter launcher that has a safer and more modern firing system than its predecessor. The new model enables soldiers to attach the launcher in seconds without any tools. Moreover, it is designed to use all current 40 x 46 mm ammunition (side-loading and long cartridges) that the previous M203 model was incapable of accommodating (Gourley, 2006). Likewise, the US XM25 Individual Airburst Weapon System, currently under development by Alliant Techsystems as part of the Objective Individual

Combat Weapon (OICW) programme, features a time-fused grenade controlled by a computer. Before firing, the shooter determines the range by using a laser rangefinder. Then the computer calculates the trajectory and sets the time fuse so the grenade explodes at the pre-selected range up to 500 m (ATK, 2007). Although slated to replace the US MK19 Automatic Grenade Launcher, this weapon has been delayed several times and has yet to enter production (Kucera, 2006).

Rocket/grenade launchers and mortars

Unguided 'anti-tank' rocket launchers (including RPGs)

Unguided rocket launchers cover a wide range of multi-purpose weapons that discharge an unguided rocket and are armed with various warheads to engage and defeat a variety of targets. These weapons, which may be reloadable or disposable after a single use, typically are designed to be operated by one person.

The numerous roles designed for this type of light weapon defy a generalized description of their ranges and effectiveness. In the anti-armour role, the ubiquitous RPG-7 has an effective range of about 330 m against moving targets and 500 m against stationary targets, but generally cannot defeat main battle tanks (Jane's, 2007c, pp. 476–78). Newer models such as Spain's Alcotan-100 achieve longer ranges and are fitted with a variety of warheads that are effective against explosive reactive armour as well as bunkers and other structures. Besides engaging armoured vehicles and bunkers, versions of these weapons are also employed against people. These technological differences are expressed through the prices of these weapons' launchers: an RPG-7 costs USD 1,900–2,200 and the Alcotan-100 sells for more than USD 11,000 (FI, 2007a).

The appearance of armoured vehicles during WWI, followed by tanks equipped with more resilient armour in WWII, created demand for a light and portable infantry weapon, which continues to this day although the targets are more varied. The first shoulder-fired rocket launchers, all introduced in the early 1940s, were the US M1, better known as the 'Bazooka', the German Panzerfaust, and the British PIAT (Gander, 2000, pp. 88–100). After the Soviet army captured blueprints for the Panzerfaust in 1945, it developed the RPG-2, which closely resembled its German counterpart. Since WWII, Germany, the Russian Federation, and the United States have developed upgrades for their rocket launcher systems every decade or so. Although commonly called rocket-propelled grenades (RPGs), which happens also to be the acronym for the popular Soviet-designed weapon (Ruchnoy Protivotankovyy Granatomyot), many newer models bear little resemblance to the RPG-2 or RPG-7. The US M72 LAW (light anti-tank weapon), which followed the Bazooka, and the Swedish AT4, for example, are shoulder-launched, but differ from RPGs in that they are single-use weapons in which the projectile is pre-packaged.

Improvements to unguided rocket launcher warheads make these weapons more powerful against a wider range of targets than older munitions. The US MK 118 Mod 0 High Explosive Dual-Purpose (HEDP) warhead, for example, is designed to detonate at different times depending on the material of the target. For soft targets such as concrete and sandbags there is a fuse delay, which allows the rocket deep penetration before detonation. In contrast, the warhead explodes immediately upon impact with harder targets such as armoured vehicles (FI, 2007a).

Unguided rocket launchers are widely produced and widely procured. More than 35 countries have produced unguided rocket launchers. Of these about half have ceased production over the last few decades. As of 2006, at least

11 countries had produced licensed copies of the RPG-7, accounting for more than 13 million units produced worldwide (FI, 2007a). RPGs' low price,[32] wide availability, small size, and light weight make them attractive to non-state actors.

Future developments primarily involve improvements to the rocket's warhead. In line with current combat conditions, new designs are aimed at increasing explosive strength and penetration, while reducing the launcher size and the amount of back blast that often accompanies such improvements. The Swedish Next-generation Light Anti-tank Weapon (NLAW), expected to enter service by 2009, is the first single-soldier rocket system that is capable of destroying any type of main battle tank (MBT), and is small enough to operate in cramped quarters as a bunker buster (Saab).

Mortars

Mortars are generally smooth-bored indirect-fire weapons that enable the operator to fire from small deep pits, behind hills, or in ravines. A mortar's high-trajectory fire makes the weapon effective against similar enemy positions. There are, generally speaking, three categories of mortar: 'light' (up to 79 mm), 'medium' (80–99 mm), and 'heavy' (100 mm and above). With traditional ammunition these mortars can engage targets less than 100 m. from the firer's position to more than 7 km away (see Figure 1.1). Specialized ammunition has augmented these weapons' operational capacity in terms of both range and lethality (see below). Some light mortars can be carried and operated by a single person. But most mortars are crew-served weapons; one soldier carries the launch tube and fire-control unit, another carries the base plate, and a third carries the bipod or tripod. This three-person team can carry the requisite munitions for smaller mortars (a 60 mm mortar bomb weighs around 1 kg, for example), but larger systems typically require additional team members or light vehicles to transport the munitions (Jane's, 2007c, pp. 511–85, 707–63).

The mortar is one of the oldest forms of artillery, and its basic design has not changed much in the past 50 years. The weapon was likely used as long ago as the siege of Constantinople in 1453. Modern-day versions are based on a 1915 design by the British engineer, Wilfred Stokes. He invented what became known as the 3 in. (76.2 mm) muzzle-loading Stokes mortar for British use during WWI (Jane's, 1979, p. 405). Such mortars won wide acceptance in part because they were cheap and easy to make. In the lead-up to WWII, two firms—Britain's Stokes and France's Thomson-Brandt—became the leading mortar manufacturers of that time. Then, during the war, numerous countries began to manufacture 120 mm mortars. There have since been metallurgical advances to produce lighter launch tubes and political requirements for a mortar just under 100 mm.[33]

Nearly 50 countries have manufactured one or more types of mortars, making it the most widely produced light weapon. Only around 30 of these countries, however, continue to produce or partially produce one or more types of mortar (Jane's, 1975; 1985; 2007c). Partial producers include Canada and New Zealand, which manufacture mortar

Figure 1.1 **Mean maximum ranges for 50 mm to 120 mm mortars with standard munitions**

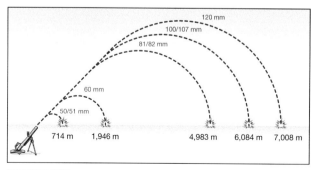

120 mm
100/107 mm
81/82 mm
60 mm
50/51 mm

714 m   1,946 m   4,983 m   6,084 m   7,008 m

Source: Wilkinson (2008)

> ## Box 1.6 Mortar developments: precision guidance and extended ranges
>
> Traditionally, mortars have been 'guided' only in the sense that with skill one could calculate the distance, and in which direction, a mortar shell would travel. A spotter could relay information to the individual or team firing the weapon, and subsequent refinements would enable the target to be effectively engaged—often with a salvo of mortars. In recent years, however, munitions have been developed that permit a single mortar to obtain a degree of precision previously impossible to achieve—and at distances previously beyond reach.
>
> Four types of precision guidance system exist for mortars. As these systems have been developed since the late 1990s, it is perhaps misleading to speak of them as comprising separate 'generations'. But their developments mirror those of MANPADS in the sense that early systems used infrared technology and more recent systems use radio frequencies (RFs), laser-beams, and fibre optics. IR (and RF) systems have the advantages of fire-and-forget targeting, but can mistake similar 'signatures' for the intended objective. Systems using laser beams can provide the user with a higher degree of reliability but require someone within a kilometre of the target and with an unobstructed view to illuminate the mark so that the projectile can latch on to it. A system utilizing fibre-optic technology allows the operator to be far from the target (or the launch site). Global positioning system (GPS) software is also being used—sometimes on its own and also in conjunction with other forms of terminal guidance. The first precision mortar system—the 120 mm IR-guided Saab Bofors Strix—entered service in 1994 (and had an unexceptional range of 7 km). Other precision mortars since produced or under development include the British ODAM, French ALFO, Israeli Fireball, Russian Gran, and US PGMM. These subsequent models employ the different guidance systems noted above and range in size from 60 to 120 mm, with some systems having more than one version.
>
> Most precision mortars are also equipped with technological improvements that extend their ranges. Changes include booster rockets, deployable fins, and extendable wings. It is not uncommon for ranges to be extended two or more times the distance of traditional mortars. (Some mortars that do not employ terminal guidance have extended ranges using similar features.)
>
> Source: Bonomo et al. (2007, pp. 20-38)

fire control units but do not produce complete mortars or their requisite ammunition. Canada offers a full line of mortar sight units. New Zealand is one of the few countries that have developed a computer system that utilizes global positioning system (GPS) technology. This allows operators at secured posts to engage targets from single or multiple mortar locations (Jane's, 2004, pp. 550–52, 555). Computerized fire-control systems not only reduce the time needed to calculate necessary changes to aim the mortar but in some cases can adjust the mortar tube automatically (Bonomo et al., 2007, pp. 34–37). Given their availability, longevity, ease of operation, and low cost, mortars appeal to non-state armed groups (as noted above, by their use in Former Yugoslavia and in Liberia). More recently, in September 2007, an unidentified Sudanese armed group used mortars, among other small arms and light weapons, to kill ten African Union peacekeepers in Darfur (CNN, 2007).

Besides the improvements to control units noted above, other important developments concern the mortar construction and munitions. For example, light carbon fibre composite barrels are being developed that could enable a single person to transport and operate a mortar as large as 120 mm. New designs are permitting systems to be deployed more easily. Mortar shells are also undergoing significant changes and are no longer constrained by 'simple' ballistics (see Box 1.6).

CALCULATING VALUES AND VOLUMES FOR LIGHT WEAPON PRODUCTION

What is the volume and value of production of the light weapons identified in this chapter? Manufacturers and government officials are not particularly open about individual or overall sales figures. Analysts who follow the industry closely are more inclined to forecast future growth for a specific product and that system's or that company's potential overall market share than they are to discuss actual recipients, numbers sold, and unit values. Measures to encourage transparency in reporting have been adopted by organizations such as the Economic Community of West African States (ECOWAS) and the Organization for Security and Co-operation in Europe (OSCE). Yet, even when reporting is kept confidential among peers, the information that states choose to share tends to be selective and partial.

How then does one determine the number of light weapons produced and their value?

To date, the Small Arms Survey has utilized customs data to ascertain the value of the authorized transfer of certain weapons. This sheds some light on production values and volumes, but is an imperfect indicator at best. Customs data does not distinguish between newly produced weapons and those that may represent excess stockpiles or second-hand goods. Moreover, customs data tracks trans-border transactions, not domestic acquisitions. A further limitation that concerns light weapons (and not small arms) is that some existing categories include both light weapons and major conventional weapon systems, and cannot be disaggregated. For these and other reasons, estimates of the volumes and values of new production can be based on customs data only in exceptional cases.

General media and trade reports sometimes provide the details of a sale. While in some instances this can shed light on the value and volume of production and transfer, there are limits to the use of such information. Often the information provided refers to 'packages' including different types of weapons, support equipment, and spare parts. It is not unusual for a single order to encompass numerous missiles of different ranges, warheads, guidance systems, and platforms. Furthermore, the number of spare parts will often differ between contracts. One country may buy sufficient spare parts for the expected time of operation of a particular system, but another may buy only an initial set of spare parts. A repeat customer may require fewer spare parts than a new purchaser. Offsets (see Box 1.5) can also affect a system's unit sales value. For guided weapons, the ratio between a firing post (FP), containing the launch control unit (LCU), thermal sights, and tripod, and the missiles it fires will differ among recipients. As the LCU is considerably more expensive than the individual missile, this creates challenges to calculating values. This is a partial, but representative, list of concerns.[34]

Despite these challenges, the Survey believes that sufficient information exists to make some general calculations and provide rough estimates that will shed light on a matter that has until now remained mostly in the shadows. For example, there are methods for estimating the mix of firing posts and missiles in a contract even where specific information is not available. A useful ratio can be generated from knowledge of doctrine and previous procurement. General price data for these components is sometimes reported. One can extrapolate from a small number of examples to make some general statements about other sales for which less information is available. And it might be possible to make some assumptions about how that weapon has fared in comparison with competing countries and systems to get a sense of the price a system can fetch in a competitive market.

Moreover, one can estimate the number of systems produced and delivered on a yearly basis by averaging a recipient's expected deliveries over the duration of a contract. Distinguishing launchers from missiles (in instances where the two are distinct and the launcher is reusable) is also often possible or can be estimated based on doctrine or examples of certain countries. By adding the estimated annual total units delivered and multiplying the total firing posts and missiles by an average price, one can shed considerable light on both the value and the volume of production for that system. With a view to testing some of these estimation techniques, we have developed a production worksheet for the Spike anti-tank guided weapon (see Table 1.3).

We have based our assessment of Spike ATGW production on a thorough review of open source information. Where we had no information on procurement rates for specific years, we assumed transfers of firing posts and missiles to

Table 1.3 Production worksheet for the Spike ATGW based on reported sales and estimates (2001-05)

Recipient	Contract signed	Period of delivery	Totals		Deliveries of firing posts (FPs) and missiles (Ms), in units								
			FPs	Ms	2001		2002		2003		2004		
					FPs	Ms	FPs	Ms	FPs	Ms	FPs	Ms	FPs
Chile	2003	2003-06	20	1,000					25	250	25	250	25
Czech Rep.	2006	2007-12	80	80									
Finland	2000	2001-05	120	1,000	24	200	24	200	24	200	24	200	24
Finland	2005	2008-09	?	?									
Israel	1990s	1995-?	?	?	0	50	0	50	0	50	0	50	
Italy	2005	2007-11	50	500									
Netherlands	2001	2001-05	250	2,400	50	480	50	480	50	480	40	480	50
Poland	2003	2004-13	264	2,675							2	20	24
Romania	1997	1999-2002	200	200	50	50	50	50					
Romania	1998	2002-05	80	160			20	40	20	40	20	40	20
Singapore	1999	2001-06	100	1,000			16	167	16	167	16	167	1
Slovenia	2006	2007-09	35	500									
Spain	2006	2008-?	260	2,600									
Totals					124	780	160	987	135	1,187	127	1,207	15

Key: FP = firing post; M = missile (MR, LR, and ER models); ? = insufficient data to base estimate
Source: Berman (2008)

be constant over the course of a multi-year delivery period. As Spike firing posts and missiles are easily interchange-able among firing platforms, we include in our analysis Spikes that may be mounted on 8 x 8 armoured wheeled vehicles (such as the Austrian Pandur or the Finnish Patria), or the tracked armoured infantry fighting vehicles (such as the Romanian MLI-84), or on helicopters (such as the Augusta A129). In other words, the fact that the weapon is man-portable or designed to function on a light vehicle is of greater significance for our purposes than the recipient's particular doctrine and intended use.

We base our calculations on an assessment of Spike missile costs by Forecast International, specifically that the MR (medium-range) version costs USD 97,000, the LR (long-range) version USD 115,000, and the ER (extended-range) version USD 129,500 (FI, 2007c). We assume that the firing post costs around USD 250,000. As the majority of missiles are of the LR and ER versions, for the purposes of our calculations we take USD 125,000 to be the average value of a Spike missile. Thus, between 2001 and 2005 the average annual sales value for this system may be esti-mated to be USD 170.4 million (i.e. 705 firing posts at USD 250,000 a piece for a total of USD 176.2 million, and 5,408 missiles at USD 125,000 each for a total of USD 676 million divided by five). This does not take into account production of spare parts and supporting equipment such as simulation systems. Spare parts can involve fairly large production values particularly for systems that have been in use for some time. There is, however, very little information on production of spare parts.

These figures are for sales values. Thus they include production costs, as well as taxes and profits. In the case of the Spike, parts of which are produced in many countries, it is difficult to say how much individual companies earn from production. It is important to underscore that almost every customer nation requires some form of compensation ('offset') for the purchase, usually a combination of direct and indirect offsets. In Poland, for example, Mesko is responsible for much of that country's procurement, just as General Dynamics Santa Bárbara Sistemas (GDSBS) will build components to fulfil the Spanish order, or the German firms Diehl BGT Defence (DBD) and Rheinmetall Defence Electronics (RDE) as part of the EuroSpike consortium play a leading role in supporting sales elsewhere in Europe. Since all these companies produce parts for many other weapon systems, it is difficult to obtain any further information from public company data.

Collecting data on the Spike is a first step towards generating a more complete picture of the production of light weapons. Next steps might include an analysis of Spike's competitors such as the Javelin, the TOW, and the MILAN, which could shed light on the Spike's market share and therefore allow one to gauge the larger market for anti-tank guided weapons from detailed knowledge of a single system. Each weapon system could be analysed separately and aggregated if sufficient information existed. It could also be possible to make an appraisal of the market based on information on quantities of ATGWs sold together with an assessment of the average value of this type of weapon system. Or, if prices were known for other ATGWs along with their comparable characteristics, then parametric cost estimation could be used to generate the broader picture for production values of this type of weapon. Parametric cost estimation, which is well established, is an especially promising technique for calculating unknown prices on the basis of physical characteristics, such as weight, range, accuracy, and complexity. With the use of known values and major physical characteristics that are closely linked to price differences, a price function could be estimated that could then be used to arrive at figures for individual weapons whose prices are not known. The multiplication of prices and quantities would result in estimates of sales values.

Such approaches—though meritorious—are beyond the scope of this initial exercise. For the purposes of generating an initial estimate of the market for ATGWs, we have taken Forecast International's projected market share for the Spike for the period 2007–11—roughly 15 per cent—and accepted that it broadly reflected the period 2001–05. With the Spike's annual sales for 2001–05 estimated to be USD 170.4 million, as noted above, this gives us a projected total for the anti-tank guided weapon market to have averaged USD 1.1 billion (i.e. USD 170.4 million x 6.67) for this five-year period.

CONCLUSION

In this chapter we have largely accepted the approach and categorization of the 1997 UN Panel of Experts when it comes to 'light weapons'. Focusing on portability as the overarching criterion, we have amended the Panel's listing to include mortars up to 120 mm, and various craft-produced materiel such as improvised explosive devices and man-portable rail-launched rockets.

Light weapons pose a demonstrable threat to societies and states. Their potential for causing political and economic instability and exacerbating armed violence is very real. The temporary cessation of British Airways flights to Kenya because of a perceived threat underscored MANPADS' effects even when they were not used. A single mortar shell fired into a crowded market in Sarajevo killed and wounded more than a hundred people. A one-day barrage of shells against the Liberian capital Monrovia resulted in thousands of casualties. RPGs and IEDs are responsible for the majority of US casualties in Iraq.

Some actions can be taken to counter the threat posed by some light weapons and help reduce the extent to which they proliferate, but some dangers cannot be neutralized or meaningfully mitigated. For example, technological countermeasures can be developed to impede a missile's ability to acquire or defeat its target (although perhaps not always in an economically viable manner). Moreover, improving states' abilities to manage their stockpiles of these weapons, combating their illicit trade, and strengthening oversight of licensing agreements can make a positive difference. Certain materials for producing light weapons, however, are available commercially and cannot easily be monitored or restricted. And it is nearly impossible to defend against some light weapons such as limpet mines, anti-materiel rifles, or indirect-fire weapons.

Fifty-nine countries either have produced one or more of the eight types of guided and unguided light weapons covered in this chapter, or have manufactured components or system upgrades for these types of weapon. More than half of these countries have undertaken production of guided weapons or their components: 28 currently produce MANPADS or their components, and 25 produce ATGWs or significant parts thereof. Generally speaking, light weapon systems are becoming cheaper to produce and acquire, easier to operate and transport, and more capable of engaging their targets at greater distances. The number of countries capable of producing light weapons far exceeds those that presently do so. For many of the light weapons covered in this chapter the technology required to manufacture them is simple to acquire, and 'barriers' to entry into such markets are self-imposed. It is simply cheaper and easier to procure the weapon from others than to undertake production on one's own.

The value of light weapons production exceeds several billion dollars annually. This chapter has focused on assessing just one of the UN Panel's eight light weapons item types: anti-tank guided weapons. We estimated that the annual sales for ATGWs averaged USD 1.1 billion for the period 2001–05. While much of this production results in local procurement and stockpiling, a sufficient percentage is sold to foreign customers to suggest that the long-standing estimate of USD 4 billion (Small Arms Survey, 2006, p. 67) for the authorized trade in small arms, light weapons, and their ammunition may be an underestimate.

Relatively few countries possess the know-how and industrial capacity to develop and produce on their own the most technologically sophisticated systems, but this does not stop them from obtaining the necessary capabilities. Many guided weapons considered advanced in the 1980s are now widely produced through reverse engineering or licensed production. If history is any indication, then it is only a matter of time before many countries produce new technologies such as guided mortars, which would have serious security implications, especially if they fell into the hands of terrorist groups.

Moreover, light weapon systems are widely held among non-state armed groups. Politicized reporting and the opaqueness of the black market make it difficult to ascertain the exact number of armed groups in possession of such materiel. But sufficient evidence exists to establish that dozens of such groups hold numerous guided light weapons. At least two groups have also obtained .50 calibre (12.7 mm) anti-materiel rifles (from civilians in the United States, where it is legal to purchase them). Many of these groups also produce their own light weapons, including mortars as well as grenade and rocket launchers. The sophistication of these weapons is growing, as is the threat they pose. Improvised explosive devices have proven effective against the most advanced armour. Man-portable rockets have increased in range, and it is believed to be only a matter of time before advances in the design of their propellant will enable them to be fired in large numbers rather than in small batches.

The combination of increased lethality and portability, together with reduced training requirements and barriers to production, suggests that greater attention should be paid to light weapons. ◼

ANNEXE 1.1

Guided light weapons reportedly held by non-state armed groups, 1996–2007*

Country or territory/area in which groups are active	Non-state armed group ■ Active as of Dec. 2007 ■ Defeated, dormant, or seized/joined government as of Dec. 2007	MANPADS Unspecified	SA-7	SA-14	SA-16/SA-18	Redeye	Stinger	HN-5	Blowpipe	Other**	ATGWs Unspecified	AT-3 Sagger	AT-4 Spigot	AT-5 Spandrel	AT-13 Saxhorn-2	AT-14 Spriggan	Toophan	Raad-T	Other**
Afghanistan	■ Jamiat-e-Islami		●	●															
	■ Jumbish-e-Milli		●																
	■ Northern Alliance (NA)										●								
	■ Taliban		●				●	●	●										
Algeria	■ Armed Islamic Group (GIA)						●												
	■ Salafist Group for Preaching and Combat (GSCP)		●																
Angola	■ National Union for the Total Independence of Angola (UNITA)		●	●	●	●	●												●
Chad	■ Union of Forces for Democracy and Development (UFDD)		●																
Colombia	■ National Liberation Army (ELN)	●					●												
	■ Revolutionary Armed Forces (FARC)		●	●	●														
Côte d'Ivoire	■ Patriotic Movement of Côte d'Ivoire (MPCI)	●																	
Democratic Republic of the Congo	■ Unspecified				●		●												
	■ National Congress for the Defense of the Congolese People (CNDP)						●												
Ethiopia	■ Oromo Liberation Front (OLF)	●																	
Guinea	■ Unspecified		●																
Iraq	■ Unspecified	●	●	●	●				●										●
Kashmir	■ Harkat ul-Ansar (HUA)		●																
	■ Hizbul Mujahideen (HM)						●												
Kenya	■ Unspecified		●																
Kosovo	■ Kosovo Liberation Army (UÇK)		●																
Lebanon	■ Hezbollah		●	●	●		●		●			●	●	●	●	●	●	●	●
	■ Popular Front for the Liberation of Palestine-Gen. Command (PFLP-GC)	●	●																
Liberia	■ Liberians United for Reconciliation and Democracy (LURD)		●																

Country	Group	1	2	3	4	5	6	7	8	9	10	11	12	13	14	15	16	17	18
Macedonia	National Liberation Army (NLA)		●		●							●							
Moldova	Unspecified		●	●															
Myanmar	United Wa State Army (UWSA)		●					●											
Northern Ireland	Irish Republican Army (IRA)		●																
Occupied Palestinian Territory	Islamic Resistance Movement (Hamas)						●												
	Palestinian Authority (PA)		●				●					●							
Pakistan	'Army of the Pure': Lashkar-e-Tayyiba (LeT)	●																	
Russian Federation	Chechen rebels		●		●		●		●										
Saudi Arabia	Al-Qaeda		●																
Sierra Leone	Armed Forces Revolutionary Council (AFRC)		●						●				●						
	Revolutionary United Front (RUF)		●	●					●				●		●				
Somalia	Shabaab	●	●		●						●								
	Islamic Courts Union (ICU)	●	●		●						●								
	Somali National Alliance (SNA)	●																	
	Transitional National Government (TNG)										●								
	Transitional Federal Government (TFG)										●								
	United Somali Congress/Somali Salvation Alliance (USC/SSA)	●																	
Spain	Basque Homeland and Freedom (ETA)		●																
Sri Lanka	Liberation Tigers of Tamil Eelam (LTTE)		●	●			●	●											
Sudan	Sudan People's Liberation Army (SPLA)		●																
Turkey	Kurdistan Workers' Party (PKK)		●				●												
Uganda	Lord's Resistance Army (LRA)		●								●								
TOTALS	Specific system reported to be, or have been, in groups' stockpiles	10	31	8	9	2	14	3	4	2	6	3	3	1	2	1	1	1	3
	Number of groups believed to be holding, or to have held, this type of weapon	42									13								

* This Annexe reflects the assumption that if a group reportedly fired a missile during the period under review, it probably has (or had) additional examples of the same system.
** The category 'other' includes reports of the Misagh (or Mithaq) in service with Iraqi armed groups, and the Vanguard and Misagh among Hezbollah's MANPADS holdings. As for ATGWs, Hezbollah is believed to possess the MILAN and TOW; these weapons are also reported to have been in service with UNITA.
Source: Lazarevic (2008)

ANNEXE 1.2

Global overview of countries producing light weapons (1947–2007)

No.	Country	MANPADS			ATGWs			HMGs/AAGs		Mortars			Grenade launchers			Recoilless rifles/guns	Anti-materiel rifles	Rocket launchers
		LBR	IR	CLOS	MCLOS	SACLOS	FaF	12.7 mm	14.5–20 mm	<79 mm	80–99 mm	100–120 mm	Hand-held	Under-barrel	Automatic			
1	Argentina				●	■				●	●	●	●			●		
2	Australia																●	
3	Austria									■	■	■				●	■	●
4	Belarus			▲														
5	Belgium							■	●		●		■				○	●
6	Bosnia and Herz.									●	●	●				●		●
7	Brazil				●	■				■	■	■				●		●
8	Bulgaria		■		●	■		■	■	●	■	■	■	■		■		■
9	Canada					▲				▲	▲	▲		●	▲			
10	Chile									■	■	■						
11	China		■		■	■		■	■	■	●	●	■	■	■	■	■	■
12	Croatia									■	●	■	●	●		●	■	●
13	Cuba																■	
14	Czech Republic		■						●	●	●	●	■			●	●	■
15	Denmark		▲								●	●						
16	Egypt		■			●				■	■	■		■	●			■
17	Finland						▲			●	●	●				●	○	●
18	France		■		○	■			●	■	■	■	■	■		●	■	●
19	Georgia									●	●	●					●	
20	Germany	▲	■		●	●	■		■				■	■		●		■
21	Greece		●					○		■	■	■		●	■	●	●	●
22	Hungary										●	●					■	
23	India		▲		●	■	■	■		●	●	●				■		■
24	Indonesia									■	■		■	■			■	
25	Iran		■		■	■			●	■	■	■				■		■
26	Iraq									●	●	●			●			●
27	Israel		▲		■	■				■	■	■	■					■
28	Italy				●	●					■			●		●	●	

#	Country	1	2	3	4	5	6	7	8	9	10	11	12	13	14	15	16	17
29	Japan		■		●	■	■				●					■		
30	Kazakhstan							●										
31	Macedonia																	■
32	Netherlands		●				◣											
33	New Zealand									◣	◣	◣						
34	Nigeria									●	●							●
35	North Korea		■			●		●										
36	Norway	◣			◣													■
37	Pakistan	■	■		●	■		■		■	■	●	■	●		■		■
38	Philippines									●	●			●				
39	Poland		■		●		◣	■	○	■	●		■	■	■		■	●
40	Portugal									●	■							
41	Romania		■			■		■	●	■	■	■	■			●		■
42	Russia		■		●	■		■	●	■	■		■	■		●		
43	Serbia		●			■				■	■					●		
44	Singapore		■				●	■		●	●	■	■	■				●
45	Slovak Republic		■			■					●			●				■
46	Slovenia															●		
47	South Africa					■				■	■		■	■	■		■	■
48	South Korea		■							■	■		■		■			
49	Spain					■	■			●	●	●			■	●		■
50	Sweden	■			●	■	○	●		●	●	●				■		
51	Switzerland		■		●	■				●	●	●	■			●		●
52	Taiwan				●			■		■	●		■					
53	Thailand									■	■	●						●
54	Turkey		◣		●		○			■	■	■	■	●	■			■
55	Ukraine		◣		◣	◣	◣	●			●						●	
56	United Kingdom	■		■	●	■		■		●	●	■	●	■		●	■	●
57	United States		■		●	■	■	○		■	■	■	■	■	●	■	●	■
58	Vietnam		■								■							
59	Zimbabwe									●								
TOTALS* (at least one type)		5	27	2	20	26	11	16	9	40	48	33	17	21	20	25	19	36
		31			33			20		49			31					

* Totals refer to countries that have undertaken partial or full production of the light weapon in question at one point over the past 60 years. A system that was still reportedly in research and development in 2007 is not included.
Key: AAG = anti-aircraft gun; HMG = heavy machine gun; ■ = (essentially) full production; ◣ = partial/assembly production; ○ = research and development; ● = production complete/dormant/status unclear
Source: Berman and Leff (2008)

ABBREVIATIONS

ATGW	Anti-tank guided weapon	MCLOS	Manual command to line-of-sight
CLOS	Command to line-of-sight	MILAN	Missile d'Infanterie léger antichar
EFP	Explosively formed projectile (or penetrator)	NATO	North Atlantic Treaty Organization
		NLAW	Next-generation Light Anti-tank Weapon
FaF	Fire and forget	QCB	Quick-change barrel
FARC	Revolutionary Armed Forces of Colombia	RF	Radio frequency
		RPG	Ruchnoy Protivotankovyy Granatomyot; Rocket-propelled grenade
GPMG	General-purpose machine gun		
GPS	Global positioning system	SACLOS	Semi automatic command to line-of-sight
IED	Improvised explosive device	TFG	War-front workshops
IR	Infrared	TOW	Tube-launched, optically tracked, wire-guided missile
LCU	Launch control unit		
MANPADS	Man-portable air-defence system(s)	WWI	First World War
MBT	Main battle tank	WWII	Second World War

ENDNOTES

1   This section focuses on the definition developed by the UN Panel of Governmental Experts in its 1997 report (UNGA, 1997). For a discussion of other definitions, see Small Arms Survey (2005, pp. 123–27; 2006, pp. 103–04).

2   In December 1997 the Convention on the Prohibition of the Use, Stockpiling, Production and Transfer of Anti-Personnel Mines and on Their Destruction (commonly known also as the Mine Ban Treaty or the Ottawa Convention) was concluded and opened for signature. It entered into force the following year. See <http:www.icbl.org>

3   The word 'operated' here does not include ancillary (although often necessary) personnel, including spotting or security details that usually accompany the deployment of light weapons, such as MANPADS and mortars.

4   By contrast, the US High Mobility Multi-purpose Wheeled Vehicle (widely known as a Humvee) and the British Land Rover can transport more than twice that payload. The Toyota Hilux, a 4 x 4 civilian vehicle that is ubiquitous in UN peace operations, and has been seized by rebel groups in numerous missions, has a payload greater than a UAZ-3151.

5   Thirteen countries—Burma, China, Cuba, India, Iran, Nepal, North Korea, Pakistan, Russia, Singapore, South Korea, the United States, and Vietnam—are believed still to produce anti-personnel mines or have yet to indicate that they will refrain from further such activity (LM, 2007, p. 13).

6   Some 30 countries are reported to have produced anti-vehicle landmines: Argentina, Austria, Belgium, Brazil, Chile, China, Czech Republic, Denmark, France, Germany, Greece, Hungary, Italy, Japan, the Netherlands, Pakistan, Peru, Poland, Portugal, Romania, Slovak Republic, South Africa, the former Soviet Union, Spain, Sweden, Thailand, the United Kingdom, the United States, and the former Yugoslavia (see Hiznay and Goose, 2000; HRW, 2002).

7   However, 120 mm mortar ammunition is heavy, which brings into question the utility of this system.

8   Pistols and revolvers that fire calibres in excess of 10 mm have also appeared in both civilian and military markets in recent years. These weapons include the .50 calibre (12.7 mm) Action Express-chambered 'Desert Eagle' pistol developed by Israel Military Industries (IMI) and the .50 calibre Smith and Wesson 'Model 500' series of revolvers. While these weapons have similar calibres to some heavy machine guns and anti-materiel rifles, the case length of the ammunition that they employ is considerably shorter, resulting in lower-velocity ballistics.

9   This chapter does not, therefore, consider the Finnish Lapua Magnum rifle to be a light weapon even though it fires a .338 in. (8.6 mm) cartridge, which is significantly larger, and capable of engaging targets from greater distances more effectively, than the 7.62 mm rifles that are traditionally conceived of as 'small arms'.

10   See Pézard and Anders (2006).

11   The company that sells this item, Machine Guns New Zealand, advises that a full-scale six-barrel model will soon be available. See <http://www.machineguns.co.nz/products.shtml>

12   Vickers did produce 12.7 mm machine guns, but an Internet search yielded no evidence that replicas of this particular model are being produced.

13   The type of ground, as well as the type and size of warhead, will affect the mortar's lethality.

14   EFPs have reportedly been used in just three per cent of all roadside bombings against US soldiers, but have resulted in 17 per cent of US fatalities through such attacks (Atkinson, 2007d). According to *The New York Times,* EFPs accounted for fully one-third of the deaths of US soldiers killed in action in Iraq in July 2007 (Gordon, 2007).

15   For example, Afghan rebels reportedly used MANPADS to shoot down more than 250 Russian and Afghan aircraft in the 1980s (Kuperman, 1999, p. 246). More recently, in August 2002 a Russian military Mi-26 transport helicopter was hit with a MANPADS missile in Khankala, on its approach to Grozny, the capital of Chechnya, killing 85 of the 117 soldiers on board (Fiszer, 2002).

16   While the terrorists that day failed to down the civilian aircraft, they succeeded in attacking an Israeli-owned hotel in Mombasa, killing ten Kenyans and three Israeli tourists (Lacey, 2002). But it was the subsequent threats to civilian aviation that continued to make international headlines and make Kenya a less attractive holiday destination for prospective tourists.

17   This statement was made by the Kenyan Tourist Board despite the loss in tourism experienced after the August 1998 US embassy bombing in Kenya that resulted in hundreds of deaths.

18   Al-Qassam rockets, like most craft-produced weapons noted here, differ slightly as they are not mass-produced with precision equipment and moulds. Each small production facility produces the weapons slightly differently.

19   Information on this aspect was gathered from two main sources: a presentation given by Colombian intelligence and law enforcement and presentations at a Conference on Small Arms and Light Weapons organized by the United Nations Center for Peace, Disarmament and Development in Latin America and the Caribbean UN-Lirec and the Government of Panama, Panama, 13–15 November 2002; and an interview with Colombian intelligence and law enforcement experts held in Bogotá, Colombia in July 2003.

20   The rocket was named after an LTTE officer who died in combat. Written correspondence with Seunghwan Yeo, 13 February 2008. The authors would like to thank Seunghwan Yeo, a master's student in the Coexistence and Conflict program at Brandeis University, for sharing a draft of his master's thesis on the conflict in Sri Lanka with us and for his insights into the LTTE's craft production of small arms, light weapons, and explosive devices.

21   Short-range surface-to-air-missiles denote those with maximum ranges of less than 10,000 m. Medium- and long-range surface-to-air-missiles have maximum ranges up to ten times the distance of short-range models (TGC, 2007).

22   Some modern missiles use a combination of laser beam-riding technology and IR homing for locking on to the target at different stages in flight (Jane's, 2006a).

23   Slant range is the 'line of sight' distance between the weapon and target (in contrast to the vertical altitude of the target).

24   Only about ten per cent of SA-7s fired during the Vietnam War actually destroyed their intended target. Most successful attacks were against small planes and helicopters. Such weapons would have a hard time downing larger aircraft such as 747s, 757s, and 767s, with engines built to endure several thousand kilograms of thrust (Dunnigan, 2007a).

25   Strela is Russian for 'arrow'. Moscow designated it the 9K32M, but this text refers to it as the North Atlantic Treaty Organization (NATO) designated SA-7 or Grail, by which it is commonly known. Copies of the weapon are known as the Hongying 5 or HN-5 in China, the Anza in Pakistan, the Ayn-al-Saqr in Egypt, and the CA-94M in Romania (Jane's, 2006a, pp. 3–50).

26   For example, a Greek industrialist affiliated with the licensed production of the Stinger shared proprietary information on the missile to the Soviets (Anastasi, 1987a; 1987b).

27   The authors wish to thank Adrian Wilkinson for his insights into these dynamics.

28   In 28 major battles during the 1980s, ATGWs were used against tanks 4 per cent of the time (in a defensive role), whereas they were used for offensive fire 75 per cent of the time (TGC, 2007).

29   A Canadian soldier firing a .50 calibre rifle (a McMillan Tac-50) reportedly successfully engaged an enemy combatant at 2,430 m in Afghanistan in 2002, besting a record for sniping in combat that had stood for more than a quarter of a century (Friscolanti, 2006).

30   The US Fifty Caliber Shooters Association (FCSA), for example, boasts more than 4,000 members from more than 20 countries since it was established in 1985 (FCSA, 2007).

31   The Davis Gun was used by the Air Force for ground attack. Hitting a tank from the sky at high speeds was difficult. Only a direct hit could neutralize a tank, and direct hits were rare (Gander, 2000, p. 178).

32   It is not uncommon for variants of the RPG-7 to sell for as little as USD 10 in many of the world's arms bazaars (Dunnigan, 2007b).

33   In an effort to abide by restrictions on state production and holdings of mortars 100 mm and larger under the 1990 Treaty on Conventional Armed Forces in Europe (CFE Treaty) while attaining heightened capabilities, Poland and the Slovak Republic have produced a 98 mm mortar.

34   Additional examples include sales that may involve upfront payment for after-sale services. Warranties can also make a difference in price: a customer asking for a multi-year warranty will have to pay more than one accepting weapons without a warranty. As well, ordering weapons in bulk tends to reduce unit costs. Some contracts call for trainers or simulators, which can be very expensive, while others do not. And so on.

BIBLIOGRAPHY

Anastasi, Paul. 1987a. 'Missile Coup Laid to Russian Spies.' *The New York Times*. 28 October.

—. 1987b. 'Athens Charges Greek With Giving Stinger Missile Secrets to Soviet.' *The New York Times*. 29 October.

ASN (Aviation Safety Network). 2007. <http://aviation-safety.net/database/record.php?id=19790212-1> (accessed in February 2008).

ATK (Alliant Techsystems Inc). 2007. 'XM25 Airburst Weapon System.'

     <http://www.atk.com/Customer_Solutions_MissionSystems/cs_ms_w_fp_xm25.asp> (accessed in February 2008).

Atkinson, Rick. 2007a. 'The IED problem is getting out of control. We've got to stop the bleeding.' *Washington Post*. 30 September, p. A13.

—. 2007b. 'There was a two-year learning curve . . . and a lot of people died in those two years.' *Washington Post*. 1 October, p. A01.

—. 2007c. 'You can't armor your way out of this problem.' *Washington Post*. 2 October, p. A01.

—. 2007d. 'If you don't go after the network, you're never going to stop these guys. Never.' *Washington Post*. 3 October, p. A 01.

BBC (British Broadcasting Corporation) News. 2003. 'Kenyan Tourism Faces Meltdown.' Web edition, 19 June.

     <http://news.bbc.co.uk/2/hi/business/3003148.stm> (accessed in March 2008).

Ben-David, Alon. 2006. 'Hamas Deploys Improved Qassam.' *Jane's Defense Weekly*. Coulsdon: Jane's Information Group. 12 July.

Berman, Eric G. 2008. *Production Worksheet for the Spike Anti-Tank Guided Weapon*. Unpublished background paper. Geneva: Small Arms Survey. February.

— and Jonah Leff. 2008. *Global Overview of Countries Producing Light Weapons*. Unpublished background paper. Geneva: Small Arms Survey. February.

Blair, David. 2007. 'US Presents "Evidence" that Weapons from Iran are Being Used in Iraq.' *Daily Telegraph*. Web edition, 12 February.

     <http://www.telegraph.co.uk/news/main.jhtml;jsessionid=RZ42LR3F4EDD3QFIQMFCFF4AVCBQYIV0?xml=/news/2007/02/12/wiran12.xml> (accessed in February 2008).

Blanche, Ed. 2003. 'Hamas Boosts the Range of Qassam Rockets.' *Jane's Missiles and Rockets*. Coulsdon: Jane's Information Group. 1 September.

Boatman, Robert H. 2004. *Living with the BIG .50*. Boulder, Colorado: Paladin Press.

Bonomo, James, Giacomo Bergamo, David R. Frelinger, John Gordon IV, and Brian A. Jackson. 2007. *Stealing the Sword: Limiting Terrorist Use of Advanced Conventional Weapons*. Santa Monica: RAND Corporation.

Chalk, Peter. 1999. *Liberation Tigers of Tamil Eelam's (LTTE) International Organization and Operations – A Preliminary Analysis*. Commentary No. 77. Ottawa: Canadian Security Intelligence Service.

Chivers, C.J. 2007. 'Pilots Say Missile Was Fired at Airliner in Northern Iraq.' *The New York Times*. 14 August.

Chow, James et al. 2005. *Protecting Commercial Aviation Against the Shoulder-Fired Missile Threat*. Rand Corporation.

     <http://www.rand.org/pubs/occasional_papers/2005/RAND_OP106.pdf> (accessed in February 2008).

CNN (Cable News Network). 2007. 'U.N Condemns Deadly Darfur Attack.' Web edition, 1 October.

     <http://edition.cnn.com/2007/WORLD/africa/10/01/darfur.peacekeepers/index.html> (accessed in February 2008).

CRS (Congressional Research Service). 2006. 'Homeland Security: Protecting Airliners from Terrorist Missiles.' 16 February.

     <http://www.fas.org/sgp/crs/terror/RL31741.pdf> (accessed in February 2008).

Davis, Anthony. 2003. 'Philippine Security Threatened by Small Arms Proliferation.' *Jane's Intelligence Review*. Coulsdon: Jane's Information Group. 1 August.

Dreyfus, Pablo. 2005. *Political Economy of Illegal Arms Acquisitions*. Unpublished background paper. Geneva: Small Arms Survey. June.

Dunnigan, James. 2007a. 'Poor Little Missiles Have Lost Their Prey.' *Strategy Page*. Web edition, 22 September.

     <http://www.strategypage.com/dls/articles/2007922221713.asp> (accessed in February 2008).

—. 2007b. 'China's Hot New RPG Warhead.' *Strategy Page*. Web edition, 5 May.

<http://www.strategypage.com/dls/articles/200753013324.asp> (accessed in February 2008).

Eagle Picher. 2003. 'Thermal Batteries'. Web edition.

<http://www.eaglepicher.com/NR/rdonlyres/FEB03316-8021-4DBD-AB3F-1E9E3E7D193C/0/ThermalAboutUs.pdf> (accessed in February 2008).

FAS (Federation of American Scientists). 1999. 'Javelin Antitank Missile.' *Military Analysis Network,* 6 August.

<http://www.fas.org/man/dod-101/sys/land/javelin.htm> (accessed in February 2008).

FCSA (Fifty Caliber Shooters Association). 2007. <http://www.fcsa.org/> (accessed in February 2008).

FI (Forecast International). 2007a. 'Ordnance and Munitions Forecast.' September.

—. 2007b. 'Worldwide Missile Inventories.' October.

—. 2007c. 'Missile Forecast.' November.

Fiszer, Michal. 2002. 'Russian Helicopter Downed by MANPADS.' *Journal of Electronic Defense*. Web edition, 19 August.

<http://findarticles.com/p/articles/mi_go2581/is_200210/ai_n7271205> (accessed in February 2008).

Friscolanti, Michael. 2006. 'We Were Abandoned.' Macleans.ca. Web edition, May.

<http://www.macleans.ca/canada/national/article.jsp?content=20060515_126689_126689> (accessed in February 2008).

Gander, Terry. 2000. *Anti-tank Weapons*. Wiltshire: Crowood Press.

General Dynamics. 2007. 'XM312'. <http://www.gdatp.com/products/PDFs/XM312.pdf> (accessed in February 2008).

Gordon, Michael. 2007. 'US Says Iran-supplied Bomb Kills More Troops.' *The New York Times*. 8 August.

Gourley, Scott R. 2006. 'Soldier Armed: XM320 Grenade Launcher Module and XM26 Modular Accessory Shotgun System.' *Army Magazine*. 2 January.
Web edition. <http://www.ausa.org/webpub/DeptArmyMagazine.nsf/byid/KHYL-6L7MAD> (accessed in February 2008).

Guardian. 2007. 'Rainbow Warrior Ringleader Heads Firm Selling Arms to US Government.' 25 May. Web edition.

<http://www.guardian.co.uk/environment/2007/may/25/usnews.france> (accessed in February 2008).

Gyürösi, Miroslav. 2003. 'Shlem Command System Can Co-ordinate Nine MANPADS.' *Jane's Missiles and Rockets*. Coulsdon: Jane's Information Group.
1 September.

Hiznay, Mark and Stephen Goose. 2000. 'Antivehicle Mines With Antihandling Devices.' *Human Rights Watch Fact Sheet*. January.

Hogg, Ian. 1999. *The Greenhill Military Small Arms Data Book*. London. Greenhill Books.

Holdanowicz, Grzegorz. 2004. 'Poland Wins Contract to Build Spike-LR Anti-tank Missiles.' *Jane's Missiles and Rockets*. Coulsdon: Jane's Information
Group. 1 February.

—. 2007. 'ZM Mesko Completes Spike-LR Missile Tests.' *Jane's Missiles and Rockets,* 1 November.

HRW (Human Rights Watch). 2002. 'Antivehicle Mines with Sensitive Fuzes or Antihandling Devices.' Backgrounder. 25 February.

—. 2003. *Weapons Sanctions, Military Supplies, and Human Suffering: Illegal Arms Flows to Liberia and the June–July 2003 Shelling of Monrovia*.
Briefing Paper. 3 November. <http://www.hrw.org/backgrounder/arms/liberia/liberia_arms.pdf> (accessed in February 2008).

IA (International Alert). 2005. *Small Arms Control in Moldova*. <http://www.international-alert.org/pdfs/MISAC_MoldovaStudy.pdf> (accessed in
February 2008).

India Today. 1997. 'Procurement of War Material and its Smuggling by LTTE from Tamil Nadu.' <http://www.india-today.com/jain/vol6/chap40.html>
(accessed in February 2008).

Jane's. 1975. *Jane's Infantry Weapons 1975*. Coulsdon: Jane's Information Group.

—. 1979. *Jane's Infantry Weapons 1979–1980*. Coulsdon: Jane's Information Group.

—. 1985. *Jane's Weapon Systems 1985–1986*. Coulsdon: Jane's Information Group.

—. 2000. *Jane's Military Vehicles and Logistics 2000–2001*. Coulsdon: Jane's Information Group.

—. 2004. *Jane's Infantry Weapons 2004–2005*. Coulsdon: Jane's Information Group.

—. 2005. 'Polish Live-firing Debut for Rafael's Spike-LR.' *Jane's International Defense Review*. Coulsdon: Jane's Information Group. 1 April.

—. 2006a. *Jane's Land Based Air Defence 2006–2007*. Coulsdon: Jane's Information Group.

—. 2006b. 'Iraqi Insurgents Found with Rockets.' *Jane's Missiles and Rockets*. Coulsdon: Jane's Information Group. 1 February.

—. 2006c. 'Production dawns for Red Sky-2.' *Jane's Missiles and Rockets*. Coulsdon: Jane's Information Group. 1 February.

—. 2007a. 'Rocket powered "Hamastan".' *Jane's Terrorism and Security Monitor*. Coulsdon: Jane's Information Group. 11 July.

—. 2007b. *Jane's Ammunition Handbook 2007–2008*. Coulsdon: Jane's Information Group.

—. 2007c. *Jane's Infantry Weapons 2007–2008*. Coulsdon: Jane's Information Group.

Koorey, Stephanie. 2007. *Craft Production and Possession of Light Weapons by Armed Groups: A Case Study of South and Southeast Asia*. Unpublished background paper. Geneva: Small Arms Survey. November.

Kucera, Joshua. 2006. 'US Army Delays Next-generation Infantry Weapons.' *Jane's Defence Weekly*. 26 April. Coulsdon: Jane's Information Group.

Kuperman, Alan J. 1999. 'The Stinger Missile and U.S. Intervention in Afghanistan.' *Political Science Quarterly*, Vol. 114, No. 2. Summer, pp. 219–63.

Lacey, Marc. 2002. 'Threats and Responses; Kenyans Release Name of Suspect in Mombasa Hotel Bombing.' *The New York Times*. Web edition, 12 December. <http://query.nytimes.com/gst/fullpage.html?res=9C01E4DC123AF931A25751C1A9649C8B63&n=Top/News/World/Countries%20and%20 Territories/Kenya> (accessed in February 2008).

LM (Landmine Monitor). 2007. 'Landmine Monitor Report 2007: Toward a Mine-Free World.' *Executive Summary*. International Campaign to Ban Landmines.

Lazarevic, Jasna. 2008. *Guided Light Weapons Reportedly Held by Non-State Armed Groups (1996–2007)*. Unpublished background paper. Geneva: Small Arms Survey. February.

Leff, Jonah. 2007. *For Sale: .50 Caliber Rifles in the US*. Unpublished background paper. Geneva: Small Arms Survey. November.

Machineguns New Zealand. 2007. <http://www.machineguns.co.nz> (accessed in February 2008).

Moser-Puangsuwan, Yeshua. 2007. *Non-state Armed Groups and Improvised Explosive Devices*. Unpublished background paper. Geneva: Small Arms Survey. October.

NYT (*The New York Times*). 1912. 'Aeroplane, Gun, Scores, Successes: Commander Cleland's Novel Weapon to be Displayed at the Palace Aviation Show.' 7 April.

Parsch, Andreas. 2002. 'General Dynamics FIM-43 Redeye.' *Directory of U.S. Military Rockets and Missiles*. <http://www.designation-systems.net/dusrm/m-43.html> (accessed in February 2008).

Pézard, Stephanie and Holger Anders. 2006. *Targeting Ammunition: A Primer*. Geneva: Small Arms Survey.

Richardson, Doug. 2002. 'IDF hunts Qassam-II rocket workshops.' *Jane's Missiles and Rockets*. Coulsdon: Jane's Information Group. 1 April.

—. 2004a. 'Sderot Strike Used Nasser 3 Rockets.' *Jane's Missiles and Rockets*. Coulsdon: Jane's Information Group. 1 September.

—. 2004b. 'Upgraded Stinger Could be Deployed in 2007.' *Jane's Missiles and Rockets*. Coulsdon: Jane's Information Group. 1 September.

—. 2007. 'Quds 4 Configuration Reveals Challenges Facing Gaza Activists.' *Jane's Missiles and Rockets*. Coulsdon: Jane's Information Group. 1 September.

SAAB. <http://www.saabgroup.com/en/Capabilities/weapon_systems.htm> (accessed in February 2008).

Schroeder, Matt. 2007. 'Countering the MANPADS Threat: Strategies for Success.' *Arms Control Today*. September.

SEESAC (The South Eastern and Eastern Europe Clearinghouse for the Control of Small Arms and Light Weapons). 2006. *SALW Survey of Moldova*. Belgrade: SEESAC.

Small Arms Survey. 2004. *Small Arms Survey 2004: Rights at Risk*. Oxford: Oxford University Press.

—. 2005. *Small Arms Survey 2005: Weapons at War*. Oxford: Oxford University Press.

—. 2006. *Small Arms Survey 2006: Unfinished Business*. Oxford: Oxford University Press.

—. 2007a. *Small Arms Survey 2007: Guns and the City*. Cambridge: Cambridge University Press.

—. 2007b. *Responses to Pastoral Wars: A Review of Violence Reduction Efforts in Sudan, Uganda, and Kenya*. HSBA Issue Brief No. 8. Geneva: Small Arms Survey.

Smith, Tony. 1994. 'Shelling of Sarajevo Market Kills 66; More Than 200 Wounded.' *Washington Post*. 6 February.

Sullivan, Stacy. 2004. *Be Not Afraid, For You Have Sons in America*. New York: St. Martin's Press.

TGC (Teal Group Corporation). 2007. 'World Missiles and UAVs Briefing 2006–2007.' Fairfax: Teal Group Corporation.

UNGA (United Nations General Assembly). 1992. *An Agenda for Peace: Preventive Diplomacy, Peacemaking and Peace-keeping*. A/47/277 – S/24111 of 17 June.

—. 1995. *Supplement to an Agenda for Peace: Position Paper of the Secretary-General on the Occasion of the Fiftieth Anniversary of the United Nations*. A/50/60 – S/1995/1 of 3 January.

—. 1997. *Report of the Panel of Governmental Experts on Small Arms*. A/52/298 of 27 August.

UNSC (United Nations Security Council). 2007. *Letter from the Chairman of the Security Council Committee established pursuant to resolution 751 (1992) concerning Somalia addressed to the President of the Security Council*. S/2007/436 of 18 July.

USDoD (United States) Department of Defense. 2007. 'Iraqi, Coalition Troops Begin Clearing Operation in Ramadi.' 26 March.

USDoS (United States Department of State). 2005. 'The MANPADS Menace: Combating the Threat to Global Aviation from Man-Portable Air Defence Systems. 20 September. <http://www.state.gov/t/pm/rls/fs/53558.htm> (accessed in February 2008).

USFNS (United States Federal News Service). 2007. 'Hearing of the Senate Foreign Relations Committee.' 5 September.

Vobejda, Barbara and David Ottaway. 1999. 'The .50-Calibre Rifle.' *Washington Post*. 17 August.

Wezeman, Siemon. 2007. *The Case That Was and The Case That Wasn't*. Unpublished background paper. Geneva: Small Arms Survey.

— et al. 2007. 'International Arms Transfers.' In *SIPRI Yearbook 2007: Armaments, Disarmament and International Security*. Oxford: Oxford University Press, ch. 10.

Wilkinson, Adrian. 2008. *Maximum Distances and Mean Averages of Mortars*. Unpublished background paper. Geneva: Small Arms Survey.

ACKNOWLEDGEMENTS

Principal authors

Eric G. Berman and Jonah Leff

Contributors

James Bevan, Michael Brzoska, Stephanie Koorey, Jasna Lazarevic, Yeshua Moser-Puangsuwan, Matt Schroeder, Barbara Gimelli Sulashvili, Siemon Wezeman, Adrian Wilkinson

AKM-pattern assault rifles seized by Indian troops
from rebel forces in Gurez, India, May 2006.
© Tauseef Mustafa/AFP/Getty Images

Arsenals Adrift
ARMS AND AMMUNITION DIVERSION

2

INTRODUCTION

Diversion lies at the heart of illicit arms proliferation. In northern Kenya, 40 per cent of ammunition on the illicit market has leaked from Kenyan armed forces. Across the world, theft from civilian owners may result in the unlawful acquisition of as many as 1 in every 1,000 weapons. These are examples of diversion: the unauthorized transfer of arms and ammunition from the stocks of lawful users to the illicit market.

Across the world, the diversion of arms and ammunition sustains the activities of non-state armed groups, terrorist organizations, and armed criminals. It includes, but is not limited to: large, international transfers organized by corrupt military officials; low-level, localized theft and resale by military and police forces; and the loss of civilian weaponry through home burglary and other forms of theft.

Diversion can present a serious threat to the safety of civilian populations and even to the security of the state itself. In some countries it threatens the state's monopoly on the use of force by allowing armed groups that are denied other sources of weaponry to challenge state authorities. For these reasons, diversion has the potential to thoroughly undermine any measures taken to strengthen domestic and international regulations governing the arms trade—making it an increasingly important field of both national and international concern. Among this chapter's principal observations are:

- Diversion is largely a self-inflicted problem that stems from negligence by states, militaries, and civilians.
- Weapons that are diverted from state stockpiles or from civilian hands can fuel crime as easily as they can fuel insurgency or international terrorism.
- Diversion can often be addressed by relatively low-cost improvements to accounting, monitoring, and the physical security of arms and ammunition.
- Measures to curtail diversion must be comprehensive, addressing both security force stocks and civilian holdings.

The chapter addresses diversion in two parts: the unauthorized acquisition of arms and ammunition held by state security forces, and the acquisition of legally held civilian stocks by criminals. It emphasizes that diversion operates at many different levels. Tackling the problem therefore requires comprehensive controls over all arms and ammunition—regardless of where they are stored or used.

DIVERSION IN CONTEXT

Stockpile diversion can occur from any legally held quantity of small arms and ammunition, whether in military or in civilian hands. Before analyzing diversion, however, it is useful to sketch a number of 'baseline' features of stockpiles.

Stockpiles

'Stockpile' (or simply 'stocks') refers to any collection of arms and ammunition, of any scale, and under the possession of any actor. The term, as used in this chapter, should therefore not be confused with the stereotypical, mass
storage depots that militaries use to house munitions, although the term does encompass these facilities. This chapter
deals with two, analytically distinct, stockpiles: the state-owned or 'national stockpile' and civilian stocks—the 'civilian
stockpile' (see Figure 2.1).

The *national stockpile* encompasses every item of arms or ammunition under the control of—or destined for—a
state's defence and law and order apparatus. Its components range from munitions stored in manufacturing facilities
to large arms and ammunition depots and the weapons and ammunition issued to individual soldiers and police
officers. It also includes the weapons and ammunition of paramilitary personnel that are nominally under state control. Diversion can, and does, occur anywhere in the national stockpile.

Figure 2.1 **Avenues of diversion from national and civilian stockpiles**

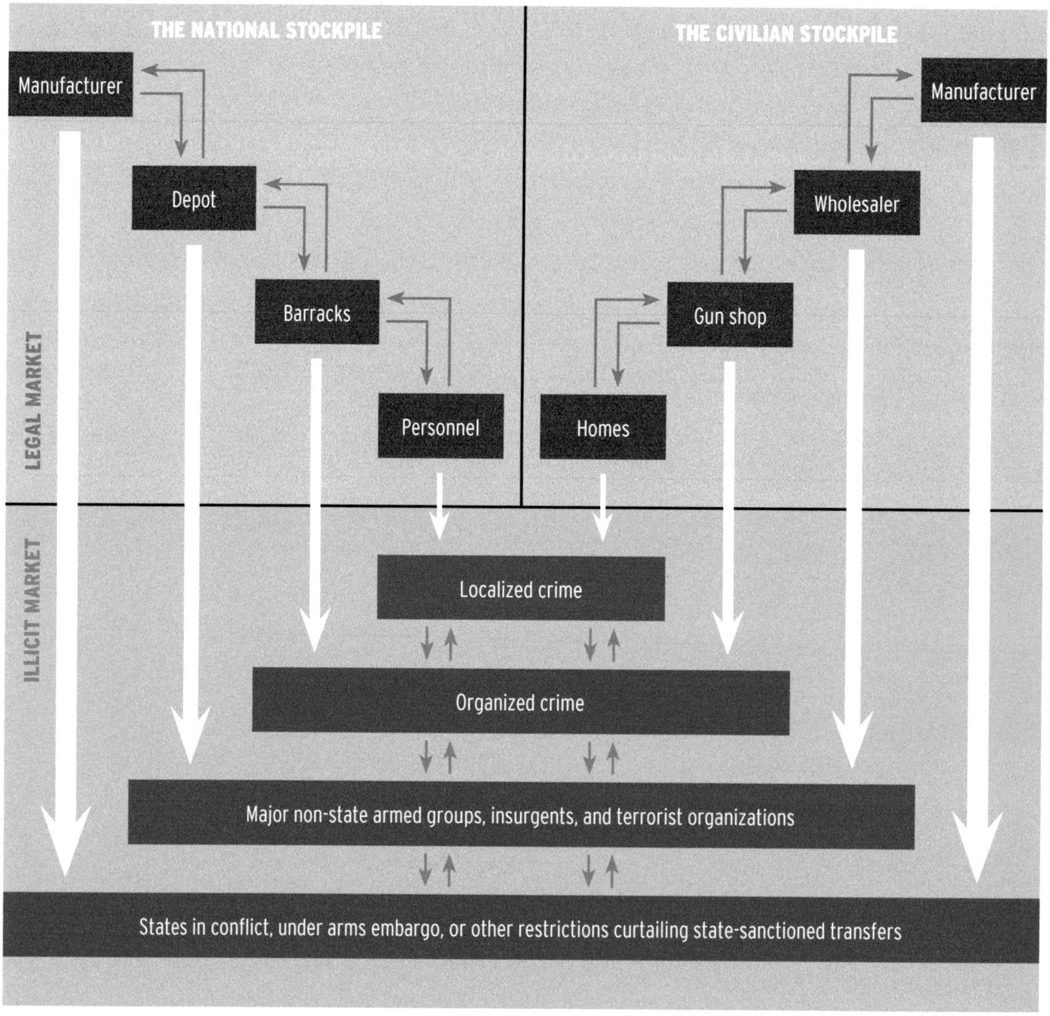

The *civilian stockpile* includes all arms and ammunition that are in the hands of—or destined for—authorized civilian users. Its components include weapons located in manufacturing facilities (which may be the same as those that supply the security forces); arms and ammunition stored by wholesale firms, which supply smaller businesses in the arms trade; weapons and ammunition held in gun shops and sports shooting associations; and those that are stored by private users at home (civilian holdings). Again, stocks anywhere in the civilian stockpile can be subject to diversion.

Arms and ammunition flows

Weapons and ammunition are not static and do not usually reside permanently in any one place. In the state-owned national stockpile, they flow throughout the security apparatus in response to patterns of deployment, changing demand, and the need to 'return' items for repair or alteration. Similar dynamics apply in the civilian market, as weapons and ammunition are sold, resold, or, in the case of ammunition, consumed.

Both in the national stockpile and among civilian stocks, ammunition is notably 'mobile' because it is a rapidly consumable good and needs to be regularly replenished when used—whether expended during training or combat or for recreational purposes. In the case of national stockpiles, for example, a single round of ammunition may be stored under tight security in a military depot. However, if it is transferred to a barracks or a police station with ineffective physical security measures, the ammunition risks being lost or stolen and thereby diverted to the illicit market. The same is also true of weapons that are transferred from one locale to another or from one set of users to others.

Ammuni-
rapidly c
good.

This flow effect, which is present in both national stockpiles and civilian holdings, means that efforts to prevent diversion at any one point in the supply chain can be undermined by weaknesses at other points. Effective physical security needs to apply to arms and ammunition everywhere and not just to certain parts of either stockpile.

A multiplicity of sources

The diversion of arms and ammunition can have serious consequences regardless of whether it originates from the state-owned national stockpile or from civilian stocks. Diversion from either source—whether military or civilian—can provide illicit users with compatible weapons and ammunition because there are relatively few common small arms calibres, and frequently these are used by both militaries and civilians.

For example, a military assault rifle can fire civilian-marketed ammunition and vice versa. Common military calibres, such as the 5.56 x 45 mm SS109 rifle and 9 mm Parabellum pistol rounds, are widely used by civilian shooters in many Western countries (in the case of 5.56 x 45 mm, the civilian equivalent is the .223 Remington).[1] It is often relatively easy for illicit users to find appropriate calibres to suit diverted small arms or, conversely, the small arms to fire diverted ammunition.

Clear evidence of the impact of calibre compatibility comes from seizures of ammunition by the Police of Rio de Janeiro (see Figure 2.2). Not only do there appear to be relatively few calibres in use on the illicit market, but these calibres have both military and civilian applications. While all are 'restricted use' and therefore subject to some control (Bevan and Dreyfus, 2007, pp. 303–04), they are nevertheless used by a wide range of actors including sporting shooters, hunters, collectors, and various branches of the Brazilian state security forces (Presiência da República, 2000, arts. 16, 17, chs. VIII and IX of Title V; 2004, art. 19).

In some countries there are even fewer calibres in service among both military and civilian users than in the case of Brazil. For example, most civilian users in East Africa are equipped with military assault rifle ammunition (such as the 7.62 x 51mm and 7.62 x 39 mm calibres in Figure 2.2). They rarely use pistols, and hence pistol calibres (9 mm, .38, etc.), which means that there is very little difference between the arms and ammunition used by civilians and the military.[2] In these cases, minimal calibre diversity makes it easier for illicit users to obtain the required types of ammunition as a result of diversion from either civilian or military sources.

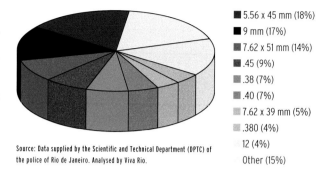

Figure 2.2   **Ammunition calibres seized by police from criminal factions, Rio de Janeiro 2003-06 (n = 2860)**

- ■ 5.56 x 45 mm (18%)
- ■ 9 mm (17%)
- ■ 7.62 x 51 mm (14%)
- ■ .45 (9%)
- ■ .38 (7%)
- ■ .40 (7%)
- ▨ 7.62 x 39 mm (5%)
- ▨ .380 (4%)
-   12 (4%)
-   Other (15%)

Source: Data supplied by the Scientific and Technical Department (DPTC) of the police of Rio de Janeiro. Analysed by Viva Rio.

Paths of diversion

The diversion of arms and ammunition takes many forms and ranges from thefts that involve high-level decision-maker complicity to low-level pilfering by petty criminals. Its contributing factors are various, and extend from private motivations, such as the need for hard cash by underpaid security personnel, to major political changes that affect the entire structures of states and their capacity to secure national stockpiles.

Table 2.1   **Categories of diversion and regulatory frameworks**

Stockpile	Type of diversion	Dynamic	Description	Reach	Regulatory framework
National stockpile	Low-order	Intra-security force theft	Theft by members of the armed forces	Localized	Stockpile management
		Extra-security force theft	Theft through unauthorized access to stocks or attack	Regional to international	Stockpile management / security sector reform
	High-order	High-level corruption	Defence sector officials orchestrate diversion	International	Institutional capacity building / combating corruption / security sector reform
		Mass looting or dispersal	State or security sector collapse leading to the dissolution of stockpiles	Regional to international	Political (domestic governments prior to collapse, possibly occupying powers)
Civilian stockpile	Low-order	Theft from users	Theft from persons, homes, and vehicles	Localized	National firearms laws (ownership, carrying, and storage)
		Unauthorized sales	Sale to unauthorized users	Localized	National firearms laws (commerce and resale)
	High-order	Theft from gun shops, wholesalers, and factories	Targeted thefts by organized crime and other organized non-state groups	Regional to international	National firearms laws (commerce and security thereof)

Source: Bevan (2008a)

Faced with such divergent conditions, the following sections present a typology of diversion, its contributing factors, and measures that can be applied to limit its occurrence (see Table 2.1). They address diversion from civilian and security force (national) stocks separately—in recognition of the often different illicit markets each can feed and the differing sets of responses that are required.

In each case the sections make a simple dichotomy by assigning high and low orders to diversion. These orders recognize a number of factors including: differing scales of diversion (quantities diverted); the 'reach' of diverted munitions (whether transferred locally or internationally); and the impact of diversion (for example, enabling small-scale armed crime or larger-scale organized crime or armed insurrection) (see Table 2.1).

DIVERSION FROM THE NATIONAL STOCKPILE

The diversion of state-owned arms is not a new phenomenon. As early as the third century BC, weapons looted from Roman armouries and transferred via illicit arms deals were used to arm Germanic war bands (Penrose, 2005, p. 210). The national stockpile has always been a source of weapons for non-state armed groups with few other sources of weaponry. Moreman (2006), for instance, notes the pivotal role that diversion by members of the armed forces played in supplying groups along the Northwest Frontier Province of India in the late 19th and early 20th centuries. In recent times, cases ranging from the Tuareg Rebellion in Mali (Florquin and Pézard, 2005, p. 51) to the streets of Rio de Janeiro (Bevan and Dreyfus, 2007, pp. 301–11) demonstrate that diversion is still a major problem leading to the loss of state stocks and the acquisition of arms and ammunition by armed groups and civilians.

The dive
state-ow
is not a r
phenome

Low-order national stockpile diversion

Low-order diversion of the national stockpile is the theft of relatively minor quantities of weapons and ammunition by individuals and small groups of people. It may occur at all levels of the national stockpile, but is generally characterized by its links to localized illicit trade rather than regional or international transfers. The problem is largely a result of microeconomic demand factors combined with poor stockpile management. It is often facilitated by the concealability and portability of small arms.[3] In addition, two factors make small arms, light weapons, and their ammunition particularly susceptible to low-order diversion.

First is their wide distribution throughout security force stockpiles (see Figure 2.3). While larger conventional arms, such as artillery and missile systems, are rarely deployed to smaller units of a country's security forces, small arms and light weapons feature in all levels of the national stockpile. This wide distribution results in a greater number of potential opportunities for diversion, ranging from the manufacturing facility to military depots, barracks, and deployed personnel.

Second, the fact that small arms and light weapons tend to be distributed at 'lower' levels than larger weapons can lead to diminishing security measures and an increased risk of diversion. When command and control is weak, oversight over arms and ammunition is likely to be progressively weaker when weapons are dispersed throughout progressively smaller units of the security forces.

Weak oversight and poor physical security measures facilitate several forms of diversion, including theft by both personnel (intra-security force diversion) and 'external' actors (extra-security force diversion).

Figure 2.3 **The distribution of conventional arms and ammunition within the national stockpile**

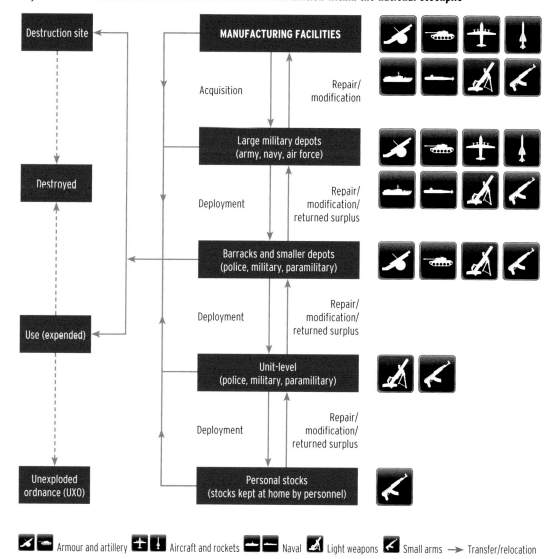

Armour and artillery   Aircraft and rockets   Naval   Light weapons   Small arms   → Transfer/relocation

Intra-security force diversion

Lower-order, intra-security force theft involves the diversion of arms and ammunition by military, police, or paramilitary personnel, and can take two forms—theft from arms and ammunition storage facilities, and illicit transfers from the individual stocks of security force members.

Theft from storage sites

Diversion is often orchestrated by the stockpile security personnel who are themselves charged with monitoring and securing stocks from theft. Small facilities, such as police stations and military barracks, may be particularly suscep-tible if few personnel are responsible for record-keeping and the physical inventorying of stocks. Illustrative in this regard is the case of Papua New Guinea, where the diversion of arms and ammunition from the Royal Papua New

Guinea Constabulary (RPNGC) has been particularly prominent. A 2004 audit estimated that around 30 per cent of the RPNGC's stocks of small arms had been sold onto to the illicit market. The problem prompted authorities to issue weapon safes to the smaller police stations—many of which, like the weapons they were designed to protect, were subsequently stolen (Alpers, 2005, pp. 49–50).

At larger storage facilities the problem of diversion may be similarly problematic and, from a public security perspective, perhaps more so, given that these facilities are likely to stock explosive light weapons. In Sydney, Australia, for instance, military personnel, including a munitions technical officer, stole an estimated eight M-72 LAW rocket launchers from military stockpiles between 2002 and 2007. These light weapons were sold to one or a number of Sydney's criminal networks (AAP, 2007; Braithwaite et al., 2007). Light weapons such as these can pose both an elevated risk of diversion (if that kind of explosive firepower is in high demand by certain users) and, as a result, an elevated risk once they have been diverted (Box 2.1).

In virtually all cases where individuals, or small groups of military personnel, appear to have been able to divert arms and ammunition, their actions have been facilitated by two factors. First, they frequently perform duties that give them regular access to stocks and to stock accounting systems. Russian military supply officers in Chechnya, for instance, have been implicated in 'writing-off' weapons as destroyed and then selling them (JIG, 2005). Second, in some cases, such as Papua New Guinea, personnel have access to stocks that are poorly inventoried. Both of these factors are made critical because the personnel concerned are poorly monitored by peers or superiors—facilitating both theft and account-tampering.

Diverted FN FAL rifles, stolen from a military base and recovered by Brazilian authorities, Rio de Janeiro, March 2006. © Antonio Scorza/AFP/Getty Images

Box 2.1 Prioritizing the security of certain types of ammunition

Different varieties of ammunition and their component parts present different security risks if lost or stolen from stockpiles. These risks are proportional to: 1) the operational (i.e. tactical and destructive) potential of the ammunition in question; and 2) the ease and speed with which persons illicitly acquiring the ammunition can make it operational and use it. While it is clear that all arms and ammunition pose risks to security when in the wrong hands, certain states have attempted to prioritize risks for different types and allocate specific security measures accordingly.

For these reasons, the United States Department of Defense (USDoD, 1989, p. 30) classifies conventional ammunition according to 'the degree of protection needed against loss or theft by terrorists or other criminal elements'. As a result the DOD ranks ammunition higher in sensitivity (see Table 2.2) when it is explosive, can threaten high value military assets, and can be deployed quickly.

For example, Code 1 munitions include man-portable air defence systems (MANPADS) and anti-tank guided weapons (ATGW) that are either stored or transported as a complete system (missile and launcher) or sufficiently proximate to one another to enable quick assembly into a functioning weapon system. Code 2 ammunition includes explosive munitions that are either ready to use (such as grenades and mines); or could be improvised for other purposes (such as raw explosives and missiles). All of these weapons could either be used quickly and with great effect or used in weapons that already circulate on the illicit market.

This accounting system is designed to ensure that weapons listed under Code 1 are subject to enhanced security at all times. Measures include specific regulations on physical security, such as guard levels at storage facilities, modes of perimeter security, and communications equipment to alert authorities of a loss or theft of weapons (USDoD, 2000, pp. 24-25).

It is worth noting that the Department of Defense ranks small arms ammunition as Code 4 (low sensitivity), despite the often ready availability of arms capable of firing military calibres. Given the potential destabilizing impact of leakages of most types of ammunition, it is probably safe to conclude that security measures should be as comprehensive as possible for all categories. While the codes listed in Table 2.1 prioritize protective measures to prevent loss or theft, they do not entail different accounting standards. The United States stockpile management and security system dictates comprehensive accounting of *all* stocks–regardless of assigned codes.

Table 2.2 United States military ammunition and explosives security risk codes

Code	Designation	Category of ammunition included
1	Highest sensitivity	Ready-to fire (ammunition and weapon) missiles, including Hamlet, Redeye, Stinger, Dragon, LAW, and Viper. This category includes non-nuclear missiles and rockets in a *ready-to-fire* configuration. It also applies when the launcher (tube) and the associated explosive rounds, though not in a ready-to-fire configuration, are stored or transported together.
2	High sensitivity	The following items are included: (a) Grenades, both high explosive and white phosphorous. (b) Antitank and antipersonnel mines with an unpacked weight of 100 lbs or less each. (c) Explosives used in demolition operations, such as C-4, military dynamite, TNT, and the like. (d) Explosive rounds for missiles and rockets other than Category I that have an unpacked weight of 100 lbs or less each.
3	Moderate sensitivity	(a) Ammunition, .50 calibre and larger, with explosive-filled projectile and having an unpacked weight of 100 lbs or less each. (b) Incendiary grenades and grenade fuses. (c) Blasting caps. (d) Detonating cord. (e) Supplementary charges. (f) Bulk explosives.
4	Low sensitivity	(a) Ammunition with non-explosive projectiles and having an unpacked weight of 100 lbs or less each. (b) Fuses, except those in Category III. (c) Grenades, illumination, smoke and practice, and CS/CN (tear producing). (d) Incendiary destroyers. (e) Riot control agents in packages of 100 lbs or less.

Source: Adapted from USDoD (1989, pp. 30-36)

All of these risk factors can be attenuated by effective, rule-based stockpile management procedures. As a result of the theft of M-72 LAWs, for instance, the Australian defence forces have enforced a strict 'two-person policy' whereby personnel are prohibited unsupervised access to weapons and explosives stores (Blenkin, 2007). Other countries already have such measures in place. In the United States, personnel tasked with storage functions are not allowed access to records. Similarly, record-keeping personnel are prohibited from conducting physical inventories without the supervision of storage personnel (USDOD, 2002, p. 8). These 'check and balance' procedures also ensure that law-abiding personnel are better protected from blame should a loss or theft occur.

Diversion of individual stocks

A second type of intra-force theft occurs when members of a state's armed forces or other state agents divert *issued* stocks of arms and ammunition to the illicit market.

Issued weapons are those that are required by personnel to perform their duties. They rarely include light weapons, and, in most countries, consist of small calibre weapons and ammunition, such as pistols and assault rifles,

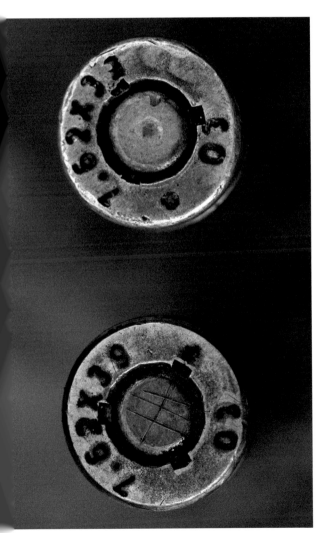

which comprise the individual weapons of police, military, paramilitary, and other government agents. While many states issue arms and ammunition only in time of need, others allow individual weapons (and their ammunition) to remain in the hands of security force personnel, whether on or off duty.

Because these issued stocks are already in the charge of personnel, and access to them is not subject to entry to an armoury or other weapons storage facility, they can pose a particular risk of diversion—particularly in the case of ammunition. In northern Kenya, for instance, 7.62 x 39 mm assault rifle ammunition circulates widely among Turkana pastoral communities and can be attributed to diversion from Kenyan security forces, most notably the Kenya Police Reserves (KPR), which has a track record of 'losing' arms and ammunition.[4] In northern Uganda the situation is similar, with paramilitary Local Defence Units (LDU) as well as members of the Uganda People's Defence Forces (UPDF) implicated in diversion (Bevan and Dreyfus, 2007, pp. 288–301).

Reasons for low-order diversion

Low-order diversion, whether directly from weapons storage facilities or from the issued stocks of security force personnel, is generally a response to localized illicit demand.

A common feature of low-order diversion is that the security force personnel make very local contacts with

Ammunition on the loose: 7.62 x 39 mm 'AK' ammunition photographed in the hands of non-state groups in northern Kenya, January 2008. © James Bevan

Box 2.2 The particular case of ammunition diversion

Unlike a soldier's weapon, such as an assault rifle or pistol, the disappearance of ammunition is often unnoticed or can easily be explained to superiors. Where security forces do not have to account for the ammunition they expend in engagements or training, when commanding officers cannot oversee the use of weapons, and where no records are kept of the numbers of rounds issued: ammunition is easily diverted. In many countries the scale of diversion remains unclear for precisely these reasons.[6]

Although the impact of such small-scale diversion may seem relatively slight when viewed from the perspective of individual transactions–major legal ammunition shipments often run into millions of rounds–on aggregate low-level diversion can assume very large proportions. In Rio de Janeiro a stockpile manager was convicted in 2005 for diverting around 10,000 rounds to drug-trafficking organizations (Bevan and Dreyfus, 2007, p. 310). Similarly, in March 2007 four army personnel, including one warehouse guard, were arrested in Albania for diverting around 100,000 rounds of ammunition (JIG, 2007a). In Peru, in 2006 and 2007 alone 80,000 assault rifle rounds were recovered after having been diverted in a number of instances from police and military stocks. The ammunition was believed to be destined for the Colombian Fuerzas Armadas Revolucionarias de Colombia (FARC) (JIG, 2007c).

Even the smallest of trades, of perhaps three or four rounds, can reach large proportions when sufficient numbers of personnel are involved for long periods of time. In northern Kenya, for instance, research by the Small Arms Survey suggests that around 40 per cent of 7.62 x 39 mm ammunition circulating illicitly in the region can be attributed to diversion from Kenyan security forces. In this case individual instances of diversion are small in volume, but when combined they have a strong impact on the propensity for armed violence.[7]

the illicit market. Such transfers can be relatively large in scale. For example, in 2002 four Israeli soldiers were charged with the theft of around 60,000 5.56 x 45 mm assault rifle rounds, destined for Palestinian factions in the Hebron region (BBC, 2002; Greenberg, 2002). But more often than not they are small transfers.

These may take the form of interaction with criminal gangs in cities and towns, as in the Australian M-72 case (Braithwaite et al., 2007). In the Israeli case it appears to have involved Israeli Arabs with social ties to Palestinian factions, and included other illicit activity including the smuggling of non-military goods (Greenburg, 2002). In Kenya and Uganda diversion by paramilitary personnel often occurs between members of the same clan or sub-clan (Bevan and Dreyfus, 2007, p. 299).

For the most part, the motive behind these locally connected thefts is personal economic gain. The value of such transactions may run into many hundreds of thousands of dollars or it may be confined to very small trades. In northern Kenya, for instance, a round of 7.62 x 39 mm ammunition sells for around 200 Kenyan shillings (around USD 3 or the price of a beer).[5]

The attractiveness of such small trades cannot be overestimated. In many developing countries security force personnel receive extremely low or intermittent pay. Small arms, and ammunition in particular (Box 2.2), can provide a ready currency with which to purchase items required for daily subsistence, such as foodstuffs or perhaps a pair of boots or a new shirt.

Policy implications

Accounting and oversight are two fundamental pillars of arms and ammunition management that can be employed to address low-order diversion. Effective accounting covers three basic processes:

1. Stocks issued: The numbers and types of arms and ammunition issued to security forces (at all levels) are recorded and this information is stored securely at progressively higher administrative levels.

2. Stocks expended: The numbers and types of arms and ammunition expended or rendered unfit for use (whether in training or combat) are documented and the circumstances of such expenditure specified.

3. Stocks audited: All stocks are thoroughly audited and the balance checked against reports detailing issuance and expenditure.[8]

These three procedures are contingent on functioning command and control within security force administrations.[9] Where there is little oversight, it is unlikely that such measures will operate effectively.

If internal monitoring of personnel is weak, however, external monitoring can be employed to detect instances of diversion and trace thefts back to the security forces responsible—particularly with respect to ammunition. Lot-marking is one such measure, whereby ammunition is assigned a code that specifies the particular unit within a state's security apparatus to which it has been issued. Lot-marking can be an effective way to highlight instances of diversion and remedy theft within security forces, in addition to deterring theft in the first place. Few countries, however, directly lot-mark small arms ammunition. Austria, Brazil, Colombia, France, and Germany are exceptions whereby national regulations require that all or certain security forces use only lot-marked ammunition (Anders, 2006, p. 212; Bevan and Dreyfus, 2008).

Extra-security force diversion

Low-order, extra-security force theft involves diversion from national stockpiles by non-state actors. These unlawful users may target weapons storage facilities or the personal stocks of members of the security forces. In either case their access to arms and ammunition is often contingent on lax stockpile management practices—including stockpiles that are made vulnerable to violent attack by minimal investments in security and a lack of planning on the part of relevant authorities.

Diversion via unauthorized entry

Stockpile facilities that are extremely poorly guarded allow the entry of unauthorized personnel and the theft of arms and ammunition. Direct, unaided entry by non-state actors is probably rare for larger stocks of weapons, such as those held in barracks and larger security force facilities, because intruders have to confront relatively large numbers of state agents before gaining access to arms and ammunition. However, cases such as the theft in 1999 by local teenagers of man-portable air defence systems (MANPADS) from a state factory in Poland suggest that large facilities can be prone to the most basic incursions (Golik, 1999; PNB, 2000).

For the most part, however, smaller stockpiles appear to be the most vulnerable to non-violent thefts by unauthorized personnel. For example, Capic (2003, pp. 97–109) noted the ease with which national stockpiles in a number of Pacific states could be accessed by outsiders. Among the risks he identified were: hundreds of assault rifles secured only by single doors with single padlocks, and, in the worst cases, weapons stored on floors, or simply leaning against walls, in unlocked, unguarded rooms.

The Pacific states were, and are, not unique. Numerous reports from South-east Asia suggest that many weapons and ammunition storage facilities are left unguarded and in an almost comical state of repair—one, for instance, was described as having a locked door, a roof, but only three walls.[10] Certain parts of Africa display similar problems. One US State Department Official recalled a 2003 case in Monrovia, Liberia, in which a monitoring team found four MANPADS inside a shed 'guarded only by a chicken with no tail feathers'.[11]

Storage conditions such as these require little concerted effort on the part of thieves. Diversion can be a relatively passive process whereby local people simply walk into the stockpile and help themselves to arms and ammunition. Although such pilferage may be localized, the easy availability of high-value weapons such as MANPADS, which are in great demand by some non-state groups, suggests the potential for these local dynamics to link with the international trade in illicit weaponry.

Diversion by force

The above cases are illustrative of situations in which security has been sufficiently lax to enable the unchallenged entry of unauthorized personnel into storage facilities, but there are also cases where non-state actors gain access to arms and ammunition by force.

State forces often inadvertently provide large quantities of arms and ammunition to opposing non-state armed groups. Diversion via capture from state security forces—whether on the field of battle or through direct assault on military facilities—is a major source of illicit arms and ammunition. As Florquin and Berman (2005) note, in seven out of nine West African countries where armed groups have operated in recent years, the groups in question have acquired arms and ammunition through one or both of these means.[12]

Captured weapons are often pivotal in allowing insurgencies to gain momentum through a process described by Bevan (2005, pp. 186–87) as the 'acquisition spiral'. One example of this phenomenon described by Humphreys and ag Mohammed (2003, p. 247) was the rapidly strengthening position of the Malian Mouvement Populaire de Libération de l'Azawad, as it used successively larger quantities of captured weapons and ammunition to launch attacks on military facilities—thereby obtaining yet greater amounts of arms and ammunition.

State stockpiles are tempting targets for many groups—whether criminally or politically motivated—that wish to augment their firepower. The long-term impact of such attacks can be devastating when large numbers of weapons and ammunition are released onto the illicit market. In 1979, for instance, the Matheniko Karimojong sub-clan of northern Uganda overran a Ugandan Army barracks in Moroto, resulting in the capture of an estimated 60,000 assault rifles and extensive stocks of ammunition (Mkutu, 2007a, p. 36). Many of the rifles and ammunition of that period still circulate in the region and help sustain armed violence that claims many hundreds of lives annually.[13]

se police officer with military-issue AUG assault rifles looted by
violence in May 2006. Balibar-Aileu district, East Timor, June 2006.
s/AFP/Getty Images

The impact of such attacks can be particularly pronounced when this form of diversion comprises the only source of arms for non-state actors. The Solomon Islands provide a fairly unique, self-contained case. Almost all of the factory-manufactured weapons and ammunition that proved pivotal in intensifying the 1998–2003 conflict were captured from stocks of the Royal Solomon Island Police (RSIP) and there were few such weapons in civilian hands at the outbreak of the conflict (Muggah and Bevan, 2004, p. 8).

The capture of arms and ammunition often continues throughout conflicts and enables otherwise poorly equipped non-state armed groups to sustain military offensives. In East Timor, for instance, the rebel faction led by Alfredo Reinado has consistently targeted security forces as a source of arms and ammunition. In February 2007 the group attacked police stations along the East Timor–Indonesian border, resulting in the capture of around 17 assault rifles (BBC, 2007).

Even troops that are stationed to prevent or end hostilities can help sustain them when their weapons are forcibly diverted. In September 2007, for instance, the African Union Mission in Sudan (AMIS) base at Haskanita in southern Darfur was overrun by rebels, resulting in the loss of weapons and ammunition (JIG, 2007b).

Not all diversion by force is large in scale. United Nations security reports from northern Uganda, for instance, indicate numerous instances in which soldiers have been waylaid by groups of criminals, resulting in the theft of arms and ammunition.[14] Similarly, in 2003 an attack in Venezuela blamed on 'common criminals' resulted in the deaths of four National Guard soldiers and the theft of their weapons (Olson, 2003). Soldiers, operating alone or in small units, can be an attractive target specifically because they carry weapons and ammunition.

Policy implications

Diversion by unauthorized access to national stockpiles is preventable through the application of basic physical security components of stockpile management.

Physical security refers to the protection of ammunition, weapons, and explosives against any malevolent actions, including theft, sabotage, damage, or tampering. The most effective means to ensure security is by restricting access by unauthorized personnel and installing measures to *detect, slow, and counteract* intrusion. Multiple fences and locked doors slow intruders, regular patrolling detects incursion, and police or troops stationed within easy reach of a facility can intervene to counter unauthorized access.

Additions such as electronic surveillance systems, perimeter lighting, and electrical alarms make facilities safer; but in many states the most basic, low-cost stockpile security procedures could be applied with minimal expenditure[15] and sufficient political will. The first step in this process is to draft a plan detailing security measures, their requirements, and actions to take in the event of malfeasance (Annexe 2.1).

Basic se◼
procedu◼
applied ◼
expendi◼

While these measures can detect, slow, and counteract unauthorized entry, it is important to note that monitoring and accounting procedures must also be in place to dissuade stockpile management personnel from facilitating unauthorized access to facilities. Physical security is only as reliable as the personnel charged with keeping it, which again underlines the need for effective oversight and accountability. In 2004, for example, the chief armourer of a Moldovan military brigade's storage facility was sentenced to three years in prison for allowing unauthorized access to military facilities. Although the armourer did not personally take possession of the munitions, his actions enabled the theft of 200 grenades, 31 grenade-launchers, and more than 90,000 rounds of ammunition (SEESAC, 2006, pp. 101–02).

However, it is not just the facilities themselves that account for unauthorized entry and theft. Very often diversion results from negligence on the part of state agents working in otherwise secure environments. Diversions of this kind include the theft of unsecured weapons from the homes or vehicles of security force personnel,[16] or the theft of weapons and ammunition that have been left unattended on desks in security force facilities.[17]

Safe storage is critical in the case of theft from homes and vehicles. Even in the most organized of security forces, procedures related to securing deployed weapons may be inadequate. In 2005, for instance—in an event that was far from isolated—a service weapon was stolen from the car of a Washington Police Chief (AP, 2005). Although members of the US police readily admit that stolen police weapons are usually used in other crimes (Klein and Dvorak, 2006), the official in this case, having left his weapon in a locked car, broke no rules (AP, 2005).

The problem may be more pronounced elsewhere. Many security force personnel in developing countries do not have the physical security measures to protect their own homes, let alone their weapons and ammunition. Military and police forces in East Africa, for instance, are often deployed to villages where an earth or wicker wall is all that protects valuables—including weapons—from theft. Short of carrying an assault rifle into a local bar at night, often the only option for off-duty service men and women is to leave the weapon in the care of a friend or relative.[18]

The logical solution, in these cases, would be to enforce a strict policy that weapons cannot leave military or police facilities if they cannot be secured. Given that many such facilities, however, remain less secure than people's homes, this will not always be appropriate.

In the case of violent attack resulting in diversion it may be difficult for security forces to guard against such assaults. This is particularly the case in attacks against individual personnel. However, the same basic tenets of physical security that apply within stockpile facilities—detect, slow, and counteract—also apply to how they are situated and protected in a broader sense. These include: 1) adequate garrisons of well-equipped forces to slow potential attacks and lessen the likelihood that they will result in diversion; 2) communications channels to warn against potential attack or seek assistance in the event of assault; and 3) the proximity of forces that are able to repel attacks should they occur.

Very often the susceptibility of stocks to attack is commensurate with the insecurity facing members of the security forces in many countries, who are often deployed far from central control—sometimes in dangerous border regions—with little support from other state forces. As with many factors associated with diversion, vulnerability in these cases often stems from weaknesses in broader security sector management.

High-order national stockpile diversion

High-order stockpile diversion involves the theft of large volumes of arms and ammunition, sometimes running into many hundreds of tonnes of weaponry. Like low-order diversion it is often facilitated by poor stockpile management practices, but in many cases it results from factors that are much broader than the management of arms and ammunition per se.

Weak state structures, a lack of accountability within political and military administrations, and associated loopholes in transfer regulations, conspire to present often highly placed individuals with the opportunity to divert weapons. As the following sections note, however, curbing high-order diversion is not beyond the scope of arms management, and there are certain basic measures that can be adopted to dissuade illicit activity. For the most part these involve taking steps to ensure that the departments responsible for intra-state arms and ammunition transfers are accountable to central authorities and that these flows are well documented. The greatest danger of high-order diversion arises where individuals, departments, and military units are able to misuse the authority granted them by the state to divert arms and ammunition in their charge, while still receiving a supply of weapons from the national stockpile.

Official conspiracy in high-order diversion

In 1992 the value of Ukraine's military stocks was estimated at USD 89 billion. By 1998 around USD 32 billion had been stolen and much of it resold abroad.[19] Loss on this scale does not simply result from the kind of low-order diversion described earlier. It occurs because large parts of a state's stockpile management system become opaque, allowing senior individuals—and sometimes entire departments—unregulated control over the management and transfer of weapons and ammunition.

This 'personalized control' facilitates illicit diversion and can result from a number of factors, including: administrative breakdown following major political upheaval (for example, Ukraine and other eastern European states in the early 1990s); loss of control over large parts of the security sector (such as Cambodia and Russia in the 1990s); and ad hoc arms management systems that give unregulated actors control over key parts of the military supply chain (for example, contemporary Iraq, described in detail below).

In all of these instances high-order diversion does not necessarily result from breaches in security or lax accounting in a particular depot or facility—although this may often occur under the same conditions. Rather, it is characterized by the wholesale redirection of large volumes of weaponry out of the state's arms management system and onto the illicit market.

Several interacting factors appear to be pivotal in facilitating high-order diversion.

First, political instability and economic downturn prompt short-term gain-seeking activities among all levels of security force personnel (and indeed society at large). Second, nationwide illicit activity rises as the state and its institutions weaken, creating increased illicit demand for military materiel by organized crime or non-state armed groups. Third, and pivotally, security force oversight and accounting mechanisms become weak and prove unable to prevent or identify diversion.

'Persona

control'

diversior

Turbiville's (1995) analysis of rising crime in the Russian armed forces in the late 1980s and early 1990s is illustrative. The collapse of the Soviet system prompted a general increase in all forms of crime within the security forces (around 14.5 per cent between 1988 and 1989). A parallel, flourishing black market provided a ready demand for all forms of stolen state assets. To compound this, the institutions responsible for curtailing intra-military crime (namely, military counterintelligence operating under the KGB) were ill-equipped to deal with it, and were quickly dissolved, along with the KGB, in 1991. Incidences of weapons theft, in particular, grew dramatically under this permissive environment, rising 50 per cent between 1989 and 1990 and a further 64 per cent between 1992 and 1993 (Busza, 1999, p. 565).

Very often it was the 'compartmentalization' of arms management responsibilities that appeared to have the greatest bearing on diversion. Highly placed military officials were able to capitalize on their personal command of military finances, equipment, and personnel—and the fact that their units continued to receive military equipment—to plunder state assets. Russian parliamentary investigations in 1994, for instance, charged the Soviet/Russian Western Group of Forces (WGF) commander-in-chief with creating an environment 'in which illegal commercial activities by his senior commanders were unrestricted if not actively encouraged' (Turbiville, 1995).

Similar situations have arisen elsewhere when senior military officials have been able to use their personal control over parts of the military to divert arms and ammunition, while still receiving a ready supply of weapons from the national stockpile. In 1990s Cambodia, for instance, military officers were able to sell entire armouries belonging to 'phantom' military units, which existed only on paper (JIG, 2000).

At higher levels in the defence establishment this compartmentalization of control can result in massive cases of diversion. In April 1997, for instance, Russian authorities noted that arms worth over USD 1 billion had been transferred to Armenia since 1992 without any state-to-state agreement or formal government permission. Among other things, the shipments included more than 230 million rounds of small arms ammunition. While the defence minister

Figure 2.4 **Arms management responsibilities in Iraq, 2004–2005**

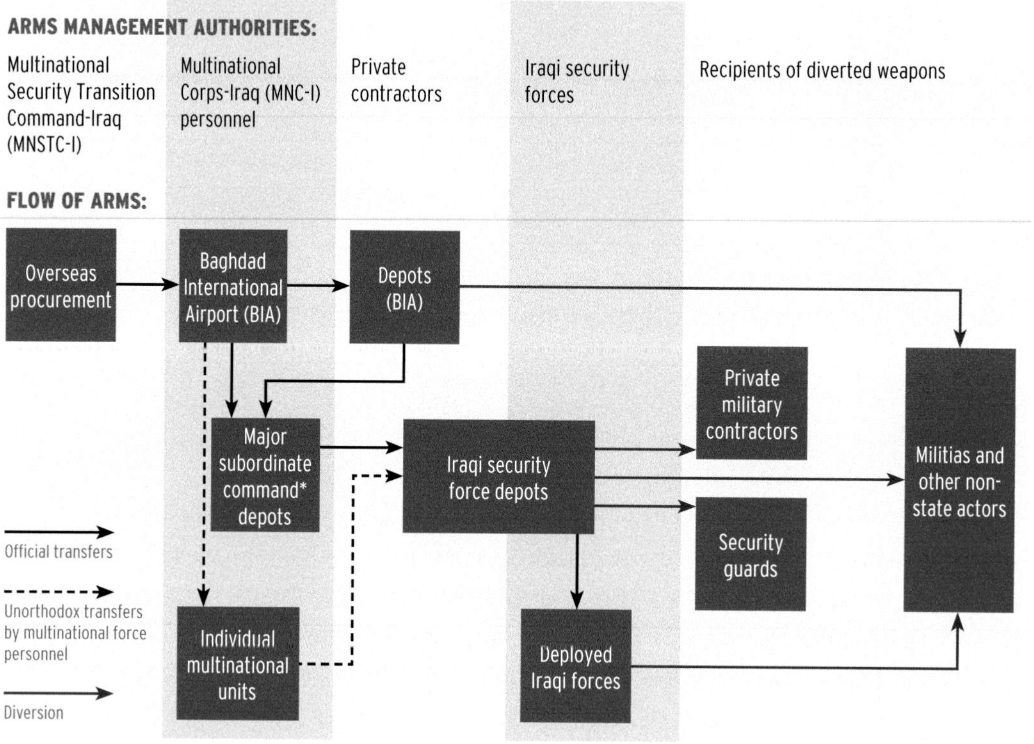

ARMS MANAGEMENT AUTHORITIES:

| Multinational Security Transition Command-Iraq (MNSTC-I) | Multinational Corps-Iraq (MNC-I) personnel | Private contractors | Iraqi security forces | Recipients of diverted weapons |

FLOW OF ARMS:

[Diagram showing flow of arms:]

Overseas procurement → Baghdad International Airport (BIA) → Depots (BIA)

Major subordinate command* depots → Iraqi security force depots → Private military contractors → Militias and other non-state actors

Individual multinational units

Security guards

Deployed Iraqi forces

→ Official transfers
- - -> Unorthodox transfers by multinational force personnel
→ Diversion

* Multinational divisions responsible for seven different geographic areas of operations.
Sources: USGAO (2007); Schmitt and Thompson (2007)

at the time claimed no knowledge of the transfers, the chief of the general staff was aware of the policy, which had commenced under the former defence minister (JIG, 1997).

Opacity and the associated compartmentalization of arms management responsibility can be strong risk factors in diversion. They are not always confined to states that experience major systemic failure, and can occur in the most efficient military systems when those systems are subverted. Even when highly organized modern military systems are nominally responsible for arms management, control over arms and ammunition can become fragmented when insufficient attention is paid to ensuring transparency and accountability for weapons.

In July 2007, for instance, the US Government Accountability Office (USGAO, 2007, pp. 10–11) noted that the Department of Defence and Multinational Force in Iraq could not account for more than 190,000 weapons reportedly issued to Iraqi security forces between June 2004 and September 2005. As a result of a failure to institute an effective accounting system, many of these weapons may have entered the illicit market (TRANSFER DIVERSION). But as one director at the GAO later reported to *The New York Times*, the problem went beyond accounting practices (Schmitt and Thompson, 2007).

As Figure 2.4 sketches, in the Iraq case a lack of oversight and accounting was compounded by the fact that arms and ammunition moved relatively unchecked between a number of disparate authorities, ranging from multinational forces to private contractors and Iraqi security forces. The lack of oversight and the unorthodox measures some military units adopted in order to shorten a lengthy supply chain made it impossible to establish where many weapons and ammunition were stored, and in what quantities. As a result, entire arsenals were diverted en route between one nominal authority and another (Schmitt and Thompson, 2007).

Policy implications

High-order diversion is a systemic problem, involving the plunder of all types of state assets, ranging from theft of military funds to illegal loans of government capital, the use of military aircraft for commercial charter, and the expropriation of military facilities and land. Taken at face value, controlling diversion of this magnitude appears to be contingent on very broad structural changes to state administrations and has linkages to wider issues such as good governance and accountability. But relatively simple arms management procedures could do much to control high-order diversion.

The Iraq case is one in which accounting procedures and effective oversight could have both deterred diversion and made its detection and policing much more effective. However, these measures were not implemented because military officials deemed that the rapid transfer of weapons and ammunition was more important than ensuring the security of those arms. As the USGAO report (2007, p. 9) noted:

> *Until December 2005, no centralized set of records for equipment distributed to Iraqi security forces existed . . . a fully operational distribution network was not established until mid-2005, over 1 year after [the multi-national force] began distributing large quantities of equipment to the Iraqi security forces. [The multi-national force] did not have the personnel necessary to record information on individual items distributed to Iraqi forces. Further, according to [multi-national force] officials, the need to rapidly equip Iraqi forces conducting operations in a combat environment limited [the multi-national force's] ability to fully implement account-ability procedures.*

The other cases noted above, in particular that of Ukraine, demonstrate that curtailing diversion may sometimes be a more challenging task and one related to deeper reforms of state security and defence-export sectors. In these cases high-order diversion may be particularly difficult to eradicate because officials use their positions to direct extant stockpile security systems—and the broader arms management system—to their personal advantage. The problem may not be one of stockpile management per se, because arms can be well secured in their particular facilities and among military units, but that departments may act in isolation from the rest of the government appa-ratus to engage in illicit transfers that *appear* to be sanctioned by the state. In such cases officials typically divert arms and ammunition using the network of international contacts, supply chains, and resources of the state itself.

However, curtailing high-order diversion is not an insurmountable challenge. Addressing it requires detecting it in the first place. Effective stockpile management and, in particular, accounting procedures have the potential to play a critical role in identifying corrupt officials and weak points in the national stockpile. High-order diversion may be a deep structural problem in the defence sectors of some states, but relatively basic management mechanisms may be pivotal in combating it in others.

Centralized record-keeping is one example where records of transactions made by all departments are stored by one, central authority—thereby minimizing the risks that those departments, or individuals within them, can gain relatively unchecked power to divert munitions. The United Kingdom, for instance, gives particular branches of the armed forces arms management—notably accounting—responsibilities for certain weapons systems. Each branch is responsible for all weapons of its allocated category within the national stockpile, regardless of which other branches use the weapons. This measure is in place for logistical reasons.[20] However, it arguably illustrates how cross-departmental systems of responsibility could potentially minimize the risk of any department gaining unchecked power over weapons and ammunition—particularly in countries where the risks of high-order diversion are very much greater than in the United Kingdom.

Military collapse

Military collapse provides the most favourable conditions for large-scale diversion of arms and ammunition. State forces lose control over stocks or disband, resulting in the dispersal of these weapons throughout society. Sometimes military collapse is associated with the collapse of the state itself, such as in Liberia and Somalia in the 1990s. In other cases it results from militaries briefly losing control of national stockpiles (such as Albania in 1997) or from armed forces disbanding yet retaining their weapons (for example, Iraq in 2003).

sections
national
become
ivatized.

While such large-scale 'external' shocks to military control over arms and ammunition may appear to pose an insurmountable challenge to curtailing diversion, as the following sections note, the risk is aggravated—and even bred—by the adoption of arms management polices that fundamentally weaken existing accounting and oversight systems.

Policies prior to collapse

One of the most striking aspects of diversion resulting from military collapse is that it is often closely linked to the factors that prove pivotal in the collapse itself. In cases where states have dissolved into a morass of competing armed factions, many of these factions have been armed by the state in question.

Faced with non-state challenges to their monopoly on violence, the response of numerous state administrations has been to further erode this monopoly by arming 'aligned' civilian factions. In Haiti, for instance, this process occurred under both the Aristide and Cédras presidencies of the 1990s. While nominally under state control at one time, many militias subsequently became embroiled in localized, politically motivated violence and crime that continues to challenge the creation of a strong state (Muggah, 2005, pp. 1–7, 50–52).

Diversion occurs in these contexts, not necessarily because state parties act unlawfully in distributing arms (although they may) but because they retain little or no control over state-provided weapons, resulting in a hazy delimitation between legal and unlawful uses. Large sections of the national stockpile become privatized and subject to diversion or illicit use. Minimal control over state-armed groups often leads to their use of weapons in contravention of the objectives of the state or in direct opposition to it.

Whether symptomatic of military collapse or precipitating it, state-armed militia groups have proved pivotal in sustaining armed conflict following the most extreme cases of state collapse, including Liberia, Sierra Leone, and Somalia.[21] These practices can prove costly when governments and international agencies have to fund disarmament programmes that are aimed explicitly at removing weapons from such militia groups.[22]

Dealing with the aftermath

Dealing with the large volumes of arms released by collapsing militaries is critical to ensuring that the weapons do not become diverted to illicit users.

In 2004 the Small Arms Survey estimated that more than 4 million small arms alone were released into Iraqi society from the stocks of state security forces (Karp, 2004, p. 49). This was technically not a case of diversion. There is no law against possession of military weapons in Iraq; they did not cross a legal–illicit threshold when the Iraqi army disbanded.

Box 2.3 Diversion and improvised explosive devices

Improvised explosive devices (IEDs) can be made from any explosive material, including items with explicitly civilian applications, such as compounds derived from nitrate-based agricultural fertilizers, and military explosives, such as TNT[23] and RDX[24] (DHS, 2005; TRADOC, 2007). Many of these ingredients are readily available to non-state armed groups around the world.

Diversion of light weapons ammunition from state stocks, however, poses a particular threat because it involves the release of weapons with specific military capabilities onto the illicit market. These weapons can be used, in their entirety or as components, to manufacture IEDs. They differ from civilian explosives because they are designed exclusively for military applications. Light weapons ammunition (as well as ammunition for larger conventional weapons) can be used in the following ways:

- removal of explosives from warheads and subsequent use in home-made bombs and projectiles;
- remote firing of projectile weapons, such as mortars and rocket launchers and ammunition thereof;
- adaptation of existing ammunition, such as mortar bombs, to detonate under pressure (mines); and
- use of shaped charges from anti-armour weaponry to increase the penetrative capacity of IEDs.

These features make national stockpiles attractive targets for non-state armed groups, allowing them to drastically increase both the speed with which they can manufacture IEDs and the capacity of these weapons against modern military targets. They have proven especially deadly in Iraq (LIGHT WEAPONS).

However, what happened to those weapons after the event is critical. By dramatically increasing the gross volume of weaponry in society, military collapse or disbandment also increases the numbers that are available to illicit users, including criminals and insurgent groups. In Iraq former state-owned weapons have been used in attacks ranging from small arms shootings to MANPADS attacks on civilian airliners (Bevan, 2004, p. 84) and roadside bombings. Notably, the ready availability of conventional ammunition with specific military capabilities has greatly facilitated the development of effective improvised explosive devices (IEDs), as Box 2.3 illustrates.

The dispersal of arms following military collapse illustrates how important it is for states to maintain effective control over national stockpiles, even at times of internal strife. Any weapons and ammunition that become subject to minimal oversight (whether through deliberate state distribution policies or military collapse) pose a threat to states, societies, and international peace and stability. Many states continue to rely on militia forces for the suppression of armed insurrection. History proves that, in cases ranging from the Congo to Colombia, it is a dangerous game to play, and groups that are subject to little state oversight and arms management can direct violence towards the state that created them.

In states where the national stockpile has already diffused into society, recovering weapons and ammunition should be a matter of priority. In Iraq, for instance, US military officials estimated that between 540,000 and 900,000 metric tonnes of ammunition and explosives were stored in around 130 sites

Sign in a gun shop window in the aftermath of Hurricane Charley, Port Charlotte, Florida, August 2004. © Mario Tama/Getty Images

in autumn 2003. However, by December 2003 only 227,000 metric tonnes had been partially secured by coalition forces and the rest remained at high risk of diversion or was already on the black market (Klingelhoefer, 2005).

DIVERSION FROM THE CIVILIAN STOCKPILE

The civilian stockpile (see Figure 2.1) encompasses a wide range of arms and ammunition storage locations, ranging from manufacturers and wholesalers to gun shops and weapons stored at home or in vehicles. Diversion from any one of these locales has the potential to contribute to unlawful use, armed crime, and violence.

In particular, the diversion of civilian-owned weapons and ammunition provides a ready source of weapons that are later used in crime. The following sections focus primarily on this phenomenon—dividing it into higher and lower orders of magnitude, as outlined for the case of military stockpiles above.

At one end of the spectrum arms and ammunition are particularly susceptible to theft when inadequately stored in homes and vehicles. In these cases of low-order diversion, weapons often enter the illicit market as a by-product of other illegal activity, such as burglary and car theft. At the other end of the spectrum, relatively large quantities of weapons held in gun shops and wholesale warehouses can be attractive targets for organized crime, often with links to the international illicit market. These high-order cases of civilian weapons diversion can in some instances be a source of arms and ammunition for insurgent and terrorist groups

Low-order civilian stockpile diversion

ery 1,000
weapons
.bject to
.version.

Low-order civilian stockpile diversion is the theft of relatively minor quantities of arms and ammunition from gun shops, civilian homes, and vehicles. It also includes cases where firearms sellers have sold arms and ammunition to persons who are unauthorized under national legislation to possess firearms (PUBLIC HEALTH APPROACH). Low-order diversion serves a relatively localized market, although it may have cross-border dimensions.

Theft from civilian holdings releases many hundreds of thousands of legally owned arms onto illicit markets each year. Data for ten countries[25] suggests that around 1 in every 1,000 weapons in civilian hands may be subject to diversion (Karp, 2004, p. 63). Taken at face value, this number may seem small, but, given a global civilian stockpile of around 650 million firearms (Karp, 2007, p. 39), diversion from civilian stocks is, cumulatively, a grave problem. At a diversion rate of 1:1,000 civilian weapons, annual losses could total 650,000 weapons.

Illegal sales or resales are also a significant source of diversion. In the United States, for instance, licensed gun dealers are prohibited from selling weapons to a convicted felon, a person convicted of a domestic violence misdemeanour, or a person previously committed to a mental institution. This interdict does not prevent some dealers from selling to an eligible intermediary, who then immediately resells to a prohibited purchaser—a process known as 'straw purchasing'. Straw purchasing is easier because civilian-owned firearms are typically not registered, so immediate retransfer entails little or no risk for the intermediary. Technically, if this kind of private sale is conducted with the dealer's knowledge that the end-user is ineligible, the transaction is illegal and constitutes diversion. There is no federal law requiring the intermediary to obtain proof of the final purchaser's eligibility, although some states require these secondary sales to go through a formal background check. Straw purchasing is particularly problematic because many US criminals have a preference for brand-new weapons, which can be obtained only from licensed gun dealers (LeBrun, 2007) (PUBLIC HEALTH APPROACH).

Despite unlawful practices such as straw purchasing, however, most arms and ammunition diversion from civilian holdings appears to originate from home burglaries. An Australian study by Mouzos and Sakurai (2006, p. 35), for instance, notes that more than 70 per cent of stolen firearms in the reporting period (February–July 2004) were taken from private residential premises. Motor vehicles comprised the second-largest source (14 per cent), and business premises the third (10 per cent). The situation in the United Kingdom is similar (see Figure 2.5). Data for the United States, while aggregated differently, suggests that domestic burglary is responsible for a comparable 60 per cent of all stolen weapons (Rand, 1994).

Most such thefts appear to accompany other, economically motivated crime. In the Australian case 58 per cent of weapons were stolen at the same time as other goods, leading Mouzos and Sakurai (2006, p. 39) to conclude that opportunistic household burglary was a major source of diversion.

Low-order diversion from the civilian stockpile appears to respond to highly localized (and in some sense ad hoc) demand.[26] Its primary beneficiaries appear to be petty criminals. Studies in the United States, for instance, reveal that as many as 50 per cent of criminals in correctional facilities have stolen a weapon at some point in their career (Zawitz, 1995, p. 3).

Potentially more serious cases arise where criminals have explicitly targeted homes and gun shops in order to acquire arms and ammunition. In Australia, for instance, 40 per cent of cases in which a weapon was stolen targeted *only* arms and ammunition and no other commodities (Mouzos and Sakurai, 2006, p. 39), suggesting that arms acquisition was the sole motive for the theft.

Arms and ammunition that enter the illicit market as a result of theft from the civilian stockpile typically feed local crime, but can also have much wider impacts. In May 2007 Florida law-enforcement officials made arrests over the theft of weapons from gun shops in the United States, which were later shipped via Florida International Airport to Puerto Rico (UPI, 2007). There are other international dimensions to domestic diversion. According to a report by the Mexican National Defence Commission, for instance, an estimated 99 per cent of weapons confiscated from criminals in Mexico had been sourced in the United States (Núñez, 2007). There is evidence to suggest that the United States–Mexico cross-border arms trade is often organized by criminal gangs linked to the drugs trade (Roig-Franzia, 2007).

High-order civilian stockpile diversion

High-order diversion of civilian holdings occurs when criminal groups target larger, non-state arms and ammunition storage facilities, such as gun shops and wholesalers. This chapter labels the process 'high-order', not because it shares structural similarities with high-order diversion of military stocks, but simply because it is very much larger in scale than the often petty thieving from civilian holdings described above. High-order civilian diversion is often linked to large organized criminal networks and can sometimes be used to fuel insurgency.

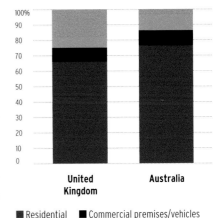

Figure 2.5 **Proportion of locations from which firearms were stolen in Australia (n = 372) and the United Kingdom (n = 4697)**

■ Residential ■ Commercial premises/vehicles
■ Private car ■ Other

Notes: Australian data for period 1 February-1 July 2004; UK aggregated from years 1999-2006.
Sources: Mouzos and Sakurai (2006, p. 37); UKHO (2000; 2001; 2003; 2004; 2005; 2006; 2007)

In countries with high civilian firearm ownership rates, organized criminal gangs can source weapons and ammunition through illicit trade that has its origin in the kinds of small-scale theft noted above. However, where access to firearms is more difficult, or certain types of weapon are scarcer, criminals have robbed more difficult targets such as larger gun shops and other secure warehouses. Often these attacks are orchestrated by organized criminal gangs, which have the necessary resources to engage in this form of robbery.

In September 2007, for instance, thieves stole weapons and ammunition from a gun shop in Ipswich, Australia, in a sophisticated robbery that involved piercing the roof of the building, disabling the alarm system, and removing the hard drive of the computer surveillance system. The theft involved more than 50 firearms and large quantities of ammunition. Police were reportedly concerned that the robbery exhibited the hallmarks of organized crime (ABC, 2007; Swanwick, 2007).

In other instances the prospect of gaining access to specific types of weapon seems to have prompted criminal organizations to target commercial establishments. In October 2007 criminals robbed a gun shop in Florida. The robbery was notable because the weapons stolen were selected by type. The thieves in question took only semi-automatic versions of military assault rifles, including 57 Armalite- and Kalashnikov-pattern weapons. These high-velocity weapons are reportedly favoured by organized crime (Curtis, 2007).

High-order diversion can therefore be a transition point whereby criminal factions gain access to far greater firepower—enhancing their status and offensive capacity via-à-vis other factions, but also presenting a greater challenge to the forces of law and order. In Rio de Janeiro, for instance, there has been a marked increase in the acquisition of high-powered rifles and sub-machine guns by the city's organized drug factions since the late 1980s (Dowdney, 2003, pp. 96–97), not least because of their offensive capacity against security forces (Bevan and Dreyfus, 2007, pp. 304–05).

In some cases the challenge to the state posed by high-order diversion may not be restricted to organized crime. Gun shops and other civilian storage facilities are tempting targets for non-state armed groups—particularly those that experience supply difficulties. In 2005, for instance, Chechen fighters in the town of Nalchik targeted two shops as part of a wider attack that included an assault on a police station (Chivers, 2005).

In many countries, therefore, the availability of large quantities of relatively poorly secured civilian arms and ammunition poses a latent threat to states and societies.

Securing civilian holdings

Many civilian holdings are insecure and present criminals with easy opportunities to divert arms and ammunition. The main reason for such accessibility is poor physical security of arms and ammunition—primarily in homes.

Firearms are stored, unlocked, in 40 per cent of US homes. In around 30 per cent of these unlocked cases, weapons are stored while loaded, with a further 15 per cent of unlocked weapons stored alongside ammunition (RAND, 2001). There is no reason to suspect that the United States differs from many other countries, and the figures are clear: it is relatively easy for criminals to acquire weapons, including ready-to-fire weapons.

The United Kingdom, for instance, has particularly low levels of civilian weapons holdings, and yet more than 700 weapons are stolen annually.[27] Most of these thefts are the result of criminal access to inadequately secured weapons.[28] While UK legislation stipulates that weapon must be kept 'safe and secure' (Box 2.4), it does not specify measures required to achieve this or minimum storage standards. Such vagueness as to what constitutes adequate security appears to lead to the uneven application of security measures in many countries.

Table 2.3 Modes of firearms theft from secured containers in Australia, February–July 2004 (n = 189)

Forced open	45%
Removal of whole safe	12%
Keys found and used	12%
Locks cut	10%

Source: Mouzos and Sakurai (2006, p. 11)

Around 60 per cent of weapons stolen from Australian homes are 'secured' in safes and other locked receptacles that comply with Australian laws on firearms storage. The findings displayed in Table 2.3 suggest, however, that these storage practices are insufficient, and thieves had the time to break into safes, cut locks, or locate keys. In some cases safes could be removed and broken into at a later date.

Box 2.4 Evidence of increased physical security? The United Kingdom post-1997

The United Kingdom has experienced a dramatic decline in the number of reported shotgun thefts since 1997, a trend that is arguably illustrative of increasing physical security of weapons in the country.

Figure 2.6 (see overleaf) plots reported thefts of shotguns and handguns in the United Kingdom between 1986 and 2006. It illustrates a pronounced decline in the number of thefts of each type of weapon reported to the police following the 1996 shooting of 16 children and a teacher in Dunblane, Scotland. The shooting resulted in the 1997 Firearms Amendment Act, which banned virtually all[29] handguns from private ownership (UK, 1997).

Taken at face value, the data in Figure 2.6 appears to reflect the impact of the 1997 Act. However, the Act did not significantly affect civilian shotgun possession, which suggests that other factors may be responsible for the rapidly diminishing reports of shotgun thefts.

There is reason to suspect that overall shotgun ownership rates did not fall particularly dramatically after 1997–and certainly not as fast as handgun ownership, which was, by contrast, highly restricted by the Act. The marked (30 per cent) decrease in shotgun theft reporting rates in Figure 2.6 is therefore unlikely to result from a decline in opportunity for theft.

The selective scope of the Act suggests that the theft of shotguns may have diminished as a result of non-legislative factors, including increased public awareness of the dangers of weapons and, pivotally, the fact that authorities responsible for issuing firearms licences made the process contingent on the security of weapons–including spot checks of domestic security arrangements.

The 1997 Act did *not* impose tighter controls on shotgun storage practices beyond those of previous Acts, which merely specified weapons should be 'kept safe and secure' at all times. As the Metropolitan Police (2007) notes:

The Firearms Acts are not specific regarding security except to state that the weapons must be kept safe and secure at all times so as to prevent unauthorised access, as far as is reasonably practical . . . It therefore follows that the issuer of the certificate [the Police] must set the standards to be met, within the limitations of the Acts. . . . all shotguns and firearms should be kept in bona-fide gun cabinets. That is, cabinets which are purpose built for the keeping of shotguns and firearms. The cabinets must be located within the confines of the house and not stored in a garage or outbuilding. They should be rawl-bolted to a solid brick wall and out of sight of casual callers. Section 1 ammunition should be stored separately and securely from Section 1 weapons. BS7558 is a British Standard for gun cabinets since 1992 which practically all cabinets, sold by reputable Registered Firearms Dealers, will meet.

Given the dramatic decline in UK shotgun thefts post-1997 (see Figure 2.6), policies such as these appear to have played a critical role in increasing the security of firearms and preventing diversion.[30] Although UK arms and ammunition storage standards are far from optimal, applying a relatively simple set of storage criteria appears to be one of the key reasons for a reduction in reported shotgun theft.

Figure 2.6 **Shotguns and handguns stolen in the United Kingdom: 1986–2005 (n = 15,063)**

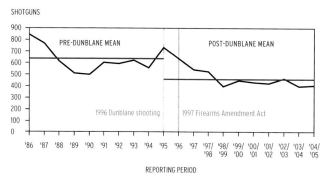

SHOTGUNS

PRE-DUNBLANE MEAN   POST-DUNBLANE MEAN

1996 Dunblane shooting   1997 Firearms Amendment Act

'86 '87 '88 '89 '90 '91 '92 '93 '94 '95 '96 '97 '97/ '98/ '99/ '00/ '01/ '02/ '03/ '04/
'98 '99 '00 '01 '02 '03 '04 '05

REPORTING PERIOD

HANDGUNS

1996 Dunblane shooting   1997 Firearms Amendment Act

PRE-DUNBLANE MEAN   POST-DUNBLANE MEAN

'06 '87 '88 '89 '90 '91 '92 '93 '94 '95 '96 '97 '97/ '98/ '99/ '00/ '01/ '02/ '03/ '04/
'98 '99 '00 '01 '02 '03 '04 '05

REPORTING PERIOD

Note: Event separators are drawn at the beginning of the year in which the event occurred and in which data collection for that year commenced.
Source: UK (2006)

The same principles that apply to securing military stockpiles apply equally to civilian stocks. As Table 2.4 illustrates, most basic stockpile management approaches that can be applied to national security force stockpiles have civilian equivalents. But the findings in this section, and Table 2.4, show that in many (if not all) countries civilian stockpile management and security does not even begin to meet the basic tenets of security applicable to national stockpiles, particularly with respect to ammunition.

Civilian stockpile management falls far short of military standards, for several reasons. First, and despite the fact that many states have national registration systems for firearms, ammunition is almost always poorly regulated. Diverted ammunition cannot be traced back to its original owners, making it difficult to establish either the scale of ammunition diversion or the nature of security weaknesses for civilian holdings.

Table 2.4 **Standard military stockpile security measures and civilian equivalents** (particular weak points marked in red)

Military stocks	Civilian stocks
Accounting	*Firearms registration*
Records of stocks issued	Firearms/ammunition registration
Records of stocks expended	n/a
Monitoring	*Periodic registration*
Physical inspection	Periodic (yearly) registration of arms
Stock audits	Inspection of registered weapon (yearly)
Stock loss/theft reports	Mandatory reports of theft to police
Lot-marking by unit	Lot-marking by retailer and records of sales
Stock security	*Domestic/commercial security*
Perimeter security; secure doors and access routes; lockdown of portable weapons	Weapon safes; secure doors; keys stored elsewhere
Separation of arms and ammunition	Separation of arms and ammunition
Guards, dog patrols, and random patrols	Electronic alarms
Proximate additional security forces	Electronic alarms (perhaps linked to police stations)

Second, only in a handful of countries is there anything approaching the kind of stock audit expected within functional stockpile management systems of national stockpiles. Very few states have systematic checks or periodic re-registration which might enable law-enforcement officials to determine whether private holdings have been lost or stolen, and to take appropriate measures. Theft reporting is mandatory in effective military stockpile management systems, but this is not the case with most thefts from civilian holdings.

Third, the physical security of civilian holdings remains poor. Measures taken to *slow, detect,* and *counteract* intrusion reduce the risk of diversion. Some states, such as Australia and the United Kingdom, specify storage criteria. Yet even these may be insufficient. In the United Kingdom, for instance, between 1999 and 2006 the rate of reported small arms loss or theft from military establishments was 1 in 29,000.[31] The rate of civilian loss or theft was approximately 1 in 400 firearms.[32] A safe or gun cabinet is not sufficient in many cases to prevent theft.

In the absence of measures to detect and counteract theft, such as alarm systems, thieves may be able to spend considerable time penetrating safes and other storage systems. It is worth noting that only one of the premises in the Australian study was fitted with an alarm (Mouzos and Sakurai, 2006, p. 47).

Lessons from national stockpile security suggest that physical security extends beyond locks and doors to regular patrolling and the stationing of security forces to rapidly interdict the theft of arms. This is not feasible in the case of civilian holdings, but there is arguably some justification for claiming that electronic alarms—and particularly systems that notify security forces of thefts of registered weapons—could do much more to bring civilian diversion within acceptable limits.

The security of homes, vehicles, or any other repositories of civilian weapons holdings remains substandard in most countries. Whether through changes in national legislation, regulatory measures, or awareness campaigns focusing on secure storage, curtailing diversion will be contingent on effectively securing civilian holdings. Although there are critical variations in the scale and types of stock, physical measures adopted to control diversion from the civilian holdings differ very little from those that are required for national stockpiles.

CONCLUSION

Diversion lies at the heart of illicit arms proliferation. In varying degrees of severity, in almost all countries it facilitates the acquisition of arms and ammunition by criminals, terrorist organizations, and non-state armed groups. By providing a source of arms and ammunition to users who might otherwise have difficulty acquiring arms, it intensifies armed conflict and criminality, threatening communities, societies, and the state itself.

This chapter is deliberately wide in scope, recognizing that diversion of munitions operates at many different levels. It highlights the fact that all forms of diversion play a mutually supporting role in sustaining illicit proliferation. In recognition of this fact, the chapter emphasizes the need for comprehensive, mutually reinforcing controls over the security of all stocks of arms and ammunition—whether in the hands of civilians or state agents.

Effective control requires measures at a number of levels. It may involve tightening national stockpile security through the more effective management of military and police stockpiles. Equally, it requires comprehensive attention to national firearms laws and non-legislative regulations governing how civilians store their weapons at home.

In some instances controls may extend to broader changes in the way states manage arms and ammunition. Security sector reform to improve accountability within administrations is one measure that could protect national stockpiles from high-order diversion. In other cases, controls are contingent on improving national and international regulations over the export of arms and ammunition.

Although resources play a critical role in the lack of progress towards enhanced stockpile security in many countries, a growing number of states participate in bilateral and multilateral initiatives that are designed to assist states with enhancing stockpile security. Recipients of this kind of support, however, remain few in number, and there is a clear need for donors to better advertise such initiatives and the fact that they can make a tangible difference to stockpile security.

The most severe cases of diversion—such as can occur with state collapse—are dependent on broader political factors that may seem beyond the scope of small arms and light weapons control. Nevertheless, even in these catastrophic instances, diversion can be alleviated by concerted efforts to address weak points in national stockpile management at the earliest possible moment, and by ensuring that any subsequent rearmament occurs under effective arms management systems.

Some measures to control diversion are relatively easy to apply—such as placing a padlock on a door, installing a gun safe at home, or posting a guard at a weapons storage facility. But in many countries, whether as a result of insufficient political will or through a lack of awareness, these small issues remain unaddressed. The primary barrier to preventing most cases of diversion is not expenditure but foresight.

The interface between the legal and illicit arms markets lies at home: with private citizens and state security forces. Diversion is not a product of shadowy deals in the world's crime and conflict zones, but a problem that stems directly from the negligence of legal users. Unless greater attention is paid to this fact, states and societies will continue to 'shoot themselves in the foot'. ▰

ANNEXE 2.1

Model security plan

	Item	Comments
1.	Registration of the name, location, and telephone number of the establishment security officer.	One, single security authority. This person, or a deputy, must be contactable 24 hours a day.
2.	Scope of the plan.	What does the plan cover: which areas, individuals, and possible scenarios?
3.	Content of the stockpile.	Types of weapon. Types of ammunition nature.
4.	Security threat.	What sorts of interests might try to remove weapons and when (e.g. nightly theft, armed robbery, children).
5.	Detailed geographic map of the site location and its surroundings.	This should clearly indicate fences, access roads, bunkers/storage areas, and access routes.
6.	Detailed diagram of the layout of the site, including locations of: • all buildings and structures • entry and exit points • electricity generators/substations • water and gas main points • road and rail tracks • wooded areas • hard- and soft-paved areas • guard points	Ideally a proper survey map of the site at around 1:5,000 scale or less.
7.	Outline of the physical security measures to be applied to the site, including, but not limited to, details of: • fences, doors, and windows • lighting • perimeter intruder detection systems • intruder detection systems • automated access control systems • guards • guard dogs • locks and containers • control of entry and exit of persons • control of entry and exit of goods and material • secure rooms • hardened buildings • closed-circuit television	
8.	Security responsibilities (including, but not limited to, the following personnel, as applicable): • security officer • guards and guard commanders • transport officer • inventory management and verification personnel • all personnel authorized to have access to the site	The greatest possible specificity of responsibilities, even on a case-by-case basis—e.g. 'In the event of an attempted break-in, the security officer shall be responsible for...' Even personnel with no specific security brief (transport officer, other personnel) may have security responsibilities—e.g. 'You are responsible for locking all doors you have previously unlocked.'

9.	Security procedures to be followed in: • stock reception areas • pre-storage processing • bunkers • during all stock withdrawals	For example, how are people to be admitted to perform these functions? What security procedures should be followed when withdrawing stocks?
10.	Control of access to buildings and compounds.	Detail fences, gates, and how they operate, for whom they are to be opened, etc.
11.	Transport procedures	• Who provides security? • How is handover to another authority to be secured? • How are external recipients to be identified?
12.	Control of security keys (those in use and their duplicates).	• Where are keys to be located? • Who can have them? It is often a good idea to attach keys permanently to large metal key tags so that they are highly visible. New technologies such as embedded Radio Frequency Identification (RFI) chips can aid in locating keys.
13.	Security education and staff briefing.	• How are the staff to be briefed? • When? • By whom? New personnel must be briefed as soon as possible. Refresher briefings should be conducted as a matter of course.
14.	Action on discovery of loss.	• The security aspects of every loss must be investigated. • Lessons must be drawn and amendments made to the security plan if necessary.
15.	Details of response force arrangements (e.g. size, response time, orders, means of activation and deployment).	How and when to activate the site's guard response force? Expected response times and actions. How to contact the police/security forces? How long will it take them to respond?
16.	Actions to be taken in response to activation of alarms.	Who must deploy where when an alarm is sounded?
17.	Security actions to be taken in response to security emergency situations (e.g. robbery, attack).	Clear instructions on the use of force, on alerting police and security services, and on post-event investigation.
18.	Security actions to be taken in response to non-security emergency situations (e.g fire or flood).	You must have procedures in place to coordinate activities of rescue and emergency teams with the security needs of the site (access in times of emergency, securing keys, avoiding theft during the confusion).

Sources: This plan has been adapted from the OSCE (2003a) 'Best Practice Guide on National Procedures for Stockpile Management' by Michael Ashkenazi of the Bonn International Centre for Conversion (BICC) and is part of a chapter on stockpile security in Bevan (2008a).

LIST OF ABBREVIATIONS

DoD	(United States) Department of Defense	MANPADS	Man-portable air defence systems
IED	Improvised explosive device	RPNGC	Royal Papua New Guinea Constabulary
LAW	Light anti-tank weapon		

ENDNOTES

1   It is worth noting that the SS109 and .223 Remington are not entirely interchangeable. The military SS109 differs from the civilian .223 in having a higher gas pressure. This means that, while the .223 can be fired from weapons intended for the civilian market, when fired from military rifles it delivers lesser performance than the SS109. Conversely, firing the SS109 from civilian-specification rifles can cause excessive stresses to the weapons and may present a danger to the user.

2   Field research in Kenya, Uganda, and Sudan. Conducted by James Bevan, 2005–08.

3   Size should not be overemphasized as a factor in diversion. In 1997, for instance, one person was convicted of stealing a Sheridan light tank, 17 armoured personnel carriers, and 136 other vehicles from the Fort McCoy Army Base (JIG, 2000).

4   Field-based ammunition tracing conducted by James Bevan for the Small Arms Survey, 2006–08.

5   Field-based ammunition tracing conducted by James Bevan for the Small Arms Survey, 2006–08.

6   See for instance the United Nations Sanctions Committee report on the Democratic Republic of Congo, which noted: 'The failings in the establishment, management and sharing of arms inventories in the Democratic Republic of the Congo are factors that facilitate illegal appropriations or diversions. The few databases that do exist are too inaccurate to enable an efficient enquiry' (UNSC, 2006, para. 24).

7   Field-based ammunition tracing conducted by James Bevan for the Small Arms Survey, 2006–08.

8   For further information on accounting, see OSCE (2003a, p. 8; 2003b, p. 4).

9   Diversion of this type is not restricted to domestic security forces. In September 2006, for instance, the South African Defence Minister, Mosiuoa Lekota, reported that '50,000 rounds of ammunition, 97 mortar bombs, 46 R-4 assault rifles, three light machine guns, two pistols and two grenades had been lost or stolen in the course of [South African] peace-support missions' in Burundi, the Democratic Republic of Congo, and Sudan (Glatz and Lumpe, 2007, pp. 85–86).

10 Presentation by Dr Owen Green to the Joint Arms Control Implementation Group (JACIG), RAF Henlow, United Kingdom, 19 September 2007.

11 State Department Official cited in Stohl, Schroeder, and Smith (2007, p. 124).

12 The seven countries noted by Florquin and Berman (2005) are: Côte d'Ivoire (p. 249), Guinea-Bissau (p. 290), Liberia (p. 302–03), Mali (p. 313), Nigeria (p. 341), Senegal (p. 362), and Sierra Leone (p. 372).

13 See Bevan and Dreyfus (2007, p. 296) for a breakdown of ammunition by age alongside political events in Ugandan history (Figure 9.4). See also Bevan (2008b) for an assessment of the distribution and impact of armed violence in Karamoja.

14 UN daily, weekly, and monthly security summaries kindly provided by the UN Field Security Office, Gulu.

15 Expenditure is a relative concept, and it is worth noting that some states have minimal budgets for enhancing the security of national stockpiles. A growing number of stockpile assistance programmes, however, offer technical assessments of security requirements and can provide states with advice concerning potential donors for security enhancements.

16 See, for instance, the case of a Dallas police officer whose 9 mm pistol and 46 rounds of ammunition were stolen after he had left his gun belt on the seat of his vehicle while playing basketball (Eiserer, 2007).

17 See, for instance, Klein and Dvorak (2006) for a reported theft from a desk within a police station. The gun was later used in at least three shooting incidents and a robbery.

18 Field research conducted by James Bevan in Kenya, Sudan, and Uganda, 2005–07.

19 Report of a Ukrainian state-instigated investigation cited in Kuzio (2002). See also JIG (2002) and interviews conducted with Ukrainian officials at the Ministry of Foreign Affairs, with former government officials at the Ministry of Economy by International Alert (von Tangen Page, Godnick, and Vivekananda, 2005).

20 These logistical reasons stem from economies of scale in which it is more effective for the branch of the armed forces that uses the majority of a particular type of weapon to assume responsibility for managing all stocks of that system in the national stockpile.

21   See, for instance, analysis of the role of state-armed militias in the collapse of the Somali state by Clapham (2007, pp. 231) and Compagnon (1998, pp. 76–77).

22   See, for example, UNICEF and Guinean government programme to disarm, demobilize, and reintegrate members of the Guinean government-supported 'Young Volunteers' militia (Florquin and Berman, 2005, pp. 280–81).

23   Trinitrotoluene.

24   Cyclotrimethylenetrinitramine.

25   These countries were Australia, Canada, England and Wales, Finland, Norway, Philippines, South Africa, Spain, Sweden, and the United States. See table on page 63 of Karp (2004).

26   It is important not to overlook theft from homes that is not associated with burglaries. One of the best-publicized examples has been the use of diverted arms and ammunition in school-related shooting incidents in the United States. Between 1992 and 1999, for instance, around 37.5 per cent of firearms used in school-related shootings that resulted in homicide involved weapons that had been sourced from the home of the perpetrator (Reza et al., 2003, p. 1626). Available evidence suggests that many juveniles had access to arms and ammunition because of poor domestic security.

27   Mean average of shotgun, rifle, and handgun thefts for the years 1986-2005. Data from UKHO (2000; 2001; 2003; 2004; 2005; 2006; 2007).

28   UKHO (2000; 2001; 2003; 2004; 2005; 2006; 2007).

29   The Act did not ban muzzle-loading guns, pistols produced before 1917, or pistols of historical or aesthetic interest.

30   Normative changes in the way British society views firearms in the aftermath of the March 1996 Dunblane shooting are difficult to assess, but cannot be ignored as another potential source of reduced firearm theft. It is quite plausible that many firearm-owning residents began increasingly to view firearms as dangerous and either disposed of them or took steps to ensure that they were better secured, regardless of national regulations or police policies. Either course of action could have an impact on gun theft rates.

31   Thefts: UKHO (2000; 2001; 2003; 2004; 2005; 2006; 2007). Firearm inventory estimate: correspondence with Aaron Karp. The figure 1,179,056 is an estimate used to generate findings for the Small Arms Survey (2006, pp. 37–63).

32   Thefts: UKHO, (2000; 2001; 2003; 2004; 2005; 2006; 2007). Firearm inventory estimate: Small Arms Survey (2004, p. 63). Firearm inventory refers to pre-1997 Act numbers (1996) and probably overestimates civilian holdings.

BIBLIOGRAPHY

ABC (Australian Broadcasting Corporation). 2007. 'Qld Police Investigate Gun Store Robbery.' Sydney: ABC. 23 September.
    <http://www.abc.net.au/news/stories/2007/09/23/2040972.htm?section=Justin>

AAP (Australian Associated Press). 2007. 'NSW: Army Captain is Behind Rocket Launcher Thefts.' AAP Newsfeed. Sydney: AAP. 5 April.

Alpers, Philip. 2005. *Gun-running in Papua New Guinea: From Arrows to Assault Weapons in the Southern Highlands*. Small Arms Survey Special Report No. 5. Geneva: Small Arms Survey. June.

Anders, Holger. 2006. 'Following the Lethal Trail: Identifying Sources of Illicit Ammunition.' In Pézard, Stéphanie and Holger Anders. *Targeting Ammunition: A Primer*. Geneva: Small Arms Survey, pp.207–28.

AP (Associated Press). 2005. 'Seattle, Washington Police Chief's Gun Stolen in Car Prowl.' New York: Associated Press. 4 January.
    <http://www.officer.com/web/online/Top-News-Stories/Seattle--Washington-Police-Chiefs-Gun-Stolen-in-Car-Prowl/1$19938>

BBC (British Broadcasting Corporation). 2002. 'Israeli Soldiers "Sold Arms to Militants".' London: BBC. 18 July.
    <http://news.bbc.co.uk/2/hi/middle_east/2136798.stm>

—. 2007. 'Indonesia Shuts Border after East Timor Rebels Seize Arms.' BBC Monitoring Asia Pacific–Political. London: BBC. 26 February.

Bevan, James. 2004. 'Big Issue, Big Problem? MANPADS.' In Small Arms Survey. *Small Arms Survey 2004: Rights at Risk*. Oxford: Oxford University Press, pp. 77–98.

—. 2005. 'Violent Exchanges: The Use of Small Arms in Conflict.' In Small Arms Survey. *Small Arms Survey 2005: Weapons at War*. Oxford: Oxford University Press, pp. 179–203.

—, ed. 2008a. *Conventional Ammunition in Surplus: A Reference Guide*. Geneva: Small Arms Survey.

—. 2008b. *Crisis in Karamoja: Armed Violence and the Failure of Disarmament in Uganda's Most Deprived Region*. Occasional Paper. Geneva: Small Arms Survey.

— and Pablo Dreyfus. 2007. 'Enemy Within: Ammunition Diversion in Uganda and Brazil.' In Small Arms Survey. *Small Arms Survey 2007: Guns and the City*. Cambridge: Cambridge University Press, pp. 289–315.

——. 2008. 'Small Arms Ammunition Lot Marking.' In Bevan, James, ed. *Conventional Ammunition in Surplus: A Reference Guide*. Geneva: Small Arms Survey.

Blenkin, Max. 2007. 'Defence Moves to Tighten Weapons Security.' Canberra: Australian Associated Press. 25 September.

Braithwaite, David and Dylan Welch with Deborah Snow, John Garnaut, and Les Kennedy. 2007. 'Rocket Launchers "Stolen for Gangs"; Officer and Ex-Soldier Face Charges.' *The Age* (Melbourne). 6 April.

Busza, Eva. 1999. 'From Decline to Disintegration: The Russian Military Meets the Millennium.' *Demokratizatsiya: The Journal of Post-Soviet Democratization,* Vol. 7, No. 4, pp. 561–72.

Capie, David. 2003. *Under the Gun: The Small Arms Challenge in the Pacific.* Wellington: Victoria University Press.

Chivers, Christopher. 2005. 'At Least 85 Slain as Rebels Attack in South Russia.' *New York Times.* 14 October.

Clapham, Christopher. 2007. 'African Guerrillas Revisited.' In Bøås, Morten and Kevin Dunn, eds. *African Guerrillas: Raging Against the Machine.* Boulder: Lynne Rienner, pp. 221–33.

Compagnon, Daniel. 1998. 'Somali Armed Units: The Interplay of Political Entrepreneurship and Clan-Based Factions.' In Clapham, Christopher, ed. *African Guerrillas.* Oxford: James Currey, pp. 73–90.

Curtis, Henry. 2007. '3 Men Arrested after 16 Guns Found from Orange City Theft.' *Orlando Sentinel.* 23 October.

DHS (Department of Homeland Security). 2005. 'Awareness Level WMD Training: Explosive Devices.' Washington, DC: Department of Homeland Security, Office for Domestic Preparedness. 9 June. <http://cryptome.org/ieds.pdf>

Dowdney, Luke. 2003. *Children of the Drug Trade: A Case Study of Children in Organized Armed Violence in Rio de Janeiro.* Rio de Janeiro: 7 Letras.

Eiserer, Tanya. 2007. 'Police: Gun Belt Stolen from Car while Officer Played Basketball.' *Dallas Morning News.* 22 May. <http://www.dallasnews.com/sharedcontent/dws/dn/latestnews/stories/DN-officer_22met.ART.State.Edition2.438d634.html>

Florquin, Nicolas and Eric Berman, eds. 2005. *Armed and Aimless: Armed Groups, Guns, and Human Security in the ECOWAS Region.* Geneva: Small Arms Survey.

Florquin, Nicolas and Stéphanie Pézard. 2005. 'Insurgency, Disarmament, and Insecurity in Northern Mali, 1990-2004.' In Florquin, Nicolas and Eric Berman, eds. *Armed and Aimless: Armed Groups, Guns, and Human Security in the ECOWAS Region.* Geneva: Small Arms Survey, pp. 46–73.

Glatz, Anne-Kathrin and Lora Lumpe. 2007. 'Probing the Grey Area: Irresponsible Small Arms Transfers.' In *Small Arms Survey 2007: Guns and the City.* Cambridge: Cambridge University Press, pp. 73–115.

Golik, Piotr. 1999. 'Arms Theft: Missing Missiles.' *Warsaw Voice.* 11 October.

Greenberg, Joel. 2002. 'Shock at Charges Arabs were Sold Israeli Munitions.' *New York Times.* 19 July.

Humphreys, Macartan and Habaye ag Mohamed. 2003. 'Senegal and Mali.' Paper presented at the 'Civil Conflict Workshop' organized by the World Bank and the International Peace Research Institutes, Oslo (PRIO). <http://www.columbia.edu/~mh2245/papers1/hm2005.pdf>

JIG (Jane's Intelligence Group). 1997. 'Russia Details Illegal Deliveries to Armenia.' *Jane's Defence Weekly,* Vol. 27, Issue 15. Coulsdon: Jane's Information Group. 16 April.

——. 2000. 'Clandestine Trade in Arms: A Matter of Ways and Means.' *Jane's Intelligence Review,* Vol. 12, Issue 5. Coulsdon: Jane's Intelligence Group. 1 May.

——. 2002. 'Ukraine: An Inside Report (Part 3).' *Jane's Intelligence Digest.* Coulsdon: Jane's Intelligence Group. 27 September.

——. 2005. 'Dealing with the Russian "Arsenal of anarchy".' *Jane's Intelligence Review.* Coulsdon: Jane's Intelligence Group. 1 February.

——. 2007a. 'Small-Arms, Big Problem – Light Weapons Trafficking in Albania.' *Jane's Intelligence Review.* Coulsdon: Jane's Intelligence Group. 1 October.

——. 2007b. 'Peacekeepers Killed as Guerrillas Attack AMIS Base in Darfur.' *Jane's Defence Weekly.* Coulsdon: Jane's Intelligence Group. 10 October.

——. 2007c. 'FARC Rearms from Peru, Eyes Venezuela.' *Jane's Terrorism & Security Monitor.* Coulsdon: Jane's Intelligence Group. 10 October.

Karp, Aaron. 2004. 'From Chaos to Coherence: Global Firearm Stockpiles.' In Small Arms Survey. *Small Arms Survey 2004: Rights at Risk.* Oxford: Oxford University Press, pp. 43–76.

——. 2007. 'Completing the Count: Civilian Firearms.' In Small Arms Survey. *Small Arms Survey 2007: Guns and the City.* Cambridge: Cambridge University Press, pp. 39–71.

Klein, Allison and Petula Dvorak. 2006. 'Gun Stolen From D.C. Officer Used In Crimes.' *Washington Post.* 7 July. <http://www.washingtonpost.com/wp-dyn/content/article/2006/07/06/AR2006070601614.html>

Klingelhoefer, Mark. 2005. *Captured Enemy Ammunition in Operation Iraqi Freedom and Its Strategic Importance in Post-conflict Operations.* Carlisle Barracks, Pennsylvania: US Army War College, Strategy Research Project. 18 March. <http://www.strategicstudiesinstitute.army.mil/pdffiles/ksil72.pdf>

Kuzio, Taras. 2002. 'Ukraine's Decade-long Illegal Trade in Arms.' *RFE/RL Crime, Corruption, and Terrorism Watch,* Vol. 2, No. 1. 10 January. <http://www.nisat.org/default.asp?page=/search.asp>

LeBrun, Emile. 2007. *Recent Innovative Approaches to Preventing Criminal Access to Firearms in the United States*. Background paper. Geneva: Small Arms Survey. October.

Metropolitan Police. 2007. 'Firearms Enquiries: Security.' London: Metropolitan Police. <http://www.met.police.uk/firearms-enquiries/security.htm>

Mkutu, Kennedy. 2007a. 'Impact of Small Arms Insecurity on the Public Health of Pastoralists in the Kenya–Uganda Border Regions.' *Crime, Law and Social Change,* Vol. 47, No. 1. February, pp. 33–56.

—. 2007b. 'Small Arms and Light Weapons Among Pastoral Groups in the Kenya-Uganda Border Area.' *African Affairs,* Vol. 106, No. 422. January, pp. 47–70.

Moreman, Tim. 2006. 'The Arms Trade on the N.W. Frontier of India 1890–1914.' Articles on the Indian Army. King-Emperor. <http://www.king-emperor.com/article5-armstrade.htm>

Mouzos, Jenny and Yuka Sakurai. 2006. *Firearms Theft in Australia: A Six-Month Exploratory Analysis.* Technical and Background Paper No. 20. Canberra: Australian Institute of Criminology. <http://www.aic.gov.au/publications/tbp/tbp020/tbp020.pdf>

Muggah, Robert. 2005. *Securing Haiti's Transition: Reviewing Human Insecurity and the Prospects for Disarmament, Demobilization, and Reintegration.* Small Arms Survey Occasional Paper No. 14 (updated). Geneva: Small Arms Survey. October.

— and James Bevan. 2004. *Reconsidering Small Arms in the Solomon Islands.* Background paper. Geneva: Small Arms Survey. October.

Núñez, Claudia. 2007. 'México aumentará vigilancia fronteriza: El propósito es combatir el tráfico de armas que procede de EU.' *La Opinión* (Los Angeles). 9 October. <http://www.laopinion.com/supp7/?rkey=00071008214049446122>

Olson, Alexandra. 2003. 'Four Soldiers Ambushed and Killed in Western Venezuela.' New York: Associated Press. 20 December.

OSCE (Organization for Security and Cooperation in Europe). 2003a. *Handbook of Best Practices on Small Arms and Light Weapons: Best Practice Guide on National Procedures for Stockpile Management and Security.* FSC. GAL/14/03/Rev.2. Vienna: OSCE. 19 September.

—. 2003b. *OSCE Document on Stockpiles of Conventional Ammunition.* FSC.DOC/1/03. Adopted at the 407th Plenary Meeting of the OSCE Forum for Security Co-operation. Vienna: OSCE. 19 November.

Penrose, Jane. 2005. *Rome And Her Enemies: An Empire Created And Destroyed by War.* Oxford: Osprey.

PNB (Polish News Bulletin). 2000. 'Teenagers Reportedly Stole Missiles.' Warsaw: PNB. 15 February.

Presidência da República do Brasil. 2000. Decreto N° 3665 de 20 de Novembro de 2000. Dá Nova Redação ao Regulamento para a Fiscalização de Protudos Controlados (R-105). Brasília: Casa Civil, Subchefia para Assuntos Jurídicos. <http://www.planalto.gov.br/ccivil_03/decreto/D3665.htm>

—. 2004. Decreto N° 5123 de 1 de Julho de 2004. Regulamenta a Lei N° 10826, de 22 de dezembro de 2003, que dispõe sobre registro, posse eco-mercialização de armas de fogo e munição, sobre os Sistema Nacional de Armas—SINARM e define crimes. Brasília: Casa Civil, Subchefia para Assuntos Jurídicos. <http://www.planalto.gov.br/ccivil_03/_Ato2004-2006/2004/Decreto/D5123.htm>

RAND. 2001. 'Guns in the Family: Firearm Storage Patterns in U.S. Homes with Children.' Research Highlights. RB-4535 (2001). Santa Monica: RAND Corporation. <http://www.rand.org/pubs/research_briefs/RB4535/index1.html>

Rand, Michael. 1994. 'Guns and Crime: Handgun Victimization, Firearm Self-Defense, and Firearm Theft.' Bureau of Justice Statistics Crime Data Brief. NCJ-147003. Washington DC: U.S. Department of Justice, Office of Justice Programs, Bureau of Justice Statistics. April. <http://www.ojp.usdoj.gov/bjs/pub/ascii/hvfsdaft.txt>

Reza, A., et al. 2003. 'Source of Firearms Used by Students in School-Associated Violent Deaths-United States, 1992–1999.' *Journal of the American Medical Association.* Vol. 289, No. 13. 2 April, pp. 1626–27. <http://jama.ama-assn.org/cgi/reprint/289/13/1626>

Roig-Franzia, Manuel. 2007. 'U.S. Guns Behind Cartel Killings in Mexico.' *Washington Post.* 29 October. <http://www.washingtonpost.com/wp-dyn/content/article/2007/10/28/AR2007102801654_pf.html>

Schmitt, Eric and Ginger Thompson. 2007. 'Broken Supply Channel Sent Arms for Iraq Astray.' *New York Times.* 11 November.

SEESAC (South Eastern and Eastern Europe Clearinghouse for the Control of Small Arms and Light Weapons). 2006. 'SALW Survey of Moldova.' Belgrade: SEESAC. July.

Small Arms Survey. 2004. *Small Arms Survey 2004: Rights at Risk.* Oxford: Oxford University Press.

Stohl, Rachel, Matt Schroeder, and Dan Smith. 2007. *The Small Arms Trade: A Beginner's Guide.* Oxford: OneWorld.

Swanwick, Tristan. 2007. 'Crime Gang Blamed for Firearms Robbery.' *Courier Mail* (Brisbane). 25 September. <http://www.news.com.au/story/0,23599,22473920-421,00.html>

TRADOC (US Army Training and Doctrine Command). 2007. *A Military Guide to Terrorism in the Twenty-First Century.* 'Appendix E (not available on Web site): Improvised Explosive Devices.' Fort Leavenworth: TRADOC Intelligence Support Activity–Threats. 15 August, pp. E1–E14. <http://www.au.af.mil/au/awc/awcgate/army/guidterr/app_e.pdf>

Turbiville, Graham. 1995. *Mafia In Uniform: The Criminalization of the Russian Armed Forces.* Fort Leavenworth: Department of Defence, Foreign Military Studies Office. <http://leav-www.army.mil/fmso/documents/mafia.htm>

UK (United Kingdom). 1997. 'Firearms (Amendment) (No. 2) Act 1997: An Act to extend the class of prohibited weapons under the Firearms Act 1968 to include small-calibre pistols.' 27 November. <http://www.opsi.gov.uk/acts/acts1997/ukpga_19970064_en_2>

—. 2006. 'Foreign Criminals'. *United Kingdom Parliament Publications and Records*. House of Commons Hansard Written Answers. 4 September. <http://www.publications.parliament.uk/pa/cm200506/cmhansrd/vo060904/text/60904w2277.htm>

UKHO (United Kingdom Home Office). 2000. *Criminal Statistics England and Wales 1999: Statistics relating to Crime and Criminal Proceedings for the year 1999*. London: Stationery Office. 8 December.

—. 2001. *Criminal Statistics England and Wales 2000: Statistics relating to Crime and Criminal Proceedings for the year 2000*. December.

—. 2003. *Crime in England and Wales 2001/2002: Supplementary Volume*. Research Development and Statistics Directorate. ISSN 1358–510X. January.

—. 2004. *Crime in England and Wales 2002/2003: Supplementary Volume 1: Homicide and Gun Crime*. National Statistics. January.

—. 2005. *Crime in England and Wales 2003 / 2004: Supplementary Volume 1: Homicide and Gun Crime*. National Statistics. ISSN 1358–510X. January.

—. 2006. *Violent Crime Overview, Homicide and Gun Crime 2004/2005*. National Statistics. ISSN 1358–510X. 26 January.

—. 2007. *Homicides, Firearms Offences and Intimate Violence 2005/2006*. National Statistics. ISSN 1358–510X. 25 January.

UNSC (United Nations Security Council). 2006. 'Letter dated 15 June 2006 from the Group of Experts on the Democratic Republic of the Congo addressed to the Chairman of the Security Council Committee established pursuant to resolution 1533 (2004).' S/2006/525 of 18 July.

UPI (United Press International). 2007. 'Fla. Gun Smuggling Linked to Burglary Ring.' Washington, DC: UPI. 20 May.

USDoD (United States Department of Defense). 1989. *Single Manager for Conventional Ammunition (Implementing Joint Conventional Ammunition Policies and Procedures)*. DoD 5160.65-M. 'Chapter 12: Security.' Washington, DC: Department of Defense, Assistant Secretary of Defense (Production and Logistics). April.

—. 2000. 'Physical Security of Sensitive Arms, Ammunition, and Explosives.' DoD 5100.76-M. Washington, DC: Assistant Secretary of Defense for Command, Control, Communications and Intelligence. 12 August.

—. 2002. 'Marine Corps Ammunition Management and Explosives Safety Policy Manual.' MCO P8020.10A 'Chapter 4: Security and Accountability.' Washington, DC: Department of Defense, Department of the Navy, Headquarters United States Marine Corps. April.

USGAO (United States Government Accountability Office). 2007. *Stabilizing Iraq: DOD Cannot Ensure That U.S.-Funded Equipment Has Reached Iraqi Security Forces*. GAO-07-711. Washington, DC: GAO. July. <http://www.gao.gov/new.items/d07711.pdf>

von Tangen Page, Michael, William Godnick, and Janani Vivekananda. 2005. *Implementing International Small Arms Controls: Some Lessons from Eurasia, Latin America and West Africa*. 'Small Arms Control in Ukraine' (Appendix published as a CD-Rom). London: International Alert. <http://www.international-alert.org/pdfs/MISAC_UkraineStudy.pdf>

Wilkinson, Adrian, James Bevan, and Ian Biddle. 2008. 'Improvised Explosive Devices (IEDs): An Introduction.' In Bevan, James, ed. *Conventional Ammunition in Surplus: A Reference Guide*. Geneva: Small Arms Survey.

Zawitz, Marianne. 1995. *Guns Used in Crime*. NCJ-148201. Washington, DC: U.S. Department of Justice, Office of Justice Programs, Bureau of Justice Statistics. July. <http://www.ojp.usdoj.gov/bjs/pub/pdf/guic.pdf>

ACKNOWLEDGEMENTS

Principal author

James Bevan

A Semi-automatic Process?
IDENTIFYING AND DESTROYING MILITARY SURPLUS

3

INTRODUCTION

Although precise comparisons are impossible, the world seems to be witnessing the largest systematic destruction of excess small arms and light weapons since the end of the Second World War. Dozens of internationally sponsored destruction or security enhancement projects are currently under way: from the destruction of a few dozen light weapons, more than a million small arms, or thousands of tons of ammunition to the construction of better fences around stockpiles. They may destroy corroded rifles from the First World War or state-of-the-art anti-aircraft missiles.

Although surplus destruction is well established in the international security-building repertoire of donor governments, it remains in many respects experimental. This chapter reviews the successes and failures of small arms and ammunition destruction projects. What barriers must be overcome? When are they most likely to succeed? Among the major findings are the following:

- Definitional issues are the sine qua non of surplus military small arms, light weapons, and ammunition destruction.
- Destruction of surplus military small arms averages about 430,000 units annually. This probably is less than new military production.
- Out of some 200 million military firearms worldwide, at least 76 million are surplus.
- The world harbours approximately 100 to 140 million tons of military ammunition, of which some 20 to 30 million tons are for military small arms.
- Although the UN *Programme of Action* and other international instruments create a predisposition to eliminate surpluses through destruction, in practice exports are often preferred.
- The most systematic progress in surplus destruction involves man-portable air defence systems (MANPADS), where the United States has secured extensive cooperation.
- Two mechanisms that greatly increase short-term willingness to destroy surpluses are the promise of membership in regional organizations and security sector reform.
- Donors can facilitate surplus destruction beyond providing financial and technical help by taking steps to enhance international legitimacy.

Surplus arsenals can be vast, as illustrated below. Experiences with conflicts as diverse as Iraq, Liberia, and Somalia show that the loss of control over government arms depots can be catastrophic. Destroying surplus weapons and ammunition is the only fully reliable way of guaranteeing control. It ensures that excess equipment will not end up where it should not be. It reduces the scale of small arms and light weapons management problems, risks of environmental contamination, and the constant danger of ammunition depot explosions. There are other ways to reduce surplus weapons dangers, especially secure storage (Greene, Holt, and Wilkinson, 2005, pp. 19–20), but destruction alone ensures certainty and finality.

DESTRUCTION, NOT DISARMAMENT

Small arms are certainly not the only weapons being routinely destroyed today. Better known processes include Start I and the Moscow Treaty for the destruction of nuclear delivery systems. Signatories of the 1993 Chemical Weapons Convention continue working to eliminate those weapons, and destruction of anti-personnel landmines continues under the 1997 Ottawa Convention on the Prohibition of the Use, Stockpiling, Production and Transfer of Anti-Personnel Mines and on Their Destruction.

Destruction of surplus small arms, light weapons, and ammunition is not unique, but, unlike other disarmament processes, it is not guided by a binding treaty obligation. It builds on principles codified in several international agreements, but relies on unilateral decisions by governments or their armed services. They are often encouraged and supported by donor countries, usually working with multilateral organizations. Four major groups have dedicated offices to facilitate small arms and ammunition destruction: the European Union (EU, Brussels), NATO (through the NATO Supply and Maintenance Agency in Luxembourg), the Organization for Security and Co-operation in Europe (OSCE, Vienna), and the United Nations Development Programme (UNDP, Geneva and New York). The mere existence of these offices helps ensure that internationally sponsored small arms and ammunition destruction will continue for years to come (Halperin and Clapp, 2006, pp. 25–61).

The clearest sign of distinctiveness is the phenomenon's very name. Surplus *destruction* is not the same as *disarmament*. In small arms parlance, disarmament is a term typically reserved for the collection of weapons from ex-combatants—usually non-state ex-combatants—in disarmament, demobilization, and reintegration (DDR) programmes. Only exceptionally does it refer to the collection of civilian guns. It is one of the ironies of this field that disarmament often emphasizes only collection; in some cases the weapons may be retained for later redistribution.

This chapter does not examine small arms disarmament through DDR or the collection of unwanted or illegal civilian guns. Both topics have been treated extensively elsewhere (Faltas, McDonald, and Waszink, 2001; Karp, 2003). Although excluded here, such programmes are neither exceptional nor small. Some of the largest undertakings—in Australia, Brazil, and the United Kingdom—eliminated hundreds of thousands of unwanted or illegal civilian guns. The destruction of tens of thousands of weapons in the Democratic Republic of the Congo, Liberia, and Sierra Leone is more controversial. Some observers see these as instrumental, directly inhibiting resumption of warfare; others maintain they are more symbolic.[1]

The focus of this chapter, therefore, is on the conditions that lead to the destruction of government-owned—especially military—small arms, light weapons, and ammunition. Surplus destruction is fully established on the international agenda. Here to stay, it has made major contributions to alleviating small arms and light weapons problems. But it is far from automatic or comprehensive.

...struction
same as
...mament.

SURPLUS CHOICES: STORAGE, DESTRUCTION, OR TRANSFER?

What to do with unneeded guns and ammunition? Several international documents codify a presumption in favour of destroying such weapons, but there are other ways to deal with surpluses. These can be understood as a hierarchy of aggressiveness, from the least to most absolute:

- **Secure storage** requires investments in rigorously guarded facilities and enhanced procedures, including routine accounting to ensure that weapons and ammunition stay where they are and only leave when properly authorized.

- **Surplus disposal** involves measures that end a state's responsibility for ensuring the security of surplus weapons (and prevent their diversion). Disposal methods include domestic or international transfer, as well as destruction.

- **Surplus destruction** is the specific form of disposal preferred for surplus management, since it precludes questionable transfer or future misuse.

Table 3.1 Stockpiled small arms and light weapons transferred to Afghanistan and Iraq, 2004–07

Supplier	Year	Quantity
Bosnia and Herzegovina	2004-06	290,000
Czech Rep.	2007	30,650
Montenegro	2007	1,600
Poland	2005	47,000
Slovenia	2006	10,000
Total		**379,250**

Note: This list does not include shipments of newly manufactured weapons.

Sources: Bosnia and Herz.: Christian Science Monitor (2006); Czech Republic: Dickerson (2007); Slovenia: The New York Times (2007); Montenegro: South East European Times (2007); Poland: Poland (2006, p. 3)

Box 3.1 Belarus, Kaliningrad, and the riddle of political ripeness

The political difficulties of weapons destruction can be seen in the cases of Belarus and Kaliningrad in the Russian Federation. Surplus small arms destruction is overwhelmingly affected by shifting attitudes and opportunities. Seemingly identical plans may be acceptable one moment and impossible the next, as moments of political ripeness mature and dissipate (Haass, 1990). Two unsuccessful destruction projects illustrate this problem of timing.

In 2000-04 Belarusian officials showed enthusiasm for multilateral cooperation to reduce excess inventories. In July 2002 the Ministry of Defence was ordered by President Lukashenko to implement the *OSCE Document on Small Arms and Light Weapons* (Belarus, 2002). This led to a series of small arms initiatives, culminating in a formal request in July 2003 for OSCE-sponsored assistance to destroy and secure excess equipment. The initial plan called for the destruction of 316,000 small arms, mostly Second World War vintage. In 2004-05, Belarus invited the OSCE to undertake major surveys of the country's munitions depots, the largest small arms-related assessments it has ever undertaken.[3]

The destruction project began with enthusiastic support. But once preparatory work was complete, momentum dissipated. Whether weak high-level commitment by political leaders or lack of concomitant military restructuring and downsizing was more important is hard to say. Although symbolic projects continued—notably, destruction of 29 MANPADS—Belarusian officials became less responsive.[4] In November 2005 the Foreign Ministry formally withdrew its request for destruction assistance, a reversal that still remains unexplained. The OSCE concluded: 'SALW [small arms and light weapons] destruction is not a priority at the moment for the MoD' (OSCE, 2007a). It would appear that the Belarusian Ministry of Defence decided that the weapons, old as they are, still contribute to national goals. The stockpile security project survives and began in August 2007 to improve management and security of 16 sites, although actual progress has been slow (OSCE, 2007b).[5]

Although there is less information on its premature end, a similar OSCE project to destroy 100,000 tons of ammunition in the Russian Federation's Kaliningrad *oblast* (administrative unit) ceased in much the same way. Following an invitation from *oblast* officials, initial assessments were completed. This too ended abruptly when the request was withdrawn in March 2007 (OSCE, 2007b). In this case, differences between regional officials in Kaliningrad and national leaders in Moscow may have contributed to the premature ending of the project, reinforced by renewed Kremlin interest in restoring the Red Army presence in Kalingrad (Itar-Tass, 2008).

Box 3.2   Serbia and the choice between destruction and export

Defence reform often results in large weapons surpluses, but not necessarily their destruction. After massive cuts made possible by the end of the Serb-Croat and Serb-Bosnian conflicts in 1995, the Serbian armed forces began a gradual reduction in
personnel numbers, a process that accelerated after their defeat in Kosovo in 1999 (*Vecernje Novosti*, 2007). By mid-2007, formal
reorganization was scheduled to leave only 28,000 personnel. Conscription should end completely by 2010 (*Vecernje Novosti*,
2007). After years of decline, however, Serbian defence budgets are increasing. New funding reportedly is going not into new
procurement, but overhaul of old equipment and especially salaries, with the goal of matching salaries of regional neighbours
(VIP News Service, 2007a; 2007b). Serbia has a large weapons surplus on its hands, with no need for most of its 789,000 military firearms (as of 2004) and a MANPADS arsenal estimated at 30,000 to 80,000 missiles, of which at least 5,000 have been
destroyed (see Table 3.10). But there are difficult choices to be made, choices that must be mediated through national politics.

Unwanted equipment has emerged as a major source of controversy in Belgrade. Under President Vojislav Koštunica, who
replaced Slobodan Milošević in October 2000, military reform was minimal. Army Chief of Staff Nebosja Pavkovic asserted
the continuing importance of territorial defence and the need for the ability to mobilize large forces rapidly. Weapons in
storage were not surplus (Griffiths, 2008a, p. 9). The situation began to change after the election victory of reformist Zoran
Djindjic, prime minister from January 2001, who facilitated several foreign-sponsored destruction projects, including United
States-sponsored MANPADS destruction, UNDP-sponsored destruction of 23,000 Ministry of Interior weapons, and NATO-
sponsored elimination of 27,530 small arms (Griffiths, 2008a, p. 11; Woo, 2004, p. 6).

This was only a tentative beginning. Serbian uncertainty was clearest in the choice of weapons for the NATO project, which
the Serbs described as 'useless' and 'obsolete', and not suitable for export (Griffiths, 2008a). After Djindjic was assassinated
in March 2003, the willingness of the Ministry of Defence to cooperate with destruction projects declined rapidly. The government formed by Koštunica in 2004 expressed no direct interest in the issue. The exceptions are MANPADS, where persuasion
and financial support from Washington have been instrumental. The Ministry of the Interior, which remained more cooperative,
undertook smaller destruction projects on its own, eliminating some of its MANPADS (Griffiths, 2008a, pp. 12-16).

With defence reform on the Serbian agenda again, surplus material has become politically visible. Selling off military
property for additional income remains extremely tempting. While weapons exports receive the most attention internationally,
controversial efforts to dispose of real estate have provoked bigger scandals at home (VIP News Service, 2007a; 2007b). On
top of such pressures, the effect of losing sovereignty over Kosovo must be considered. The fate of Serbia's surplus military
small arms is unclear.

Weapons are destroyed in a furnace in Smederevo,
Serbia, April 2003. © Mikica Petrovic/AP Photo

Improving the security of surplus weapons and ammunition is often the least controversial response. Even when they rule out destruction, governments are often willing to permit internationally sponsored improvement in storage safety and security (e.g. see Box 3.1).

The 2001 UN *Programme* and other international instruments create a presumption in favour of eliminating surpluses through destruction (UNGA, 2001, para. II.18). But other forms of disposal are often preferred in practice. Government agencies routinely maintain large surpluses for national security, especially emergency mobilization. Excess weapons also have economic value. Military weapons can be transferred domestically to other government agencies (other armed services or law enforcement) or private buyers. Small arms from storage are prominent on global markets, often in highly controversial deals. Circumventing the temptation to export to questionable destinations is the major rationale behind destruction programmes.[2]

While surplus destruction is supposed to be preferred, foreign transfer often is more appealing financially. This tension fuels widespread official ambivalence (see Box 3.2). The United States offers a prominent example of this. The US government has simultaneously encouraged governments to deal with their surpluses through both destruction and export (Waltz, 2007). One manifestation of US policy is destruction programmes, supported by the US State Department. In 2007 the State Department marked its destruction of one million surplus small arms and light weapons, including 21,000 MANPADS (USDoS, 2007a).

Across the Potomac River, the US Department of Defense encourages countries to manage their surpluses through export to other US clients. The Pentagon purchased or solicited donation of over 500,000 firearms for the indigenous security services of Iraq alone and more for Afghanistan (*New York Times,* 2006). At least 379,250 of these are identified here as surplus, mostly AK rifles purchased or donated from Eastern Europe (see Table 3.1). The purchases have had the unintended effect of fuelling regional expectations, making governments less willing to permit additional surplus destruction (Griffiths, 2008a). This policy may have changed. In late 2006 the Pentagon ordered 123,544 newly manufactured M16 rifles for Iraqi security services (Reuters, 2007). Whether this signals the end of Eastern European AK acquisitions is unclear.

The key t
destruct
the defin
'surplus'

WHAT IS A SURPLUS? THE PROBLEM OF SURPLUS IDENTIFICATION

The key to surplus destruction is the definition of 'surplus'. How are required weapons distinguished from excess? What is a reasonable military requirement? The two most prominent documents on surplus management—the 2001 UN *Programme* (UNGA, 2001) and the 2003 *OSCE Handbook of Best Practices on Small Arms and Light Weapons,* commonly known as the *OSCE Best Practices Handbook* (OSCE, 2003a)—do not deal directly with surplus identification. Instead, they focus on the creation of a *predisposition to destroy* surplus military and law enforcement small arms and light weapons. The *Programme* established an international obligation to safeguard the security of surplus weapons and a preference to eliminate them through destruction, committing countries:

> To regularly review, as appropriate, subject to the respective constitutional and legal systems of States, the stocks
> of small arms and light weapons held by armed forces, police and other authorized bodies and to ensure that
> such stocks declared by competent national authorities to be surplus to requirements are clearly identified, that
> programmes for the responsible disposal, preferably through destruction, of such stocks are established and
> implemented and that such stocks are adequately safeguarded until disposal. (UNGA, 2001, para. II.18)

The *Programme* does not, however, explain how a surplus is defined; that is left to national governments, free to apply criteria of their own. Similar approaches can be found in regional agreements, notably the *Bamako Declaration* of 2000 (sec. 3.A.iv), the *Southern African Development Community Protocol* of 2001 (art. 10), and the 2004 *Nairobi Protocol* (art. 8). The *OSCE Best Practices Handbook* deals with surplus management at greater length, but from the principle that 'It is for each State to assess its own security situation . . . to decide on the size and structure *of military and security forces* . . . [and] to decide how these forces are to be equipped' (OSCE, 2003a, p. 2; original emphasis). This leaves determination of when a surplus exists up to the home country government, as inferred in its definition:

> . . . surplus *is defined as the quantity of SALW exceeding the defence stockpile, i.e. the total number of (a) SALW assessed nationally as needed by active and reserve units of all military and security forces, plus (b) SALW in the reserve stock.* (OSCE 2003a, pp. 3, 12; original emphasis)

Definitional issues are the sine qua non of surplus military weapons and ammunition destruction. A definition can close further action, or it might establish long-term destruction goals. Current international norms and definitions grant ownership or control over basic surplus policy questions entirely to home governments.

Alternative definitions would give more influence to donor groups. There are several ways to define the surplus component of a military small arms arsenal. Surplus identification can be based on any of several criteria:

- **Declaratory:** This is the most common method, whereby a surplus is what the home government says it is. This grants the home government complete control of the issue. Donor governments and international organizations can request inclusion of additional weapons, but the home country decides.
- **Technical:** Equipment becomes surplus when it is replaced by more desirable equipment. The difficulty here is that even ageing weaponry may retain potential functions, such as use in training or equipping secondary reserves.
- **Economic:** Destroying unneeded surplus eliminates the expense and opportunity costs of maintaining and guarding inventories. A common sign is when a country tries to sell unwanted equipment.
- **Strategic:** This applies when national leaders reduce military personnel, rendering weapons redundant. Strategic surpluses mean there are fewer personnel to arm.
- **Doctrinal:** This applies when the armed forces alter armament policy to operate more effectively. Doctrinal surplus is created when fewer small arms and light weapons are needed for each person in uniform.

Estimates of surplus inventories have been calculated using all of these techniques. Virtually all previous internationally assisted destruction projects were based on declaratory methods, giving predominant voice to the host country alone. Alternative definitions permit outside actors to play greater roles in surplus decision-making by facilitating introduction of outside standards. In lieu of convincing reasons to the contrary, it usually can be assumed on technical criteria that ageing firearms—bolt-action rifles, military revolvers, and vintage submachine guns—are superfluous to current requirements. If a country lacks the economic ability to ensure the security of its military small arms, they probably weaken its security more than they help. And declining force levels or armament policies, whether strategically or doctrinally guided, will generate readily calculated excess equipment.

Often one surplus identification criterion is enough: most programmes rely on a host government's declaration alone. In Cambodia, various strategic criteria were applied. But even a priori, one would expect surplus destruction to be most aggressive when several criteria militate in that direction simultaneously. For example, the convergence of technical, economic, strategic, and doctrinal factors seems to have been involved in the examples of Montenegro and Papua New Guinea (PNG) discussed here.

The way surpluses are identified has major implications for what happens next. Acceptance of declaratory criteria typically leads to programmes that are small or focused on less important weapons and ammunition. When negotiating with host countries for inclusion of one or more advanced weapons, donors often stress economic criteria, since the financing issue resonates with many host governments.[6] Technical criteria emphasize particular categories of equipment, such as the oldest or most lethal. Doctrinal or strategic change can be sweeping enough to mandate redundancy of even the most advanced equipment. Doctrinal criteria have enormous potential for accelerating surplus destruction because the armed forces are usually the actual owners of the stockpiles under consideration here.

Without a clear international definition of surplus, destruction processes tend to be dominated by home governments. If definition is a unique national decision, home governments effectively control the process. Foreign donors mostly just fund their choices. This has some advantages. The home government can act with complete confidence that the process supports national interests, and domestic adversaries cannot criticize the decision as readily as a foreign recommendation. But it also permits home countries to truncate surplus management arbitrarily. Other definitions give donor governments a stronger role.

Without a standard, shared definition of surplus or criteria for distinguishing required from excess equipment, donors can only ask to broaden lists of items marked for destruction. In practice, as seen in the examples of Belarus (see Box 3.1) or Kazakhstan (see Box 3.5), donors can ask for more or more advanced equipment to be included. But such appeals tend to win only symbolic additions. The most important exception to this rule is MANPADS, as explored below.

SURPLUS IDENTIFICATION UNCERTAINTIES

Since most countries do not make information on their small arms and light weapons inventories public, outsiders are compelled to rely on estimates of supply and need. Estimation procedures provide insights into military small arms requirements, inventories, and surplus shares. The results are approximate, based on rule of thumb rather than specific national conditions. As illustrated here by the example of South America, this method can be applied globally, albeit with varying reliability and reproducibility. Any estimating technique confronts limits. For surplus small arms estimation, the role of military reserves is especially troublesome.

Estimating surplus

National surpluses of military firearms can be estimated by subtracting estimated national requirements from estimated inventories. Requirements can be readily calculated, based on armed forces personnel levels and doctrinal assumptions. Inventories are more elusive, since they develop over decades and are subject to many factors, such as rounds of modernization, imports and exports, breakage, deterioration, and loss.

Based on recent research by the Small Arms Survey, this technique is illustrated here by the example of South America. For the 12 independent countries of the region, current military requirements have been estimated generously, to favour the largest legitimate weapons inventories given the current number of military personnel.

This review bases requirements on the relatively high equipment levels associated with the Clausewitzian doctrine for state-to-state warfare (Small Arms Survey, 2006, ch. 2). Industrial warfare on this scale may not be the most deadly, but it undoubtedly consumes the most hardware. The assumption that the state requires forces able to defeat other states in a war to the finish is unrealistic for South America, where such wars are unusual.[7] The Clausewitzian level of 2.5 firearms per soldier is used here, not as an accurate description of need, but as the highest of all justifiable thresholds. Anything above is indisputably surplus. The legitimate firearms requirements of other armed services are estimated at lower rates: for the air force and navy, 0.5 firearms per uniformed personnel member; 1.2 for first-line ground forces reserves (reserves that regularly drill); and 0.5 for secondary or inactive reserves. These levels are calculated to reflect not the actual level of armaments, but the highest legitimately justifiable requirements.

Since no South American military actually is configured for Clausewitzian operations, a more accurate image of requirements would be generated by lower ratios. Most South American ground forces would be more appropriately armed at levels closer to constabulary forces, i.e. 1.8 firearms per soldier and marine (Small Arms Survey, 2006, ch. 2). This is especially true where state-to-state warfare is a distant possibility and operations are more likely to be peacekeeping or disaster assistance. Because they are based on maximum assumptions, the model used here establishes the *minimum* dimensions of each country's military firearms surplus, as shown in Table 3.2. The surplus weapons identified here serve no practical domestic military role: their only use is foreign or domestic sale, military assistance, or nostalgia.

Out of approximately 3.4 million modern military firearms in South America, the region's armed forces have legitimate requirements for as many as 2.25 million, summarized in Table 3.2. The other 1.15 million military firearms appear to be superfluous to any reasonable need. Not included in this conservative estimate of surplus are obsolescent

Table 3.2 **Estimated South American modern military firearms and surpluses, 2007**			
	Est. modern firearms	**Est. current requirement**	**Est. surplus firearms**	**% surplus**
Argentina	550,000	127,000	425,000	77
Bolivia	67,000	66,000	1,000	1
Brazil	1,100,000	840,000	271,000	25
Chile	358,000	193,000	175,000	49
Colombia	600,000	535,000	66,000	11
Ecuador	134,000	68,000	66,000	49
Guyana	19,000	3,200	15,500	82
Paraguay	40,000	16,500	23,700	59
Peru	201,000	120,000	83,000	41
Suriname	7,000	3,700	3,300	47
Uruguay	60,800	46,500	14,000	23
Venezuela	233,000	233,000	0	0

Note: Country totals do not add up precisely due to rounding.
Source: Karp (2007, pp. 10-11)

weapons. The total number of older weapons acquired, like bolt-action rifles and revolvers, can be estimated, but decades of sell-offs, theft, and breakdown make it much harder to evaluate the number remaining.

These surpluses are the result of two opposite vectors: the growth of arsenals through sequential waves of modernization, combined with reduction in the number of military personnel. Guided by the long-established Latin American doctrine of the national security state, which calls for maximizing state power, South America's armed forces have almost always been unwilling to destroy weapons they replace or those made redundant by new procurement (Pion-Berlin, 1989).[8] As these armed forces are highly autonomous institutions, until recently facing little civilian pressure for reform, this resistance has not been expressed literally. Rather, it emerges implicitly, through the accumulation of weapons themselves.

About half of this surplus is located in Argentina, home to an estimated 552,000 unneeded military small arms. Argentina stands out partially because it has reduced its armed forces more than any other country in the region. But Argentina is also a prominent example because of its transparency. Unlike many of its neighbours, the country does not conceal its surpluses behind an inflated reserve system: it has no reserves whatsoever (IISS, 2007). If other countries were equally frank, the regional surpluses would be substantially larger and more equally distributed.

Brazil, Chile, and Peru also have exceptionally large surplus stockpiles in absolute terms, but they do not approach Argentina proportionally. While some 77 per cent of all Argentine military armaments appear to be surplus, massive force cuts have left Guyana unable to make reasonable use of roughly 83 per cent of the weapons in its arsenal, proportionately the largest surplus in South America (Karp, 2007, p. 4). Both pose serious risks of loss and diversion. But international small arms policy is ultimately about numbers—scale matters. Argentina has the ability to flood local, regional, and even international markets. The much smaller Guyanese military firearms surplus is a threat, but mostly to itself and its immediate neighbours.

The easie
military i
to justify
of surplu
expand t
reserve

Reserve exaggeration

The easiest way for military institutions to justify retention of surpluses is to expand reserve components. Whether or not surplus justification is an explicit goal of reserve exaggeration, it has significant effect. Reserves can be mature organizations, with full-time officers, dedicated facilities, and equipment and personnel who drill routinely. Others are mobilization reserves, lists of discharged or retired personnel, or draft-age cadres legally eligible for mobilization. A prominent example is the Russian Federation, with a 20-million strong titular reserve (Weitz, 2007, pp. 109–20). Still others appear to be little more than expressions of resolve, proclaiming military potential in an era of cutbacks.

Keeping excess equipment even for titular reserves may be of great importance to national commanders. An exaggerated reserve system is, in effect, a weapons sink. There is no direct evidence of countries exaggerating their reserves specifically to justify large material requirements, but in many cases, as numbers of active personnel decrease, reserves increase, a trend illustrated in recent years by Ecuador and Paraguay (Aguirre and Orsini, 2007; Urrutia, 2007). Whether by design or effect, large reserves justify the retention of equipment that otherwise could be eliminated.

An extreme example is Venezuela, where President Hugo Chavez recently established a Territorial Guard with a goal of 1.5 million members, largely as an alternative to the armed forces he mistrusts (Nascimento, 2007, pp. 27–28). Even if never established, this force creates a permanently unfulfilled requirement for small arms, ensuring that Venezuela will never be compelled to define any of its official weapons as surplus. Venezuela is extreme, but Brazil,

Specials Forces instructor demonstrates combat methods to a
ard member at base outside Caracas, Venezuela, April 2006.
ano/AP Photo

Ecuador, and Paraguay also have exceptionally large reserve systems, effectively absorbing any small arms or light weapons unneeded by active-duty forces. The same practice is common in the former Soviet Union (IISS, 2007, p. 195). So long as reserve exaggeration persists, surplus size will be very controversial.

HOW MANY MILITARY SMALL ARMS ARE ENOUGH?

Evaluation of global surpluses would be much easier and more reliable with comprehensive data on each country's military requirements and inventories. Currently, such information is available only for a handful of countries, such as PNG, Peru, and the United States. For other countries, the scale of military surpluses can only be roughly estimated.

Surpluses are estimated here through a combination of *strategic* and *doctrinal* techniques, previously applied by the Small Arms Survey to estimate total inventories (Small Arms Survey, 2006, ch. 2). Two techniques are shown here. Global surpluses can be seen most readily by comparing troop levels over time. As a result of strategic adjustment since the end of the cold war, the number of soldiers, sailors, and airmen/-women has declined in most countries, dropping an average of 38 per cent, from peak year totals of almost 112 million military personnel (1987–91 for most countries) to fewer than 69 million today, including almost 20 million active and 49 million reservists (see Appendix 1).

Assuming no major changes in combat doctrine, small arms requirements should drop proportionately. Based on changes in military personnel, at least 76 million of the 200 million modern military small arms thought to be in existence today can no longer be used effectively by the armed services that own them (Small Arms Survey, 2006, ch. 2). They will stay in storage unless lost, transferred, or destroyed. A small proportion of weapons—which cannot

Table 3.3   Ranking selected military small arms inventories

Country	Year	Total military personnel	Total military small arms	Small arms/person
Peru	2006	268,000	200,889	0.8
PNG	2007	2,300	2,300	1.0
Finland	2003	462,000	531,000	1.1
United States	2002–05	2,673,300	3,054,553	1.1
Norway	2000	248,700	295,070	1.2
Central African Rep. (CAR)	2003	4,442	5,552	1.3
Malaysia	1987	156,600	255,000	1.6
Jamaica	2004	3,783	7,000	1.9
Switzerland	2004	175,000	324,484	1.9
Canada	2000	102,400	233,949	2.3
Serbia	2004	345,300	789,016	2.3
German Dem. Rep. (GDR)	1990	460,700	1,205,725	2.6
South Africa	2004	115,750	350,636	3.0
Estonia	2005	15,300	83,550	5.5
Ukraine	2007	1,187,600	7,000,000	5.9
Czech Republic	2003	49,450	500,000	10.0

Note: The data in this table, with varying base years, is not strictly comparable. It is intended, rather, to illustrate the range of known military stockpiling.
Sources: Small arms data from Small Arms Survey (2006, ch. 2), except: PNG: Alpers (2008); Ukraine: Griffiths (2008b) and IISS (2007); Peru: Obando (2007); personnel data: IISS, The Military Balance of the year(s) in question

be estimated—will be lost in storage. But the vast majority remain, although the reliability of ammunition will decline as it decomposes chemically.

This crude analysis leaves no doubt that global surpluses are substantial, but it may minimize their scale. A more nuanced picture emerges from evaluation of national requirements. The approximate number of military small arms and light weapons each country needs can be determined independently by comparing estimated stockpiles and requirements. How much is sufficient to meet requirements depends not only on personnel levels (national strategy), but also on the number of weapons required per person (military doctrine). As shown in Table 3.3, even among countries for which we have reliable reports, there is a broad spectrum of answers to the question: How many military small arms are enough? While many armed forces are content with roughly one firearm per person, others seem to prefer a thick cushion, with 2.5 to 4 or even more firearms per person in uniform.

The scale of global surpluses—and, correspondingly, those of any particular country—can be estimated at any of the levels shown here. If there are 20 million active duty soldiers, sailors, and airmen/-women worldwide and 49 million reservists, required and surplus proportions of the world's 200 million modern military firearms can be estimated.

Figure 3.1 **Small arms per person, selected armed forces**

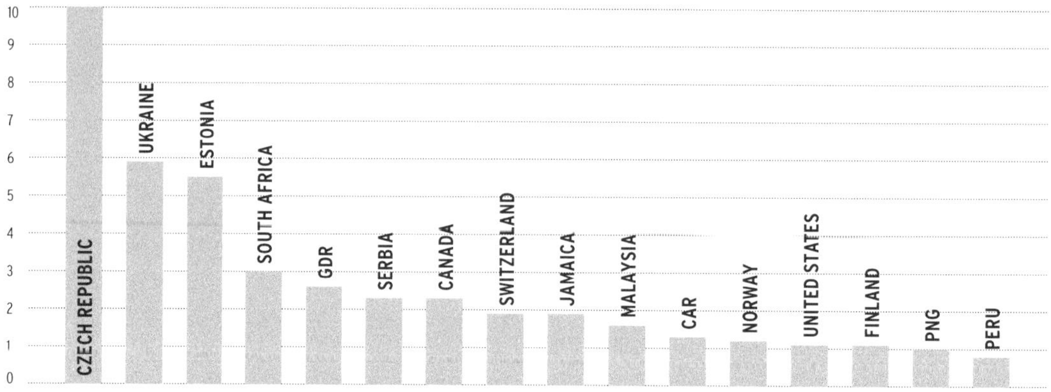

Source: Table 3.3

The key is the level of required firearms per person. Applying the lowest levels from known military requirements, such as those found in Peru or the United States, Table 3.4 (high requirement) shows that about 60 per cent of all current military firearms worldwide are excess. Even at more generous levels, typified here by Switzerland or Canada, about 20 per cent are surplus.

Surplus identification is largely about requirement setting. If requirements are set high enough, everything is needed. At military inventories of three firearms per person or more, surpluses evaporate everywhere, as shown in Table 3.4 by the estimates in red. Misconceived surplus criteria can justify additional procurement instead of reduction. This demonstrates the vital importance of rigorous criteria to guide surplus estimation.

Reserve forces are especially important to surplus estimation, as shown in Table 3.4. Extrapolating from the firearms ratios here leads to a wide range of possible global requirements and surpluses. The highest levels, illustrated by the Czech Republic and Ukraine, are legacy phenomena, the result of arsenals inherited from the cold war era. These can be dismissed as statistical outliers, unsuitable for global extrapolation. The same is true of the lowest known national requirements, in Peru and PNG, respectively. At more typical requirement levels—1.2 to 1.9 firearms per person—the world's military arsenal of some 200 million firearms includes roughly 69 to 117 million surplus military firearms.

These are crude estimates, though, exaggerating requirements for reserve units, which is a major problem for requirement and surplus calculations. Reserve components are the most readily manipulated contributor to small arms surpluses. If all countries equipped their reserves at no more than 1.2 firearms per person, global requirements shrink and surpluses grow dramatically, as illustrated by the adjusted requirements and surplus columns on the right side of Table 3.4.

A related problem is exaggeration of reserve rolls, which push small arms requirements up as well. Just as many countries absorb surpluses through exaggerated reserve structures, others generate excess by chopping reserves. Millions of firearms lost their intended role when China cut its 16 million-personnel reserve of the 1970s and 1980s to just 800,000 personnel, when Romania went from 565,000 reservists to 45,000, or Argentina from 250,000 reservists to none (see Appendix 1). If legitimate reserve components number no more than active duty forces and are equipped at no more than 1.2 small arms and light weapons per person, total global military firearms requirements shrink further, to 40 to 70 million, and surpluses grow to 130 to 160 million out of a total of 200 million military guns.

Column	A	B	C	D	E	F
Country	**Firearms/ person**	**Equivalent global requirement**	**Equivalent global surplus**	**% surplus**	**Requirement after reserve adjustment**	**Surplus after reserve adjustment**
Peru	0.8	55,200,000	144,800,000	72	55,200,000	144,800,000
PNG	1.0	69,000,000	131,000,000	66	69,000,000	131,000,000
Finland	1.1	75,900,000	124,100,000	62	75,900,000	124,100,000
United States	1.1	75,900,000	124,100,000	62	75,900,000	124,100,000
Norway	1.2	82,800,000	117,200,000	59	82,740,000	117,260,000
CAR	1.3	89,700,000	110,300,000	55	84,725,000	115,275,000
Malaysia	1.6	110,400,000	89,600,000	45	90,680,000	109,320,000
Jamaica	1.9	131,100,000	68,900,000	34	96,635,000	103,365,000
Switzerland	1.9	131,100,000	68,900,000	34	96,635,000	103,365,000
Canada	2.3	158,700,000	41,300,000	21	104,575,000	95,425,000
Serbia	2.3	158,700,000	41,300,000	21	104,575,000	95,425,000
GDR	2.6	179,400,000	20,600,000	10	110,530,000	89,470,000
South Africa	3.0	207,000,000	-7,000,000	0	118,470,000	81,530,000
Estonia	5.5	379,500,000	-179,500,000	0	168,095,000	31,905,000
Ukraine	5.9	407,100,000	-207,100,000	0	176,035,000	23,965,000
Czech Republic	10.0	690,000,000	-490,000,000	0	257,420,000	-57,420,000

Table 3.4 Hypothetical breakdown of global military firearms, required v. surplus

Note: Columns B and C assume active and reserve elements both arm at the rate shown in column A. Columns E and F are adjusted to show the effect of arming reserve elements at no more than 1.2 weapons per person.

HOW MUCH IS ENOUGH? MILITARY AMMUNITION

While few countries are transparent in their reports on stockpile elements, more have made available the total scale of their ammunition stockpiles. Contested terms like ton create serious problems here (Box 3.3). But general comparison is feasible, although a more precise definition remains an important goal (see Table 3.6). One conclusion is that many countries do not have a formal sense of how much ammunition is enough. The amount of ammunition per uniformed military personnel shows the divergence of national procurement and strategic policy. Although ammunition logistics usually are based on tons—an imprecise term, as indicated above—these comparisons are still revealing.[9] Former Soviet and Warsaw Pact countries inherited massive legacy arsenals, unrelated to contemporary requirements. Force modernization has exaggerated these surpluses by further reducing personnel. Shaped more by happenstance and inertia than by design, their ammunition surpluses bear little resemblance to conventional military needs. These excesses have become the nexus of disarmament activity supported by NATO, the OSCE, and donor governments.[10]

Box 3.3 How much is a ton?

Unlike weapons, which are procured and transferred as units, ammunition is often handled by the ton, especially for destruction. To discuss ammunition is to discuss tons, and therein lies a vital conundrum. Despite its importance as the basic unit of ammunition policy, the ton is an unpredictable term.

Tons can be metric or avoirdupois, long or short. While metric tons are used throughout this chapter unless otherwise specified, other problems are tougher to resolve. A ton can be calculated to include the number of pieces of ammunition, filled cases, pallets, or truckloads. A ton may include shells alone, or packaging and shipping containers too. Even within a single military service, rival definitions can prevail. This is illustrated by examples from Ukraine, the one case in which comprehensive descriptions of inventories are publicly available (see Table 3.5). These document both tonnage and number of units, but show differences as great as several orders of magnitude in the meaning of a ton of rifle bullets. Hand grenade and rocket-propelled grenade (RPG) rounds per ton differ by as much as 100 per cent.

In Ukraine, the differences are probably due to procedural eccentricities. The Ministry of Defence and the armed services demonstrated openness and goodwill. But the imprecision is a warning for policy-making in more antagonistic cases, illustrating the need for uniform criteria for quantifying national surpluses.

Crushing a Kalashnikov in Ukraine, January 2007.
© Sergei Supinsky/AFP/Getty Images

Table 3.5 How much is a ton?[1]

Unit:		A1588	A2985	A3845	A3870	47158	55238
Location:		Rozsishky	Novobogdanivka	Slavuta	Briukhovychy	Bilen'ke	Ushomyr
Type		Units/ton	Units/ton	Units/ton	Units/ton	Units/ton	Units/ton
Rifle cartridges	5.45 mm	94,894	96,984	267,940	0	0	119,150
Rifle cartridges	7.62 mm	45,392	5,451	52,074	0	58,945	62,626
Pistol cartridges	9 mm	0	100,003	99,903	0	100,036	102,400
Hand grenades	Various	2,210	2,030	3,007	0	1,777	2,049
HMG[2] cartridges	12.7 mm	7,932	7,648	7,757	0	7,704	7,480
RPG rounds	RPG-7	600	552	429	529	0	477
RPG rounds	RPG-16	0	489	0	0	0	0
RPG rounds	RPG-18	710	385	0	0	0	0
Mortar rounds	BM-37 82 mm	0	0	310	209	0	286

[1] Based on stockpiles declared for destruction in Ukraine.
[2] Heavy machine gun.
Source: Figures calculated from data in OSCE (2003b)

Table 3.6	**Military ammunition stockpiles of selected countries, in metric tons**				
Country	**Year**	**Total tons**	**Total mil. personnel**	**Tons/ person**	**Notes**
US Army[1]	2003	540,000	1,199,500	0.5	600,000 short tons converted to metric
Iraq	2003	600,000+	1,000,000	0.6+	Personnel 1990
GDR	1990	295,430	460,700	0.6	Includes AT[2] and AP[3] landmines
Montenegro	2007	9,000	7,300	1.2	
Ukraine	2003	2,448,000	1,187,600	2.1	13.1 tons/person without reserves
Bosnia and Herzegovina	2005	33,500	11,865	2.8	
Kazakhstan	2007	200,000+	65,800	3.0	
Moldova	2007	40,000	6,750	5.9	
Albania	2002	180,000	27,000	6.7	
Transdniester	2007	21,500	1,400	15.4	22,000 tons previously moved to Russian Federation

[1] Whereas the data in Tables 3.3 and 3.4 is for the US armed forces as a whole, here it is only for the US Army.
[2] Anti-tank.
[3] Anti-personnel.
Note: The data in this table, with varying base years, is not strictly comparable. It is intended, rather, to illustrate the range of known military stockpiling.
Sources: Albania: Greene, Holt, and Wilkinson (2005, p. 14). Bosnia and Herz.: UNDP (2007); GDR: Nassauer (1995, p. 50); Iraq: CIA (2004, p. 35) and Klingelhoefer (2005, p. 2); Kazakhstan: Ashkenazi (2008, p. 7); Moldova: SEESAC (2005, p. 115); Montenegro: Vijesti (2007); Transdniester: Itar-Tass (2007); Ukraine: Griffiths (2008b); US Army: Erwin (2003); military personnel (active and reserve): IISS (2007); except GDR and Iraq: IISS (1990, pp. 49, 105); Albania: IISS (2002, p. 63); US Army: IISS (2002, pp. 16-17)

Countries that tailor procurement to strategy can maintain much smaller stockpile ratios, illustrated here by the US Army. The ammunition used to train each soldier leads to the question of annual training requirements. Prior to the 2003 invasion of Iraq, the US Army reportedly required 80,000 short tons of ammunition of all kinds for its annual qualification training, or 60 kilos per soldier (Farrell, 2002). Of course, few military commanders feel they have enough. An example is the US Navy, where small arms ammunition became a precious resource after the bombing of the destroyer USS *Cole* in October 2000, which led to much greater emphasis on the use of small arms and light weapons for ship security.[11]

A major source of doubt overshadows the comparability of each country's figures, not only because of the vague meaning of 'ton', but also due to problems regarding what gets included or excluded. The US Army's pre-Iraq stockpile of 540,000 metric tons of ammunition should be compared to the total US pre-war military stockpile of 1.65 million metric tons of deliverable munitions.[12] The latter total appears to be inflated by including air-dropped ordnance for the US Air Force and Navy, naval mines, and torpedoes, items not always regarded as ammunition.

As the examples in Table 3.6 show, size is not everything when it comes to stockpile problems. Iraq's arsenal was not huge compared to others. Its absolute size, at 0.6 tons per person, was hardly exceptional. Even if not excessive relatively, Iraq's arsenal was remarkably dispersed, with over 10,000 caches (CIA, 2004, pp. 33–35). This exacerbated complete loss of control after the 2003 invasion, creating an almost limitless reservoir for improvised explosive devices (more commonly known as IEDs) (Klingelhoefer, 2005).

Sentry duty on the rebuilt USS Cole, April 2001. © Rogelio Solis/AP Photo

From the range of national inventories—illustrated as tons per person in Figure 3.2—one can speculate on recommendations for legitimate requirements. Going further with these examples, it is possible to envisage negotiations on international rules for ammunition stockpile dimensions. Emulating previous multilateral achievements, an agreement limiting ammunition possession could be modelled on the 1990 Treaty on Conventional Armed Forces in Europe (CFE), the agreement that established national limits for major weapons (Croft, 1994; Sharp, 2006). An ammunition agreement would be a natural counterpart to CFE, which regulates possession of the systems that consume a large proportion of all stockpiled ammunition.

Not enough countries furnish data on their total stockpiles and surplus to project an estimate of global ammunition surpluses. There are only four complete examples, all former Soviet or Yugoslav republics, notorious for huge munitions inventories. These examples may be relevant to other countries that inherited Soviet-style armed forces,

Figure 3.2 **Ammunition tons per person, selected armed forces**

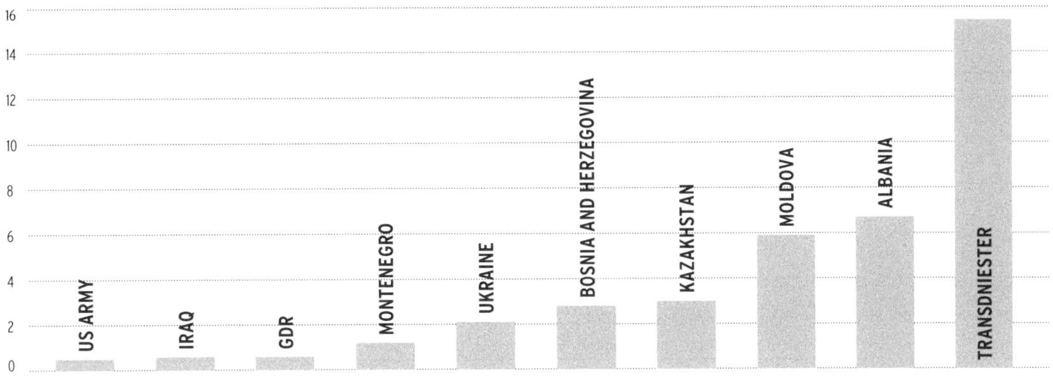

Source: Table 3.6

but they do not speak to global estimation. Consequently, at the time of writing, we can estimate total global ammunition, but not the surplus share.

Multiplying each example to show its global equivalent generates an initial range of feasible totals. As shown in Table 3.7, the estimates vary widely, from 34.5 million to hundreds of millions of metric tons. Most examples cluster at approximately 1.5 to 2 metric tons per person in uniform. Multiplied by the 69 million active and reserve military personnel worldwide today (see Appendix 1), this suggests there are 100 to 140 million metric tons of ammunition of all kinds around the world.

Compared to these estimated totals, only 4.3 million tons of ammunition were documented in Table 3.6. Even allowing for smaller cases that have been overlooked and the fact that many of the munitions listed here already have been destroyed (especially in the GDR and Iraq), this is a small proportion of the estimated global total of 100

Table 3.7 **Estimating the global ammunition inventory***

Base country	Tons/person	Equivalent global tons
US Army	0.5	34,500,000
GDR	0.7	48,300,000
Montenegro	1.2	82,800,000
Iraq	0.6	41,400,000
Ukraine	2.1	144,900,000
Bosnia and Herzegovina	2.8	193,200,000
Kazakhstan	3.0	207,000,000
Moldova	5.9	407,100,000
Transdniester**	8.3	572,700,000
Albania	16.3	1,124,700,000

* Based on projections from known countries.
** Transdniesterian ammunition is for the Operational Group of Russian Federation forces.
Source: Tonnage from Table 3.6, multiplied by global troop numbers (active and reserve) from IISS (2007)

to 140 million tons. The distribution of the rest can only be surmised, but probably corresponds to the global distribution of military weapons among major regions, as reviewed in Small Arms Survey (2006, ch. 2).

Unfortunately, it is not possible to establish the proportion of the global ammunition stockpile made up specifically of small arms and light arms ammunition. The best-studied example is the former GDR (East Germany). Upon reunification in 1990, the German government inherited some 300,000 tons of GDR munitions, of which 22 per cent was small arms and light weapons ammunition (Nassauer, 1995, p. 50). Applied globally, this single example would suggest roughly 20 to 30 million metric tons of small arms ammunition.

This global total of approximately 100 to 140 million tons of ammunition of all kinds can be imagined by comparison to Iraq, where an inventory of some 650,000 tons was lost (CIA, 2004, pp. 33–35), which was less than 1 per cent of the world total. Ukrainian munitions dumps, widely regarded as extraordinary, total some 2.5 million tons (*New York Times,* 2005, p. A1).

By comparison, the total tonnage of bombs dropped by British and US air forces in the Second World War was roughly 3.3 million tons. In Vietnam, the US Air Force and US Navy dropped 7 million tons.[13] Neither figure includes artillery, other munitions, or deliverable ordnance used by other combatants. Similarly, the largest nuclear weapon ever detonated, the Soviet Tsar Bombe, or Big Ivan, tested on 30 October 1961, was equal to 50 million tons of TNT, or half to one-third of the world's current presumed conventional arsenal (Adamsky and Smirnov, 1994; Sakharov, 1990, pp. 215–25).

If the world harbours approximately 100 to 140 million tons of ammunition, of which some 20 to 30 million tons are for small arms, what proportion is surplus? This depends on how much is reasonably required. The examples above provide no reliable threshold for estimating global ammunition surpluses. If the training rates and stored equipment of the US Army are used for comparison, there is a requirement for roughly 34.5 million tons worldwide, leaving two-thirds to three-quarters of the global stockpile militarily superfluous. The world has substantial excess ammunition.

ORIGINS OF SYSTEMATIC SMALL ARMS DESTRUCTION

Surplus small arms and ammunition destruction continues to be affected by its historical roots in anti-personnel landmine destruction. More explicitly than other areas of small arms policy, surplus small arms, light weapons, and ammunition destruction is an outgrowth of previous experience eliminating anti-personnel landmines (APLs). All major international organizations and many government agencies involved in international small arms destruction previously were heavily involved in implementation of the Ottawa Convention. For the EU, NATO, and the OSCE, lists of completed destruction projects are still dominated by landmine projects (EU, 2006; NAMSA, 2007, p. 1; OSCE, 2007b).

After rapid progress with APL destruction in the 1990s, resources gradually became available for other types of unwanted munitions in the early 2000s. The transition was logical, but required strong efforts by advocates to bring about. From the start, many NGOs and government agencies involved in APL destruction also destroyed small arms, light weapons, and ammunition when it was convenient as part of their other work.[14] Over time, as APLs have become less common, and more aggressive efforts were needed to ferret out the last of them, destruction activities moved closer to war zones, encountering more small arms, light weapons, and ammunition.[15] Among host countries, the government agencies and officials usually were the same, as were many destruction skills. Some of the mechanisms established to eliminate landmines are heavily involved today in the disposal of toxic rocket fuel and the destruction of small arms, light weapons, and ammunition (Courtney-Greene, 2008; Kryvonos and Kytömäki, 2008).

Contrary to the biological metaphor, though, the ontogeny of small arms destruction no longer recapitulates its phylogeny.[16] Shifting to small arms and ammunition necessitated fundamental changes in doing destruction. The vital difference between landmines and small arms and light weapons is the attitude of host governments. As parties to the 1997 Ottawa Convention, most states are uninhibited in support of landmine eradication, and donors did not have to persuade hosts to cooperate. Small arms and light weapons do not arouse the same attitude. While international norms encourage surplus destruction, as discussed below, host governments routinely view small arms and light weapons stockpiles as a source of security or financial value.

Instead of declaring entire inventories for destruction, as was the case with landmines, host countries usually declare a portion of their total, often quite small. Or they offer only guns seized from criminals or rebels (e.g. Tajikistan). Or they present their oldest and least useful equipment (e.g. Belarus, Romania). Like Ukraine, they can sell large quantities as they destroy others (see Box 3.4). More salient weapons get added only with special pleading by donor government officials.[17]

This can achieve meaningful results, most strikingly through addition of MANPADS (see below). Often, though, the result of such appeals has been largely cosmetic, with host country officials agreeing to add a few hundred

---

Box 3.4 Scale v. comprehensiveness: surplus destruction lessons from Ukraine and Montenegro

While it is natural to focus disproportionate attention and resources on the largest destruction projects, smaller undertakings can be much more ambitious and no less important, especially for domestic security. The largest projects eliminate greater absolute numbers, but often leave extraordinary quantities behind. The remnants can be more than enough to perpetuate serious risks at home, where weapons can be put to deadly use or ammunition depots blow up, and abroad, where they can be transferred. Projects in smaller countries can more readily achieve comprehensiveness, guaranteeing permanent elimination of particular risks.

Designed to eliminate 133,000 tons of ammunition and 1,531,664 small arms, the Ukraine destruction programme is far larger than any international destruction project ever undertaken (Brown, 2005b, p. 4). Only Germany's unilateral programme is bigger, having eliminated 2,076,442 small arms and light weapons through 2006 (Germany, 2007, p. 21). Even so, the Ukraine project eliminates only 5 per cent of the country's total ammunition and 20 per cent of its military small arms out of an inventory of 2,448,000 tons of ammunition and roughly 7 million small arms (Griffiths, 2008b). Destruction has been limited partially by the slow pace of military reform, but even more by financial pressure (Ulrich, 2007, pp. 4-8, 17). This suggests that much more may be possible. If reforms continue and additional foreign funding becomes available, destruction of the Ukraine surplus could continue for decades. Meanwhile, massive diversion from Ukraine remains a risk, as does the possibility of unpredictable legal exports. In 2006, while destruction was under negotiation, Ukraine reportedly exported 320,000 military firearms (Defense and Security, 2007). It has the ability to flood markets with much more.

Although Ukraine has by far the largest surplus destruction programme, the most comprehensive example belongs to Montenegro. The small state (population 620,000) became independent from Serbia in 2006. Under President Filip Vujanović, military reform immediately rose to the top of the national agenda (Cagorovic, 2006). The country's armed forces, once over 50,000 men, numbered 7,300 at independence (Eger, 1996; IISS, 2007, p. 170). Conscription ended, and military personnel fell to 2,400. Some commentators expect the troop total to fall below 1,000 (*South East European Times*, 2006).

The OSCE, UNDP, and donor governments came in to assist Montenegro with destruction of excess equipment. On the list were 47,747 small arms and light weapons. Of Montenegro's 9,000-ton munitions stockpile, 6,000 to 7,000 tons are scheduled for destruction. The remaining 2,000 to 3,000 tons are being consolidated for safe storage.[18] The destruction of 66 to 80 per cent (by mass) of Montenegro's ammunition and the securitization of the rest make this the most complete ammunition surplus destruction ever.

modern weapons. Examples of the latter include Kazakhstan, which added 464 modern firearms (341 AKMs and 123 RPK-74s) to its small arms listed for destruction (see Table 3.9). It is clear that even countries willing to engage in international destruction show considerable ambivalence towards it.

DESTROYING SMALL ARMS: DO IT YOURSELF OR WITH HELP?

There are two major forms of small arms destruction: domestic and internationally sponsored. Both were fully established after the First World War, the first time that former parties to war engaged in massive destruction of wartime inventories. Much of this was done unilaterally, as countries cleared their own inventories. The former Allies also presided over destruction of the arsenals of defeated Austria and Germany. This practice continued after the Second World War and irregularly since: Vietnam, for example, did not destroy the 1.6 million US-made weapons it captured in 1975, but the allied coalition did get rid of most of the Iraqi equipment it took in 1991 (Towle, 1997, pp. 183–87).

Today, domestic destruction continues, having accelerated with the end of the cold war (see Table 3.8). Germany has done the most to eliminate excess inventories, certainly in terms of raw numbers and probably as a proportion of total military inventories (Beeck, 2008, p. 1). The Russian Federation, South Africa, Ukraine, and the United States have destroyed large stockpiles as well. Domestic military surplus destruction is largely autochthonous: military commands do this themselves—unprompted and often without outside recognition—for reasons of their own. But this quiet process eliminated most of the 7,292,000 military weapons recorded here, an average of about 430,000 annually for 17 years (this does not include the contribution of programmes that destroyed less than 15,000 firearms, quantities that still may be very significant locally). By comparison, the Small Arms Survey (2006, p. 7) estimates new production at 700,000 to 900,000 military firearms annually. Globally, destruction probably does not offset stockpile growth from new production, although it does in specific countries.

Internationally sponsored destruction—illustrated in Table 3.8 by leading hosts like Albania, Bosnia and Herzegovina, Cambodia, and Romania—is very different. Previously associated with military conquest, international destruction was a synonym for military defeat. This changed radically in 1999–2000, when international actors began promoting destruction support. The breakthrough was Cambodia, where the Hun Sen government, consolidating stability after defeating other claimants to power, welcomed EU help to eliminate about half the country's small arms (Roberts, 2008; Wille, 2006). In 2001 Bulgaria and Romania accepted US support to reduce their cold war weapons inheri-

ASEAN officials observe small arms destruction in Cambodia's province, May 2007. © Chor Sokunthea/Reuters

Table 3.8 Selected military surplus small arms destruction programmes, 1991–2007

Country	Source of weapons	Quantity destroyed	Programme sponsorship	Years	Sources
Germany	Military	2,076,442	Domestic	1990–2006	Germany (2007, p. 21)
Russian Federation	Military	1,110,000	Domestic	1994–2002	Faltas and Chrobok (2004, p. 115)
United States	Military	830,000	Domestic	1993–96	Small Arms Survey (2002, p. 85)
Ukraine	Military	700,000	Domestic	1990s	Griffiths (2008b, p. 17)
United Kingdom	Military	543,000	Domestic	1992–95	Faltas and Chrobok (2004, p. 37)
South Africa	Military	262,667	Domestic	1998–2001	Lamb (2004, p. 155)
Bosnia and Herz.	Military	250,000	International	2002–07	UK (2006, pp. 15, 32)
Albania	Military	222,918	International	1997–2005	Holtom (2005, p. 7)
Cambodia	Military	198,148	International	1999–2006	EU ASAC (2006)
Romania	Military	195,510	International	2002–03	Romania (2003, p. 10)
Netherlands	Military	143,632	Domestic	1994–96	Small Arms Survey (2004, p. 58)
France	Military	140,000	Domestic	1998–2000	France (2003, p. 10)
Serbia	Military	117,269	International	2001–03	Small Arms Survey (2004, p. 58)
Belarus	Military	126,407	Domestic	2003–04	Belarus (2005, p. 13)
Bulgaria	Military	97,751	International	2001–04	Faltas (2008, p. 104); USDoS (2003)
Panama	Military	77,553	International	1991	USDoS (2001)
Philippines	Military	57,826	International	2003?	USDoS (2003)
Uganda	Military	57,000	Domestic	2006	Monitor (2006)
Angola	Military	40,000	International	2003?	USDoS (2003)
Italy	Military	37,371	Domestic	2005	Italy (2006, p. 3)
Switzerland	Military	19,270	Domestic	2001	Faltas and Chrobok (2004, p. 63)
Croatia	Military	18,389	Domestic	1998–2005	Pietz (2006, p. 50)
Guinea	Military	15,000	International	2003?	USDoS (2003)

Notes: Bosnian weapons designated for surplus destruction may be among those subsequently transferred to Iraq. Albanian and Cambodian totals include an unknown proportion of civilian firearms. The possibility of civilian guns in the Belarusian, Cambodian, and Ugandan totals cannot be excluded. The UK figure is based on predictions.

tance. Similar, initially ad hoc, often bilateral projects became more organized and international in 2003, when NATO and the OSCE began to offer more systematic support (Courtney-Greene, 2008; Kryvonos and Kytömäki, 2008).

The roots of surplus destruction in victors' elimination of spoils of war help explain lingering sensitivity. As explained already, surplus destruction is not disarmament, yet even contemporary projects are vulnerable to politicization and nationalist criticism. As illustrated in this chapter by the example of Bolivia (Box 3.6), publicity can be bad for destruction.

A more practical difference between domestic and international destruction projects is the kinds of actors involved in decision-making. Domestic destruction appears to be handled most often as a routine, internal matter for military and law enforcement organizations. As seen in Germany and the United States in the 1990s, decision-making authority belonged to mid-level officials. Their decisions were reported to their immediate superiors, but often were otherwise unknown (Beeck, 2008). International destruction appears to work best, however, with direct involvement of the highest level decision-makers. Cambodian destruction appears to have occurred with the explicit approval of Prime Minister Hun Sen (Roberts, 2008). Without the active involvement of national leaders, especially in home governments, projects are vulnerable to loss of interest or the rise of unexpected opposition. They can stall prematurely, sometimes with little or nothing accomplished (see Boxes 3.1 and 3.5).

Box 3.5 Kazakhstan: the triumph of domestic politics

The dominance of domestic over international politics in surplus small arms and light weapons destruction is illustrated by on and off destruction efforts in Kazakhstan. Although its high-level politics are notoriously opaque, the effects of bureaucratic tension also may be at work. Surplus destruction was emphasized initially by the Kazakh Foreign Ministry, which supplied information to the UN and hosted a prominent regional conference on this issue (IRIN, 2004; Kazykhanov, 2004). The Ministry of Defence was noticeably less forthcoming.[19] With the possible exception of the Foreign Ministry, the Government of Kazakhstan did not view military surpluses as a problem (Ashkenazi, 2008, p. 1). The gap between official government spokespersons and the agencies with actual control is a routine problem for international small arms and light weapons policy (Small Arms Survey, 2005). In this case, the difference may have misled foreign expectations.

Energized by UN processes and promised assistance from NATO, the OSCE, and donor governments, the Government of Kazakhstan became active on this issue in 2003, with a memorandum of understanding signed in Brussels on 1 July (Ashkenazi, 2008, p. 3). Feasibility studies were completed, and funds were made available by Washington. Other forms of weapons destruction occurred. According to Kazakhstan's Ministry of Foreign Affairs, 36,000 seized civilian weapons were destroyed unilaterally in 2001–04 (Heathershaw et al., 2004, p. 26). Other sources suggest that only 5,708 of these were actually destroyed (Ashkenazi, 2008, p. 4).

In contrast to the willingness to deal with civilian gun problems, destruction of military weapons was contingent on foreign assistance and domestic politics. A total of 19,472 small arms and light weapons were designated for NATO destruction, although these were mostly obsolescent (see Table 3.9). Even so, initial efforts led nowhere. As early as 2004, an assessment concluded: 'The absence of a weapons destruction programme creates the perception of a lack of political will to address the issue of stockpile management within Kazakhstan' (Heathershaw et al., 2004, p. 23). Despite reassurance, there was no action for over four years. In Kazakhstan's closed political system, nothing could be learned about why the project had stalled.[20] All that could be deduced was that surplus destruction held little intrinsic importance for the Government of Kazakhstan (Ashkenazi, 2008, p. 1).

Without warning, this changed in April–June 2007. Transformation began when President Nazarbaev appointed a new defence minister and pledged to modernize military power with new equipment and doctrine. One month later, the new defence minister, Daniyal Akhmetov, announced that additional spending would be invested in modernization, training, and professional development (RFE 2007a; 2007b). Modernization may not be a prerequisite for surplus elimination, but, as this example and other examples from the Balkans, Cambodia, and PNG show, it clearly helps.

Suddenly, the destruction deal was recalled. Parliament ratified the long-stalled NATO agreement. The importance of the vote was emphasized by the deputy defence minister (*Kazakhstan Today*, 2007; Vremya, 2007). Leaving no doubt that this was a major policy shift, a few days later parliament passed legislation tightening civilian gun ownership (Interfax, 2007). Given past experience, some scepticism is in order. But the shift creates the impression that President Nazarbaev is now personally committed.

Table 3.9 Weapons designated by Kazakhstan for NATO destruction, 2005	
Weapon	**Quantity**
Handguns/pistols	468
RPG 73 mm	90
RPG 40 mm	153
Grenade launcher 30 mm	208
Machine guns 14.5 mm	399
Machine guns 12.7 mm	347
Machine guns 7.62 mm	2,231
Sub-machine guns 7.62 mm	3,553
Carbines 7.62 mm	551
AK-47 rifles 7.62 mm	479
AKM rifles 7.62 mm	341
RPK-74 light machine guns 5.45 mm	123
Miscellaneous rifles	10,529
Total	**19,472**

Source: NATO (2005)

MANPADS IMPLICATIONS

The greatest exception to the problem of defining surpluses and stressing destruction is MANPADS. In this area, donors have been able to secure much more systematic cooperation. Whether this is because the budgets are larger, because host countries are more cognizant of the terrorist dangers, or because they are swayed by more intense donor pressure is hard to say.

Despite much greater unit costs, countries have permitted destruction of more of their MANPADS. Out of a global inventory estimated to be 'well in excess of 500,000' interceptor missiles (Small Arms Survey, 2004, p. 83), over 24,000 (about 5 per cent) have been eliminated since 2003, mostly through US-led projects (USDoS, 2008). Projects responsible for destruction of some 15,700 of these are detailed in Table 3.10. The national origins of the other 8,300 have not been made public. The largest documented cases are in Eastern Europe. By comparison, total firearms destruction through comparable international projects has eliminated roughly three million military firearms, no more than 1.5 per cent of the global total of at least 200 million military firearms (Small Arms Survey, 2006, ch. 2).

Not all MANPADS (LIGHT WEAPONS) are alike, though, and governments have varying attitudes toward their fate. Older MANPADS have been the first to go. But there has been greater willingness to destroy these than other small arms and light weapons. A unique confluence of considerations leaves armed services and governments willing to permit their destruction:

- Since older MANPADS have limited military uses—they usually cannot hit fast jets—it is hard to justify keeping them.
- There are limited opportunities for legitimate export, especially for older systems. Thus, home governments are not giving up economic opportunity either.
- Fear of loss is a factor, since MANPADS tempt pilferage by corrupt personnel and raiding by outsiders, including separatists and terrorists.
- The lesser quantities compared to firearms minimize logistical problems of destruction.
- There is greater pressure and financial incentives from donor governments, especially the United States.

Convincing governments to give up their older versions of weapons, like Soviet SA-7s and Chinese HN-5s, has been difficult enough. More advanced weapons, by comparison, remain highly capable for air defence. They are also much more costly. Fewer governments have been willing to part with them, except in token quantities. Instead, it has been much easier improving inventory control and security. When destruction is impossible, the US Department of Defense operates a parallel programme to enhance stockpile security (Johnson, 2007).

Although MANPADS destruction is somewhat easier, it is not immune to the typical problems of surplus destruction. While most MANPADS destruction stresses ageing weapons, more modern weapons may also be superfluous. Because of the greater media prominence of MANPADS compared to other light weapons, moreover, there is also a special danger of politicization. This is illustrated here by the case of Bolivia (Box 3.6). Much the same could be said of Nicaragua, where a bilateral project was brought to a halt and redesigned in response to similar forces (Schroeder, 2006).

A US Army officer prepares surplus SA-7 missiles for detonation in Bosnia and Herzegovina, March 2004. © Amel Emric/AP Photo

Table 3.10   International MANPADS missile destruction, 2003–present

Country	Year	Type	Total destroyed	Total planned destruction	Remaining	Support	Sources
Afghanistan	2005?	SA-7	101	0	n/a	USDoS	Pico (2006)
Albania	2006?	HN-5	79	n/a	n/a	USDoS	Porth (2006)
Belarus	2005	Strela-2M	15	29	n/a	OSCE	NTI (2005)
Bolivia	2005	HN-5	28	0	n/a	USDoS	Pagina (2005, p. 12)
Bosnia and Herzegovina	2003–04	n/a	6,000	n/a	n/a	NATO	Hillen (2006, p. 7)
Burundi	n/a	SA-7?	n/a	0	n/a	USDoS	USDoS (2008)
Cambodia	2004	SA-7?	233	0	0	USDoS	Hillen (2006, p. 7)
Chad	n/a	SA-7?	n/a	0	n/a	USDoS	USDoS (2008)
Czech Republic	n/a	n/a	n/a	1,359	n/a	USDoS	ČTK (2007)
Greece	2007	Redeye	573	0	n/a	Germany	Personal communicatio
Guinea	n/a	SA-7?	n/a	0	n/a	US	USDoS (2008)
Hungary	2005	SA-7	1,540	0	n/a	NATO	USDoS (2005b)
Kazakhstan	2008	SA-7, SA-14, SA-16	0	400	n/a	NATO, US	Brown (2005a)
Liberia	2003	SA-7?	45	0	0	USDoS	USDoS (2005a)
Moldova	2003?	n/a	70	0	n/a	Russian Fed.	Wood (2006)
Nicaragua	2004–05	SA-7, SA-14	1,000	651	1,051	USDoS	*Seattle Times* (2007); AP*
São Tomé and Príncipe	n/a	SA-7?	n/a	0	n/a	US	USDoS (2008)
Serbia	2004–07	Various	5,000	n/a	30,000	NATO	Griffiths (2007a)
Sudan	2005?	SA-7?	21	0	n/a	USDoS	Pico (2006)
Tajikistan	2006	SA-7	8	0	n/a	OSCE	Kryvonos (2007, p. 17)
Ukraine	2006	SA-7, SA-14, SA-16, SA-18	1,000	3,099	5,000	NATO	Brown (2005b); Griffiths
Total			**15,713**	**5,538**			

* Private communication to the author from government official, 6 April 2007.

Notes: Reported estimates in italics. **Total** refers to missiles only, not gripstocks (an aiming and triggering device attached to the missile storage and launch canister), but there may be confusion on this distinction, making some total figures less certain.

Box 3.6   The politics of surplus destruction: Bolivia's MANPADS affair

Bolivia's MANPADS affair of 2005–06 illustrates the political risks that can be involved in surplus small arms and light weapons destruction. The US-sponsored disarmament project ignited an unanticipated political crisis, becoming one of the most notorious of recent years (Pagina, 2005). Only the dispute over Nicaraguan MANPADS is comparable (*Miami Herald,* 2005). The irony is that the Bolivian controversy came after the weapons ceased to exist.

The small missile arsenal was apparently acquired as part of a package negotiated with China in 1992–95 (IISS, 1994). The deal included some 28 HN-5 missiles and a number of gripstocks (launch units). No publicly available source recorded their existence until after their destruction ten years later.[21] The HN-5s (Hongying or Red Tassel) were militarily obsolescent when delivered to La Paz, with limited capability except in very specific circumstances (Small Arms Survey, 2004, p. 80). While military missions could be found, they would be much more dangerous in the hands of terrorists likely to aim them at more vulnerable civilian aircraft.

The anarchic atmosphere in La Paz in 2005 played a role as well. Political instability in May and June over a new hydro-carbons law (on ownership and sale of fossil fuels) led to mass demonstrations, often violent. President Carlos Mesa was forced from office. Public chaos raised unprecedented incentives to dispose of weapons posing special risks of theft and misuse. The impending presidential victory of populist-nationalist candidate Evo Morales and his party, Movimiento al Socialismo, may also have contributed (Karp, 2007, p. 21).

In this atmosphere, a bilateral agreement to eliminate the HN-5s was reportedly signed on 30 September 2005 by US offi-cials and Bolivia's then-deputy defence minister. Exceptionally, the arrangement called for the missiles to be shipped to the United States for destruction (*Washington Post,* 2006). As reported in the press, this resembled cooperative operations previously used to remove fissile nuclear material from Eastern Europe and the former Soviet Union (Porth, 2006). A few days later, the missiles were loaded onto a US Air Force transport plane and removed for destruction (*Washington Post,* 2006).

As elections loomed, Morales charged the guardians of national security with treason, abandoning the country to foreign enemies and cooperating with the enemy of Latin America's underclass. In response to the pressure, President Rodriguez relieved the army commander of his duties (AP, 2006). Within days of being sworn in, President Morales, citing the deal, forced the retirement of 56 generals and admirals. Treason charges were filed against his immediate predecessor, former defence minister Gonzalo Mendez, and military commander Admiral Marco Antonio Justiniano (*Washington Post,* 2006). In response, the US State Department spokesman said: 'This was done at the request of the Bolivian Government and it was done in partnership and consistent, I would note, with an Organization of American States resolution on the matter' (McCormack, 2005; Gollust, 2005; Hillen, 2006).

The Bolivian HN-5s are a curious example of weapons more influential after their destruction than before. The destroyed missiles helped Morales strengthen his nationalist credentials and compel military subservience. But Morales' partisanship was not cost-free: it has inspired unprecedented Paraguayan interest in acquiring MANPADS of its own (Aguirre and Orsini, 2007).

Bolivian chief commander Admiral Marco Antonio Justiniano speaks to journalists at the presidential palace in La Paz, December 2005. © David Mercado/Reuters

INCENTIVES FOR SURPLUS DESTRUCTION

Surplus management is largely about context. Some of the most important forces affecting surplus disposal decisions do not come from programmes directly designed to deal with these issues. Rather, they are an indirect result of broader political reform. Although the links are largely circumstantial, two sources of reform appear to have great effect in the short run on willingness to improve surplus management: the promise of membership in regional organizations and security sector reform. Donors have a role in facilitating surplus destruction as well. Beyond providing financial and technical help, they can specifically enhance the legitimacy of destruction.

Membership expansion

Expansion of the EU and NATO compelled candidate countries to reform extraordinary swaths of public law, practice, and even official attitudes. While implementation of the 35 chapters of the EU *acquis communautaire* is the most demanding formal part of the process, the indirect and more intangible effects of membership are especially relevant to surplus weapons issues. Beginning with the *acquis* for the Former Yugoslav Republic of Macedonia, questions have been included about small arms and light weapons.[22] All potential members face pressure for across-the-board reform. With the overwhelming goal of EU membership guiding them, applicant countries found previously unimagined capability for reform. The ten countries that joined the EU in its 'Big Bang' of March 2004—Cyprus, the Czech Republic, Estonia, Hungary, Latvia, Lithuania, Malta, Poland, Slovakia, and Slovenia—felt enormous pressure to accommodate Western expectations by cleaning up backward government practices and corruption (Rehn, 2006, pp. 45–53).

European flags are prepared for the ceremony marking the expansion of EU membership from 15 to 25 countries in Dublin, 30 April 2004. © Yves Herman/Reuters

The impetus was reinforced by pressure from NATO. Focusing almost exclusively on each country's ministry of defence and armed forces, NATO has a more immediate effect on small arms requirements. Although membership requirements had few direct small arms and light weapons implications, the requirement for military modernization created widespread redundancy. Applicants modernized their forces to NATO standards, trading size for professionalization. In 1999 NATO admitted the Czech Republic, Hungary, and Poland. Seven more countries joined in March 2004: Estonia, Latvia, Lithuania, Slovenia, Slovakia, Bulgaria, and Romania. Most new NATO members ended or curtailed conscription, thus reducing personnel. In some cases, the response was wholesale security sector reform (Gallis, 2003). By rendering legacy arsenals largely superfluous, membership tends to inflate surpluses. NATO programmes also directly support surplus destruction.

For both the EU and NATO, however, there have been limits to the achievements of expansion. Since 2004 fatigue has become evident. The admission of Bulgaria and Romania to the EU on 1 January 2007 is regarded by critics as premature, since the two countries were not fully ready to adapt to European practices (*Financial Times,* 2007). It has been widely observed that, once they joined, conditionality weakened and incentives for reform diminished and slowed dramatically (Rehn, 2006, pp. 55–63). It is no surprise that the interest of new members in surplus destruction has abated. Neither Bulgaria nor Romania currently has major destruction projects under way.

More countries may join the EU or NATO in the next few years, creating pressure to clean up surplus weapons and ammunition. Croatia is likely to be the next to join the EU (Dudrap and Freedman, 2007; EurActiv, 2007). The membership of other EU candidates—Albania, Bosnia and Herzegovina, Macedonia, Montenegro, Serbia, and Turkey—is more distant. NATO has membership dialogues with Albania, Croatia, Georgia, Macedonia, Montenegro, and Ukraine, but these countries' prospects are uncertain (Perepelytsia, 2007; IWPR, 2006).

Security sector reform (SSR)

Restructuring armed forces is typically intended to improve political accountability, reduce costs, and enhance capability. While surplus management may not be explicitly emphasized, SSR often reaches this far, at least by implication. As armed forces are transformed from large conscript organizations into smaller, fully professional organizations, large legacy munitions stockpiles become unnecessary. This can create major opportunities and dangers for surplus

Box 3.7   Papua New Guinea: security sector reform first

In absolute terms, military small arms and ammunition destruction in PNG was small stuff, smaller than the purely symbolic efforts of countries like Belarus and Kazakhstan. But in relative terms, the accomplishment is extraordinary, made possible by a combination of foreign advocacy and domestic support, including sweeping military reforms. Both ingredients were essential.

The country faced a major problem from its loss of control over state arsenals. Of roughly 10,000 military firearms acquired since the early 1970s, only 5,700 remained under state control in 2004. Poverty, corruption, ethnic conflict, and a culture of sharing made it difficult to keep weapons under lock and key. Mounting violent crime, especially homicide, and increasingly fatal ethnic conflict left no doubt about the seriousness of the problem (Alpers, 2005). But, the scale of the problem alone was not sufficient to bring action.

Weapons security and destruction came instead through rationalization of the PNG Defence Force. A *Defence White Paper* in 1999 called for a significant reduction in personnel (Alpers, 2008, p. 9). Small arms were barely mentioned; efficiency was the essential theme. In early 2001 this was followed by the report of the Commonwealth Eminent Persons Group, calling specifically for slashing military personnel from 4,500 to 1,900 (Commonwealth Eminent Person's Group, 2000, p. 13). It also drew attention to lack of control over weapons (Brown, 2001). The report was vulnerable to attack as outside interference, but it had the support of a reform faction in the armed forces. When their leader, Commodore Peter Ilau, was appointed armed forces commander in October 2001, change could begin. His influence was enhanced in March 2002, when former soldiers ransacked a military installation of 128 firearms (Alpers, 2008, pp. 6, 10).

Prior agreement within the Defence Ministry on defence reform further strengthened the case for surplus destruction. Australian assistance was essential to making reform possible, but the bilateral programme was a magnet for nationalist opposition. As the instigator of personnel reductions and weapons destruction, Ilau was excoriated by the parliamentary opposition, accused of undermining national security and independence by accepting Australian destruction aid. Citing previous ministerial commitments to defence reform, however, he was able to parry such objections (Alpers, 2008, pp. 15-17).

With Australian financing and technical assistance, secure armories were built and oversight procedures made routine. This apparently ended large-scale haemorrhaging of weapons and ammunition (*Post-Courier,* 2006a; 2006b). Small arms and light weapons inventories were reduced by 60 per cent, from 5,700 weapons in August 2004 to 2,300 in 2007. Ammunition inventories were cut proportionately (Alpers, 2008, p. 14).

management. Reform can exacerbate surplus problems by increasing unneeded equipment; it also can be part of the solution by facilitating greater willingness to take responsibility for institutional problems.

In former Soviet and Warsaw Pact countries, restructuring usually means dramatic cuts. Outdated strategies based on massed infantry operations are replaced with contemporary network-centric operational concepts. Restructuring leaves no obvious role for massive reserve components, which can be jettisoned outright. Active forces may be reduced exponentially (Keridis and Perry, 2004). Among the most immediate results are redundant people, facilities, and equipment. The same is true of reforms elsewhere in the world, in countries as diverse as PNG, Paraguay, and South Africa (Aguirre and Orsini, 2007; Alpers, 2008; Lamb, 2004).

Two recent examples with major implications for small arms surplus management are defence reform in PNG and Serbia. Both have involved foreign-sponsored surplus destruction. Both have engaged in negotiations for broader small arms, light weapons, and ammunition destruction, but progress has been uneven. In PNG, commitment to defence reform led directly to more rigorous stockpile management and surplus destruction (Alpers, 2008). In Serbia, reform only expanded the weapons surplus; whether it leads to destruction or increased exports has yet to be seen (Griffiths, 2008a).

Enhancing donor legitimacy

Donor countries need to be no less concerned with enhancing the legitimacy of their support for surplus destruction. Some of the early international small arms, light weapons, and ammunition destruction projects were conducted bilaterally, with support from a single donor.[23] Practical considerations limited what could be achieved this way. Multinational collaboration emerged from necessity: donor governments lacked the personnel, expertise, or budgets to adapt to rising possibilities among host countries.[24]

Small arms destruction has been a shoestring operation. Even the best endowed programme, sponsored by the United States, had a total budget of no more than USD 8.7 million until October 2007, when the annual allocation rose to USD 44.7 million (see Table 3.11). Reflecting US counter-terrorism priorities, most of this has gone to MANPADS destruction alone. By comparison, US support for managing fissile materials in the former Soviet Union (through the Nunn–Lugar Cooperative Threat Reduction Program) averages USD 1 *billion* annually in recent years (Pomper, 2004).

Table 3.11 **US Department of State annual budgets for small arms and light weapons destruction (USD millions), 2004–08**			
Fiscal year	**Total**	**MANPADS**	**Small arms, light weapons, and ammunition**
2004	4.0	2.0	2.0
2005	6.9	?	?
2006	8.7	7.3	1.4
2007	8.6	?	?
2008	44.7	36	8.7

Sources: USDoS (2005c, p. 162; 2006, p. 179; 2007b, p. 90); Johnson (2007)

Donor coordination multiplies budget reach. But there are more profound effects of collaboration. While bilateral arrangements have the greatest celerity and flexibility, they tend to achieve less. The examples of Bulgaria and Romania show that bilateral projects lack the authority of their multilateral counterparts. Although the evidence is limited, bilateral projects seem less likely to permanently affect attitudes toward surplus destruction in host countries, and they are less likely to lead to follow-on projects. They can also more easily arouse nationalist resistance from critics who see destruction as foreign meddling, illustrated explicitly in Bolivia and PNG (Boxes 3.6 and 3.7, respectively). The stronger the international support for a specific destruction initiative, the better it can be insulated from nationalist criticism and domestic politics. Collaborative projects, such as the EU in Cambodia or NATO in Ukraine, have been almost immune to such criticism (Griffiths, 2008b; Roberts, 2008).

stronger ernational pport for ction, the it can be ated from criticism.

CONCLUSION: OVERCOMING BARRIERS TO SURPLUS IDENTIFICATION AND DESTRUCTION

Almost 20 years since the end of the cold war, countries worldwide have reduced their armed forces personnel by almost 40 per cent (see Appendix 1). An unintended consequence is massive stockpiles of excess small arms and ammunition, as estimated here. Dealing with these mountains has become an enduring part of international security building. Surplus destruction is here to stay, but not only because excess inventories need to be kept secure, often at considerable expense. Equally important are principles in multilateral agreements, institutional commitments from multilateral organizations, and the non-proliferation aims of donor governments.

The process of surplus small arms, light weapons, and ammunition destruction has acquired an independent momentum, but the force behind it is not very strong. There may be at least 76 million surplus firearms sitting in the world's military arsenals, and possibly considerably more, but even after years of effort, destruction programmes are not reaching more than a small proportion. Destruction is organized, but not systematic. It is enduring, but it is not growing. It is highly legitimate, but not authoritative.

Although exact numbers are wanting, it appears that destruction of small arms is offset by new military production. As a result, despite the scale of destruction, surplus stockpiles are probably not shrinking; they actually still could be growing. Nor are surpluses always being carefully stewarded: it appears that many countries with surpluses are as likely to export their unwanted equipment as to destroy it. This is partly due to the ambivalence of outside actors, most prominently the United States, who simultaneously encourage cooperative host governments to both destroy and export their surpluses.

Lack of financing for destruction is a major problem. Compared to other areas of international disarmament, spending on small arms, light weapons, and ammunition is remarkably small. But lack of money is not the only barrier. As stressed here, vague definitions and weak standards are serious problems as well.

Surplus identification and destruction are heavily influenced by the broader international and domestic political contexts. Domestic military reform can be instrumental. Even ostensibly unrelated processes like EU and NATO expansion affect them fundamentally. International cooperation is an invaluable lubricant for surplus destruction, allowing donors to work more efficiently by enhancing legitimacy and insulating projects from political criticism. When it comes to dealing with surplus small arms and ammunition, bilateral action is good, but multilateral action is better.

In this field, definitions are tantamount to policy. As shown here, surplus identification and destruction are unlikely to accelerate or become more systematic until international organizations and donor governments gain more influence over definitions and standards. Above all, there is a profound need for a cooperative military requirement setting. Nothing will facilitate surplus identification as much as shared understandings of how much equipment is reasonable and what is excessive. Such understandings might be codified through formal negotiations like those that led to the CFE Treaty for major conventional weapons. They might emerge less formally through multilateral dialogue. But without wider agreement on how much is enough, surplus destruction seems likely to remain sporadic. ✒

LIST OF ABBREVIATIONS

APL	Anti-personnel landmine	OSCE	Organization for Security and Cooperation in Europe
CAR	Central African Republic		
CFE	Treaty on Conventional Armed Forces in Europe	PNG	Papua New Guinea
		RPG	Rocket-propelled grenade
DDR	Disarmament, demobilization, and reintegration	SALW	Small arms and light weapons
		SSR	Security sector reform
EU	European Union	UNDP	UN Development Programme
GDR	German Democratic Republic	USD	US dollar
MANPADS	Man-portable air defence system		

ENDNOTES

1   The author wishes to thank Guy Lamb for this distinction.

2   Author interviews with Mark Adams, Washington, DC, 3 August 2006; Steve Brown, Arlington, Virginia, 22 February 2007; Peter Courtney-Greene, Geneva, 12–13 April 2007; and Richard Kidd, Washington, DC, May and October 2007.

3   Author interview with international official, Washington, DC, 22 February 2007.

4   Author interview with international official, Washington, DC, 22 February 2007.

5   Written comments to the author by Adrian Wilkinson, 2 January 2008.

6   Author interviews with Mark Adams, Washington, DC, 3 August 2006 and Peter Courtney-Greene, Geneva, 12–13 April 2007.

7   Since the resolution of its independence struggles in 1824, only four major inter-state wars have taken place in the region: the war of the Triple Alliance that found Paraguay simultaneously challenging Argentina, Brazil, and Uruguay (1864–70); the war of the Pacific, pitting Chile against Peru and Bolivia (1879–83); the Chaco War between Bolivia and Paraguay (1932–35); and the Falklands War between Argentina and the United Kingdom (1982). Regional intra-state war has been much more common.

8   The author would like to thank Pablo Dreyfus for emphasizing this point.

9   Ammunition is usually procured in rounds. Daily ammunition expenditure rate is calculated in the same way. Tonnage is used for logistic planning, including destruction (written comments to the author by Adrian Wilkinson, 2 January 2008).

10 For example, see NAMSA (2007) and USDoS (2008).

11 Author interview with the commander of the USS *Mahan* (DDG 72), Norfolk, Virginia, 25 May 2007.

12 The 600,000 short ton figure for the US Army is from Erwin (2003). The 1.8 million ton US Department of Defense figure is from Scavetta (2004).

13 The figure of 3.3 tons (2 million tons, US Army Air Corps; 1.3 million tons, Royal Air Force) is from USAAF (1945) and USSBS (1947). The 7 million tons Vietnam figure is from *Vietnam War Timeline* (2008). Other sources estimate total aerial tonnage in Vietnam at between 8 and 15 million tons (Franklin, 1988).

14 Author interview with Steve Wilson of Mine Action Group, Washington, DC, 2–3 August 2006.

15   Author interview with Richard Kidd, Washington, DC, May and October 2007.

16   Following the theory formalized by zoologist Ernst Haeckel in 1866 of ontogeny (the development of an individual organism) recapitulating phylogeny (the development of a species or group of organisms), that the embryonic development of species passes through stages resembling the physical appearance of less evolved species (Haeckel, 1900).

17   Author interviews with Mark Adams, Washington, DC, 3 August 2006 and Richard Kidd, Washington, DC, May and October 2007.

18   Sources differ on the figures for Montenegrin ammunition. All agree that Montenegro inherited 9,000 tons, but sources differ on the amount to be destroyed (Garčevic, 2007; Montenegrin Press Agency, 2007; *Vijesti*, 2007). For a list of items scheduled for destruction, see Perović (2007).

19   Author interview with Col Assylbek A. Mendygaliyev, Kazakhstan's defence, military, naval, and air attaché to the United States, Arlington, Virginia, 22 February 2007.

20   Author interviews with Steve Brown, Arlington, Virginia, 22 February 2007 and Col Assylbek A. Mendygaliyev, Kazakhstan's defence, military, naval, and air attaché to the United States, Arlington, Virginia, 22 February 2007.

21   Private communications from Pieter Wezeman, Stockholm International Peace Research Institute.

22   Written comments to the author by Adrian Wilkinson, 2 January 2008.

23   Author interview with Mark Adams, Washington, DC, 3 August 2006.

24   Author interview with Susan Pond, Arlington, Virginia, 22 February 2007.

BIBLIOGRAPHY

Adamsky, Viktor and Yuri Smirnov. 1994. 'Moscow's Biggest Bomb: The 50-megaton Test of October 1961.' *Cold War International History Project Bulletin*. Fall, pp. 3, 19–21.

Aguirre, Katherine and Yadaira Orsini. 2007. *Paraguay*. Unpublished background paper. Geneva: Small Arms Survey.

Alpers, Philip. 2005. *Gun-running in Papua New Guinea*. Special Report No. 5. Geneva: Small Arms Survey.

——. 2008. 'Papua New Guinea: Small Numbers, Big Results.' *Contemporary Security Policy*, Vol. 29, No. 1.

AP (Associated Press). 2006. 'Bolivia's Army Chief Fired over Missiles.' 19 January.

Appendix 1. Small Arms Survey Web site. <http://www.smallarmssurvey.org/files/sas/publications/yearb2008.html>

Ashkenazi, Michael. 2008. 'Kazakhstan: Where Surplus Arms Are Not a Problem.' *Contemporary Security Policy*, Vol. 29, No. 1.

Beeck, Christina. 2008. 'Identifying Surplus Military Small Arms. Case Study: Germany.' *Contemporary Security Policy*, Vol. 29, No. 1.

Belarus. 2002. 'On Implementation by the Republic of Belarus of International Commitments Ensuing from the *OSCE Document on Small Arms and Light Weapons*.' Decree No. 383. 15 July.

——. 2005. *Republic of Belarus Report on the Implementation of the United Nations Programme of Action to Prevent, Combat and Eradicate the Illicit Trade in Small Arms and Light Weapons in All Its Aspects*. New York: UN.

Brown, Gary. 2001. 'Crisis in Papua New Guinea: Military Mutiny and the Threat to Civilian Democratic Rule.' Research Note 27 2000-01. Canberra: Parliament of Australia, Foreign Affairs, Defence and Trade Group. 3 April.

Brown, Steve. 2005a. 'Kazakhstan Project Feasibility Study Technical Briefing.' Presentation to the OSCE Forum for Security Cooperation. FSC. DEL/164/05 of 4 May. Vienna: OSCE.

——. 2005b. 'Ukraine II Project Technical Proposal Briefing.' Presentation to the OSCE Forum for Security Cooperation. FSC.DEL/165/05 of 4 May. Vienna: OSCE.

——. 2007. 'Ukraine II Project: MANPADS Destruction.' Presentation to ACCS MANPADS Workshop, Brussels, 12–13 June.

Cagorovic, Ljubika. 2006. 'Europe's Newest State Trims the Army.' *Defense News*. 30 August.
      <http://www.defensenews.com/story.php?F=2069510&C=navwar>

Christian Science Monitor (Boston). 2006. 'Bosnia's Leftover Guns: Sell, Give, Destroy?' 10 July.

CIA (Central Intelligence Agency). 2004. *Comprehensive Report of the Special Advisor to the DCI on Iraq's WMD (Iraq Survey Group Final Report), Vol. 3: Iraq's Chemical Warfare Program*. McLean: Central Intelligence Agency. 30 September.

Commonwealth Eminent Person's Group. 2000. *Commonwealth Eminent Person's Group Review of the Papua New Guinea Defence Force*. Unpublished report.

Courtney-Greene, Peter. 2008. 'NATO PfP Trust Funds for Demilitarization of Surplus Weapons and Ammunition.' *Contemporary Security Policy*, Vol. 29, No. 1.

Croft, Stuart. 1994. *The Conventional Armed Forces in Europe Treaty: The Cold War Endgame*. Aldershot: Dartmouth.

ČTK (Czech News Agency). 2007. 'Czech Government Approves Agreement on Disposal of Missiles.' 27 July. <http://www.ctk.cz/>

Defense and Security (Moscow). 2007. 'Ukraine Supplied Almost 320,000 Pieces of Small Arms to 12 Countries in 2006.' 15 October.

Dickerson, Larry. 2007. 'Czechs Donate Small Arms to Afghanistan'. Forecast Intelligence Center. 6 November.
      <http://www.forecastinternational.com>

Dudrap, Thomas and Richard Freedman. 2007. 'Croatia: Good Progress towards Accession and Some Issues Remain.' European Parliament Press Service, ref. 20070420IPR05684. 25 April. <http://www.euractiv.com>

Eger, Christopher. 1996. 'The 1914 Army of Montenegro: The Postage Stamp Sized Kingdom that Fought for Every Hill in World War One.' In *Armies of the Balkan States 1914–1918*. London: Imperial War Museum. Reprint of *Military Forces of Bulgaria, Greece, Montenegro, Romania, and Servia* (sic). London: General Staff, War Office, n.d. (1918?).

Erwin, Sandra. 2003. 'Army Not Producing Enough Ammunition.' *National Defense*. May.

EU (European Union). 2006. *Small arms and Light Weapons (SALW) Projects*. Brussels European Commission, External Relations Directorate General. FSC.DEL/67/06 of 29 March. Vienna: OSCE.

EU ASAC (European Union's Assistance on Curbing Small Arms and Light Weapons in the Kingdom of Cambodia). 2006. Weapons Destruction Table. Brussels: EU ASAC. <http://www.eu-asac.org/programme/weapons_destruction/weaponsDestructionTable.pdf>

EurActiv. 2007. 'Rehn: Croatia Will Not Join EU before 2010.' 9 June.
<http://www.euractiv.com/en/enlargement/rehn-croatia-join-eu-2010/article-156042>

Faltas, Sami. 2008. 'Surplus Identification and Destruction Decision-Making in Bulgaria.' *Contemporary Security Policy,* Vol. 29, No. 1.

—— and Vera Chrobok, eds. 2004. *Disposal of Surplus Small Arms: A Survey of Policies and Practices of OSCE Countries*. London: Saferworld.

Faltas, Sami, Glenn McDonald, and Camilla Waszink. 2001. *Removing Small Arms from Society: A Review of Weapons Collection and Destruction Programmes*. Geneva: Small Arms Survey. July.

Farrell, Lawrence. 2002. 'U.S. Facing Alarming Ammunition Shortfalls.' *National Defense*. April.

Financial Times. 2007. 'Europe's Errant Entrants.' 13 June, p. 9.

France. 2003. *Rapport National de la France*. Paris: Ministry of Foreign Affairs. ASD/DT/FG, April.

Franklin, H. Bruce. 1988. 'How American Management Won the War in Vietnam.' *American Quarterly,* Vol. 40, No. 3. September, p. 423.

Gallis, Paul. 2003. *NATO Enlargement*. Washington, DC: Congressional Research Service. 5 May.

Garčević, Vesko. 2007. 'Statement under "Any Other Business" Delivered by Ambassador Vesko Garčević, Representative of Montenegro.' Presentation to the 512th meeting of the FSC, OSCE, Vienna, 25 April.

Germany. 2007. *National Report on the Implementation of the United Nations Programme of Action*. Berlin: Auswärtiges Amt. 15 April.

Gollust, David. 2005. 'US Denies Removal of Bolivian Missiles Was Secret.' *Voice of America News*. 23 December. <http://www.voanews.com>

Greene, Owen, Sally Holt, and Adrian Wilkinson. 2005. *Ammunition Stocks: Promoting Safe and Secure Storage and Disposal*. Biting the Bullet Briefing No. 18. London: International Alert. February.

Griffiths, Hugh. 2008a. 'Surplus Decision-Making in Serbia.' *Contemporary Security Policy,* Vol. 29, No. 1.

——. 2008b. 'Negotiated Surplus Decision-Making in Ukraine.' *Contemporary Security Policy,* Vol. 29, No. 1.

Haass, Richard. 1990. *Conflicts Unending: The United States and Regional Disputes*. New Haven: Yale University Press.

Haeckel, Ernst. 1900. *Riddle of the Universe at the Close of the Nineteenth Century*. New York: Harper.

Halperin, Morton and Priscilla Clapp. 2006. *Bureaucratic Politics and Foreign Policy,* 2nd edn. Washington, DC: Brookings Institution.

Heathershaw, John, et al. 2004. *Small Arms Control in Central Asia*. London: International Alert.

Hillen, John. 2006. 'Testimony before the House International Relations Committee, Subcommittee for International Terrorism and Nonproliferation.' Washington, DC: US House of Representatives. 30 March.

Holtom, Paul. 2005. *Turning the Page*. London: Centre for Peace and Disarmament Education and Saferworld. December.

IISS (International Institute for Strategic Studies). 1990. *The Military Balance 1990–1991*. London: Brassey's.

——. 1994. *The Military Balance 1994–1995*. London: Brassey's.

——. 2002. *The Military Balance 2002–2003*. Oxford: Oxford University Press. October.

——. 2007. *The Military Balance 2007*. Abingdon: Routledge. January.

Interfax. 2007. 'Kazakh Senate Passes Gun Control.' 29 June.

IRIN (Integrated Regional Information Networks). 2004. 'Central Asia Regional Conference on Arms Proliferation Underway.' 17 March.

Italy. 2006. *United Nations Resolution No. 60/81 'The Illicit Trade in Small Arms and Light Weapons in All Its Aspects' Information Provided by Italy*. Rome: Ministry of Foreign Affairs.

Itar-Tass (Information Telegraph Agency of Russia—Telegraph Agency of the Soviet Union). 2007. 'Russia Has No Plans to Withdraw Munitions from Moldova's Rebel Region.' 5 April.

——. 2008. 'Russian Military May Reconfigure Kaliningrad Troops.' 30 January.

IWPR (Institute for War and Peace Reporting). 2006. 'Is NATO Ready for Georgia?' 23 November.

Johnson, Matthew. 2007. 'Shoulder-fired Missile Supply Shrinking but More Money Requested.' *CQ Homeland Security*. 23 May.

Karp, Aaron. 2003. 'Dunblane and the International Politics of Gun Control.' In Stuart Nagel, ed. *Policy and Peacemaking*. Lanham: Lexington Books, ch. 8.

——. 2007. *Mapping South American Small Arms Stockpiles and Surpluses: Vol. I, Summary Findings*. Unpublished background paper. Geneva: Small Arms Survey. 30 September.

Kazakhstan Today. 2007. 'Kazakhstan Ratifies NATO Arms Disposal Deal.' 28 June.

Kazykhanov, Yerzhan. 2004. 'Kazakhstan's Efforts to Improve United Nations "Machinery".' *UN Chronicle*. March–May.

Keridis, Dimitris and Charles Perry. 2004. *Defense Reform, Modernizations and Military Cooperation in Southeastern Europe*. Dulles: Brassey's.

Klingelhoefer, Mark. 2005. *Captured Enemy Ammunition in Operation Iraqi Freedom and Its Strategic Importance in Post-Conflict Operations.* Carlisle, Pennsylvania: US Army War College. 18 March.

Kryvonos, Yurii and Elli Kytömäki. 2008. 'Surplus SALW and Conventional Ammunition and the OSCE.' *Contemporary Security Policy,* Vol. 29, No. 1.

Lamb, Guy. 2004. 'South Africa.' In Chandre Gould and Guy Lamb, eds. *Hide and Seek: Taking Account of Small Arms in Southern Africa.* Pretoria: Institute for Security Studies.

McCormack, Sean. 2005. 'Daily Press Briefing.' Washington, DC: US Department of State. 22 December.

Miami Herald. 2005. 'Nicaragua to Reveal Details about Stockpiled Weapons.' 27 February.

The Monitor (Kampala). 2006. 'Ugandan Army Destroys 57,000 Surplus Guns.' 22 May 2006.

Montenegro News Agency (Podgorica). 2007. 'Montenegro, OSCE, UNDP Sign Surplus Arms Reduction Programme.' BBC Monitoring Service. 19 April.

NAMSA (NATO Maintenance and Supply Agency). 2007. *Status of Trust Fund Projects—9 October 2007.*
    <http://nids.hq.NATO.int/pfp/trust-fund-projects.pdf>

Nascimento, Marcelo de Sousa. 2007. *Venezuela.* Unpublished background paper. Geneva: Small Arms Survey.

Nassauer, Otfried. 1995. 'An Army Surplus: The NVA's Heritage.' *Coping with Surplus Weapons.* BICC Brief No. 2. Bonn: Bonn International Conversion Center, p. 50.

NATO (North Atlantic Treaty Organization). 2005. *Kazakhstan Project Feasibility Study Technical Briefing.* FSC.DEL/164/05 of 4 May. Vienna: OSCE.

New York Times. 2005. 'Ill-secured Soviet Arms Depots Tempting Rebels and Terrorists.' 16 July, p. A1.

——. 2006. 'The Untracked Guns of Iraq.' 31 October.

——. 2007. 'Russia's Trademark Gun, but Others Grab Profits.' 15 July, p. A1.

NTI (Nuclear Threat Initiative). 2005. *Belarus Destroys MANPADS in Cooperation with OSCE.* Washington, DC: NTI. 25 May. <http://www.nti.org/>

Obando, Enrique Arbulú. 2007. *Peru.* Unpublished background paper. Geneva: Small Arms Survey. March.

OSCE (Organization for Security and Cooperation in Europe). 2003a. *Handbook of Best Practices on Small Arms and Light Weapons.* Vienna: OSCE.

——. 2003b. *Questionnaire regarding the Provision of Assistance to Ukraine under the OSCE Document on Stockpiles of Conventional Ammunition, Permanent Mission of Ukraine to the International Organizations in Vienna.* FSC.DEL/536/03 of 17 December. Vienna: OSCE.

——. 2007a. *Report on SALW Destruction Facility Visit to Belarus.* SEC.GAL/122/07 of 27 June. Vienna: OSCE FSC Support Section.

—— 2007b *Synopsis of Status of SALW and Conventional Ammunition Projects in the OSCE in 2000.* FSC.GAL/81/07 of 2 July. Vienna: OSCE Conflict Prevention Centre.

Pagina (Argentina). 2005. 'Misterio en Bolivia por 28 misiles que se habrían llevado los EE.UU.' 21 November, p. 12.

Perepelytsia, Grigoriy. 2007. 'NATO and Ukraine: At the Crossroads.' *NATO Review.* Spring.

Perović, Ljubiša. 2007. 'Address by Mr. Ljubiša Perović Deputy Minister for Defence Policy of Montenegro.' Presentation to the 509th meeting of the FSC, OSCE, Vienna, 28 February.

Pico, Stephanie. 2006. 'U.S. Assistance in Destruction Programs.' Presentation to the OAS Seminar on Stockpile Management and Destruction, Santiago, Chile, 9–10 November.

Pietz, Tobias. 2006. *SALW Survey of Croatia.* Bonn and Belgrade: Bonn International Conversion Center and SEESAC. 1 December.

Pion-Berlin, David. 1989. 'Latin American National Security Doctrines: Hard and Softline Themes.' *Armed Forces & Society,* Vol. 15, No. 3, pp. 411–29.

Poland. 2006. *2005 Report to the UN Conventional Arms Register.* New York: UN. 25 May.

Pomper, Miles. 2004. 'Bush Stresses Importance of Nunn-Lugar Programs but Cuts Funds in 2005 Budget Request.' *Arms Control Today.* March, p. 18.
    <http://www.armscontrol.org/act/2004_03/NunnLugarFunding.asp?print>

Porth, Jacquelyn. 2006. 'State's Joseph Says "a Nuclear Armed Iran Is Unacceptable to Us".' *Washington File.* 9 February.

Post-Courier (Port Moresby). 2006a. 'Rebuilding Our Defence Force.' 12 May.

——. 2006b. 'Guns Cull Defended.' 27 June.

Rehn, Olli. 2006. *Europe's Next Frontiers.* Baden-Baden: Nomos.

Reuters. 2007. 'US Eyes Weapons Sales Worth up to $2.3 bn to Iraq.' 26 September.

RFE (Radio Free Europe). 2007a. 'Kazakh President Shakes up Defense Ministry.' 18 April. <http://www.rferl.org/newsline/>

——. 2007b. 'Kazakh Defense Minister Says Country to Become "Military Power" within Five Years.' 22 June. <http://www.rferl.org/newsline/>

Roberts, Rebecca. 2008. 'Surplus Identification and Destruction Decision-Making in Cambodia.' *Contemporary Security Policy,* Vol. 29, No. 1.

Romania. 2003. *Report on implementation of the Programme of Action to Prevent, Combat and Eradicate the Illicit Trade in Small Arms and Light Weapons (SALW) in All Its Aspects.* Bucharest: Ministry of Foreign Affairs.

Sakharov, Andrei. 1990. *Memoirs.* New York: Alfred A. Knopf.

Scavetta, Rick. 2004. 'Civilian Contractors Work Nonstop to Blow up Iraq's Ordnance Stockpile.' *Stars and Stripes.* 25 January.

Schroeder, Matt. 2006. 'Nicaragua Agrees to Destroy More MANPADS.' Washington, DC: Federation of American Scientists. 18 July.
    <http://www.fas.org/blog/ssp/2006/07/nicaragua_agrees_to_destroy_mo.php>

Seattle Times. 2007. 'U.S. Ready to Discuss Nicaragua Missile Swap.' 10 August.

SEESAC (South Eastern and Eastern Europe Clearinghouse for the Control of Small Arms and Light Weapons). 2005. *Clearing Guns.* Belgrade: SEESAC. April.

Sharp, Jane. 2006. *Striving for Military Stability in Europe: Negotiation, Implementation and Adaptation of the CFE Treaty.* London: Routledge.

Small Arms Survey. 2002. *Small Arms Survey 2002: Counting the Human Cost*. Oxford: Oxford University Press.

——. 2004. *Small Arms Survey 2004: Rights at Risk*. Oxford: Oxford University Press.

——. 2005. *Small Arms Survey 2005: Weapons at War*. Oxford: Oxford University Press.

——. 2006. *Small Arms Survey 2006: Unfinished Business*. Oxford: Oxford University Press.

South East European Times (Stuttgart). 2006. 'Dividing up Serbia-Montenegro's Army: Montenegro's Perspective.' 21 September.

——. 2007. 'Montenegro, Other Balkan Nations Donate Guns, Ammunition to Afghanistan.' 23 August.

Towle, Philip. 1997. *Enforced Disarmament: From the Napoleonic Campaigns to the Gulf War*. Oxford: Oxford University Press.

UK (United Kingdom). 2006. *UK Implementation and Support for the UN Programme of Action on SALW*. London: Foreign and Commonwealth Office.

Ulrich, Marybeth. 2007. *Ukraine's Military between East and West*. Carlisle, Pennsylvania: US Army War College, Strategic Studies Institute. May.

UNDP (UN Development Programme). 2007. *Bosnia and Herzegovina: Small Arms and Light Weapons (SALW) and Ammunition Control and Destruction*. Geneva: UNDP. <http://www.undp.ba/?PID=25&RID=22>

UNGA (UN General Assembly). 2001. *Programme of Action to Prevent, Combat and Eradicate the Illicit Trade in Small Arms and Light Weapons in All Its Aspects*. 20 July. Reproduced in UN document A/CONF.192/15. <http://disarmament.un.org/cab/poa.html>

Urrutia, Nicolás. 2007. *Ecuador*. Unpublished background paper. Geneva: Small Arms Survey. May.

USAAF (United States Army Air Forces). 1945. *Army Air Forces Statistical Digest; World War II*. Washington, DC: USAAF, Office of Statistical Control. <http://www.usaaf.net/digest/t140.htm>

USDoS (US Department of State). 2001. *Background Paper: U.S. Policy and Programs on Destroying Excess Small Arms*. Fact Sheet. Washington, DC: USDoS, Bureau of Political-Military Affairs. 2 June.

——. 2003. *United States Assistance for Small Arms and Light Weapons (SA/LW) Destruction Projects*. Washington, DC: USDoS, Bureau of Political-Military Affairs. 1 June.

——. 2005a. *The MANPADS Menace: Combating the Threat to Global Aviation from Man-Portable Air Defense Systems*. Fact Sheet. Washington, DC: USDoS. 20 September.

——. 2005b. 'U.S., Hungary Agree to Destroy Man-Portable Air Defense Systems: Will Cooperate in Destruction of 1,540 Shoulder-fired Anti-aircraft Missiles.' Media Note. Washington, DC: USDoS, Bureau of International Information Programs. October.

——. 2005c. *Congressional Budget Justification, Foreign Operations, Fiscal Year 2006*. Washington, DC: USDoS.

——. 2006. *Congressional Budget Justification, Foreign Operations, Fiscal Year 2007*. Washington, DC: USDoS.

——. 2007a. 'United States Commemorates Small Arms Destruction Day with "Millionth Weapon Destruction" events.' Media Note. Washington, DC: USDoS. 5 July.

——. 2007b. *Congressional Budget Justification, Foreign Operations, Fiscal Year 2008*. Washington, DC: USDoS.

——. 2008. *United States Efforts to Protect International Aviation from Man-Portable Air Defense Systems Attacks*. Fact Sheet 2008/052. Washington, DC: USDoS, Office of the Spokesman. 24 January.

USSBS (United States Strategic Bombing Survey). 1947. *Final Reports of the United States Strategic Bombing Survey, 1945–1947: Statistical Appendix*. Washington, DC: USBBS. February.

Vecernje Novosti (Belgrade). 2007. 'Serbian Reorganizes Army Reduces Number of Troops, Armament.' BBC Monitoring Service. 26 July.

Vietnam War Timeline. 2008. Milwaukee, Wisconsin: 7/15th Field Artillery Association. <http://www.landscaper.net/timelin.htm>

Vijesti (Podgorica). 2007. 'Surplus of Armament Will Be Destroyed by 2009.' 19 April.

VIP News Service (Belgrade). 2007a. 'Financing the Army of Serbia.' 2 August.

——. 2007b. 'Reorganization of the Army of Serbia.' 2 August.

Vremya (Moscow). 2007. 'Kazakhstan to Destroy Obsolete Arms with NATO Help.' News programme, Channel One TV. BBC Monitoring Service. 25 June.

Waltz, Susan. 2007. 'U.S. Small Arms Policy: Having It Both Ways.' *World Policy Journal*, Vol. 24, No. 2. Summer, pp. 67–80.

Washington Post. 2006. 'Ex-Bolivia Leader: U.S. Won't Clear Role.' 17 August.

——. 2007. 'Nicaragua Offers to Give up Soviet-era Missiles for Medical Aid, Helicopters.' 1 August, p. A12.

Weitz, Richard. 2007. *The Reserve Policies of Nations: A Comparative Analysis*. Carlisle, Pennsylvania: Strategic Studies Institute, US Army War College. September.

Wille, Christina. 2006. *How Many Weapons Are There in Cambodia?* Background Paper. Geneva: Small Arms Survey.

Woo, Brian. 2004. *Countering Terrorism: OSCE Push for Implementation*. London: Parliamentary Office of Bruce George, MP. <http://www.rthonbrucegeorgemp.co.uk/pdfs/38.pdf>

Wood, David. 2006. *SALW Survey of Moldova*. Belgrade: South Eastern and Eastern Europe Clearinghouse for the Control of Small Arms and Light Weapons.

ACKNOWLEDGEMENTS

Principal author

Aaron Karp

arms dealer Viktor Bout sits in the Bangkok Criminal Court as he ansferred to a prison after his arrest in March 2008.
lang/Reuters

Deadly Deception
ARMS TRANSFER DIVERSION

4

INTRODUCTION

On 17 March 1999 a Ukrainian-registered Ilyushin-76 cargo aircraft was nearing the end of its transcontinental flight from Amman, Jordan, to Iquitos, Peru, when something very unusual happened. As the lumbering aircraft passed over southern Colombia, it disgorged several parachute-rigged pallets, which floated down into the rebel-infested jungles below. On the pallets were hundreds of surplus assault rifles ostensibly destined for the Peruvian military, but diverted by high-ranking Peruvian officials to the Revolutionary Armed Forces of Colombia (FARC), a 40-year-old insurgent group known for its involvement in drug trafficking and kidnapping. Over the next five months, the Ilyushin would make three more trips over Colombia, delivering a total of 10,000 AKM rifles to the FARC before the Jordanian government learned of the diversion from Colombian officials and impounded the rest of the weapons. Had the Colombian military failed to uncover the scheme, the FARC might have received the other 40,000 rifles—an arsenal 'comparable . . . to what a regular army might have', observed Peruvian president Alberto Fujimori, who was subsequently forced into exile after news of his regime's involvement in the diversion scheme became public (LAWR, 2000).

Few crimes capture the imagination more than the massive small arms diversions arranged by the so-called 'Merchants of Death' (Farah, 2007; Farah and Braun, 2006). These shipments, the largest of which are organized by a complex and ever-shifting web of brokers, financiers, and shipping companies scattered across the globe, stock the arsenals of terrorists and abusive governments; prolong civil war; and, when they are exposed, embroil governments in scandal. This chapter explores the phenomenon of small arms diversion in all its forms, from crates of assault rifles flown to remote jungle locations by lumbering Soviet-era cargo planes to the online sale of knock-off AR-15s illicitly assembled from legally acquired component parts.

Arms transfer diversions merit special attention because they are responsible for some of the largest illicit small arms transfers in recent years and because responsible governments are often better positioned to prevent diversions than strictly black market transfers—where opportunities for government intervention are fewer—and intentional illicit transfers organized by irresponsible governments, which are often difficult to deter, especially when the exporting government views the transfers as critical to its national security.

The objectives of this chapter are twofold: to shed light on diversions as a subset of illicit arms transfers and to identify and evaluate the tools and strategies adopted by states to detect, deter, and prevent diversions. The chapter begins by defining diversion and providing a brief overview of the sources, major players and their tactics, modes of transport, and the consequences of major diversions. Four key risk factors—the stage of the transfer, the type of transfer, the level of government involvement in the diversion scheme, and the transfer controls of the exporting state—are then explored in the context of actual cases. The chapter then assesses the various control measures pursued by governments at each stage of the transfer chain and concludes with an evaluation of the costs and benefits of key measures.

Major findings of this chapter include the following:

- Diversions occur throughout the transfer chain, from the time that the arms are loaded onto boats and planes for delivery to years after the authorized end user takes custody of them.

- The risk of diversion is not limited to major arms-exporting states. States that do not produce or export small arms are also targeted.

- Covert arms transfers to non-state groups are particularly vulnerable to diversion.

- Most diversions can be prevented with the right combination of transfer controls and, in some cases, with no more than a few telephone calls.

- The top exporters of small arms and light weapons (those with an annual export value of at least USD 100 million) according to available data and estimates for 2005—the latest year for which customs data is available for analysis— were the United States, Italy, Germany, Belgium, Austria, Brazil, the Russian Federation, and China.[1] The top importers of small arms and light weapons (those with an annual import value of at least USD 100 million)[2] for 2005 were the United States, Saudi Arabia, Canada, France,[3] and Germany. See the top and major exporter and importer tables online in the Annexe to this chapter.[4]

- The 2008 Small Arms Transparency Barometer reviews the reports of 40 'major' small arms exporters (i.e. a country believed to have exported USD 10 million or more of such material for at least one year during the period 2001–05). The 2008 Barometer, assessing the period 2005–06, shows that the most transparent major small arms exporters are the United States, Italy, Slovakia, the United Kingdom, and France. The least transparent are Iran and North Korea, both scoring zero on the Barometer.

DEFINING DIVERSION

For the purposes of this chapter, arms transfer diversions are defined as *the transfer of controlled items authorized for export to one end user, but delivered to an unauthorized end user or used by the authorized end user in unauthorized ways*. The operative word in this definition is *unauthorized*—which separates diversions from (unauthorized) black market transfers. Note that the definition used here encompasses the concept of use as well as possession— specifically where a recipient uses transferred weapons in violation of commitments it made prior to export.[5]

ions can
with the
nation of
controls.
 At first glance, the need for this distinction may not be apparent. Diversions have much in common with other illicit transfers: they often result in the delivery of large quantities of small arms to terrorists, criminals, insurgents, and embargoed countries; exploit the same modes of transport and employ the same deceptive practices; and are widely condemned by the international community. However, diversions differ significantly from other illicit arms transfers in at least one crucial area—control strategies. Preventing diversion requires a very different set of strategies and tools from other forms of illicit transfer, such as authorized but covert state-sponsored arms transfers to terrorists and insurgents. Strategies for preventing diversion include rigorous pre-shipment licence reviews, in-transit monitoring of exported shipments, and post-delivery end-use monitoring, none of which are particularly relevant to covert transfers purposefully arranged by the exporting government.

Excluded under this definition are domestic diversions (i.e. those not involving *international* transfer), and illicit transfers of domestically acquired weapons that were never authorized for export by relevant government authorities.

The *unauthorized* retransfer of imported weapons would qualify as diversion—but not in cases where the original exporter imposes no restrictions in relation to re-export.

DIVERSION: AN OVERVIEW

A survey of UN arms monitoring reports and other credible sources reveals that diversion takes many forms and occurs at different points in the transfer chain. Individual diversions range in size and content from hundred-ton shipments of military-grade small arms and light weapons to small packages of component parts for civilian firearms. The sources of diverted weapons are also diverse. While the massive surplus stocks of cold war-era weaponry in Eastern Europe have been targeted repeatedly in recent years, investigators have also documented major diversions from military and civilian stocks in Africa, Asia, the western hemisphere, and the Middle East. Even countries with little or no indigenous small arms production capacity occasionally fall victim to diversion schemes, as illustrated by the diversion of 1,000 recently imported Slovakian sub-machine guns from Uganda to Liberia in November 2000 (see Box 4.1).

Diversion occurs at most points in the transfer chain. In recent years, investigators have documented the diversion of large arms shipments: in the origin country (point of embarkation); en route to the ostensible end user (in transit); at the time of or shortly after delivery to the intended recipient (point of delivery); and some time after importation (post-delivery). Table 4.1 includes examples of each type of diversion. It is important to note that most diversions are conceived and executed across several stages of the transfer chain. Diversions that occur while the shipment is in transit, for example, are often set up well before the ship or aircraft carrying the weapons leaves the port or airport. Similarly, plots to retransfer illicitly arms received by legitimate end users are often hatched well before the first consignment of weapons is received by the original recipient. Thus, the cases in Table 4.1 are categorized according to the pivotal moment of the diversion (i.e. the moment at which physical control or custody of the shipment shifts from the exporter or authorized end user to an unauthorized third party).

The modes of transport and routing used in documented cases of diversion vary depending on the destination, the size of the shipment, and the point in the transfer chain at which the diversion occurs. The majority of in-transit and point-of-delivery diversions are transported by air or sea. Soviet-era military transport and passenger planes (e.g. Ilyushin-18s and -76s and Antonov 124s) have featured prominently in recent cases, although non-Warsaw Pact aircraft have been used as well. According to the South Eastern and Eastern Europe Clearinghouse for the Control of Small Arms and Light Weapons (SEESAC), the types of

An Ilyushin-76 cargo aircraft like this one dropped 10,000 AKM rifles to the FARC in Colombia in 1999. © Reuters

The Panamanian ship Otterloo, which was used in the November 2001 diversion of Nicaraguan assault rifles to Colombia, is seen on the north mouth of the Panama Canal in May 2002. © Tomas Munita/AP Photo

ships used in illicit transfers vary, but most are so-called 'tramp vessels'—ships with no fixed schedules or ports of call (Griffiths and Wilkinson, 2007, p. 13). Once the aircraft or ship arrives in the destination country, the weapons are often divided into smaller bundles and transported by aircraft, boat, or truck to the final recipient.

Aircraft and ships used in major diversions are often registered under flags of convenience and owned by offshore shell companies that frequently change their names and shift their locations and assets from country to country. A good example is the *Otterloo*, which was used in the November 2001 diversion of Nicaraguan assault rifles to Colombia (see Table 4.1). The *Otterloo* was the sole ship registered to Trafalgar Maritime, Inc., a front company established in Panama in July 2001, just a few months prior to the diversion. After delivering the rifles to Colombia, the *Otterloo* sailed to Panama and five months later was sold by Trafalgar, which was dissolved at around the same time (OAS, 2003).

The routing of diverted arms shipments depends upon the mode of transport, the destination, and the complexity of the diversion scheme. Some planes and ships travel directly from the source to the recipient, while other schemes involve circuitous routing that covers several continents. An example of the latter is an elaborate November 2000 diversion that resulted in the delivery of 1,000 sub-machine guns from Uganda to Liberia. The Ilyushin-18 that transported the weapons began its roundabout journey in Moldova on 4 November. From there, it flew to the United Arab Emirates (UAE) and then on to Entebbe, Uganda, where the guns were loaded onto the aircraft. It was then flown to Monrovia, arriving on 22 November—a 19-day, 7,000-mile trip to deliver weapons from a source country 3,000 miles away (see Box 4.1).

Box 4.1 Pecos, Liberia, and Uganda's sub-machine guns

In 2000, the Ugandan military imported a large consignment of sub-machine guns[6] from Slovakia through an Egyptian arms broker named Sharif al-Masri. When the weapons arrived, the military discovered that they did not meet specifications in the contract and requested that al-Masri return them to the manufacturer. Instead of arranging for the guns to be shipped back to Slovakia, however, the broker sold them to Pecos, a Guinean brokering company later linked to a series of illicit arms transfers to Liberia. Pecos then diverted the sub-machine guns to Liberia through an elaborate 'bait-and-switch' scheme that spanned three continents (UNSC, 2001).

The events that converged in the sanctions-busting delivery of 1,000 sub-machine guns to Liberia developed along two parallel tracks, one originating in Moldova and the other in Liberia (see Map 4.2). In Moldova, Vichi Air Company, a private agent of the Moldovan government, sought and received permission to charter an Il-18 airliner to another Moldovan company, MoldTransavia, which claimed that the aircraft was needed as a substitute for a damaged Tupolev-154 originally scheduled to fly passengers from the UAE to Moldova. The Il-18 departed from Moldova on 4 November. When it arrived in the UAE, however, its crew were informed that the Tu-154 had been repaired and had already flown back to Moldova with its passengers. Representatives of Vichi claim that the crew were then approached by a representative of Centrafrican Airlines, Serguei Denissenko, who offered them a new contract to fly cargo (identified as 'Technical Equipment') to Uganda and then on to Liberia. According to UN investigators, the contract was signed on 9 November, and the Il-18 departed for Uganda shortly afterwards (UNSC, 2001).[7]

Map 4.1 **One thousand sub-machine guns to Liberia**

The Liberian end of the diversion scheme appears to have been coordinated by Sanjivan Ruprah, an arms dealer with close connections to the Liberian government. On 8 November—the day before Centrafrican Airlines chartered the Ilyushin from Vichi—Ruprah signed another charter contract for the Ilyushin with Centrafrican. According to UN investigators, the charter contract listed a cargo of 14.5 tons, 'the exact weight if the plane had flown the full amount of rifles to Liberia' in two separate flights, and the same routing specified in the contract with Vichi. Ominously, the contract also referred to 'the performance of several air transportations', an apparent reference to additional arms transfers (UNSC, 2001).

Shortly after the Ilyushin arrived in Entebbe, it was loaded with 'seven tons of sealed boxes' containing 1,000 of the 2,250 sub-machine guns that the Ugandan government believed were being returned to the manufacturer in Slovakia. Instead, the plane headed west, arriving in Monrovia on 22 November. Three days later the crew returned to Uganda for the rest of the guns, only to be informed that the flight had been cancelled. Sometime during the Ilyushin's three-day trip to Liberia, the Ugandan government had learned of Masri's unauthorized side deal with Pecos. Upon further investigation, Ugandan authorities also discovered discrepancies between the purported destination (Guinea) and the flight plan, which suggested the plane was bound for Liberia. The Ugandans subsequently impounded the plane, interrupting the diversion scheme and denying Charles Taylor's embargoed regime an additional 1,250 sub-machine guns (UNSC, 2001).

Consistent with the other cases profiled in this chapter, the diversion featured a host of witting and unwitting accomplices; forged and fraudulent documentation; and extensive involvement by Viktor Bout's loose, global confederation of brokering and air transport companies. Centrafrican Airlines was reportedly owned by Bout and was run by one of Bout's protégés. MoldTransavia was managed by Pavel Popov, a former employee of Bout's 'flagship entity', Air Cess (USDoS, 2005; UNSC, 2001). Another company, West Africa Air Services, was set up specifically for smuggling operations and was represented by Sanjivan Ruprah, 'a close business associate of Bout', according to UN investigators (UNSC, 2001). UN investigators have found evidence implicating all three of these companies in other illicit arms deals.

This case also highlights the challenge for exporting states of preventing diversion after importation. Even rigorous post-delivery end-use controls, such as regular physical inventories and on-site inspections, would not have prevented this diversion. Similarly, retransfer notification requirements would have made little difference, since the Ugandan government believed it was simply returning the weapons to the Slovakian manufacturer. Instead, responsibility for preventing the diversion rested primarily with the Ugandan government, its broker Sharif al-Masri, the crew of the Ilyushin, and possibly Vichi Air Company, over which the Slovakian government had little control.

Document abuse is another hallmark of diversion, particularly those instances that occur in transit or at the point of delivery. As explained in Chapter 5 (END-USER CERTIFICATION), these documents—end-user certificates, bills of lading, flight plans, etc.—are used to create a facade of legitimacy, obscure or misrepresent key details about the shipment or the parties involved, and corroborate crucial details of the diversion scheme. They range from authentic documents issued specifically for the diversion and signed by the appropriate (but often corrupt) government officials to poor-quality forgeries created by the traffickers themselves. Some complex diversion schemes involve complete parallel sets of documentation. In one such case, brokers compiled one set of documents—manifests, bills of lading, and two Nigerian end-use certificates—aimed at convincing Yugoslav officials that a 200-ton consignment of surplus small arms and ammunition was bound for Nigeria, and a second set—compiled for the transport agent—that correctly identified Liberia as the final destination of the six shipments arranged to transport the weapons, but falsely indicated that the cargo was 'mine drilling equipment' (UNSC, 2002, pp. 18–22).

Also uniting many of these cases are the profound military and security implications of the diverted weapons. Some schemes deliver consignments of weapons to armed groups and rogue regimes that are comparable with or

Map 4.2 **Selected transfer diversion routes**

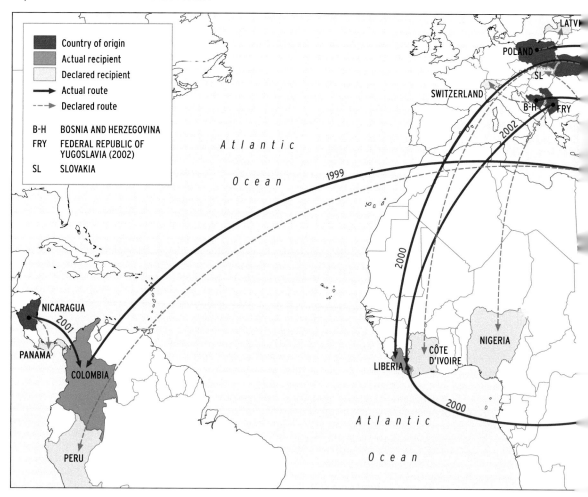

even larger in size than some government arsenals. The 5,000 assault rifles diverted to Liberia as a result of a single diversion scheme in 2002 exceed recent peak procurement rates of rifles for many militaries in small countries, including the neighbouring government of Sierra Leone, which fought a brutal civil war against rebels armed with weapons from Liberia (Small Arms Survey, 2006, p. 29). Some diversions also augment significantly the quantity and sophistication of weapons on the black market that are suitable for use in terrorist attacks. A good example is the diversion of US Stinger missiles from Afghanistan in the late 1980s and early 1990s. Of the estimated 2,500 Stingers distributed to Afghan rebels from 1986 to 1988, 600 missiles remained unaccounted for as of 1996—the rough equivalent of about 10 per cent of *all* man-portable air defence systems (MANPADS) estimated to be outside of government control in 2004 (Coll, 2004, p. 11; USGAO, 2004, p. 10).

Table 4.1 contains a list of major cases of diversion that illustrate the diversity of sources, weapons, points in the transfer chain when diversion occurs, and recipients. This list is not exhaustive and does not necessarily reflect the most common source countries, recipients, or types of diversion. The cases were selected based on their illustrative value; they are not a proportional representation of all diversions. Map 4.1 illustrates selected diversion routes.

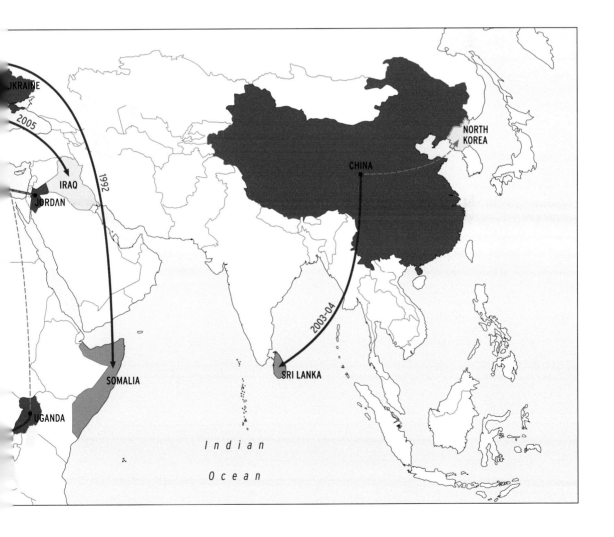

Table 4.1 Significant diversion cases, 1987–2007

Origin	Authorized recipient	Unauthorized recipient	Commodities	Type of diversion	Date
United States	Afghan rebels	Various governments and non-state groups	Surface-to-air missiles	Post-delivery	1987 onward

From 1986 to 1988 the US government sent hundreds of Stinger MANPADS to rebels in Soviet-occupied Afghanistan. The missiles proved extremely effective against Soviet and Afghan government aircraft, bringing down nearly 270 helicopters and aircraft in just two years. Even before the Soviets left Afghanistan in 1988, however, the missiles started disappearing. Despite the best efforts of the Central Intelligence Agency (CIA), dozens, possibly hundreds, of the missiles were diverted to hostile states, terrorists, and other unauthorized end users.[1] As of 1996, independent observers reported that approximately 600 of the estimated 2,000–2,500 missiles distributed to the Afghan rebels were still missing.[2]

Sources: Coll (2004); Schroeder et al. (2006); Hunter (2001); Kuperman (1999)

Poland	Government of Latvia	Somalia	Rifles, pistols, sub-machine guns, rocket-propelled grenades, mortars, and ammunition	Point of delivery	1992

According to UN investigators, in 1992 international arms broker Monzer al-Kassar and two co-conspirators arranged for the illicit retransfer of thousands of Polish weapons and millions of rounds of ammunition from Latvia to Somalia. One of the alleged conspirators was the chief of procurement for the Latvian armed forces, who signed documents falsely identifying the Latvian military as the final end user of the shipment in exchange for 300 AK-47 rifles and 250,000 rounds of ammunition. The weapons were shipped to Latvia on the MV *Nadia*, which departed from Poland on 10 June. When the ship arrived in Latvia, the procurement chief's share of the AK-47 rifles and ammunition was unloaded, and the rest of the weapons were forwarded to the coast of Somalia, where they were incrementally off-loaded onto a fishing vessel for onward delivery to Adale, Somalia.

Sources: UNSC (2003); Baltic News Service (2002)

Jordan	Peru	Colombian rebels	Assault rifles	In transit	1999

In 1999, 10,000 AKM assault rifles—part of a consignment of 50,000 surplus rifles approved for export to Peru—were diverted in transit to Colombian insurgents by high-ranking Peruvian officials, including the former head of the National Intelligence Service, Vladimiro Montesinos. The rifles were air-dropped over Colombia during four flights from March to August 1999 in a Ukrainian-registered Ilyushin-76 allegedly linked to Viktor Bout. The Colombian military seized some of the rifles shortly after the first delivery and were able to trace them back to Jordan. Upon learning of the diversion, Jordan cancelled the deal, thereby preventing the diversion of an additional 40,000 rifles.

Sources: Austin (2001); Farah (2007); Abdallah (2000); NYT (2000); Rempel and Rotella (2000)

United States	Western Europe[3]	Various countries	Components for semi-automatic rifles	Post-delivery	1999–2007

In 2007 a series of suspicious licence applications for US firearms components submitted by a European company prompted the US State Department to launch an investigation into suspected end-use and retransfer violations. Using publicly accessible online resources and information collected during interviews of the company's employees conducted by US embassy personnel, investigators uncovered an extensive operation involving the illicit manufacture of dozens, possibly hundreds, of imposter AR-15 and M4 semi-automatic assault rifles that were illegally sold over the Internet to buyers in at least six countries on two continents (see Box 4.3).

Source: Interviews with US government officials, 2007

| Uganda | Slovakia | Liberia | 1,000 sub-machine guns | Post-delivery | 2000 |

In 2000 the Ugandan military received a large shipment of Slovakian sub-machine guns that did not meet contractual specifications and requested that the Egyptian arms broker return the weapons to the manufacturer. Instead of arranging for the guns to be shipped back to Slovakia, however, the broker sold them to Pecos, a Guinean brokering company linked by UN investigators to a series of illicit arms transfers to Liberia. Pecos then diverted 1,000 of the guns to Liberia through an elaborate 'bait-and-switch' scheme that spanned three continents. An additional 1,250 guns were impounded after the Ugandan government learned of the arms broker's unauthorized side deal with Pecos (see Box 4.1).

Source: UNSC (2001)

| Ukraine | Côte d'Ivoire | Liberia | Ammunition | Point of delivery | 2000 |

In July 2000 five million rounds of 7.62 mm ammunition were legally transferred from Ukraine to Côte d'Ivoire and then illicitly re-exported to Liberia in violation of a UN arms embargo. UN reports indicate that the diversion was jointly devised and implemented by the government of Côte d'Ivoire, Liberia's ambassador-at-large, arms trafficker Leonid Minin, and an associate of Viktor Bout. In exchange for Abidjan's role in the diversion, the Ivorian military were allotted an unspecified percentage of the ammunition. The rest was divided into bundles and flown–in eight separate flights–to Monrovia, where it was delivered to the embargoed regime of then Liberian president Charles Taylor.

Source: UNSC (2001)

| Nicaragua | Panama | Colombian paramilitaries | Assault rifles and ammunition | In transit | 2001 |

Often referred to as the 'Otterloo incident' after the ship used to deliver the weapons, this in-transit diversion was organized by two Panamanian-based arms brokers, one of whom claimed to be acting on behalf of the Panamanian National Police. In 2000 the Nicaraguan government authorized the sale of 3,000 surplus AK series assault rifles and 2.5 million rounds of ammunition to the Panamanian National Police after receiving a falsified end-user certificate from one of the brokers. Instead of shipping the rifles to Panama, however, the captain of the Otterloo sailed to Turbo, Colombia, where the weapons were delivered to the United Self-Defence Forces of Colombia (AUC), an illegal paramilitary group implicated in numerous human rights abuses.

Source: OAS (2003)

| Federal Republic of Yugoslavia | Nigeria | Liberia | Rifles, pistols, machine guns, grenades, missile launchers, mines, and ammunition | In transit | 2002 |

From May through August 2002 two hundred tons of old Yugoslav small arms, light weapons, and ammunition were ferried from Belgrade to Monrovia in six separate flights. Yugoslav authorities had approved the transfer based on documents that identified the Nigerian Ministry of Defence as the end user. The Nigerian government later confirmed to UN investigators that the documentation–airport stamps, end-use certificates, and cargo manifests–were forgeries. The scheme was devised and implemented by brokers, freight forwarders, and other parties operating out of at least three different countries.

Source: UNSC (2002)

| China | North Korea[4] | Sri Lanka | Rifles, ammunition, and other weapons | Point of embarkation | 2003-04 |

According to media reports, middlemen acting on behalf of Sri Lankan rebels used North Korean documentation to divert two large consignments of Chinese assault rifles, rockets, light artillery, and ammunition to the Liberation Tigers of Tamil Eelam, a violent Sri Lankan secessionist group designated as a terrorist organization by the European Union (EU) and the United States (US Treasury, 2007). The weapons were loaded onto cargo ships in China and taken to the coast of either Thailand or Indonesia, where they were off-loaded onto smaller vessels and transported to rebel-held territory in Sri Lanka. A third shipment scheduled for spring 2007 was reportedly scuttled by Chinese officials after the president of Sri Lanka brought the scheme to their attention. The Chinese government is currently investigating the alleged transfers.

Source: AP (2007b)

Bosnia and Herzegovina	Switzerland	Iraq	Assault rifles and ammunition	Unclear	2005

In 2005 a Swiss import certificate was used in the apparent diversion of 9,400 AK series assault rifles and more than 24 million rounds of ammunition. According to SEESAC investigators, a broker supposedly operating out of Croatia used the import certificate and other Swiss documents to acquire a Bosnian export licence that was, in turn, used to procure the weaponry, which was ostensibly destined for Switzerland. However, cargo manifests and transport requests identify the Iraqi Ministry of the Interior as the final recipient. The Swiss and Belgian governments have launched investigations into this incident, including whether the weapons were delivered to Iraq.

Source: Griffiths and Wilkinson (2007, pp. 91-92)

Bulgaria and Romania	Nicaragua	Colombia	Rifles, machine guns, pistols, grenades, and surface-to-air missiles	In transit[5]	2007

In early 2006 the United States initiated an undercover operation against alleged arms trafficker Monzer al-Kassar. The operation involved a fictitious plot to divert thousands of AKM assault rifles, RPK machine guns, Dragunov sniper rifles, Makarov pistols, rocket-propelled grenade launchers and rounds, RGO-78 hand grenades, and Strela-2M MANPADS to Colombian rebels. Al-Kassar and his alleged accomplices told US government sources posing as representatives of the rebels that the weapons would be acquired from sources in Bulgaria and Romania with the help of authentic Nicaraguan end-user certificates furnished by that government for the operation. The weapons were to be delivered to Colombia on a ship, a schematic of which was provided to the Drug Enforcement Administration sources by the boat's captain, who is identified as a co-conspirator. Al-Kassar and two of his alleged co-conspirators were arrested in June 2007.

Sources: US District Court (2007); USDoJ (2007)

Notes:
[1] Information on the covert aid programme through which the Stinger missiles were delivered is classified, but public sources suggest that the missiles were acquired (or retained) illicitly by the governments of Qatar, Iran, and possibly China and North Korea, as well as Chechen separatists, the Liberation Tigers of Tamil Eelam, the Taliban, and al Qaeda (Hunter, 2001; Schroeder et al., 2006, pp. 88-89).
[2] The CIA has not revealed the number of missiles shipped to Afghanistan, but estimates range from 800 to 2,500 (Kuperman, 1999; Coll, 2004).
[3] The State Department has not released the names of the suspects or identified the country in which they operated.
[4] It is not clear from the source if the 'North Korean documents' used in the diversion were North Korean import documents or forged documents indicating a different destination country that were produced by or obtained through North Korean sources (AP, 2007b).
[5] Transfer of the fictitious weapons was supposed to take place in transit. While the diversion plot was fictitious, and no actual weapons were transferred, the traffickers' apparent access to weapons, transport, and possibly end-user certificates suggests that, despite greater government and public awareness of the threat posed by diversions, traffickers still have access to the weapons.

DIVERSION: MAJOR RISK FACTORS

While limitations on existing data sources preclude a comprehensive and definitive assessment of the variables that determine the relative vulnerability of a given arms transfer to diversion, a survey of UN, media, and NGO reports reveals four key variables, or risk factors, that appear to be particularly important: the stage of the transfer, the presence (and degree) of government involvement in the diversion scheme, the type of transfer, and the rigour of relevant national transfer controls.[8] Below is a brief assessment of each.

Stage of the arms transfer

As the cases in Table 4.1 illustrate, the arms transfer chain is only as strong as its weakest link, and major diversions occur at all points of the chain (i.e. the point of embarkation, in transit, the point of delivery, and post-delivery). For example, the shipment of 3,000 AK series assault rifles diverted to Colombian paramilitary forces en route to the

Panamanian National Police in 2001 was roughly comparable in size and significance to the five million rounds of Ukrainian 7.62 mm ammunition diverted to Liberia shortly after arriving in Côte d'Ivoire in 2000 and the 1,000 Slovakian sub-machine guns illicitly retransferred from Uganda in the same year (OAS, 2003; UNSC, 2001). All of these cases resulted in the acquisition of significant quantities of deadly small arms and ammunition by embargoed governments and groups accused of human rights abuses and other atrocities.

What does vary from link to link is the ability of exporters to combat diversion effectively. Exporting states have more tools at their disposal for detecting, preventing, and deterring diversions that occur at the point of embarkation and in transit than at the point of delivery and post-delivery. As explained in the next section, even relatively sophisticated in-transit diversions can be prevented or deterred through, *inter alia*, rigorous pre-licence checks, physical accompaniment of the weapons delivery, remote monitoring, and delivery verification procedures—control measures that are largely ineffective against diversions that occur after the shipment is delivered to the ostensible end user.

A good example of a sophisticated in-transit diversion that may have been prevented by such control measures is the delivery of Jordanian assault rifles to Colombian rebels organized by Vladimiro Montesinos (see Table 4.1). Compared to many other diversions, there were few problem indicators that would have been apparent to Jordanian officials during pre-licence reviews of the proposed transfer. Montesinos' men—some of whom were former members of the Peruvian military—furnished documentation confirming that the Peruvian armed forces were the end users, and the involvement of the former spy chief, who was a close adviser to Peruvian president Alberto Fujimori, would have buttressed the claim. Furthermore, the request for 50,000 AK series assault rifles was not inconsistent with Peru's ad hoc procurement of Warsaw Pact weaponry and was not necessarily excessive for a 115,000-member military (IISS, 1999). Furthermore, before finalizing the sale, Jordanian officials consulted a local US intelligence agent, who reportedly endorsed the transfer (NYT, 2000).

Nonetheless, the Jordanian government could have thwarted (or at least delayed) the diversion by simply sending a government representative to accompany the shipment until it was officially received and signed for by an official representative of the intended recipient, the Peruvian military. This extra step would have been warranted, given the nature and quantity of the weapons being sold, Peru's proximity to Colombia's civil war, and the attendant black market demand for military small arms, as well as the criminal history of the broker who arranged the sale. It would have cost the Jordanian government little more than the price of a return airline ticket between Jordan and Peru—a small fraction of the USD 5 million that Jordan reportedly charged for the rifles (Rempel and Rotella, 2000).

In contrast, point-of-delivery and post-delivery diversion can be significantly more difficult to prevent, as illustrated by the scheme that resulted in the diversion of five million rounds of Ukrainian ammunition from Côte d'Ivoire to Liberia in 2000. Like the Montesinos case, high-level government involvement created a facade of legitimacy and ensured that the documentation provided as part of the transfer was authentic and complete.[9] Unlike the Montesinos case, however, in-transit control measures were of little use. Apparently aware of the diversion risk associated with the transfer, the Ukrainian government sent a representative to accompany the ammunition during the trip to Abidjan, Côte d'Ivoire. Shortly after taking custody of the ammunition, however, the Ivorian military simply loaded it onto a Liberian-registered Ilyushin-18 plane, which promptly returned to Monrovia (UNSC, 2001, pp. 47–49).

The most effective way to detect and deter point-of-delivery and post-delivery diversion is through on-site physical inspections, which require a consular presence in recipient states or frequent travel abroad by inspectors from the exporting country and a willingness on the part of recipient governments to cooperate with the inspections.

However, many governments lack the network of embassies and the budgets to conduct this type of monitoring routinely or else avoid it for fear of offending importing governments. Exporting states can reduce the risk of point-of-delivery and post-delivery diversion through the adoption of strong arms transfer eligibility criteria,[10] careful pre-licence screening of individual requests, and retransfer notification requirements, but these measures are often inadequate substitutes for on-site inspections.

Government involvement

Another key factor is the involvement of high-level officials from the (ostensible) recipient government in the diversion (STOCKPILE DIVERSION). High-level or well-placed government officials support diversion schemes by furnishing authentic documentation, taking custody of the shipment at the port of debarkation, and arranging for delivery of the weapons to the actual (unauthorized) end user—key components of the diversions that would be difficult or, in some cases, impossible for private arms traffickers to arrange on their own. Montesinos' men not only provided authentic end-user certificates, letters of credit, and other documents identifying the Peruvian government as the end user, but also arranged—through a Russian military attaché in Lima—for the use of the specially modified Ilyushin-76 cargo aircraft that air-dropped the weapons over Colombia (Rempel and Rotella, 2000).[11] Similarly, the Ivorian government played an integral role in the November 2000 diversion of ammunition to Liberia, providing the necessary cover story, documentation, and staging ground for the diversion (UNSC, 2001).

In some cases, government involvement salvages schemes that otherwise would have failed, such as the 1992 diversion of hundreds of Polish small arms and millions of rounds of ammunition to Somalia (see Table 4.1). According to UN investigators, arms broker Monzer al-Kassar's first attempt to acquire the weapons ended in failure after Polish officials rejected the blatantly fraudulent documentation submitted as part of the scheme. In response, al-Kassar and his accomplice recruited the chief of procurement for the Latvian armed forces, which was scheduled to receive a large donation of small arms and ammunition from the government of Poland, to assist with the diversion. UN investigators claim that, in exchange for a percentage of the weapons, the procurement chief signed an export contract that the brokers used to secure the release of the shipment from a Polish port. When the ship carrying the weapons arrived in Latvia, the official then cleared the shipment for onward delivery to 'Yemen', i.e. Somalia (UNSC, 2003; Baltic News Service, 2002).

Diversion schemes in which officials from the ostensible recipient governments are not involved are often much easier to foil. A good example is the November 2001 diversion of Nicaraguan assault rifles to Colombia, which apparently was orchestrated without the knowledge of the authorized end user, the Panamanian National Police. Had the Nicaraguan government conducted even basic pre-licence checks, it probably would have uncovered the scheme in time to prevent the diversion. In the words of Organization of American States (OAS) investigators, '[o]ne telephone call could have prevented the entire arms diversion' (OAS, 2003).

Type of arms transfer

While all types of arms transfers are potentially vulnerable to diversion, some are clearly more vulnerable than others. At one end of the spectrum are government-to-government arms sales carried out through established, transparent, and rigorously controlled export programmes. Thousands of these transfers take place each year without incident. At the other end of the spectrum are arms transfers arranged through ad hoc or clandestine programmes that are exempt from the rules and regulations that apply to arms transferred through conventional programmes. These transfers are often extremely vulnerable to diversion, as illustrated by the disappearance of Stinger missiles provided to rebels in Soviet-occupied Afghanistan in the 1980s and, more recently, by the reported diversion of small arms provided to the Iraqi Ministry of the Interior via the US train-and-equip programme (see Table 4.1 and Box 4.2).

The diversion of the mujahideen's Stingers underscores the extreme difficulty of retaining control over weapons covertly transferred to non-state actors. Covert military aid programmes are often run by agencies and through programmes that lack the oversight and accountability afforded to routine arms transfers, increasing the likelihood of ill-conceived or mismanaged arms transfers. Not only were US export controls not applicable to weapons distributed by the CIA, but few members of Congress had access to detailed information about the covert arms programme through which the Stingers were distributed, and those who did were strictly forbidden from sharing that information with the public. To this day, the CIA has refused to divulge even basic details about the programme, including the number of missiles originally distributed and still unaccounted for.

In many cases, the nature of guerrilla warfare also precludes the application of the physical security, stockpile management, and end-use monitoring requirements imposed on arms exports to conventional end users.[12] The

---

Box 4.2 US-funded weapons in Iraq

The *Small Arms Survey 2007* called attention to reports of serious deficiencies in the stockpile security and accounting procedures for small arms and light weapons distributed as part of the US-funded train-and-equip programme for Iraqi security forces. The reports, which were compiled by the Special Inspector General for Iraq Reconstruction, indicated that the US military had failed to log properly the serial numbers of most of the 370,251 small arms purchased for the Iraqi security forces and questioned the accuracy of the military's inventories of MP-5 machine guns, 9 mm pistols, and M1-F assault rifles (SIGIR, 2006, pp. 14, 17).

Since then, government and media investigations have revealed more fully the extent of the stockpile security and accountability problems in the train-and-equip programme. In July 2007 the US Government Accountability Office (USGAO) reported that the Defense Department did not establish a centralized record of weapons distributed to Iraqi forces until December 2005 and failed to 'consistently collect supporting documents that confirm when the equipment was received, the quantities of equipment delivered, and the Iraqi units receiving the equipment' (USGAO, 2007a). The USGAO also found large discrepancies between the centralized records (the 'property books') and data compiled by the former commander of the train-and-equip programme. Based on these discrepancies, the USGAO concluded that the Defense Department 'cannot fully account for at least 190,000 weapons reported as issued to Iraqi forces' (USGAO, 2007a).[13]

While it is still unclear how many, if any, of the unaccounted-for weapons have been diverted to unauthorized end users, firearms issued to Iraqi security forces are reportedly turning up in the hands of criminals not only in Iraq, but also in neighbouring Turkey. According to Turkish officials, dozens of Glock pistols—tens of thousands of which were issued to Iraqi security forces—have been recovered from criminals and militants. Serial numbers from the seized pistols reveal that at least some of them were issued to members of the Iraqi police in 2004-05 (IHT, 2007).

Since late 2005, the US military has taken several steps to improve controls on weapons distributed to Iraqi security forces. These measures include 'implementing increased supervisory checks, balances and physical security redundancies, internal control monitoring, issuance of standing operating procedures, introduction of . . . automated tools, and collaboration with other DOD [Department of Defense] organizations on accountability-related issues' (USGAO, 2007a). Information on most of these measures is scant, but those that have been described in detail appear to be quite robust. For example, coalition forces are not only recording the serial numbers of each weapon issued, but are also taking retinal scans and fingerprints of each recipient and inserting all of the data collected through these procedures into a single database (Benjamin, 2007). The Defense Department has also started channelling small arms transfers to Iraq through the Foreign Military Sales programme, the controls on which are more clearly defined and relatively rigorous, and has launched an open-ended, on-site investigation into allegations of lax stockpile security and small arms diversion (Garamone, 2007; USDoD, 2007c). The Pentagon has also bolstered its staff on the ground in Iraq to improve oversight of weapons transfers. In December 2007 the number of staff at Multi-National Security Transition Command-Iraq's security assistance office jumped from 6 to nearly 70 personnel (AP, 2007c).

These efforts come none too soon. In May and September 2007 the Defense Department notified Congress of plans to sell an additional 575 million rounds of small arms ammunition, 120,000 M16 assault rifles, 12,000 M4 carbine rifles, 74,000 mortar rounds, 50 tons of C4 explosives, and 180,000 HEDP (high-explosive dual-purpose) grenades to Iraq—a massive influx of new weaponry that could, if not properly secured, fuel violence and criminality throughout the region (USDoD, 2007a; 2007b).

informal and often transient relationship between governments and non-state actors is another barrier to proper accountability. Shortly after the Soviet Union pulled out of Afghanistan, the alliance of convenience between the United States and the mujahideen—who shared no values and objectives other than the expulsion of the Soviet Union from Afghanistan—deteriorated until most US assistance was cut off in 1992. By the time the United States attempted to retrieve the Stingers in the early 1990s, it had no meaningful leverage over the mujahideen and, consequently, efforts to retrieve the missiles were only partially successful, despite large payouts of USD 100,000 or more per missile (Coll, 2004).

Ad hoc or newly established arms transfer programmes that lack the procedures, regulations, and safeguards of more established programmes may also be more vulnerable to diversion, as evidenced by accountability problems with weapons distributed through the US Defense Department's Iraq Relief and Reconstruction Fund. The Defense Department's decision to bypass established avenues for exporting and monitoring arms in the case of Iraq contributed to serious shortcomings in the procedures and safeguards that help to prevent diversion. While the magnitude and implications of these shortcomings are still unclear, the reported seizure of dozens of Glock pistols issued to Iraqi security forces from criminals and militants in neighbouring Turkey and anecdotal accounts of large-scale thefts from US-stocked arms depots and police armories suggests that at least some of the poorly managed and tracked weapons were diverted (IHT, 2007; NYT, 2007; see Box 4.2).

*transfer
*s may be
*erable to
diversion.

Export controls

A final, critical factor in determining (and mitigating) the risk of diversion is the exporting country's transfer control system. An analysis of the diversions in Table 4.1 reveals enough irregularities and other warning signs of diversion to have merited special scrutiny and safeguards on the part of exporters, the rigorous pursuit of which would likely have prevented at least some of the diversions.

For example, warning signs in the Peruvian diversion included:

- Peru's proximity to the civil war in Colombia and the attendant black market demand for military small arms in the region;
- attempts by Peruvian officials to pay Jordan's broker in cash;
- the retrofitting of the Il-76 to air-drop large quantities of small arms near an insurgent stronghold;
- the reported misrepresentation of retired Peruvian generals as active duty officers;[14] and
- the broker's criminal history.[15]

There were similar warning signs of the Ivorian diversion, including Côte d'Ivoire's proximity to several conflict zones, the prevalence of Western European firearms in the Ivorian military's arsenals[16] and the large size of the order.[17] In the case of the diverted Nicaraguan assault rifles, irregularities in the (forged) Panamanian purchase order, the fly-by-night nature of the shipping company,[18] and the unlikely end user (a police force) were obvious red flags, as were discrepancies between the Swiss import certificate and other documentation used in the apparent diversion of Bosnian small arms to Iraq (OAS, 2003; Griffiths and Wilkinson, 2007, pp. 91–92).

Vulnerability to post-delivery diversion is often much more difficult to detect ahead of time. It is highly unlikely that the Slovak government could have foreseen the chain of events that led to the diversion of its sub-machine guns to Liberia. In some cases, however, the danger of post-delivery diversion is fairly obvious. The routine diversion of weapons by the Afghan rebels prior to the arrival of the Stingers, for example, was a not so subtle sign that the missiles were vulnerable.

The exporting state's ability to spot the warning signs of diversion and respond effectively is therefore another critical determinant of diversion. In most cases, some combination of transfer controls would have prevented (or at least delayed) the diversion. The telephone call to the Panamanian police that OAS investigators chided the Nicaraguan military for not making is an obvious and easily implemented example (OAS, 2003). Similarly, in-transit monitoring of the small arms shipments to Peru, North Korea, Slovakia, and Nigeria would have made these diversions more difficult or prevented them outright. Preventing the Ivorian diversion of Ukrainian ammunition and the diversion of Polish arms from Latvia would have been more difficult, but the credible threat of on-site post-delivery end-use monitoring might have deterred Ivorian government officials and the Latvian procurement chief from participating in their respective diversion schemes. At a minimum, end-use monitoring would have revealed the diversion after the fact and allowed the respective exporting governments to pursue corrective and punitive measures. Controlling the Stinger missiles distributed to the Afghan rebels through conventional means would have been impossible. While the surest way to prevent the diversion of weapons distributed to armed groups is to refrain from supplying them in the first place, governments can significantly reduce the threat posed by certain types of light weapons, including MANPADS, through the development and installation of technical controls that limit the pool of permissible users, the duration of use, or the geographical region in which a weapon can be operated (Sherman, 2003; Schroeder et al., 2006, pp. 96–98; Bonomo et al., 2007, pp. 87–96).[19]

None of these measures is foolproof: even robust licensing and end-use monitoring programmes occasionally fall prey to diversion schemes, as evidenced by the diversion of AR-15 rifle components from the United States (see Table 4.1). But, taken together, these cases strongly suggest that the right transfer controls can significantly reduce the risk of diversion.

PREVENTING DIVERSION: THE KEY ROLE OF SMALL ARMS TRANSFER CONTROLS

Transfer controls are the sine qua non of national and international efforts to curtail diversion. The most rigorous systems monitor and control the end use of small arms and light weapons from 'cradle to grave', i.e. throughout their life cycle. The controls that comprise such systems can be divided into three categories that roughly correspond with the applicable stage of the transfer: (1) pre-shipment; (2) in transit and point of delivery; and (3) post-delivery. The most effective systems are also often the most transparent, as explained at the end of this section.

Transfer
are the s
of effort
diversion

Pre-shipment controls

Pre-shipment controls include the steps taken to monitor and control the end use of arms transfers prior to their arrival at a port of exit. These steps include the registration of arms exporters, brokers, and other parties to the transfer and the various checks on individual transfer requests that are part of national licensing and authorization processes.

Requiring that manufacturers, exporters, brokers, shippers, distributors, and other parties to arms transfers register with the relevant government agencies and carefully vetting these applications is important for at least two reasons. Firstly, it allows government officials to exclude potential bad actors from the pool of export applicants. Secondly, it enables authorities to take action against those actors that fail to register, but engage in arms transfers anyway. According to UN investigators, registration requirements enacted by Slovakia in 1998 had a notable effect on Joy Slovakia, an arms brokerage company implicated in illicit arms sales to Liberia. 'Since then,' reported UN investigators in 2001, 'Joy Slovakia has become less active' (UNSC, 2001).[20] Despite these advantages, many states do not require key parties, including brokers, to register. This failure not only precludes up-front exclusion of potential bad actors, but also denies the government the use of important punitive measures.

Rigorous arms transfer licensing systems are another critical tool for preventing diversion. While national licensing systems vary significantly in form and rigour, there is broad international consensus on the need for them. Most major multilateral agreements on small arms transfers call on member states to ensure effective control over them (END-USER CERTIFICATION). It appears that most countries have, in fact, established at least rudimentary systems to this end. According to data compiled by the Biting the Bullet project, 111 states had laws and procedures for controlling the export of small arms and light weapons as of 2006 (Bourne et al., 2006).

Proper documentation—and a thorough review of that documentation by trained licensing officers—is the foundation of any effective review process. Licensing applications and accompanying documents facilitate the systematic and expeditious review of arms transfer requests and the identification of debarred parties and other bad actors. These documents are also critical to the prosecution of arms export violations. As explained by former Deputy US Assistant Attorney General Bruce Swartz, licensing requirements

> mak[e] it necessary for exporters intent on circumventing the law to take affirmative steps to evade the [US Arms Export Control] Act's proscriptions—typically by lying on the license application or on shipping documents . . . thus creating a domestic evidentiary trail upon which any ensuing prosecution can be based. (US House of Representatives, 2004)

Forged and fraudulent documentation is diversion schemes.

While an international consensus on which documents should be required as part of the licensing process remains elusive, most multilateral agreements and best practice guides call for some combination of a written application, an original end-user certificate (or an international import certificate), an import licence, and a transit authorization (or a written notice from the transit state indicating that it has no objection to the transfer). These instruments often also urge states to confirm that end-user documentation is valid (END-USER CERTIFICATION), a critically important step that, if adopted by all governments, would thwart many of the least sophisticated diversion attempts. Some states, such as Argentina, already have relatively rigorous verification procedures. Before issuing an export licence, the Argentine government requires that the exporting company submit a government-issued end-user certificate or an international import certificate, which is then authenticated by Argentine consular staff in the importing country. Authentication procedures include certifying the authenticity of the signatures on the end-user certificate and confirming that the signatories are, in fact, authorized to issue import documentation (Argentina, 2007).

As illustrated by many of the cases in Table 4.1, forged and fraudulent documentation is endemic to diversion schemes. Some of these documents are quite sophisticated, while others are relatively easy to spot. A good example of the latter is an end-user certificate from the 'People's Democratic Republic of Yemen' provided to Polish authorities as part of a 1992 diversion scheme allegedly organized by Monzer al-Kassar. As UN investigators pointed out, the People's Democratic Republic of Yemen merged with the Arab Republic of Yemen two years earlier and did not exist at the time of the diversion. But, as this case attests, even glaring errors can pass undetected through lax licensing systems. According to UN investigators, the licensing officer who approved the sale later admitted that Polish authorities 'did not check the veracity of foreign documents with their foreign embassies' (UNSC, 2003).

Yet even authentic documentation issued at the highest levels of the importing government is not an iron-clad assurance of propriety, as illustrated by the diversions arranged by Ivorian government officials and Peruvian spy

Table 4.2   US Blue Lantern end-use monitoring programme basic warning flags*

Unfamiliar private end user	Commodities in demand by embargoed countries
Reluctance or evasiveness by US applicant or purchasing agent in providing end-use or end-user information	Especially sensitive commodities (e.g. night-vision equipment, unmanned aerial vehicles, or cruise missile technologies) whose diversion or illicit retransfer could have a negative impact on US national security
Payment in cash or at above-market rates	Trans-shipment through multiple countries or companies
Scanty, unavailable, or derogatory background information on end user's business	Location of end user or consignee in a free trade zone
Incomplete/suspect supporting documentation	New/unfamiliar intermediary
Unfamiliarity of end users with the product or its use	Vague or suspicious delivery dates, locations (such as PO boxes), shipping instructions, packaging requirements, etc.
End user declines usual follow-on service, installation, warranty, spares, repair, or overhaul contracts	Designation of freight forwarders as foreign consignees or foreign end users
Requested commodities or services appear excessive or inconsistent with end user's or consignee's inventory, line of business, or needs	Foreign intermediate consignees (trading companies, freight forwarders, export companies) with no apparent connection to the end user

* For a summary of the Blue Lantern programme, see Box 5.3 in Chapter 5 of this volume (END-USER CERTIFICATION).
Source: Correspondence with US State Department official, 2008

chief Vladimiro Montesinos. In these cases, the (apparently) authentic end-user certificates and other documents provided by Peruvian and Ivorian government officials created a veneer of legitimacy that actually *facilitated* the diversion (UNSC, 2001; Rempel and Rotella, 2000). Thus, robust licensing systems require export officers to do more than simply collect documentation and verify its authenticity. They also consider the national and regional political and security contexts, compare the requested items against the military doctrine and procurement history of the purported recipient, and look for specific warning signs of diversion. Through its Blue Lantern end-use monitoring programme (END-USER CERTIFICATION), the US government has developed a standard list of 16 problem indicators or 'flags' that licensing officers look for when evaluating licence requests (see Table 4.2).

The presence of one or more flags often triggers an end-use check by compliance officers, who check the bona fides of the end user or consignee, confirm that the purported end user actually ordered the items, and take other steps to confirm the legitimacy of the order and the applicant. Similarly, the European Tracking Initiative has developed detailed sets of risk factors, ratings, and checklists as part of its Arms Transfer Profiling Indicator System (ATPIS). Users of the system have access to indicators that assign risk ratings for, *inter alia*, ports of call, aircraft type, civil aviation registries, document falsification, and brokering location. ATPIS is updated frequently and is accessible to any (approved) user with access to the Internet (Griffiths and Wilkinson, 2007, pp. 54–60).

Most, if not all, of the cases profiled in Table 4.1 would have triggered (or did trigger) a Blue Lantern check. In the case involving Ukrainian ammunition exported to Côte d'Ivoire, the 7.62 mm ammunition was largely incompatible with the Ivorian military's firearms stocks (which consisted primarily of NATO-calibre weaponry), and the AK series assault rifles purportedly requested by the Panamanian National Police during the *Otterloo* incident were ill-suited for police work (UNSC, 2001; OAS, 2003). Similarly, in aggregate, the quantities of AR-15 components requested by the Western European arms dealers were excessive for any purpose other than illicit manufacture.[21] In three other

Box 4.3 The dual-edged Internet: online evidence of illicit AR-15 sales

In 2007 a series of licence requests for US firearms components from a European company caught the attention of a vigilant State Department compliance officer, who noticed that the company had no manufacturing agreement with the State Department. Concerned that the company might be engaged in the illegal manufacture and retransfer of firearms constructed with US components, the officer launched an informal online investigation into the company and its dealings. Over the course of a week, the officer collected enough information just from publicly accessible Internet sources—the company's Web site, gun blogs, forums, and commercial sites—to trigger a formal end-use check through the State Department's Blue Lantern pro-gramme (END-USER CERTIFICATION). Compliance officers in Washington then asked embassy officials to check if the company was manufacturing firearms with US-origin components. After initially refusing to talk to US officials, the proprietor of the company eventually admitted that he was indeed using legally imported US firearms components in the illicit manufacture and sale of imposter AR-15 and M4 semi-automatic assault rifles. While the full scope of the operation is still unclear, US offi-cials estimate that dozens, possibly hundreds, of the rifles—which featured US bolts, receivers, and accessories—were illegally sold over the Internet to buyers in at least six countries on two continents. According to one compliance officer, the company 'appears to have been operating in this manner for at least eight years, and had stayed out of suspicion by ordering compo-nents in small quantities'. The State Department subsequently placed the company on a watch list and put it under a 'policy of denial' for future transfers.[22]

This case highlights the Internet's potential as both a marketing tool for arms traffickers and a research tool of law enforcement and export control officials. Over the past few years, US officials have noticed a growing number of Web sites hawking specialty firearms and accessories, often without being properly registered. This observation is echoed by Griffiths and Wilkinson, who note that 'a surprising number of those involved or complicit in clandestine deliveries are to be found advertising one or more of their services on the internet' (Griffiths and Wilkinson, 2007, p. 4). At the same time, the Internet has become an increasingly rich source of data regarding the possible misuse of controlled items. Valuable information, including phone numbers, email addresses, and physical addresses of arms brokers and shipping companies and data on ships and planes used in diversions, are available online, often at no charge (Griffiths and Wilkinson, 2007).

This case also underscores the need to monitor and control the transfer of small arms components as well as fully assembled weapons. According to US officials, the frequency of suspected diversion attempts involving firearms components is growing.[23]

cases, the regional security context—Peru's proximity to Colombia's civil war, the embargoes and armed conflicts in West Africa, and the instability and sectarian strife in Iraq—would also have been grounds for heightened scrutiny.

Spotting the sometimes subtle signs of diversion requires training,[24] detailed and up-to-date information on other countries' military procurement and weapons inventories, and a wide array of regional and thematic expertise. Since few (if any) licensing bureaus have all of the necessary resources and expertise in-house, some governments have established a process whereby certain licence requests are sent to several agencies for review. In some countries, this process is formalized and provides the different agencies with significant influence over the licensing process. In Croatia, requests for import and export licences are reviewed by an interagency group consisting of representa-tives from the Ministry of Defence, the Ministry of Interior Affairs, and the Ministry of Economy, all of whom have de facto veto power over the request (Croatia, 2007).

Licensing officers also seek information from other governments, input that can have a decisive influence on decisions about specific transfers. While reviewing a licence request for the sale of 300 handguns to a Latin American company in 2005, US licensing officers learned from the host government that lost and stolen firearms were factoring heavily in a recent surge in violent crime. In response, the State Department determined that the order was excessive, given the crime surge, and persuaded the seller to reduce the size of the sale (USDoS, 2006).

Another hallmark of strong licensing systems is the routine screening of *all* parties to the transfer: exporters, freight forwarders, intermediate consignees, brokers, shipping agents, and end users. While exporters, brokers, and the ostensible end users usually get the most attention, other parties to arms exports, such as consignees, also play critical roles in diversion schemes. Furthermore, the involvement in a proposed arms transfer of certain freight forwarders and shippers implicated in other illicit transfers can serve as an important red flag for licensing officers. Searchable databases, or 'watch lists', of suspected and confirmed criminals, arms traffickers, parties on UN sanctions lists, and other questionable actors are particularly useful in this regard.

A final feature of strong licensing systems is the routine inclusion of storage, use, retransfer, and disposal requirements, or provisos, in licences and other documentation. Specific requirements vary significantly, not only from country to country, but also from item to item. Standard provisos in sales contracts for US Stinger and Javelin missiles, for example, include rigorous and exhaustive physical security requirements normally not applied to other exported small arms and light weapons. These provisos require importing governments to, *inter alia,* conduct monthly physical inventories of *all* their Stinger stocks, employ a full-time guard force (or a combination of a guard force and an intrusion detection system), and notify the US government before assembling the missiles for training, lot testing, and in the event that they are lost or stolen (USDoD, 2003). Some exporting states conduct physical inspections of the proposed recipient's facilities before weapons are shipped to ensure that the recipient is capable of implementing specific requirements. Canada, for example, requires consular staff to visit the premises of commercial enterprises seeking to import sporting firearms if the enterprise submits an end-use statement instead of a government-issued end-user certificate (Canada, 2006).

Other states restrict (or at least require notification of) the retransfer of their exported weapons.[25] Egypt requires that all retransfers be licensed and that the licence identify the serial numbers and types of weapons being retransferred, the route and time of the retransfer, and additional conditions attached to the retransfer by Egyptian authorities (Egypt, 2006). Given the prominence of surplus weaponry in diversion schemes, provisos that condition the sale of new small arms and light weapons on the destruction of old stocks are also important. These and other end-use requirements help to ensure that the end user understands the exporter's expectations concerning storage, use, retransfer, and disposal of controlled items, and—assuming that the provisos are enforceable and compliance is monitored—afford the exporting country a degree of control over exported items long after they are received by the end user.

In-transit and point-of-delivery controls

Transfer controls in this category monitor and protect weapons shipments from the time they leave the warehouse until they are officially received by the intended end user. Such controls include:

- stringent physical security requirements (e.g. transport of arms and ammunition in separate vehicles, use of vehicular alarm systems and container seals, physical inspection in transit and at the point of delivery, etc.);[26]
- scrutiny of arms shipments and documentation by customs agents in the exporting, transit, and importing states;
- close coordination (formal or informal) with the governments of the countries through which the shipment travels; and
- delivery notification.

Monitoring the location of small arms shipments en route can be accomplished in several ways, including physical accompaniment and remote monitoring via satellite. For large shipments, accompaniment by armed guards with proper security clearances and supplemented by satellite tracking is warranted, given the risk and consequences of diversion. Such arrangements would probably have prevented all four of the point-of-embarkation and in-transit diversions described in Table 4.1. For small, low-risk shipments, remote monitoring via satellite along with rigorous physical security requirements, careful screening of shipping companies, and delivery confirmation are often adequate.

Satellite tracking and container security services are available from several commercial suppliers, including Comtech Mobile Data Corporation, which offers portable systems that it claims are compatible with most aircraft, including the Ilyushins and Antonovs used in many of the diversions identified above. According to Comtech, it has sold tracking systems to more than a dozen countries, several of which use them to track munitions.[27] Other systems, such as the Powers SeaCure Satellite System, not only claim to monitor the progress of the cargo to its destination, but also automatically alert authorities of hijackings and unauthorized container breaches (Powers International, 2006).

Some exporters, like the US military, use their own transportation infrastructure and robust transport security systems to protect and monitor small arms exports. While the shipments are in the United States, they are monitored via the Defense Transportation Tracking System—a Defense Department programme that continuously tracks the movement of sensitive material, including small arms, via satellite and provides 24-hour emergency response (US Army Transportation School, 2004). After the shipments reach a US military-controlled point of embarkation, most are loaded directly onto a customer country-controlled ship or aircraft by US military personnel, who require that a high-ranking member of the carrier's crew sign for the shipment. All foreign carriers must meet minimum safety and security standards and must be pre-screened by the US military. If the weapons are classified, the purchasing country must provide a transportation plan that is approved by Defense Department officials in advance. For certain types of

FARC rebels check a machine gun near San Vicente del Caguan, Colombia, in January 1999. © AP Photo

weapons (e.g. shoulder-fired anti-tank and anti-aircraft missiles) or when clients lack the capacity to transport the arms securely themselves, the Defense Department delivers the shipment to the importing state (either to a port-of-delivery [debarkation] or to a final inland delivery point) using its own aircraft and ships (USDoD, 2004).

If the Defense Department routinely schedules an airlift of its own materiel to or through the purchaser's country (i.e. if US forces are present), the transport costs are not exorbitant. In other cases, however, the shipment must be transported via a Special Assignment Airlift Mission—US military aircraft chartered specifically for the delivery. This service is so costly (USD 500,000 or more per flight) that customers are often unwilling or unable to pay the entire fee themselves and may have to wait to receive their orders until the weapons can be consolidated with other cargo bound for the same destination. In one extreme case, a shipment of sniper rifles purchased by a sub-Saharan African military was delayed for five years and still cost the recipient approximately USD 500,000.[28]

Post-delivery controls

Post-delivery end-use monitoring includes routine on-site verification visits, annual physical inventories of exported weapons, and investigations of suspected violations of end-use and retransfer restrictions. Post-delivery end-use monitoring enables exporters to detect incidents of diversion and take steps to prevent additional diversions, such as scrutinizing future export requests from violators more thoroughly, helping violators to improve their stockpile security and export control procedures, and banning exports to egregious or uncooperative violators. Such checks also help to deter diversions in the first place. Governments are less likely to violate retransfer and end-use restrictions if the likelihood of getting caught—and thereby possibly losing access to key arms supplies—is high.

A Colombian paramilitary fighter is armed with assault rifle, February 2003. © Ja

Post-delivery end-use monitoring is particularly important in cases of diversion in which high-level government involvement renders pre-shipment and in-transit checks less effective. In the July 2000 diversion of Ukrainian ammunition to Liberia (see Table 4.1), for example, pre-licence checks by the Ukrainian government probably would have yielded few clues of the diversion, since the documentation was authentic and complete, and the Ivorian military had indeed placed the order. Even the extraordinary step of sending a representative to accompany the ammunition during the trip to Côte d'Ivoire had little effect, because the diversion did not occur until after importation. Short of denying the sales request altogether (which may have been prudent, given the many contextual red flags), the diversion could have been prevented through the credible threat of post-delivery inventory checks.

The Montesinos case is another good example of the need for post-delivery checks. Had the conspirators scratched off the serial numbers on the rifles in the first shipment, the scheme might not have been detected and exposed in time to prevent the delivery of the remaining 40,000 rifles (LAWR, 2000). An on-site verification visit by Jordanian officials soon after the weapons' supposed delivery to Peru, however, almost certainly would have revealed the diversion.

When diversions are detected (either during post-delivery checks or at any time during the arms transfer process), the capacity to sanction the offenders, be they governments or private entities, becomes essential. Punishments for diversions and related violations of transfer controls range from warning letters to fines, debarment, and imprisonment for private entities; and include

Syrian businessman Monzer al-Kassar–seen at his home in Spain in May 1998–was arrested in June 2007 on charges of conspiring to provide weapons to the Revolutionary Armed Forces of Colombia. © Paul White/AP Photo

Peru's former spy chief Vladimiro Montesinos—seen here on trial in January 2004—was sentenced to 20 years for his part in the diversion of assault rifles to Colombian rebels.
© Pilar Olivares/Reuters

Lebanese arms broker Sarkis Soghanalian—pictured in Jordan in 2003—was tried in absentia for his alleged role in the diversion for which Montesinos was sentenced.
© Christopher Anderson/Magnum Photos

demarches, extra scrutiny of future requests, provisos in future contracts, and embargos or sanctions for offending governments.

While most states have criminalized the illicit trade in small arms,[29] prosecuting violators of transfer controls is notoriously difficult, especially when the accused is not a citizen of the country in which the offence is being prosecuted and the weapons never enter the territory of the prosecuting country. Weak, narrow, or non-existent national laws on brokering; barriers to extradition; and a lack of political will can delay or derail attempts to prosecute even the most notorious arms brokers. Despite an Interpol arrest warrant, Viktor Bout remained conspicuously at large until March 2008, and it is still unclear whether he will stand trial (Farah, 2007, pp. 205, 252–53; Reuters, 2008). Famed trafficker Leonid Minin's arrest in 2000 led to a conviction for the illegal possession of diamonds, but charges stemming from his suspected role in the diversion of small arms and light weapons to Liberia were dropped after Italian judges ruled that, since the arms shipments in question never entered Italy, the courts lacked jurisdiction (AI and TransArms, 2006). Sanjivan Ruprah, who allegedly assisted with the diversion of Slovakian sub-machine guns to Liberia, was arrested in February 2002 in Belgium, but fled to Italy after being released on bail two months later. He was rearrested in Italy, but released on bond shortly afterward. Ruprah is now reportedly at large in Africa (Farah and Braun, 2006). Other representatives of front companies accused by UN investigators of contributing to the diversion of small arms to countries under UN embargoes have been arrested but have been released for various reasons, including a lack of evidence (ČTK, 2001).

Despite these obstacles, some of the arms traffickers profiled in this chapter have been tried and, in a few cases, convicted of arms trafficking-related offences. In September 2006 Peruvian spy chief Vladimiro Montesinos was sentenced to 20 years in prison for his role in the diversion of Jordanian assault rifles to Colombian guerrillas. Sarkis Soghanalian, the Lebanese arms broker accused of participating in the same diversion, was tried in absentia by the Peruvian government, which is seeking his extradition from the United States (AP, 2006). Most recently, the 'Prince of Marbella', Monzer al-Kassar, was arrested in Madrid in June 2007 after a lengthy international undercover operation. In addition to his alleged role in a fictitious plot to provide Colombian rebels with thousands of small arms, the US government claims that al-Kassar has stocked the arsenals of terrorists, rebels, and dictators in Bosnia, Brazil, Croatia, Cyprus, Nicaragua, Iran, Iraq, and Somalia over the past 30 years (USDoJ, 2007). Al-Kassar currently awaits extradition to the United States (AP, 2007a).

Transparency

Transparency is another critical component of national, regional, and international efforts to prevent diversion. Past editions of the *Small Arms Survey* have looked at several aspects of transparency in the small arms trade and chronicled the evolution of key transparency mechanisms, such as the UN Register of Conventional Arms. This section builds on this analysis by assessing the benefits of transparency in identifying, investigating, and preventing diversion. The section is followed by an update of the Small Arms Trade Transparency Barometer.

For the purposes of this chapter, transparency is relevant in relation to:

* decisions regarding authorized arms transfers;
* the policies, procedures, and practices that comprise arms export control systems; and
* failures of such systems, including cases of diversion.

Transparency in decisions to authorize arms transfers

Transparency in the authorized arms trade serves several purposes: it calls attention to potentially excessive accumulations of weaponry, increases the political cost of arms transfers to irresponsible recipients, and facilitates scrutiny of irresponsible small arms transfers, in particular those authorized despite a significant risk of diversion (Small Arms Survey, 2007, ch. 3). Detailed information about authorized transfers—including the model, manufacturer, calibre, and serial (or batch) number of weapons; the date of the transfer; and the recipient—helps intelligence and law enforcement agencies to identify quickly the origin and trans-shipment points of diverted weapons. In the Montesinos case, for example, access to information about the Jordanian assault rifles seized from Colombian rebels allowed US and Colombian intelligence officials to uncover the diversion scheme in time to prevent the 40,000 additional rifles awaiting delivery to Latin America from reaching the FARC (LAWR, 2000).

Transparency in the authorized defence trade takes many forms, including data submissions to the UN Commodity Trade Statistics Database (UN Comtrade) and the UN Register of Conventional Arms, information exchanges among members of regional or multilateral institutions, ad hoc information sharing between two or more governments, and reports issued by national governments.

Transparency in arms export control regimes

Public dissemination of the laws, policies, procedures, and practices that comprise national export control regimes also helps to prevent diversion, albeit less directly. Transparent regimes contribute to the development of multilateral

ency is a mponent prevent diversion.

agreements, international best practices, and national control regimes by providing time-tested examples of effective export controls. Transparency also facilitates intra-governmental and public oversight of national export control systems, which, as explained above, are critically important for preventing diversion. Gaps and weaknesses in licensing procedures, end-use monitoring practices, and other controls essential for preventing diversion are easier to spot and correct in transparent systems than in systems that are more opaque.[30] Transparent systems are also less vulnerable to manipulation and evisceration by small, well-connected groups that view rigorous export controls as an impediment to their own (often parochial and self-serving) goals.

Transparency in arms export regimes is achieved through the publication and broad dissemination of laws, policies, and regulations, and any changes to them; and national reports on implementation of multilateral agreements such as the UN *Programme of Action* and other regional instruments. Internal and external monitoring of the production and dissemination of these documents and reports helps to ensure that they are timely and informative.

Transparency in investigations of export control violations

Intergovernmental exchanges of information on diversions and other export violations increase awareness among intelligence and law enforcement agencies of arms traffickers and their methods and facilitate intergovernmental action against such transnational trafficking networks. Similarly, the public dissemination of non-sensitive information about diversions and other export control violations facilitates research into the illicit trade and highlights best practices and shortcomings in national export control procedures. Few countries regularly report on export control violations. One noteworthy exception is the US State Department, which compiles an annual report on its Blue Lantern end-use monitoring programme. The report provides a detailed statistical overview of 'unfavorable' determinations (e.g. end-use checks that reveal suspicious or unauthorized activity, including diversion) by geographical region, commodity category, and type of unfavorable determination. It also includes case studies and, in recent years, a 'lessons learned' section (USDoS, 2007).

In sum, transparency is crucial to investigating and preventing the diversion of weapons. Detailed information about authorized arms transfers, the export control regimes through which these transfers are approved, and the failures of these systems (i.e. cases of diversion) play an imperative role in furthering the transparency of the arms trade. However, as demonstrated below, transparency continues to be an area that can benefit from improvement.

SMALL ARMS TRADE TRANSPARENCY BAROMETER

The Small Arms Trade Transparency Barometer is a tool to assess the transparency in reporting by countries on exports of small arms, light weapons, and ammunition. It is based on governments' customs submissions to UN Comtrade[31] and annual national arms export reports.[32] Points are awarded for timeliness, accessibility, clarity, comprehensiveness, and deliveries, as well as licences granted and refused.

The scoring system remains the same as for the 2007 Barometer.[33] The 2008 Barometer includes transparency scores for all major exporters in 2001–05 (governments are given two years to report customs data to UN Comtrade). The maximum score is 25 points. Details of the scoring system are provided in the footnotes following Table 4.3. In keeping with previous practice, the UN Comtrade data includes 2005 exports,[34] and the national report data is based on 2006 exports.[35] Only national arms export reports published within the last 30 months are included.[37] As a result,

Table 4.3   Small Arms Trade Transparency Barometer 2008, covering major exporters*

	TOTAL (25 max.)	Export report** (year covered)	UN Comtrade**	Timeliness (1.5 max.)	Access (2 max.)	Clarity (5 max.)	Comprehensiveness (6.5 max.)	Deliveries (4 max.)	Licences granted (4 max.)	Licences refused (2 max.)
United States[1]	21	X (06)	X	1.5	2	4	5.5	4	4	0
Italy	20	X (06)	X	1.5	1.5	5	6.5	3.5	2	0
Switzerland[2]	19.5	X (06)	X	1.5	2	3.5	4.5	4	4	0
France	18.5	X (06)	X	1	2	4	5.5	4	2	0
Slovakia	18.5	X (06)	X	1	1.5	2.5	5.5	4	4	0
United Kingdom	18.5	X (06)	X	1	2	4	5.5	4	2	0
Finland	17.5	X (06)	X	1.5	2	3.5	5	3.5	2	0
Bosnia and Herzegovina	17	X (06)	X	1.5	2	2.5	3.5	3.5	2	2
Germany[3]	17	X (06)	X	1	1.5	4	5.5	3	2	0
Norway	17	X (06)	X	1.5	1.5	3.5	6.5	4	0	0
Serbia[4]	16	X (05–06)	X	1	2	4	5.5	3.5	0	0
Sweden	16	X (06)	X	1.5	2	4	5.5	3	0	0
Netherlands	15	X (06)	X	1	2	2.5	5	3.5	1	0
Spain[5]	15	X (06)	X	1	2	3	5.5	3	0.5	0
Australia[6]	14.5	X (02–04)	X	0.5	2	2.5	5.5	4	0	0
Canada[6]	14.5	X (03–05)	X	0.5	2	2.5	5.5	4	0	0
Czech Republic[4]	14.25	X (06)	X	1	2	3.25	5.5	2.5	0	0

Country	Score									
Austria[7]	12.5	X (06)	X	1	1.5	2.5	4.5	3	0	0
Croatia	12	-	X	0	1	2.5	4.5	4	0	0
Portugal[6]	11.25	X (05)	X	0.5	1.5	2.5	3.75	3	0	0
Brazil	11	-	X	0	1	2.5	4	3.5	0	0
Mexico	11	-	X	0	1	2.5	4	3.5	0	0
South Korea	11	-	X	0	1	2.5	3.5	4	0	0
Poland	10.5	-	X	0	1	2.5	3.5	3.5	0	0
Saudi Arabia	10.5	-	X	0	1	2.5	4	3	0	0
Turkey	10.25	-	X	0	1	2.5	3.75	3	0	0
Belgium[8]	9.5	-	X	0	1	2	3.5	3	0	0
Japan	9.5	-	X	0	1	2	3	3.5	0	0
Thailand	9.25	-	X	0	1	2.5	2.75	3	0	0
Bulgaria	9	X (06)	-	1	1.5	2	1	2	1.5	0
China	9	-	X	0	1	2	3	3	0	0
Pakistan	9	-	X	0	1	2.5	2.5	3	0	0
Israel	8.5	-	X	0	1	2	2.5	3	0	0
Romania[6]	8.5	X (05)	-	0.5	2	2	0	2	2	0
Russian Fed.	8.5	-	X	0	1	2	1.5	4	0	0
Ukraine	8.5	X (06)	-	1	1.5	3	1	2	0	0
Singapore	7	-	X	0	1	1.5	1.5	3	0	0
South Africa[6]	4.5	X (03-04)	-	0.5	2	1	1	0	1	0
Iran	0	-	-	0	0	0	0	0	0	0
North Korea	0	-	-	0	0	0	0	0	0	0

* Major exporters are those countries that export at least USD 10 million worth of small arms, light weapons, their ammunition, and associated components annually, according to UN Comtrade data. The 2008 Barometer includes all countries that were among the major exporters at least once in their reporting covering the years 2001-05. For major exporters in 2005, see Annexe 4.1 to the present chapter at <http://www.smallarmssurvey.org/files/sas/publications/yearb2008.html>; for those in 2004, see Annexe 3, Table 3.1 of Small Arms Survey (2007, ch. 3) at <http://www.smallarmssurvey.org/files/sas/publications/yearb2007.html>; for those in 2003, see Small Arms Survey (2006, pp. 68-73); for those in 2002, see Small Arms Survey (2005, pp. 102-5); and for those in 2001, see Small Arms Survey (2004, pp. 103-6).

** X indicates that a report was issued.

Scoring system

The scoring system for the 2008 Barometer has not changed from the 2007 Barometer and is thus comparable to it. The following scoring system is used to provide accurate, measurable, and consistent thresholds for each category in the Barometer. This year, we further delineate the scoring thresholds below and within the categories.

(a) Timeliness (1.5 points total; score based on national arms export reports data only): A report has been published within the last 24 months (up to 31 December 2007) (0.5 points); information is available in a timely fashion (alternatively: 1 point if within 6 months of the end of the year in question or 0.5 if within a year).

(b) Access (2 points total): Information is: available on the Internet through UN Comtrade or national export reports (1 point); available in a UN language (0.5 points); free of charge (0.5 points).

(c) Clarity (5 points total): The reporting includes source information (1 point); small arms and light weapons distinguishable from other types of weapons (1 point); small arms and light weapons ammunition distinguishable from other types of ammunition (1 point); detailed weapons description included (1 point); reporting includes information on types of end users (military, police, other security forces, civilians, civilian retailers) (1 point).

(d) Comprehensiveness (6.5 points total): The reporting covers: government-sourced as well as industry-sourced transactions (1 point); civilian and military small arms and light weapons (1.5 points); information on re-exports (1 point); information on small arms and light weapons parts (1 point); information on small arms and light weapons ammunition (1 point); summaries of export laws and regulations and international commitments (1 point).

UN Comtrade scoring on Comprehensiveness categories is as follows:

Civilian/military (six sub-categories)

One sub-category (9301, military weapons) is mixed, containing both small arms and larger conventional weapons. It was replaced by four new categories in the newest revision of the UN Comtrade Harmonized System (HS 2002), facilitating differentiation between small arms and light weapons and other weapons. Some countries still use HS 1996; therefore, the calculations on which this table is based include data from HS 2002, HS 1996, and HS 1992 to account for all transfers of military small arms and light weapons reported to UN Comtrade.

HS 1996 data (military weapons, mixed category 9301): score 0.25

Civilian sporting and hunting weapons: score 0.5

Military weapons: score 0.5

Civilian or military weapons and revolvers and pistols (civilian and military mixed category): score 0.75

Mixture of civilian and military categories: score 1

Five or more categories: score 1.5

Ammunition (two sub-categories)

Shotgun cartridges or small arms ammunition: score 0.5

Both categories: score 1

Components (three sub-categories)

One category: score 0.5

Two out of the three, or all categories: score 1

(e) Information on deliveries (4 points total): Data disaggregated by weapons type (value of weapons shipped [1 point], quantity of weapons shipped [1 point]); and by country and weapons type (value of weapons shipped [1 point], quantity of weapons shipped [1 point]). Reporting to non-NATO countries only (0.5 points). Exports to Organization for Security and Co-operation in Europe (OSCE) countries only (0.25 points).

UN Comtrade scoring on Deliveries categories is as follows:

Deliveries (four sub-categories)

Sporting and hunting weapons: score 0.5

Military weapons: score 0.5

Partial data on mixed civilian and military weapons: score 0.75

All categories: score 1

(f) Information on licences granted (4 points total): Data disaggregated by weapons type (value of weapons licensed [1 point], quantity of weapons licensed [1 point]); and by country and weapons type (value of weapons licensed [1 point], quantity of weapons licensed [1 point]). Reporting to non-NATO countries only (0.5 points). Exports to OSCE countries only (0.25 points).

(g) Information on licences refused (2 points total): Data disaggregated by weapons type (value of licence refused [0.5 points], quantity of weapons under refused licence [0.5 points]); and by country and weapons type (value of licence refused [0.5 points], quantity of weapons under refused licence [0.5 points]).

Explanatory notes

Note A: The Barometer is based on each country's most recent arms exports that were publicly available as of 31 December 2007 and/or on 2005 customs data from UN Comtrade.

Note B: Under (d), (e), and (f), no points are granted for total number of shipments or number of licences granted or denied, as such figures give little information about the magnitude of the trade. The data is disaggregated by weapons type if the share of small arms and light weapons in the country's total arms trade is delineated (x per cent of the total value of the arms exports consisted of small arms and light weapons; x number of small arms and light weapons were exported in total). The data is disaggregated both by country and by weapons type if there is information on the types of weapons that are transferred to individual recipient states (x number or x USD worth of small arms was delivered to country y).

Note C: Under (d), (e), and (f), 'weapons type' means broader weapons categories (i.e. 'small arms' as opposed to 'armoured vehicles' or 'air-to-air missiles'), not specific weapons descriptions ('assault rifles' as opposed to 'hunting rifles').

Note D: The fact that the Barometer is based on two sources—customs data (as reported to UN Comtrade) and national arms export reports—works to the advantage of states that publish data in both forms, since what they do not provide in one form of reporting they might provide in the other. Points achieved from each of the two sources are added up. However, points are obviously not counted twice (e.g. if a country provides both customs data and export reports in a UN language, it gets 1 point for this under Access, not more).

Note E: The Barometer does not include country reports to other national, regional, and international mechanisms. However, it should be noted that the following countries report nationally on small arms and light weapons on a monthly or quarterly basis: the Netherlands (monthly), Sweden (monthly), and the United Kingdom (quarterly).[36]

Note F: In some cases, countries do not export all category types of small arms and light weapons and thus only report on those categories relevant to them. In other cases, countries export more category types than they actually report. The Barometer is unable to distinguish between these cases.

Country-specific notes

[1] US reports are divided into several documents, which pose complications for scoring in a consistent manner. For the purposes of the Barometer, the US annual report refers to the State Department report pursuant to section 655.

[2] Switzerland published additional documentation on existing obligations and regulations in January 2008. This was not included in the current Barometer, as the information does not form part of its 2007 national report for 2006 exports, but is contained elsewhere on its Web site.

[3] Germany did not publish detailed information on the quantity and value of small arms exports to NATO and NATO-equivalent countries; rather, it provides this information for exports to 'third countries'. Therefore, Germany received partial points in the licences granted category.

[4] The Czech Republic and Serbia provided data in an aggregated format. Points on clarity and deliveries were not awarded for categories in which thresholds on specific details are required for scoring.

[5] Spain makes public its report on small arms and light weapons exports to the OSCE as an annexe to its arms export report. The report contains information both on licences granted (volumes by country and weapons type) and on actual deliveries (also volumes by country and weapons type). It covers only the OSCE states and, hence, a very limited number of transactions. Spain is therefore granted only part of the points on licences and deliveries. Other states make their OSCE reports public, but separately from the arms export reports. These are therefore not taken into account in the Barometer.

[6] Australia, Canada, Portugal, Romania, and South Africa published national arms export reports in 2007 that pertained to the years 2003–05 (Canada); 2005 (Portugal and Romania); and 2002–04 (Australia and South Africa).

[7] Austria's 2006 national arms export report does not contain information on its small arms exports (Austria, 2007).

[8] Belgium has not published any national arms export report since 2002, because export control was regionalized into Brussels, Flanders, and Wallonia in September 2003. Each of these produces a regional report. The score for Belgium is therefore based on customs data submissions only.

Sources

Australia (2006); Austria (2007); Bosnia and Herzegovina (2007); Bulgaria (2007); Canada (2007); Czech Republic (2007); Denmark (2007); Finland (2007); France (2007); Germany (2007); Italy (2007); Netherlands (2007); NISAT (2008); Norway (2007); Portugal (2007); Romania (2007); Serbia (2007); Slovakia (2007); South Africa (2007); Spain (2007); Sweden (2007); Switzerland (2007); Ukraine (2007); UK (2007); USDoS and USDoD (2007); UN Comtrade (2007; 2008)

the transparency of major exporting countries that have not published an annual export report in this timeframe is assessed only on the basis of their UN Comtrade reports. This is the case even if these countries have issued previous national arms export reports.

As its name indicates, the Barometer is designed to measure—and to promote—*transparency*. It does not pretend to address the *veracity* of the data provided. It is also a useful tool for highlighting trends.

The 2008 Barometer includes 40 countries' reporting on their small arms exports. This is an increase of three states from last year's account. According to UN Comtrade data, in 2005 Poland, Slovakia, and Ukraine all exported

USD 10 million or more of small arms and thus merited inclusion in our analysis.[38] Not only did Slovakia join the ranks of major exporters, but the country ranked as one of the most transparent countries: due to a tie between three of the final scores, there are six countries that fall within this category. The others included the United States—which has held the top spot for a fifth consecutive year—Italy, Switzerland, France, and the United Kingdom. Bosnia and Herzegovina broke into the 'Top 10', and, further, it is the only country to report on the value and quantity of licence refusals in a way that is consistent with the Barometer scoring criteria.[39] Bulgaria and South Africa, which received scores of zero last year, were awarded 9 and 4.5 points, respectively. North Korea retained its 'perfect' record of not reporting, while Iran joined North Korea as the only other country to receive a score of zero.[40]

Trends in reporting show some improvements this year. For example, Serbia produced its first-ever national report, and Romania has adapted its reporting structure to include more information. There is increased publishing of data by new and candidate EU member states as they officially align themselves with *EU Code of Conduct* criteria and practices on exports and reporting.[41] Canada, the Czech Republic, Slovakia, and South Africa produced annual reports after a gap of at least one year or more.[42] South Africa is the only country on the African continent to produce a national report currently. The Barometer continues to offer a standard for exporters and to provide a record of these evolutions in reporting transparency.

ents face lenges in shing and transfer systems.

PROSPECTS FOR PREVENTING DIVERSION

While data on implementation of the measures described above is incomplete, recent studies suggest that the transfer controls of most countries are insufficient to prevent, deter, and detect diversion. A comprehensive study of implementation of the UN *Programme of Action* by the Biting the Bullet project found evidence of serious shortcomings in key national transfers controls and other laws, procedures, and practices critical to preventing diversion. Of the 180 countries assessed by Biting the Bullet, only 111 have procedures and laws controlling the export of small arms and light weapons (Bourne et al., 2006). Considering that most states, even those that do not manufacture small arms, are potential exporters of surplus weapons, this is worrying. Furthermore, only a small percentage of these countries appear to have even basic elements of an effective transfer control system. Only 58 countries reportedly require authenticated end-user certificates; only 37 have enacted specific controls on brokers; and only 30, as importers, notify the exporter in advance of retransfer (and fewer still, as exporters, routinely require retransfer notification from recipients) (Bourne et al., 2006; Greene and Kirkham, 2007). Of particular importance to preventing diversion are the study's findings on pre-licence risk assessments and post-delivery checks. Only about 40 states claim that their export controls include a risk assessment of diversion, and 'few states report to use [sic] delivery and post-delivery checks' (Bourne et al. 2006).

Governments face many challenges in establishing and maintaining transfer control systems that are sufficiently robust to prevent diversion. As Greene and Kirkham point out, the task of assessing the risk of diversion is often, in practice, complex, time-consuming, and resource-intensive. The authenticity and legitimacy of all documentation must be verified, shipping routes and agents must be individually reviewed, and the willingness and capacity of the end user to safeguard and use the imported items as intended must be evaluated (Greene and Kirkham, 2007). As UN investigators have repeatedly documented, many states lack the resources and infrastructure to control their own borders and airspace, let alone possess the intelligence assets, integrated databases, and network of embassies to screen exports adequately before they are shipped and monitor their use and whereabouts after they are delivered.[43] For major exporters, this problem is compounded by the sheer volume of exports. In 2006 the US State Department processed nearly 65,000 licence requests for munitions,[44] including more than 7,400 for firearms (USGAO, 2007b).

Nonetheless, there are plenty of steps that all states can take to mitigate the risks and consequences of diversion. Some steps can be applied across the board with minimal additional cost, while budget and infrastructure constraints would limit the application of more resource-intensive steps to high-risk cases. The 2001 diversion of Nicaraguan assault rifles is just one of several recent examples of schemes that could have been foiled through basic pre-licence checks, many of which require little more than Internet access and a few telephone calls. Other control measures are more costly and difficult to implement, but even the most resource-intensive are feasible for most major producers and exporters.

An analysis of data on the US export control system sheds some light on the cost of implementing the control measures identified above, at least for governments with established export control systems and large overseas consular networks.[45] Further research, particularly with regard to governments with limited resources and other constraints, is needed to determine more precisely the costs of implementing these measures globally.

According to US officials, export requests for firearms and ammunition account for more than 11 per cent of commercial arms export licences processed by the State Department in 2007.[46] The Directorate of Defense Trade Controls (DDTC)—the office that regulates the US arms trade and issues licences for commercial arms exports—has five people solely dedicated to reviewing firearms licences, a process that routinely includes most of the pre-shipment control measures identified above (e.g. confirming the authenticity of documentation, checking parties to the transfer against watch lists, reviewing the request for warning flags, etc.).[47] In total, reviewing and processing the 9,000 small arms and ammunition licences received by DDTC in the 2007 calendar year cost approximately USD 3 million dollars, or an average of USD 330 per licence. This figure includes IT and maintenance of the IT infrastructure, DDTC personnel costs, and embassy personnel time (for Blue Lantern checks).[48]

All: Colom
2005. © U

The Blue L
and Indum
observe ar
inspection
packaging

An Indumi
inspects m

Newly mar
and sorte
ammunitio

Indumil m
the Blue L
about mar
and plant

Also illuminating is data on the US military's post-shipment end-use monitoring of Stinger MANPADS.[49] As explained in Chapter 5, Box 5.3 (END-USER CERTIFICATION), the US Defense Department subjects certain exported weaponry to particularly rigorous, or 'enhanced', end-use monitoring. In the case of Stinger missiles, this monitoring includes annual on-site physical inventories of nearly all exported missiles. The time and expense associated with such monitoring varies according to recipient country. In some countries, a single Defense Department official can inventory all the Stingers in the host government's arsenals in less than a week and with minimal travel, while inventorying large, dispersed national inventories of missiles requires extensive staffing and travel. In one extreme case in which the country's Stinger missiles are stored in 80 different locations, the Defense Department has assigned a full-time major to do nothing but inventory missiles year-round. This disparity is reflected in data on Stinger end-use monitoring compiled by the various combatant commands. According to recent data from the Defense Department, staff time and travel expenses associated with end-use monitoring for Stinger missiles range from 6 hours and USD 2,600 at the low end to 1,916 hours and USD 71,000 at the high end.[50]

Table 4.4 ranks 11 key transfer controls in terms of their approximate cost and difficulty of implementation.[51]

Figure 4.1 **Transfer controls flowchart**

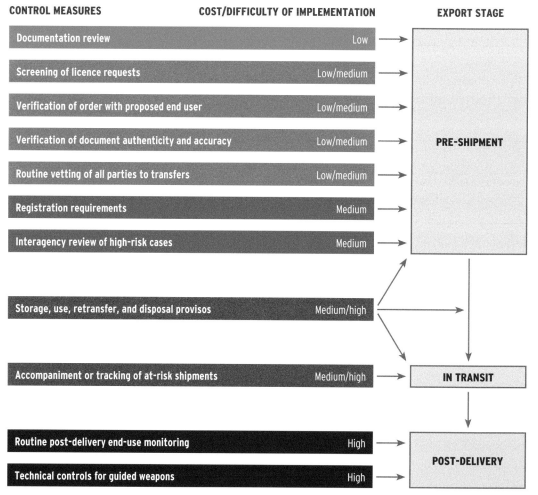

Table 4.4 Transfer controls in terms of cost and difficulty of implementation

Control measures	Export stage	Cost/difficulty of implementation
Collation and review of all documentation by a single agency	Pre-shipment	Low
Screening of licence requests against lists of warning flags	Pre-shipment	Low/medium[1]
Verification of order with proposed end user	Pre-shipment	Low/medium[1]
Verification of authenticity and accuracy of key documents, including end-user certificates	Pre-shipment	Low/medium[1]
Routine vetting of all parties to transfers against watch lists	Pre-shipment	Low/medium
Registration requirements for exporters, brokers, and other key parties	Pre-shipment	Medium[2]
Interagency review of high-risk cases	Pre-shipment	Medium
Routine inclusion and enforcement of storage, use, retransfer, and disposal provisos	Multi-stage	Medium/high[3]
Physical accompaniment or remote tracking of at-risk shipments	In transit	Medium/high[4]
Routine on-site post-delivery end-use monitoring	Post-delivery	High
Technical controls for guided weapons	Pre-delivery	High[5]

Notes:

Low: requires few resources and organizational changes.

Medium: may require some staffing and infrastructure development (e.g. database construction and management) and some organizational and procedural changes (e.g. the promulgation and implementation of new regulations and procedures).

High: involves significant staffing, infrastructure (e.g. embassies), investment in key hardware or technologies (e.g. GPS units, technical controls), and/or funding. May also have diplomatic or defence-industrial implications.

[1] The cost and difficulty of performing these checks varies depending on the licence request, i.e. simple requests for non-sensitive items from familiar applicants require fewer resources to process than requests for sensitive items from unfamiliar applicants. The volume of licence requests and complexity of the exports also have an effect.

[2] In the case of the United States, activities associated with the registration of the 5,200 registered US defence manufacturers and exporters require six full-time staff (interview with US government official, February 2008). Data on the percentage of these entities involved in the manufacture or sale of firearms is not readily available.

[3] The cost and difficulty of storage, use, retransfer, and disposal provisos varies depending on the type of proviso and the procedures adopted to monitor and enforce these provisos. For example, provisos that require 100 per cent annual on-site physical inventories of imported weapons by the exporting government are more difficult and costly to implement than retransfer notification requirements.

[4] The cost and difficulty of in-transit control measures varies from extremely resource-intensive to minimal. Deliveries made through the Department of Defense's Special Assignment Airlift Mission, for example, can cost USD 500,000 or more, while the costs of simple, informal delivery verification measures (e.g. a phone call to the intended recipient confirming that they received the items) are minimal. More research is needed to determine the costs for the full range of in-transit control measures and the optimal combination of such measures for shipments of varying levels of sensitivity.

[5] Robert Sherman, former director of the US Arms Control and Disarmament Agency's Advanced Projects Office, estimates that developing use control devices for Stinger missiles in the 1990s would have cost less than a million dollars, and that the costs of installing the devices at the time of manufacture would have been 'immeasurably small'. Verifying this estimate is difficult, however, as little has been written on technical controls for light weapons. Also factored into the cost/difficulty ranking is the fact that technical controls may have implications for foreign arms sales, especially if potential importers believe that the device could negatively affect the operation of the weapon or provide the exporter with a means of preventing the use of the weapon by the importer (Schroeder, 2006, p. 97).

CONCLUSION

As illustrated by the cases in Table 4.1 and throughout the chapter, diversion occurs at every stage in the arms transfer chain and ranges in size from multi-ton shipments of fully assembled weapons and ammunition to small quantities of component parts. The recipients of the diverted weapons also vary significantly, as do the exporting states that fall victim to diversion schemes. The sophistication and complexity of the schemes also vary from case to case. Some are simple, crude, and relatively easy to spot, while others are remarkably complex and difficult to detect. The bait-and-switch scheme organized by Pecos, for example, required precise timing and coordination by participants operating in at least four countries on three continents. Yet many of the schemes profiled above also had much in common, including the use of falsified or forged documentation, front companies established in countries known for lax oversight, and the exploitation of weak or poorly executed transfer controls.

These cases also reveal that some diversions are clearly more difficult to prevent than others. Schemes in which the ostensible government end user has no knowledge of (or involvement in) the transfer are often the easiest to foil. Even routine pre-licence checks consisting of a few phone calls to the purported recipient are likely to uncover these attempts. Diversions that occur after importation or that involve high-level government officials from the recipient state are notably more difficult to prevent. In these cases, post-delivery end-use checks may be necessary. Arms exported via unconventional transfer programmes are also more vulnerable to diversion, especially when the programmes lack transparency, oversight, and clearly defined security and accountability requirements. Weapons that are transferred covertly to non-state actors are often the most vulnerable to diversion, as illustrated by the CIA's largely futile attempt to monitor and control the Stinger missiles distributed to Afghan rebels.

While the difficulty of detecting and thwarting diversion attempts varied significantly, in most of the cases discussed in this chapter there were warning signs and contextual red flags that portended the diversion. In at least four of the cases in Table 4.1, one or more parties to the transfer had criminal or otherwise suspect histories. In two other cases, the requested weapons appeared to be excessive or incompatible with the recipient's existing inventory, and in at least one other case, the documentation submitted as part of the sale was filled with irregularities. Few of these warning signs were conclusive proof of diversion, but all of them were cause for greater scrutiny and tighter controls.

To their credit, several governments recognized these signs and disrupted the diversion schemes, preventing some or all of the targeted weapons from being diverted. In other cases, however, the exporting government's failure to conduct even the most basic of pre-licence screening or post-delivery checks resulted in the delivery of thousands of weapons to terrorists and rogue regimes. A lack of data on national export control practices precludes even a rough estimate of how many states would have spotted the diversions had their arsenals been targeted, but recent studies suggest that few governments routinely conduct even basic pre-licence checks, let alone the extensive end-use monitoring necessary to ensure that exported weapons are not misused or retransferred. Until more states put in place the essential components of an effective transfer control system, diverted weapons will continue to find their way to terrorists, criminals, and rogue regimes worldwide. ▰

LIST OF ABBREVIATIONS

ATPIS	Arms Transfer Profiling Indicator System	NISAT	Norwegian Initiative on Small Arms Transfers
CIA	Central Intelligence Agency	OAS	Organization of American States
DDTC	Directorate of Defense Trade Controls	OSCE	Organization for Security and Co-operation in Europe
EU	European Union		
FARC	Revolutionary Armed Forces of Colombia (Fuerzas Armadas Revolucionarias de Colombia)	SEESAC	South Eastern and Eastern Europe Clearinghouse for the Control of Small Arms and Light Weapons

MANPADS	Man-portable air defence system(s)	UAE	United Arab Emirates
MNSTC–I	Multi-National Security Transition Command–Iraq	USD	United States dollar
		USGAO	US Government Accountability Office

ENDNOTES

1 China and the Russian Federation report only limited, if any, customs information on their small arms and light weapons exports. In order to reflect properly these two countries' importance in the small arms trade, the Small Arms Survey does not limit itself to analysing UN Comtrade data for the period under review. See, for example, Small Arms Survey (2004, ch. 4, Annexe 4.1) and Pyadushkin (2006).

2 Cyprus, after ranking among the top major importers for the last four consecutive years (Small Arms Survey, 2004, p. 109; 2005, p. 107; 2006, p. 75; 2007, pp. 73–115) has decreased its total imports from USD 448 million (Small Arms Survey, 2004, p. 109) to USD 20 million this year.

3 France's imports from 2005 UN Comtrade data reflected USD 33 million worth of military firearms exported by Côte d'Ivoire to France. We believe that this 'exported' material was owned and in use by French peacekeeping troops during the period in question and transferred from their mission back to France or to one of the French peacekeeping depots on the continent. For this reason, Côte d'Ivoire was not included in the major exporter list (over USD 10 million).

4 Data, estimates, and sources regarding top and major exporters and importers are provided in the Annexe to the present chapter at <http://www.smallarmssurvey.org/files/sas/publications/yearb2008.html>. The methodology follows that used in both the 2006 and 2007 *Small Arms Surveys*. For detailed explanations of the methodology used to deal with the UN Comtrade data and national reports, see Small Arms Survey (2005, pp. 97–102), Glatz (2006, p. 72), and Marsh (2005).

5 The definition employed in the *User's Guide to the European Union Code of Conduct on Arms Exports* similarly includes 'function (end-use)' (EU Council, 2007, sec. 3.7.3).

6 Human Rights Watch identifies the firearms as AK-47 rifles (Human Rights Watch, 2004, p. 10).

7 While is not clear who signed the contract on behalf of Vichi, the signer apparently did not consult the Moldovan government, which claimed to know nothing of the flights to Africa until informed of them by UN investigators.

8 As with most illicit activity, data on arms transfer diversions is incomplete. Credible, publicly available accounts of illicit arms transfers are few in number and focus primarily on the areas of the world actively monitored and publicly reported on by UN monitoring groups (the mandates of which are usually limited to a handful of countries and non-state actors) and a handful of NGOs and journalists. Of these accounts, only a small percentage are detailed enough to determine if the transfer conforms to the above definition of diversion. Fewer still provide enough information to compare and evaluate all possible risk factors.

9 According to UN investigators, the end-user certificate used for the shipment was the original, was signed by the president of Côte d'Ivoire himself, and was authenticated by the Ivorian ambassador to Moscow (UNSC, 2001).

10 Eligibility criteria that limit exports to governments with good stockpile security and non-proliferation records are particularly relevant in these cases.

11 According to Sarkis Soghanalian, the broker who arranged the deal, the plane was modified specifically for the diversion. According to a report in the *Los Angeles Times*, 'the belly was refitted so that it could be depressurized at high altitude. Rollers were installed so that pallets could simply slide out through the tail cargo door' (Rempel and Rotella, 2000).

12 The incompatibility between traditional transfer controls and arms transfers to non-state actors was highlighted by US Senator Dennis Deconcini's attempt to impose on the mujahideen the same rigorous stockpile security requirements applied to typical Stinger sales. In 1986 Deconcini introduced a bill that would have required the mujahideen to adhere to the same rigorous security standards that apply to government recipients of Stinger missiles: separate storage of missiles and launchers, storage facilities that feature reinforced concrete magazines, 'class five steel doors', intruder detection systems, and restrictions that limit access to the missiles to personnel with 'the proper security clearances'—requirements that could not possibly be met by a ragtag militia fighting a guerilla war in an underdeveloped, occupied country. The bill also required an annual physical inventory of all missiles by US personnel, despite the prohibition on trips to Afghanistan by US government officials because of the need to maintain 'plausible deniability' of US involvement in the arming of the mujahideen. The bill was soundly defeated, but it did underscore the difficulty of safeguarding the missiles and their extreme vulnerability to diversion (Schroeder et al., 2006, pp. 81–83).

13 A November 2007 audit by the Defense Department's own inspector general also found significant discrepancies in weapons accountability in equipment contracts, including contracts for small arms and light weapons. In two particular contracts reviewed in the course of the audit, the

inspector general found that 'MNSTC–I [Multi-National Security Transition Command–Iraq] could not prove that ISF [Iraqi security forces] received 12,712 of the 13,508 weapons procured', which consisted of firearms, assault rifles, rocket-propelled grenades, and machine guns (USDoD, 2007a, p. 9). Additionally, the Defense Department audit revealed that MNSTC–I had only a single auditor and 16 comptrollers to oversee its USD 5.5 billion budget for the 2007 financial year (USDoD, 2007a, p. iii).

14   There is some debate over whether the 'legitimate and acting Peruvian generals' identified by the Jordanians as their contacts in this transfer were indeed 'legitimate' or 'acting'. When the story of the diversion broke in August 2000, President Fujimori claimed that one of Jordan's principal Peruvian contacts on the deal—Lucio Olivera—did not exist, i.e. there was no Peruvian army general by that name. Soghanalian also reportedly acknowledged that the individuals were former soldiers representing themselves as active-duty officers (AFP, 2000; *Los Angeles Times,* 2000).

15   In 1981, Soghanalian was indicted on three counts of fraud associated with the sale of .50 calibre machine guns to Mauritania and sentenced to five years' probation (NYT, 1985). Ten years later, he was sentenced to six years in prison for conspiring to sell helicopters and missiles to Iraq (Austin, 2001).

16   According to *Jane's Infantry Weapons,* the Ivorian military had four types of rifles in its inventory at the time of the transfer: the 5.56 mm SIG 540, 7.5 mm MAS 49/56, 7.62 mm G3, and 7.62 mm FN 30-11, none of which is chambered for the 7.62 x 39 mm Ukrainian ammunition. The fact that the Ivorian military received a small portion of the ammunition may suggest that it had Warsaw Pact firearms as well, but most of the arms appear to have been incompatible with the large quantity of imported ammunition (Gander and Cutshaw, 2000; UNSC, 2001).

17   According to the International Institute for Strategic Studies, Côte d'Ivoire's armed forces consisted of an army of 6,800, a navy of 900, an air force of 700, and 12,000 reserves at the time of the diversion. While not necessarily out of line with the annual ammunition needs of a military that size, it appears excessive given the large number of NATO-calibre weapons in the military's inventory at the time (IISS, 2000).

18   Trafalgar Maritime, Inc. appears to have been established specifically and solely for the purpose of diverting the assault rifles to the Colombian paramilitaries. It was established shortly before the diversion under a well-known open registry, had only one ship to its name, and was dissolved several months after the diversion (OAS, 2003).

19   Proposals for technical controls for MANPADS date back at least to the mid-1980s. One such proposal calls for the development of a chip-level device for the missile's guidance system that would require the entry of an electronic code in order for the missile to function properly. The device, which is reportedly similar to anti-theft technology used in car radios, would allow legitimate end users to enable the missile for any period of time—days, weeks, or months—but after the code expires, the missile would be inoperable until the code is re-entered. If widely adopted, such devices (often referred to as controllable enablers) would reduce the lifespan of diverted missiles for unauthorized users from many years to a few months or less. To date, however, there is no publicly available evidence that any MANPADS producer has developed controllable enablers or similar technology (Sherman, 2003; Schroeder et al., 2006, pp. 96–98).

20   Registration requirements themselves rarely shut down the operations of arms traffickers, who simply shift their operations to countries with less rigorous controls. When Slovakia tightened its laws on arms traffickers, the owner of Joy Slovakia simply relocated his operations to Guinea, where his new company, Pecos, allegedly organized the diversion of Slovakian rifles from Uganda to Liberia (UNSC, 2001).

21   Interviews with US government officials, September and October 2007.

22   Interviews with US government officials, 26 September and 3 October 2007.

23   Interviews with US government officials, 26 September and 3 October 2007.

24   Training programmes are not only useful for government officials. Private sector parties to arms transfers—shippers, brokers, aircraft crew members, airport employees, etc.—are often privy to telltale signs of diversion that licensing officers and other government officials are not. Teaching these individuals to recognize these signs and to alert the proper authorities when they encounter them therefore make up a critical component of national and international efforts to prevent diversions.

25   Thirty governments have reported that they notify the exporting country in advance of retransferring small arms and light weapons (Greene and Kirkham, 2007).

26   See OSCE (2003, pp. 9–10).

27   Interview with Comtech spokesperson John Pylant, January 2008.

28   Interview with US Army official, January 2008.

29   The Biting the Bullet project concluded that, as of 2006, at least 119 countries had criminalized the illicit trade in small arms and light weapons (Bourne et al., 2006, p. 178).

30   A difficult dilemma associated with transparency is that transparent systems tend to receive more scrutiny and negative attention than less transparent ones. Countries with more transparent exports and export controls are scrutinized (and criticized) much more frequently by the media and civil society than other major arms exporters, even though these countries often exercise more restraint in their arms sales and monitor the delivery and end use of their weapons more closely. Examples include the United States, the United Kingdom, France, and Norway.

31   For more information, see UN Comtrade (2007).

32   The Barometer includes countries' national export reports that have been published in the public domain. It does not include countries' reporting to other mechanisms, such as the EU Council, the Wassenaar Arrangement, or the UN Register of Conventional Arms. EU member states are required to report their arms exports in accordance with Operative Provision 8 of the *EU Code of Conduct on Arms Exports*. The *EU Code of Conduct* is a regional mechanism, and non-EU countries would be at a disadvantage if data from its reports were included in the Barometer. The same is true for the Wassenaar Arrangement and the Organization for Security and Co-operation in Europe. The UN Register to date is optional for countries to report on small arms and light weapons since 2003 (for further information, see <http://disarmament.un.org/cab/register.html>).

33   The internal notes used for awarding partial points (0.25 and 0.75) were not published in previous years, but are now found in the explanatory notes at the end of the Barometer.

34   The most recent and complete UN Comtrade data available is for 2005.

35   Some countries did not produce a 2007 report with their 2006 export data. Therefore, the most recent published export reports available were used to score.

36   For further information on monthly reports, see <http://www.sipri.org>, and for UK quarterly reports, <http://www.smallarmssurvey.org>.

37   The cut-off dates for the Barometer are 31 December 2007 for national arms export reports and 15 January 2008 for UN Comtrade data.

38   For the situation regarding Côte d'Ivoire's exports, see endnote 3.

39   Several countries provide some information on licence refusals; however, it is not in accordance with our Barometer scoring criteria and thus does not score points in this category.

40   Iran received 10.5 points in the 2007 Barometer. As of the 15 January 2008 UN Comtrade cut-off date, Iran had not reported its 2005 data.

41   For further information on the *EU Code of Conduct* and criteria, see <http://www.smallarmssurvey.org/files/portal/issueareas/measures/Measur_pdf/r_%20measur_pdf/European%20Union/EUCodeofConduct%20080698.pdf>.

42   Major exporters that produced a national report are Austria, Bosnia and Herzegovina, Bulgaria, Canada, the Czech Republic, Finland, France, Germany, Italy, the Netherlands, Norway, Portugal, Romania, Serbia, Slovakia, South Africa, Spain, Sweden, Switzerland, Ukraine, the United Kingdom, and the United States. Canada and South Africa published national arms export reports in 2007 that pertained to the years 2003–05 (Canada) and 2002–04 (South Africa). Slovakia produced two reports in 2007 that pertained to transfers in 2005 and 2006, respectively. The Czech Republic published a report in 2005 and in 2007.

43   Even governments with established and comparatively well-funded export control programmes often struggle to balance the often-conflicting need for robust screening and expeditious processing of requests. The US Directorate of Defense Trade Controls, for example, has struggled to meet target times for processing the 60,000+ licence requests it receives each year, despite a staff of over 130 full-time and contract personnel and an annual budget of around USD 10 million (USDoS, 2007). The delays have prompted calls from the defence industry for a relaxation of US defence trade controls, which are often held up as models for preventing illicit arms trafficking, including diversions (Schroeder, 2007).

44   Commodities categorized as munitions by the US government are listed on the US Munitions List, which is available at <http://pmddtc.state.gov/docs/ITAR/2007/official_itar/ITAR_Part_121.pdf>.

45   It should be noted that the US system is not necessarily representative of transfer control systems worldwide. The rigour and scope of US controls, the volume of transport requests received and processed each year, and the assets and infrastructure available to US officials that coordinate arms exports and export controls (e.g. military transport networks, an extensive global network of embassies, etc.) exceed those of most exporters.

46   This data includes only firearms and ammunition authorized for export through the State Department's Direct Commercial Sales Program. Arms transferred through the Foreign Military Sales Program, through which the Defense Department arranges government-to-government arms transfers, and other, more minor, arms export programmes are not included.

47   In each case, licensing officers review the licence itself and other required documents, including the government-issued import certificate (an original or certified copy when available—several countries do not issue import certificates), the contract (or purchase order or letter of intent), and technical information. All parties identified on these documents are manually screened against watch lists. (DDTC is currently evaluating word-matching software that would automate this process, but does not currently have this capacity.) The request is reviewed to ensure that the type and quantity of items requested are appropriate for the requested end user and the requested end use. If so, the validity of the paperwork is then checked. For example, import certificates are compared against examples of authentic certificates from various countries that the State Department has on file and screened for telltale signs of forgery or falsification. An experienced licensing officer can review a simple firearms licence request in roughly 30–45 minutes (on average), but more complex or potentially problematic cases can take much longer (interview with US government official, February 2008). If the ostensible end user is an unfamiliar private entity or the request is suspicious in other ways, a pre- or post-shipment end-use check may be conducted under the Blue Lantern Program (END-USER CERTIFICATION). In 2006

the State Department initiated 613 end-use checks, including an undisclosed number of cases involving firearms and ammunition (USDoS, 2007, p. 3). Embassy personnel often perform these checks, which consist, *inter alia,* of visits to the end user's delivery address.

48   Interview with State Department official, February 2008.

49   Stinger missiles are fired from several different platforms, not all of which are man-portable. All Stinger missiles are subjected to enhanced end-use monitoring, however.

50   Interview with Defense Department official, 31 January 2008. The official did not name the two combatant commands.

51   The chart is based on data from interviews with current and former US government officials conducted in January and February 2008. However, the rankings are the opinion of the author and are not endorsed by the government officials or their agencies.

BIBLIOGRAPHY

Abdallah, Sana. 2000. 'Jordan Insists Arms Sales to Peru Were Legal.' United Press International. 31 August.

AFP (Agence France Presse). 2000. 'False Name Signed on Jordanian Arms Request: Peruvian Official.' 2 September.

AI (Amnesty International) and TransArms. 2006. *Dead on Time: Arms Transportation, Brokering and the Threat to Human Rights.* London: Amnesty International. <http://web.amnesty.org/library/pdf/ACT300082006ENGLISH/$File/ACT3000806.pdf>

AP (Associated Press). 2006. 'Peru's Ex-spymaster Sentenced to 20 Years in Prison for International Arms Trafficking.' 22 September.

——. 2007a. 'Syria Denies Report It Threatened to Attack Spanish Peacekeepers in Lebanon.' 25 December.

——. 2007b. 'Sri Lanka's Tamil Tiger Rebels Run a Global Fundraising and Weapons-smuggling Network.' 5 November.

——. 2007c. 'Pentagon to Boost US Personnel in Understaffed Iraq.' 21 December.

Argentina. Permanent Mission of the Argentine Republic to the United Nations. 2007. *Report of the Argentine Republic on the Implementation of the United Nations Programme of Action to Prevent, Combat and Eradicate the Illicit Trade in Small Arms and Light Weapons in All Its Aspects.* Buenos Aires. 20 June. <http://disarmament.un.org/cab/nationalreports/2007/ArgentinaE.pdf>

Austin, Kathi. 2001. *Arms Trafficking: Closing the Net. A Test Case for Prosecution under the U.S. Law on Arms Brokering.* Washington, DC: The Fund for Peace.

Australia. 2006. *Annual Report: Exports of Defence and Strategic Goods from Australia: Financial Years 2002–03 and 2003–04.* Canberra: Department of Defence, Defence Trade Control and Compliance, Strategy Group. February.

Austria. 2007. *Österreichische Exportkontrolle für konventionelle Militärgüter: Politische und rechtliche Rahmenbedingungen.* Vienna: Federal Ministry of Foreign Affairs. <http://www.bmeia.gv.at/fileadmin/user_upload/bmeia/media/2-Aussenpolitik_Zentrale/4586_detailbericht_exportkontrolle_konventionelle_waffen.pdf>

Baltic News Service. 2002. 'Latvia's Formin to Request Additional Info from UN on Weapons Embargo Violation.' 18 July.

Benjamin, Mark. 2007. 'Guns, not Roses, for Iraq.' Salon.com. 18 September.

Bonomo, James, et al. 2007. *Stealing the Sword: Limiting Terrorist Use of Advanced Conventional Weapons.* Santa Monica: RAND Corporation.

Bosnia and Herzegovina. 2007. *Annual Arms Export and Import Report: Information on Licences Issued for Brokering of Arms, Military Equipment and Dual-Use Products in 2006.* Sarajevo: Ministry of Foreign Trade and Economic Relations, Department of Foreign Trade and Investments. June.

Bourne, Mike, et al. 2006. *Reviewing Action on Small Arms 2006: Assessing the First Five Years of the UN Programme of Action.* Biting the Bullet. <http://www.iansa.org/un/review2006/redbook2006/index.htm>

Bulgaria. 2007. *Report on Arms Export Control 2006.* Sofia: Ministry of Economy and Energy.

Canada. 2006. *Canadian Report on the Implementation of the United Nations Programme of Action to Prevent, Combat and Eradicate the Illicit Trade in Small Arms and Light Weapons in All Its Aspects.* 21 June. <http://disarmament.un.org/cab/nationalreports/2006/Canada%20National%20Report%20-%20August%2010%202006.pdf>

——. 2007. *Report on Exports of Military Goods from Canada 2003–2005.* Ottawa: Exports Controls Division, Export and Import Controls Bureau, Foreign Affairs and International Trade Canada.

Coll, Steve. 2004. *Ghost Wars: The Secret History of the CIA, Afghanistan, and Bin Laden, from the Soviet Invasion to September 10, 2001.* New York: Penguin Books.

Croatia. 2007. *Report of the Republic of Croatia on the Implementation of the United Nations Programme of Action to Prevent, Combat and Eradicate Trade in Small Arms and Light Weapons in All Its Aspects for 2006.* <http://disarmament.un.org/cab/nationalreports/2007/Croatia.pdf>

ČTK (Czech News Agency). 2001. 'Man Accused of Illegal Export of Arms Released from Custody.' 13 December.

Czech Republic. 2007. *Annual Report on Export Control of Military Equipment and Small Arms for Civilian Use in the Czech Republic in 2006.* Prague: Ministry of Foreign Affairs of the Czech Republic. <http://www.sipri.org/contents/armstrad/CZR_06.pdf/download>

Denmark. 2007. *Udførsel Af Våben Og Produkter Med Dobbelt Anvendelse Fra Danmark 2006.* Copenhagen: Ministry of Foreign Affairs. April. <http://www.sipri.org/contents/armstrad/DEN_06.pdf/download>

Egypt. 2006. *Report on Implementation by Egypt of the United Nations Programme of Action to Prevent, Combat and Eradicate the Illicit Trade in Small Arms and Light Weapons in All Its Aspects.* 28 April. <http://disarmament.un.org/cab/nationalreports/2006/egypt.pdf>

EU Council (Council of the European Union). 2007. *User's Guide to the European Union Code of Conduct on Arms Exports.* Doc. 10684/1/07 REV 1 (en) of 3 July. <http://register.consilium.europa.eu/pdf/en/07/st10/st10684-re01.en07.pdf>

Farah, Douglas. 2007. *Merchants of Death: Money, Guns, Planes, and the Man Who Makes War Possible.* Hoboken: John Wiley.

—— and Stephen Braun. 2006. 'The Merchant of Death.' *Foreign Policy.* 1 November. <http://www.foreignpolicy.com/story/cms.php?story_id=3600>

Finland. 2007. *Annual Report According to the EU Code of Conduct on Arms Exports: National Report of Finland for 2006.* Helsinki: Ministry of Defence. <http://www.sipri.org/contents/armstrad/FIN_06.pdf/download>

France. 2007. *Rapport au parlement sur les exportations d'armement de la France en 2006.* Paris: Ministry of Defence. November. <http://www.sipri.org/contents/armstrad/FRA_rapport_06.pdf/download>

Gander, Terry and Charles Cutshaw. 2000. *Jane's Infantry Weapons 2000–2001.* London: Jane's Information Group.

Garamone, Jim. 2007. 'IG Team to Look at Weapons Accountability Issues in Iraq.' American Forces Press Service. 29 August. <http://www.defenselink.mil/news/newsarticle.aspx?id=47224>

Germany. 2007. *Bericht der Bundesregierung über ihre Exportpolitik für konventionelle Rüstungsgüter im Jahre 2006 (Rüstungsexportbericht 2006).* Berlin: Federal Ministry of Economics and Technology. <http://www.sipri.org/contents/armstrad/FRG_06.pdf/download>

Glatz, Anne-Kathrin. 2006. 'Buying the Bullet: Authorized Small Arms Ammunition Transfers.' In Stéphanie Pézard and Holger Anders, eds. *Targeting Ammunition: A Primer.* Geneva: Small Arms Survey.

Greene, Owen and Elizabeth Kirkham. 2007. *Small Arms and Light Weapons Transfer Controls to Prevent Diversion: Developing and Implementing Key Programme of Action Commitments.* Biting the Bullet Policy Report. UK: Saferworld and University of Bradford. August. <http://www.saferworld.co.uk/publications.php?id=275>

Griffiths, Hugh and Adrian Wilkinson. 2007. *Guns, Planes and Ships: Identification and Disruption of Clandestine Arms Deliveries.* Belgrade: SEESAC. August. <http.www.seesac.org>

Human Rights Watch. 2004. *Ripe for Reform: Stemming Slovakia's Arms Trade with Human Rights Abusers.* Human Rights Watch Report, Vol. 16, No. 2(D). February. <http://www.hrw.org/reports/2004/slovakia0204/slovakia0204.pdf>

Hunter, Thomas. 2001. 'The Proliferation of MANPADS.' *Jane's Intelligence Review.* 1 September.

IISS (International Institute for Strategic Studies). 1999. *The Military Balance 1999–2000.* London: Oxford University Press.

——. 2000. *The Military Balance 2000–2001.* London: Oxford University Press.

IHT (*International Herald Tribune*). 2007. 'U.S. Weapons, Given to Iraqis, Move to Turkey.' 29 August.

Italy. 2007. *Relacione Sulle Operazione Autorizzate e Svolte per il Controllo dell'Esportazione, Importazione e Transito dei Materiali di Armamento, Nonché dell'Esportazione e del Transito dei Prodotti ad Alta Tecnologia (Anno 2006).* Rome: Camera dei Deputati. 30 March.

Kuperman, Alan. 1999. 'The Stinger Missile and U.S. Intervention in Afghanistan.' *Political Science Quarterly,* Vol. 114, No. 2. Summer, pp. 219–63.

LAWR (*Latin American Weekly Review*). 2000. 'Scale of FARC's Arms Buildup Revealed; Jordan–Peru Connection "Broken up" by Lima.' 29 August.

Marsh, Nicholas. 2005. *Accounting Guns: The Methodology Used in Developing Data Tables for the Small Arms Survey.* Background paper. Oslo: PRIO/NISAT. 14 November.

Netherlands. 2007. *Annual Report on The Netherlands Arms Export Policy 2006.* The Hague: Ministry of Economic Affairs and Ministry of Foreign Affairs. 13 September. <http://www.sipri.org/contents/armstrad/NET_06.pdf/download>

NISAT (Norwegian Initiative on Small Arms Transfers). 2007. *Calculations from the NISAT Database on Authorized Small Arms Transfers.* Unpublished background paper. Geneva: Small Arms Survey.

——. 2008. *Data from the NISAT Database on Authorized Small Arms Transfers.* Unpublished background paper. Geneva: Small Arms Survey.

Norway. 2007. *Eksport av forsvarsmateriell frå Noreg i 2006, eksportkontroll og internasjonalt ikkje-spreiingssamarbeid.* Oslo: Ministry of Foreign Affairs. <http://www.sipri.org/contents/armstrad/NOR_06.pdf/download>

NYT (*The New York Times*). 1985. 'U.S. Aides See Gun Smugglers as Low Priority.' 26 September.

——. 2000. 'C.I.A. Links Cited on Peru Arms Deal that Backfired.' 6 November.

——. 2007. 'A Broken Supply Channel Sent Arms for Iraq Astray.' 11 November.

OAS (Organization of American States). 2003. *Report of the General Secretariat of the Organization of American States on the Diversion of Nicaraguan Arms to the United Self Defense Forces of Colombia.* OEA/Ser.G CP/doc. 3687/03 of 29 January. <http://www.fas.org/asmp/campaigns/smallarms/OAS_Otterloo.htm>

OSCE (Organization for Security and Co-operation in Europe). 2003. *Handbook of Best Practices on Small Arms and Light Weapons: Best Practice Guide on National Procedures for Stockpile Management and Security.* FSC.GAL/4/03/Rev.1 of 19 September.

Portugal. 2007. *Anuario estatistico da defesa nacional 2005.* Lisbon: Ministry of Defence.

Powers International. 2006. 'Trial of a Revolutionary Container Security System with Satellite Monitoring.' Press release. 13 November. <http://www.powersintlinc.com/BremenPressReleaseNov13-2006.pdf>

Pyadushkin, Maxim. 2006. *Russian Federation's SALW Transfers in 2003–2005.* Unpublished background paper. Geneva: Small Arms Survey.

Rempel, William and Sebastian Rotella. 2000. 'Arms Dealer Implicates Peru Spy Chief in Smuggling Ring.' *Los Angeles Times.* 1 November.

Reuters. 2008. 'Foreign Ministry Protests Violation of Bout's Rights.' *The Moscow Times.* 14 April. <http://www.themoscowtimes.com/article/1010/42/361897.htm>

Romania. 2007. *Annual Report of the Romanian Arms Export Controls 2005.* Bucharest: National Agency for Export Controls, Conventional Arms Division. <http://www.sipri.org/contents/armstrad/ROM_05_ENG.pdf/download>

Schroeder, Matt. 2007. 'Licensing Exemptions, Round Two: The Defense Trade Cooperation Treaty.' *FAS Strategic Security Blog.* 20 July. <http://www.fas.org/blog/ssp/2007/07/licensing_exemptions_round_two.php#more>

—— et al. 2006. *The Small Arms Trade.* London: Oneworld Publications.

Serbia. 2007. *Annual Report on the Realization of Foreign Trade Transfers of Controlled Goods for 2005 and 2006.* Belgrade: Ministry of Economy and Regional Development. <http://www.sipri.org/contents/armstrad/SER_05-06.pdf/download>

Sherman, Robert. 2003. 'The Real Terrorist Missile Threat, and What Can Be Done about It.' *FAS Public Interest Report,* Vol. 56, No. 3. Autumn, pp. 4–5.

SIGIR (Special Inspector General for Iraq Reconstruction). 2006. *Iraqi Security Forces: Weapons Provided by the U.S. Department of Defense Using the Iraq Relief and Reconstruction Fund.* SIGIR-06-033. 28 October.

Slovakia. 2007. *Výrocná Správa o Obchode s Vojenským Materiálom za Rok 2006.* Bratislava: Slovakian Ministry of Economy. <http://www.sipri.org/contents/armstrad/SLK_06.pdf/download>

Small Arms Survey. *Small Arms Survey 2004: Rights at Risk.* Oxford: Oxford University Press.

——. 2005. *Small Arms Survey 2005: Weapons at War.* Oxford: Oxford University Press.

——. 2006. *Small Arms Survey 2006: Unfinished Business.* Geneva and Oxford: Oxford University Press.

——. 2007. *Small Arms Survey 2007: Guns and the City.* Cambridge: Cambridge University Press.

——. 2008. *National Arms Export Reports.* <http://www.smallarmssurvey.org/files/portal/issueareas/transfers/transam.html#au>

South Africa. 2007. *South African Export Statistics for Conventional Arms 2003 and 2004.* Pretoria: Directorate of Conventional Arms Control. <http://www.sipri.org/contents/armstrad/SA_03-04.pdf/download>

Spain. 2007. *Spanish Export Statistics Regarding Defence Material, Other Material and Dual-Use Items and Technologies, 2006.* Madrid: Ministry of Industry, Tourism and Trade, Secretary of State for Tourism and Trade. <http://www.sipri.org/contents/armstrad/SPA_06.pdf/download>

Sweden. 2007. *Strategic Export Controls in 2006: Military Equipment and Dual-Use Products.* Government Communication 2006/07:114. Stockholm: Ministry of Foreign Affairs. 15 March. <http://www.sipri.org/contents/armstrad/SWE_06_ENG.pdf/download>

Switzerland. 2007. *Exportations de matériel de guerre en 2006.* Bern: Secrétariat d'Etat à l'économie (SECO). <http://www.sipri.org/contents/armstrad/SWI_06.pdf/download>

UK (United Kingdom). 2007. *United Kingdom Strategic Export Controls: Annual Report 2006.* London: Foreign and Commonwealth Office. <http://www.sipri.org/contents/armstrad/UK_06.pdf/download>

Ukraine. 2007. *Information on the Scope of International Weapons Programmes in Ukraine in 2006* [author's translation]. Kiev: State Service of Export Control of Ukraine. <http://www.dsecu.gov.ua/control/uk/publish/article?art_id=40683&cat_id=34940>

UN Comtrade. 2007. *United Nations Commodity Trade Statistics Database.* Department of Economic and Social Affairs/Statistics Division. <http://unstats.un.org/unsd/databases.htm>

——. 2008. *United Nations Commodity Trade Statistics Database.* Department of Economic and Social Affairs/Statistics Division. <http://unstats.un.org/unsd/databases.htm>

UNSC (United Nations Security Council). 2001. *Report of the Panel of Experts pursuant to Security Council Resolution 1343 (2001), Paragraph 19, concerning Liberia.* Reproduced in UN doc. S/2001/1015 of 26 October. <http://www.un.org/Docs/sc/committees/Liberia2/1015e.pdf>

——. 2002. *Report of the Panel of Experts pursuant to Security Council Resolution 1408 (2002), Paragraph 16, concerning Liberia.* Reproduced in UN doc. S/2002/1115 of 25 October. <http://daccessdds.un.org/doc/UNDOC/GEN/N02/626/79/IMG/N0262679.pdf?OpenElement>

——. 2003. *Report of the Panel of Experts on Somalia pursuant to Security Council Resolution 1425 (2002)*. Reproduced in UN doc. S/2003/223 of 25 March. <http://daccessdds.un.org/doc/UNDOC/GEN/N03/259/25/IMG/N0325925.pdf?OpenElement>

US Army Transportation School. 2004. *Division Transportation Officer's Guide*, ch. 6. Reference 04-01. 1 May.
<http://www.transchool.eustis.army.mil/DTO/DTO-Chp6.htm>

US District Court. 2007. *United States of America v. Monzer Al Kassar, a/k/a 'Abu Munawar,' a/k/a 'El Taous,' Tareq Mousa Al Ghazi, and Luis Felipe Moreno Godoy*. Southern District of New York. Indictment S2 07 Cr. 354.

USDoD (US Department of Defense). 2003. *Security Assistance Management Manual*, ch. 5. <http://www.dsca.osd.mil/samm/>

——. 2004. *Defense Transportation Regulations: 4500.9-R-Part II Cargo Movement*, ch. 205, Appendix E. November.
<http://www.transcom.mil/j5/pt/dtrpart2/dtr_part_ii_app_e.pdf>

——. 2007a. 'Iraq—Small Arms Ammunition, Explosives, and Other Consumables.' News release. 4 May.
<http://www.dsca.mil/PressReleases/36-b/2007/Iraq_07-20.pdf>

——. 2007b. 'Iraq—Various Vehicles, Small Arms Ammunition, Explosives, and Communications Equipment.' News release. 25 September.
<http://www.dsca.mil/PressReleases/36-b/2007/Iraq_07-64.pdf>

——. 2007c. 'Iraq Purchases Small Arms through Foreign Military Sales.' MNSTC–I Press release. 5 December.
<http://www.mnf-iraq.com/index.php?option=com_content&task=view&id=15648&Itemid=21>

USDoJ (US Department of Justice). 2007. 'DEA Investigation Nets International Arms Dealer with Ties to Terrorist Organizations.' New release. 8 June.
<http://www.usdoj.gov/dea/pubs/states/newsrel/nyc060807.html>

USDoS (US Department of State). 2005. *Global Arms-Trafficking Network Designated by United States*. 26 April.
<http://usinfo.state.gov/ei/Archive/2005/Apr/27-279044.html>

——. 2006. *End-Use Monitoring of Defense Articles and Defense Services: Commercial Exports FY 2005*.
<http://www.pmddtc.state.gov/docs/End_Use_FY2005.pdf>

——. 2007. *End-Use Monitoring of Defense Articles and Defense Services: Commercial Exports FY 2006*.
<http://www.pmddtc.state.gov/docs/End_Use_FY2006.pdf>

—— and USDoD. 2007. *Report by the Department of State Pursuant to Section 655 of the Foreign Assistance Act of 1961, Amended*. Washington, DC: USDoS and USDoD. <http://www.sipri.org/contents/armstrad/US_655_FY06.pdf/download>

USGAO (US Government Accountability Office). 2004. *Further Improvements Needed in U.S. Efforts to Counter Threats from Man-Portable Air Defense Systems*. GAO-04-519. Report. May. <http://www.fas.org/asmp/resources/govern/GAO_04_519.pdf>

——. 2007a. *Stabilizing Iraq: DOD Cannot Ensure that U.S.-Funded Equipment Has Reached Iraqi Security Forces*. GAO-07-711. Report. July.
<http://www.gao.gov/new.items/d07711.pdf>

——. 2007b. *State Department Needs to Conduct Assessments to Identify and Address Inefficiencies and Challenges in the Arms Export Process*.
GAO-08-89. Report. November. <http://www.gao.gov/new.items/d0889.pdf>

US House of Representatives. Committee on International Relations. 2004. *U.S. Weapons Technology at Risk: The State Department's Proposal to Relax Arms Export Controls to Other Countries*, Appendix 3. 1 May.
<http://fas.org/asmp/campaigns/control/U.S.%20Weapons%20Technology%20at%20Risk/U.S._WEAPONS_Appen3.pdf>

US Treasury. 2007. 'Treasury Targets Charity Covertly Supporting Violence in Sri Lanka.' Press release. 15 November.
<http://www.treas.gov/press/releases/hp683.htm>

ACKNOWLEDGEMENTS

Principal authors

Matt Schroeder (transfer diversion); Helen Close and Chris Stevenson (Small Arms Trade Transparency Barometer)

Contributors

Katarzyna Bzdak; Thomas Jackson and Nicholas Marsh (NISAT)

Who's Buying?
END-USER CERTIFICATION

5

INTRODUCTION

For as little as USD 200, an arms trafficker can buy a blank end-user certificate (EUC) from the right (corrupt) government official. After filling in the date, supplier name, and item description, the trafficker uses this document to procure and transport war material to the destination of his choice. The blank EUC has the necessary signatures and stamps. If no one checks its authenticity—often the case—he can ship his wares to the world's hot spots with minimal risk, for maximum profit.

EUCs and other kinds of end-user documentation constitute a key line of defence against the diversion of authorized small arms transfers to unauthorized—often illicit—end-users and end uses. These documents, however, are effective only in the context of a broader system that includes a thorough consideration of diversion risks at the licensing stage, the verification of end-user documentation, and complementary post-shipment controls.

The 2007 edition of the *Small Arms Survey* focused on the criteria states need to consider when authorizing transfers of small arms and light weapons in a responsible manner. These criteria, typically rooted in international law, include respect for international humanitarian and human rights law in the recipient state (Small Arms Survey, 2007, ch. 4). Yet this is only half of the story. At the time of licensing and even beyond, it is also important that states ensure that weapons and ammunition, once transferred outside their territory, are not diverted to unauthorized end-users and end uses. This chapter examines the task of ensuring 'effective control' over small arms transfers (UNGA, 2001b, para. II.12), with a specific focus on end-user systems and documentation.

The chapter's principal conclusions include the following:

- The basic components of systems designed to prevent small arms shipments being diverted to unauthorized end-users or used for unauthorized purposes appear to be in place in the world's leading exporting states.
- It is unclear, however, whether the discretion these systems tend to grant individual licensing officials aids or impedes the diversion prevention task.
- Most governments provide very little information on the policies and practices they use in assessing diversion risks at the time of licensing.
- Nor do states indicate whether they systematically verify end-user documentation in advance of export.
- While it may make sense to devote the lion's share of resources and attention to licensing, post-shipment controls help reinforce and improve pre-shipment risk assessment.
- Practice among the ten leading exporters, however, indicates that these measures are underutilized (delivery verification) or largely neglected (end-use monitoring).
- States have yet to demonstrate that they are fulfilling their commitment under the *UN Programme of Action* 'to ensure the effective control' of small arms transfers (UNGA, 2001b, para. II.12).

The chapter examines the problem of diversion in its first section, focusing on the manipulation of end-user documentation by illicit traffickers. In subsequent sections it outlines the main features of systems designed to prevent the diversion of authorized arms transfers, reviews relevant international standards and best practices, and analyses national practices among leading exporting states. The policy implications of this discussion are elaborated in the chapter's final section and in its conclusion. The chapter concentrates throughout on end-user documentation and other elements of end-user systems. As such, it complements the broader discussion of transfers diversion and diversion prevention found in Chapter 4 (TRANSFER DIVERSION).

DIVERSION: A QUICK GUIDE

It is worth recapping some of the main features of diversion as it affects international arms transfers. These are discussed at much greater length in Chapter 4 (TRANSFER DIVERSION). While this chapter will mostly refer to the diversion of 'weapons' or 'small arms', this is merely shorthand for the diversion of small arms and light weapons, their ammunition, and parts and components.

For the purposes of this chapter, the term 'diversion' refers to a breakdown in the transfer control chain such that, either before or after arriving at their intended destination, exported weapons are transferred to unauthorized end-users or used in violation of commitments made by end-users prior to export. This definition of diversion covers both unauthorized possession and

Parts of a US-made AR-15 rifle are removed from a box at a customs warehouse in Manila as part of an investigation into an alleged coup plot, June 2005.
© Pat Roque/AP Photo

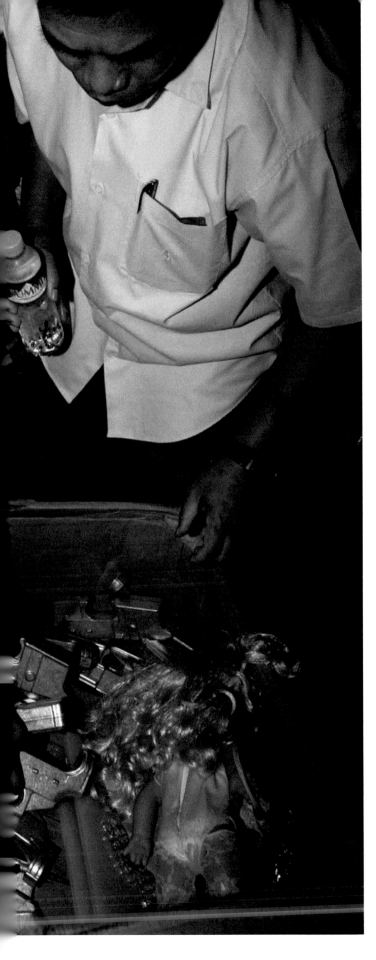

use. As understood here, diversion is not simply the movement of arms from the legal to illicit spheres, but rather an *unauthorized* change in possession or use that has this result. A deliberate government decision to transfer, or allow the transfer, of legal arms to an illicit end-user would not count as 'diversion' under this definition. Diversion occurs, rather, when a state loses control over transferred weapons and thus inadvertently—but often negligently—fuels the illicit trade.

The arms transfer chain involves a shift in control at four distinct stages: licensing, in-transit movement, delivery, and post-delivery use and retransfer. An initial opportunity to combat—indeed prevent—diversion comes at the licensing stage. Licensing criteria, procedures, and documentation are all used for this purpose—while the weapons are still under the jurisdiction of the exporting state. Opportunities for transfer diversion arise once the weapons clear customs at the port of export.

Brokers and transport agents act as intermediaries and facilitators for much of the legitimate small arms trade. In certain cases, however, these actors intervene to divert weapons as they transit between the states of export and declared import—usually by exploiting gaps in national and international regulation. Although this chapter does not focus specifically on illicit brokering and transport, the diversion methods and preventive measures it discusses are as relevant to these activities as to other aspects of the illicit trade. The 2008 transfers chapter provides additional information on diversion techniques, including those used by brokers and transport agents (TRANSFER DIVERSION).[1]

The arms consignment's arrival at its intended destination, far from representing an end to diversion risks, opens up new possibilities. The authorized end-user may use the weapons in contravention of the agreement struck with the exporter or exporting state. The end-user may also—*intentionally*—retransfer the arms in violation of initial undertakings. Alternatively, poor stockpile management and security in the originating or destination countries, often exploited by corrupt officials, may result in an *unintentional* loss of control over the material and its consequent diversion to armed criminal or rebel groups (STOCKPILE DIVERSION).

As already mentioned, this chapter focuses on systems used at the licensing stage to confirm the intended (and actual) end-user, and thereby minimize the risk of diversion. It also discusses measures, such as delivery verification and non-retransfer undertakings, that are frequently incorporated in end-user commitments. Licensing offers exporting states their best opportunity to prevent the diversion of weapons and ammunition; yet this is also where illicit traffickers focus their attention. Once they obtain an export licence, it is usually relatively easy to get weapons past the customs authorities in the exporting country and transport them to the (undeclared) destination of their choice (Griffiths and Wilkinson, 2007, sec. 6.1).

When applying for an export licence, a small arms manufacturer or dealer normally provides the national licensing authority with an end-user certificate (EUC) or similar documentation detailing the basic elements of the proposed transaction, including the type and quantity of weapons for export, as well as the end-user and end use of the goods. Illicit traffickers use false end-user documentation, or falsify information in otherwise valid documentation, to obtain such licences. Illicit EUCs take three main forms: forged, government-issued without 'follow-up service', and government-issued with 'follow-up service'.

Forged EUCs. Despite appearances, forged end-user documents are not issued by the state or other (commercial) entity they are supposed to represent. The broker that diverted Nicaraguan arms to Colombian rebels in the Otterloo case apparently acquired a blank Panamanian Police purchase order, then forged the necessary signatures to produce the sham EUC used in that deal (OAS, 2003). Obvious forgeries can still be effective. A Polish licensing officer approved the sale of weapons to Yemen (in fact, Croatia) on the basis of an EUC that was supposed to have been issued by the 'People's Democratic Republic of Yemen', even though this country had ceased to exist two years earlier (UNSC, 2003, paras. 41–45, Annex V). In some cases a genuine EUC, provided by a friendly government, is used as a model to generate a series of forgeries (UNSC, 2000, paras. 43, 49, 55).

Government-issued, no service. A second type of illicit EUC is acquired from a corrupt government official with no provision for subsequent authentification by that official. Such an EUC is issued by a government authority and signed by an authorized official who knows it will be used to facilitate an illicit transaction, but will not pretend the document is valid if questioned by export licensing authorities. EUCs of this type have been widely used in illicit arms deals, especially in Africa, during the post-cold war period. In the experience of one observer, the fee exacted by corrupt officials for these EUCs has ranged from USD 200, in the case of a Rwandan-origin document, to USD 2,000 for an EUC signed by a government official in Chad (Johnson-Thomas, 2007).

The Rwandan EUC just referred to features in a story of pseudo-illicit trafficking recounted elsewhere in this volume (COMIC STRIP). Acquired in 2003, the document was issued on Rwandan Defence Ministry letterhead and signed by an authorized representative of the ministry with crucial information omitted, including contract number, date, supplier name, and a description of the material (Johnson-Thomas, 2007). Arms traffickers subsequently fill in these details when arranging a sale to a buyer other than that declared on the EUC. The same EUC, if copied, can

Traffickers use falsified documentation to obtain an export licence.

also be used to fill more than one order, a task made easier by the simplicity of the document in question. The Rwandan EUC, with its uncomplicated letterhead and language, is similar to those issued by several other developing country defence ministries and armed forces (see Griffiths and Wilkinson, 2007, sec. 6.1).

An exporting state can easily ascertain the illicit nature of the two types of EUCs described above (forged and government-issued, no service) provided it checks the information with the declared country of import. Verification is more difficult for a third category of illicit EUC.

Government-issued, full service. This last type of illicit EUC is also procured from a corrupt government official, but in this case a full 'follow-up service' is included in the package. Though perfectly aware of the illicit nature of the transaction, the official undertakes to reassure any exporting country officials that seek such assurances that the proposed transaction is legitimate and for the benefit of the state that has issued the EUC. In these, much rarer, cases the fee for the corrupt official is far higher—in some cases a percentage of the total value of the proposed deal (Johnson-Thomas, 2007).

Simple ch
the decla
country c
will unma
illicit EUC

CONTROL MEASURES

In this section, the chapter presents norms, instruments, and systems designed to prevent the diversion of small arms transfers, with a specific focus on end-user certification and verification. It begins, however, by sketching out the basic features of transfer control systems. Although the chapter provides background information on diversion prevention measures, readers should consult Chapter 4 for a more detailed treatment (TRANSFER DIVERSION).

Transfer control basics

Before grappling with the details of end-user documentation and procedures, it is useful to situate them in broader context. Under the *UN Programme of Action* states have agreed:

> to establish or maintain an effective national system of export and import licensing or authorization, as well as measures on international transit, for the transfer of all small arms and light weapons. (UNGA, 2001b, para. II.11)

The OSCE *Handbook of Best Practices,* while noting that '[t]here is no single model for an export control system', identifies 'certain features which any export control system needs to have to be effective: a legal basis, an export policy, a decision-making mechanism, and an enforcement mechanism' (OSCE, 2003, ch. V, p. 2).

Legal basis. National transfer control systems should be based in law. This is reflected in paragraph 2, section II of the *Programme of Action,* which requires states '[t]o put in place, where they do not exist, adequate laws, regulations and administrative procedures to exercise effective control . . . over the export, import, transit or retransfer' of small arms and light weapons (UNGA, 2001b).

Export policy. National laws and regulations should reflect the state's international obligations and commitments. Additional policy guidance is incorporated in national legislation and/or policy documentation. Both the Nairobi and OSCE best-practice guides underline the importance of transparency in the formulation and implementation of national export policy. National parliaments and civil society also have a role to play in its formulation (*Nairobi Best Practice Guidelines,* 2005; OSCE, 2003).

Decision-making mechanism. The two best-practice guides state that a licence or permit should be required for any transfer of small arms or light weapons. They recommend keeping exceptions to a minimum. In such exceptional cases, a simplified licensing procedure is preferable to a complete exemption. Among their key recommendations:

- That the authorizing state ensure it receives from the state of import an import licence or other official authorization. The transfer of small arms and light weapons is, fundamentally, a shared responsibility between exporting and importing states;
- That the authorizing state ensure that appropriate transit authorizations have been issued; and
- That licensing decisions are shared across government, with all competent authorities involved (*Nairobi Best Practice Guidelines,* 2005; OSCE, 2003).

Enforcement mechanism. The Nairobi and OSCE best-practice guides note that national transfer control legislation should provide for the investigation, prosecution, and punishment of transfer control violations. This requires effective penalties—which, depending on the case, may involve the revocation of licences, fines, and/or criminal sanctions—as well as customs supervision. Customs authorities intervene, not only at the point of import, but also when the weapons leave the state's territory. The best-practice guides underline the need for information exchange and cooperation between arms licensing and enforcement officials, and also among the different agencies dealing with enforcement within the state. Cooperation among enforcement agencies in different countries is also important to the effective prosecution of transfer control violations (*Nairobi Best Practice Guidelines,* 2005; OSCE, 2003).

Best-practice guides underline the need for information exchange and cooperation.

Preventing diversion

No matter how sophisticated a country's transfer licensing system, the job is only half done if it takes no steps to prevent weapons shipments from being diverted to unauthorized end-users or used for unauthorized purposes. After presenting the normative framework at the multilateral level, this section outlines the main features of national systems designed to prevent diversion.

Multilateral measures

Section II, paragraphs 11–13 of the *UN Programme of Action* set out the basic commitments in this area (UNGA, 2001b). Paragraph 11 requires states to take account of diversion risks in authorizing small arms exports. Paragraph 12 underlines the need for 'effective control' over small arms exports and transit, making specific reference to 'the use of authenticated end-user certificates', while paragraph 13 relates to the retransfer of weapons by an initial recipient.

These provisions, applicable to all UN member states, provide a useful normative framework for the prevention of diversion. Yet they lack the level of detail and operational specificity that would foster their translation into national laws, regulations, and administrative practices (Greene and Kirkham, 2007, p. 10). There is, however, nothing more specific at the universal level in relation to small arms. Proposals for the establishment of a UN group of governmental experts on end-user certification, made at the 2006 UN Programme of Action Review Conference, did not gain consensus support despite broad acknowledgment of the issue's importance (see Small Arms Survey, 2007, p. 123).

More detailed, operationally oriented norms can be found in some regional and (non-universal) multilateral instruments. With respect to the prevention of diversion generally, these include: the *Illicit Firearms Convention* and

Model Regulations of the Organization of American States (OAS, 1997; 1998); the *OSCE Document* (OSCE, 2000); the *UN Firearms Protocol* (UNGA, 2001a);[2] the *Nairobi Protocol* (2004); and best-practice documents produced by the Wassenaar Arrangement (WA, 2000; 2002), the Organization for Security and Co-operation in Europe (OSCE, 2003), east African states (*Nairobi Best Practice Guidelines,* 2005), and the European Union (EU Council, 2007).

States have agreed to exercise especially close scrutiny over the export of man-portable air defence systems (MANPADS). Instruments adopted by the Wassenaar Arrangement (WA, 2003a), OSCE (2004a), and OAS (2005) mandate strict controls over the international transfer of MANPADS in order to minimize the risk of their diversion (see Small Arms Survey, 2005, ch. 5).

Multilateral measures focusing on end-user certification are few in number, yet important. They include the OSCE *Handbook of Best Practices* (2003, ch. V) and *Standard Elements* (OSCE, 2004b), the *Nairobi Best Practice Guidelines* (2005, sec. 2.1.e), the Wassenaar Arrangement *Indicative List* (WA, 2005), and the EU *User's Guide* (EU Council, 2007, ch. 2). The chapter does not review these instruments in detail, but instead refers to them selectively as it completes its mapping of systems—especially end-user systems—designed to prevent diversion.

Men exchange money for weapons over tea in a Baghdad home, June 2007. © Karim Kadim/AP Photo

National systems[3]

This section reviews the constituent elements of national systems designed to verify the identity of end-users and prevent arms transfer diversion. It draws on elements of (good) national practice, as well as multilateral norms and instruments.

Arms transfer licensing is instrumental in preventing diversion further down the transfers chain. An important part of the licensing task involves the thorough consideration of diversion risks before any transfer authorization (UNGA, 2001b, para. II.11). Industry has a contribution to make to such assessments (GRIP et al., 2006; WA, 2003b). Diversion risks that need to be considered at the licensing stage relate to: the intermediaries involved in the transaction, including brokers and transport agents; the capacity of the end-user and importing state to retain control over the weapons; and the intentions of the end-user regarding weapons end use and retransfer (Greene and Kirkham, 2007, p. 13). Concerns surrounding potential diversion may be sparked, for example, by an application to export weapons that are not known to be used by an importing state's armed forces, or if prospective destination countries or end-users are known—or suspected—to have illicitly trafficked arms or violated retransfer restrictions.[4]

As part of its licence application, an arms exporter normally provides the national licensing authority with documentation—such as an EUC—identifying the material to be transferred, destination country, end-user, and end use (see EU Council, 2007, sec. 2.1.2; OSCE, 2004b, para. 1). These documents often also include undertakings by the end-user regarding the use and retransfer of the weapons it receives.

In relation to end use, the recipient typically undertakes not to use the weapons for other than declared purposes (see *Nairobi Best Practice Guidelines,* 2005, sec. 2.1.e; WA, 2005). As reflected in national practice and various international instruments, undertakings concerning retransfer take a variety of forms. From most to least restrictive, these include: an absolute ban on re-export; subjecting any re-export to the prior authorization of the exporting state; allowing re-export without the authorization of the exporting state, but only to certain countries; allowing re-export provided it is authorized by the export licensing authorities in the end-user state; and mere notification of the exporting state in case of re-export (EU Council, 2007, sec. 2.1.3; *Nairobi Best Practice Guidelines,* 2005, sec. 2.1.e; OSCE, 2004b, para. 1; WA, 2005).[5]

Such undertakings tend to feature in small arms and light weapons exports to foreign state entities. Export agreements with commercial entities, on the other hand, may stipulate that transferred weapons are to be resold only on the domestic commercial market or in states identified as part of the transfer authorization.

End-user documents may originate in either the country of export or the country of import. They are signed and stamped by the prospective end-user and/or importing state government. Verification of such documentation, along with the information it contains, is an essential aspect of the licensing process (*Nairobi Best Practice Guidelines,* 2005, sec. 2.1.e; OSCE, 2004b, para. 3). A failure to verify end-user documentation and information is the primary facilitator of many cases of diversion (Griffiths and Wilkinson, 2007, sec. 6.1).

As explained earlier, an EUC may be forged or, though genuine, may not reflect the actual end-user or end use of transferred weapons. For these reasons, national licensing authorities need to check that end-user documents have been issued and signed by the right agencies. This assessment may be carried out by the exporting state's diplomatic mission in the country of prospective import (see Greene and Kirkham, 2007, p. 17). For commercial exports, licensing authorities often try to confirm that the end-user is operating a legal and reputable business in accordance with the laws of the importing state.[6] Even when thoroughly vetted, however, end-user documents cannot substitute for a broader consideration of diversion risks at the licensing stage (Anders, 2005, sec. 4.2).

Box 5.1 **Common end-user documentation**

Documentation required by national export authorities in support of a licence application usually depends on the type, destination, and end-user of transferred weapons. If small arms and light weapons are to be exported to a foreign state entity,
the latter is often asked to submit an 'end-user' (or 'end-use') certificate. Any restrictions on retransfer contained in the certificate apply to the importing state. Exports of small arms to commercial markets often necessitate the prior provision of an
'international import certificate' and sometimes an 'end-use statement'.

International import certificates are signed and stamped by the authorities of the importing state. They confirm that the
importing government is aware of, and does not object to, the proposed transfer to the commercial entity or individual. The
importing state does not commit to any restrictions in relation to such weapons. 'End-use statements' are signed and stamped
by the commercial importer. Any retransfer restrictions they contain apply to the commercial importer.

National export authorities may also ask a licence applicant to submit proof of delivery to the authorized end-user or
importer. A 'delivery verification certificate', confirming this, is issued to the exporter by the customs authorities of the
importing state. Most often, such a certificate is requested, along with an international import certificate, for exports of
small arms to a foreign commercial importer.

Source: Anders (2007)

Diversion risks are further minimized by securing, in advance of export, the cooperation of interested states. For
example, States Parties to the OAS *Firearms Convention* and the *UN Firearms Protocol* must ensure, before exporting
firearms, that the import and transit states approve the transfer, or at least indicate they have no objection to it (OAS,
1997, art. IX; UNGA, 2001a, art. 10(2)).

Diversion remains an issue long after the transfer is authorized. Post-shipment controls, such as delivery verification
and end-use monitoring, help ensure that weapons arrive at their intended destination and that end-users comply
with any restrictions on use or retransfer imposed in connection with the export. Licensing systems can play a role here
as well, establishing a framework for cooperation between exporting and importing countries after the weapons have
been exported. End-user documentation may stipulate that delivery be confirmed (EU Council, 2007, sec. 2.1.3; OSCE,
2004b, para. 1; WA, 2005). A few exporting countries also use these documents to secure permission to verify the
possession and use of exported weapons in the recipient state.

Delivery verification allows exporting states to check whether weapons have been diverted en route to the
importing country. It can also serve to deter such diversion. Yet it offers no protection against diversion occurring
after the time of delivery. End-use monitoring can be used for this purpose, but, as the next section demonstrates,
is quite exceptional in practice. When used at all, end-use monitoring tends to be ad hoc and dependent on voluntary
cooperation from the importing state. Only a small number of countries systematically provide for end-use monitoring at the licensing stage.

Ad hoc end-use checks are usually initiated in response to allegations that a specific end-user is not respecting
restrictions on end use or retransfer. This information may come from government sources, NGOs, or the media.
End-use checks may include a request by the exporting state to the importing state to clarify in writing the actual
use of exported weapons.[7] Unless end-use undertakings are included in the contract between exporter and importer,
there is often no legal remedy if they are violated. Most often, end-user undertakings take the form of a 'declaration
of honour'. The principal sanction available to export authorities when commitments of this type are breached is to
deny future export licences for the same destination or end-user. As indicated below, a few countries have made this
national policy.

NATIONAL PRACTICE

This section looks at the extent to which states are using the norms, instruments, and systems described earlier for purposes of verifying end-users and preventing diversion. The chapter uses the term 'national practice' to refer to relevant legislative frameworks (laws and regulations), as well as administrative practices.

Ten-country study[8]

This section reviews (in alphabetical order) end-user certification practices in the world's leading exporters of small arms and light weapons: Austria, Belgium, Brazil, Canada, China, Germany, Italy, Japan, the United Kingdom, and the United States (Small Arms Survey, 2007, p. 74).[9] Given the volume of their annual exports, one would expect these countries to have relatively well-developed end-user certification systems. Whether they do is the subject of the following study. Any shortcomings, especially if systematic, are likely indicators of problems among other exporters.

Austria

In Austria, the *Kriegsmaterialgesetz* (*War Material Act*; Austria, 2005a) regulates exports of 'war material', a category which encompasses semi-automatic carbines and rifles, all automatic small arms, and all light weapons (Austria, 1977, arts.1–4). Exports of weapons not considered war material, such as revolvers and semi-automatic pistols, are regulated by the *Aussenhandelsgesetz* (*Foreign Trade Act;* Austria, 2005b). Under both regimes, an export licence may be made subject to the submission of an end-use statement (Austria, 2005a, art. 3.2; 2005b, art. I, para. 28.2.1). For non-war material, a delivery verification certificate may also be required (Austria, 2005b, art. I, para. 28.2.1). Austrian licensing authorities decide whether to certify end-users or delivery on a case-by-case basis, depending on the type, quantity, or destination of the equipment, as well as any concerns that may exist in relation to end use (Austria, 2006, p. 3; EU Council, 1998).

The end-use statements submitted to the Austrian export control authorities include: a detailed description of the goods to be exported, their quantity and value, details of the supplier, the country of final destination, and details of end use, purchaser, and/or ultimate consignee (end-user). These statements are signed by the purchaser and end-user who undertake, in particular, to use the goods only as indicated in the statement and not to re-export them to third countries without the approval of the Austrian government. Weapons that are not considered 'war material' may be re-exported without Austrian government approval to EU member states, plus Australia, Canada, Iceland, Japan, New Zealand, Norway, Switzerland, and the United States (Austria, n.d.).[10] Austria rarely undertakes post-delivery checks of exported weapons.[11]

Belgium

Belgian legislation governing small arms and light weapons exports requires that licence applications be accompanied by an international import certificate or end-use certificate (Belgium, 2003b, art. 5.1). Those exporting from Belgium must also provide the exporting state[12] with proof of delivery to the destination country and importer within three months of such delivery. This may take the form of a certificate in which the customs authorities of the importing state attest that the importer has received the exported equipment (Belgium, 2003b, art. 7). The legislation also specifies that export licences may be made conditional on a commitment of no re-export without prior approval, and further that licence requests must be rejected if recipients in the country of destination have failed to comply with such commitments in the past (Belgium, 2003a, arts. 3, 4.4.e).

In practice, Belgian export authorities do not require an end-use certificate if the destination country is an EU or North Atlantic Treaty Organization (NATO) member. For exports of small arms and light weapons to these states, as well as some additional states, such as South Africa,[13] an international import certificate must be supplied. For other countries, end-use certificates must be produced by the authorities of the recipient state. These may be verified by Belgium's diplomatic services abroad, and often include a commitment not to re-export the weapons without first notifying the Belgian authorities (Belgium, Walloon Government, 2006, p. 18; EU Council, 1998). Belgian export officials have some discretion in their choice of procedures and requirements. Verification of EUCs and inclusion of no-re-export clauses are required, in principle, but exceptions are made on a case-by-case basis.[14]

Brazil

Under Brazil's *Decreto no. 3.665* (Brazil, 2000a), all exports of small arms and light weapons must be authorized by the Brazilian army. Export licence applicants need to supply an end-user certificate, international import certificate, or confirmation by Brazil's diplomatic missions abroad that the import is not subject to legal restrictions in the importing country (Brazil, 2000a, art. 178.1–2; 2005, pp. 9–10). The army determines when an end-user or international import certificate is required (see Dreyfus, Lessing, and César Purcena, 2005, p. 57). End user certificates must indicate the quantity, description, and value of the exported equipment, as well as the exporter, importer, final purchaser, and final destination. The final purchaser certifies that the imported equipment will be used only for the purposes stated in the certificate (Brazil, 2000b).

Exports of military small arms and light weapons are subject to additional controls under the *Política Nacional de Exportação de Material de Emprego Militar* (Brazil, 2005, p. 10). It is again the army that determines whether weapons are military or civilian in nature (see Dreyfus, Lessing, and César Purcena, 2005, p. 57). Information on these additional controls is not publicly available.

Canada

Canadian legislation on small arms exports derives from the *Export and Import Permits Act* (Canada, 2007a) and the related *Export Permits Regulations* (Canada, 2007b). End-use documentation is required for all licence applications. It may take the form of an end-use certificate, an international import certificate, or an import permit issued by the government of the importing country. Irrespective of the form the document takes, it must identify the exporter, importer, final consignee (recipient), and intended end use of the exported equipment (Canada, 2007b, sec. 3.1.j).

End-use statements from commercial businesses in the importing country are accepted for 'sporting' (non- and semi-automatic) firearms. Canada's diplomatic missions abroad verify whether the business is 'reputable' (Canada, 2006b, p. 9). These end-use statements must provide full information about the goods, their end-user, and intended

---

Box 5.2 State-to-state transfers

Governments often sell or supply small arms and light weapons directly to other governments, especially those that are surplus to national requirements. They may also facilitate the sale of arms to foreign governments from companies within their territory. How are end-users certified in such cases?

The following text represents a preliminary attempt to answer this question. Although its findings appear valid for the majority of EU and Wassenaar Arrangement states, no firm conclusions can be drawn in relation to the much broader range of arms-exporting countries worldwide. The research task is complicated by the fact that law and practice governing state-to-state transfers is sometimes distinct from that regulating private commercial exports. In some cases state-to-state transfer is conducted, above all, on the basis of government policy, which is less easily accessed by the public than is legislation.

In many EU and Wassenaar Arrangement states, state-to-state transfers are treated no differently from private commercial sales. Export licences are issued upon fulfilment of the same end-user certification requirements that apply to commercial exports. These requirements may be waived or relaxed for certain reasons (for example, when the purchaser is a 'friendly' government), but this is not typically influenced by the nature of the transaction, whether state-to-state or commercial.

Two cases, drawn from the principal exporters list, give some sense of current practice in this area.

United States

The United States allows foreign states to acquire US military systems or defence items by:

• purchasing items from the US government (USG) through the foreign military sales programme (FMS); or
• purchasing items directly from arms-producing companies in the United States (direct commercial sales /DCS).

Only certain states are deemed FMS eligible by the US president, and some sensitive items are designated 'FMS only', meaning they can be acquired only through that programme. The US Department of Defense provides items acquired under FMS contracts from its own stocks[15] or procures them from private contractors.

In practice, there is little difference between DCS and FMS transactions with respect to end-use or end-user undertakings. As part of their export licence application, DCS exporters must ensure that a statement is incorporated in the sales contract confirming that the items to be exported will not be transferred, transhipped, or otherwise disposed of without the prior written approval of the US government. No export licence is required for an FMS transfer, but the Letter of Acceptance (LOA) that authorizes the transaction includes a commitment from the purchaser not to transfer or dispose of the items, nor use or permit their use, for purposes other than those authorized without the written consent of the US government. In the LOA, the purchaser also agrees to permit scheduled inspections of physical inventories upon US government request, except when other forms of end-use monitoring have been mutually agreed.

Canada

Canadian government-to-government sales sometimes also involve the supply of arms that are not simply surplus to Canadian defence force requirements. The companies involved, however, must still apply for export permits and provide end-use certificates.

Most of Canada's government-to-government sales are with the United States. Under the terms of the Defence Production Sharing Agreement (DPSA), signed by Canada and the United States in 1956, an export licence is not required for many items on Canada's export control list if the final destination is the United States. Nevertheless, an export licence is required for the export of small arms and light weapons[16] to the United States. The end-use certification requirements applicable to commercial sales apply equally to state-to-state sales of such weapons.

Source: Parker (2008)

end use. They may include a declaration by the final consignee that the goods will not be re-exported or that any retransfer will respect the legislation of the country of final destination. Export authorizations for small arms and light weapons may be conditioned on the provision of a delivery verification certificate (Canada, 2006a, pp. xv–xvi).

China

China's *Arms Export Regulations* require end-use certification from the importing state for all small arms and light weapons exports (China, 2002, art. 15; 2003a, p. 4). Chinese export officials may require that the end-user and/or importing country issue end-user certificates and international import certificates for this purpose. These documents are authenticated by China's diplomatic missions abroad. They must identify the end-user and intended end use of the equipment, and may include an undertaking not to modify the end use from that stated in the certificate or transfer the goods outside the state of final destination without the permission of the Chinese government (see China, 2003b).[17]

Germany

German export control legislation distinguishes between 'war weapons'—which include semi-automatic rifles, all automatic firearms, and light weapons—and small arms, such as non-automatic pistols and revolvers (Germany, 2007a; 2007b). Applications for the export of all small arms and light weapons must include documentation identifying the recipient, the final consignee or end-user, and the end use (Germany, 2007b, arts. 5.1, 17.2). The form this documentation takes depends, in particular, on the nature of the weapons being exported. German export authorities may also require that a delivery verification certificate be provided (Germany, 2005, p. 29). Political guidelines on arms exports stipulate that licence applications to export war weapons to states that have previously failed to respect end-user undertakings will be denied until the risk of diversion has been removed (Germany, 2000, para. IV.4).

Those seeking to export war weapons must submit an end-use certificate that is provided by the government of the importing state (Germany, 2000, para. IV.2; 2005, p. 29). End-use certificates must identify the goods, their quantity and value, the supplier, and the final consignee. They include a declaration by the final consignee that the goods are for the consignee's own use, will remain in the country of final destination, and will be used only as stated in the document. They also prohibit re-export without the approval of the German government (Germany, n.d., sample form 1; 2000, para. IV.2; 2005, p. 29).

For exports of non-war weapons, Germany requires that the commercial importer furnish an end-use statement, with the importing country issuing a complementary international import certificate.[18] As provided in the end-use statement, non-war weapons can be re-exported, without German government approval, to EU member countries, Australia, Canada, Japan, New Zealand, Norway, Switzerland, and the United States (Germany, n.d., sample form 2).[19]

Officials ▪
and Germ
require p
of a deli
verificati
certifica▪

Italy

Legislation governing the export of small arms and light weapons from Italy obliges licence applicants to submit information identifying the type, quantity, and value of the equipment, the country of final destination, and the final consignee (Italy, 1990, art. 11.2.a–b). Applications for exports to states with which Italy has a 'reciprocal arms export control agreement' (those belonging to NATO and the Western European Union, WEU) are conditional on an international import certificate (Italy, 1990, art. 11.3.c.1). Applications for exports to all other states require the submission of an end-use certificate that is issued by the importing country (Italy, 1990, art. 11.3.c.2; 2003, sec. 3d). These EUCs include a declaration by the consignee that the country of final destination and the end use of the imported equipment are as stated on the certificate. They may also contain a clause prohibiting re-export without Italian government authorization. Italian diplomatic missions abroad have the task of verifying these documents (Italy, 1990, arts. 11.3.c.2, 11.4; 2003, sec. 3i).

Italian legislation also stipulates that small arms and light weapons exporters, irrespective of the destination, have to provide, within 180 days of delivery, a delivery verification certificate. The latter attests to the receipt of the exported equipment by the consignee in the country of final destination (Italy, 1990, art. 20.1.b). It appears Italy conducts no end-use monitoring after the time of delivery (Italy, 2003, sec. 3j).

An Italian policeman inspects a container after the seizure of more than 8,000 Kalashnikovs and other weapons on a ship at the southern Italian port of Gioia Tauro, April 2004. © Antonio Condorelli DJM/WS/Reuters

Japan

Under long-standing policy, Japan bans the export of small arms and light weapons for military use (Japan METI, 2002a). In practice, this means that Japan does not authorize the export of military small arms and light weapons to foreign governments or commercial importers. The export of non-military small arms is regulated by the *Foreign Trade and Exchange Law* (Japan, 1997) and its associated ordinance (Japan, 2006). Such exports require prior authorization (Japan, 1997, art. 48.1; 2006, art. 1.1). Licence applicants must submit information identifying the type of small arms for export, along with their intended end use, consignee/end-user, and country of final destination. Applicants may also be asked to submit a 'letter of assurance' from the consignee (end-use statement) regarding the country of final destination and intended end use (Japan METI, 2002b). Formal end-user certificates, signed by the authorities of the importing state, are not required (Japan, 2007, p. 11).

United Kingdom

The *Export Control Act* (UK, 2002) and its implementing orders[20] furnish the legislative framework for UK exports of small arms and light weapons. Export licence applicants must submit information identifying the exporter, consignee, exported equipment, intended end-user, and end use (UK, n.d.). Required end-user documentation may include end-user and international import certificates. The export of small arms and light weapons generally requires an end-user undertaking in which end-user and consignee provide certain written assurances concerning end use and retransfer. The consignee, for example, either certifies that the goods will not be re-exported from the country of final destination, or lists the countries to which the arms 'are likely to be transferred' (UK, n.d.). Exports of small arms to EU member states require an import permit in which the importing country confirms it has no objection to the importer's acquisition of the arms (UK, 2005, p. 12).

UK export policy requires that licensing authorities consider the 'risk that the equipment will be diverted within the buyer country or re-exported under undesirable conditions' (UK, 2000, criterion 7). The United Kingdom's strategy for preventing diversion emphasizes, above all, 'a thorough risk assessment at the licensing stage' rather than non-re-export clauses and end-use monitoring. UK licensing officials carry out checks to satisfy themselves of 'the end-user's reliability and integrity' before authorizing the export (UK, 2005, p. 13).

The UK will, however, conduct post-shipment monitoring of exported equipment, on a case-by-case basis, where it believes this 'can add value' (UK, 2005, p. 13). Desk officers in London are instructed to advise missions abroad of 'any approved arms licence that it is felt should be monitored post-export', while overseas missions have orders to inform London of 'any suspected mis-use, or diversion, of UK arms exports' (O'Brien, 2003). The UK, for example, has monitored the end use of military equipment exported to India and Israel on the condition that it not be used in Kashmir and the Palestinian territories, respectively. Diplomatic missions used information received from the UK government and other sources to determine whether any violation of end-use restrictions was occurring.[21]

The UK c■
post-ship■
monitorir
believes ▮
add value▮

United States

The *Arms Export Control Act* (US, 2005) and accompanying *International Traffic in Arms Regulations* (US, 2007) regulate the export of small arms and light weapons from the United States. Licence applicants must submit information identifying the quantity, type, and value of the equipment to be exported, the country of final destination, and the consignee, end-user, and intended end use (USDoS, 2005). Applicants must also furnish a written statement from the foreign purchaser confirming the specified end-user and end use (USDoS, 2005, p. 2). Like other leading exporters, US authorities screen licence applications with a view to identifying those exports at greatest risk of diversion or misuse. 'Indicators of concern' for the US include:

> *unfamiliar foreign parties, unusual routing, overseas destinations with a history of illicit activity or weak export/customs controls, [and] commodities not known to be in the inventory of the host country's armed forces.* (USDoS, 2007b, p. 2)

Under US legislation, contracts between arms exporters and consignees must include a clause prohibiting retransfer to a third country or a change in end use without the prior written approval of US authorities (US, 2007, art. 123.9). Export licences for fully automatic firearms, rifles with a calibre of .50 inches or greater, and other types of firearms in quantities of 50 or more require the submission of a 'nontransfer and use certificate' (USDoS, 2007a, pp. 3–4). This certificate includes commitments by the final consignee and end-user not to retransfer the exported equipment without the prior written approval of the US government (USDoS, n.d.). Export licences for small arms also require an import authorization issued by the government of the importing state (USDoS, 2005, p. 3.; 2007a, pp. 2–3).

US law also allows for the use of delivery verification certificates to confirm the receipt of small arms by commercial consignees (US, 2007, 123.14.b). In principle, the end use of exported small arms and light weapons is monitored to 'provide reasonable assurance' that recipients are complying with retransfer and end-use restrictions (US, 2005, subchapter III-A, sec. 2785.a.2.B). In practice, US authorities consistently monitor only certain types of exported light weapons. Specific measures are agreed in the export contract and can include the physical inspection of end-user stockpiles. For most types of small arms and light weapons, US export authorities initiate post-delivery checks only in response to allegations of a violation of retransfer or end-use restrictions. These are conducted in cooperation with the government of the importing state (see Box 5.3).

Box 5.3 End-use monitoring of US-origin arms

The Golden Sentry programme

Small arms and light weapons manufactured in the United States and exported to the armed forces of a foreign state may be subject to pre-licence and post-delivery controls under the Golden Sentry end-use monitoring programme. The programme is implemented by the US Department of Defense for the purposes of ensuring the recipient's compliance with restrictions on the re-export, retransfer, and end use of the equipment. The scope and intensity of verification activities are tailored to the weapons system and country of import. Certain equipment exported to 'trusted partners' may be subject to 'routine' end-use monitoring, while other equipment and destinations may require 'enhanced' monitoring. Verification activities can include visits to end-user facilities, a review of end-user records, and regular inventories of US-exported equipment. Enhanced end-use monitoring may also include physical inspections of the stockpiles where US-exported equipment is stored (USDoD, 2003, pp. 321-36).

End-use monitoring of US-manufactured MANPADS

US-exported man-portable air defence systems (MANPADS) are subject to enhanced end-use monitoring. Recipients must agree to specific verification measures in the LOA they sign for the purchase of US-origin MANPADS. US army personnel typically inspect the physical security arrangements for the MANPADS in the importing state prior to delivery. Within 30 days of delivery, the recipient and a US government representative, by means of an inspection and/or inventory, must verify receipt of the missiles, grip stocks, and other essential components by serial number. US officials also conduct an annual physical check of all imported MANPADS that includes a review of inventory records that the recipient must establish on a monthly basis (USDoD, 2003, p. 337).

The Blue Lantern programme

Commercial exports of US-manufactured small arms may be subject to pre-licence or post-shipment controls under the Blue Lantern end-use monitoring programme that is implemented by the Department of State. The controls may include requests for information and investigations by US diplomatic missions in the country of import to verify the delivery and proper end use of the equipment. Post-delivery controls may, for example, be initiated following receipt of information received post-export regarding a particular end-user and end use of US-manufactured small arms (USDoS, 2007b, pp. 1-2).[22]

The Department of State considers the programme useful to its efforts to deter diversion, assist in the disruption of illicit supply networks, and contribute to informed export licensing decisions. It cites, in particular, the effectiveness of Blue Lantern end-use checks in combating the use of fraudulent export documentation and other forms of misrepresentation for purposes of obtaining US equipment for retransfer to unauthorized end-users. During fiscal year 2006, US authorities conducted 613 Blue Lantern end-use checks, representing a little less than one per cent of all licence applications and other export requests received during that period.[23] An 'unfavorable' determination was reached in 94 of the 489 Blue Lantern cases closed in 2006 (19 per cent). Thirty-eight per cent of these 'unfavorable' checks related to applications for exports to the Americas. Firearms and ammunition were involved in over 70 per cent of the 'unfavorable' Americas cases (USDoS, 2007b, pp. 1-6).

Source: Anders (2007)

Ten-country assessment[24]

What are the key similarities and differences in the systems used by the world's principal exporters to certify end-users? The preceding study illustrates that much, in fact, depends on the type of weapons for export, as well as the destination country. Moreover, in many of these countries export licensing officials have some discretion over whether to employ various requirements and control measures.

With these caveats in mind, one can conclude that the leading exporting states typically require that export licence applicants submit information identifying the type, quantity, and value of weapons for export, as well as the country of final destination, end-user, and end use. Such documentation may be issued by the authorities of the importing state (end-user or international import certificates) and/or the end-user (end-use declarations or statements). Exports of small arms and light weapons to the armed forces of another state are often made conditional on an end-user certificate that is issued by the relevant department of the importing country. Exports of small arms to foreign commercial importers normally require an import certificate in which the importing state confirms that it does not object to the transfer, along with an end-use statement from the foreign commercial importer.

Most of the sample countries also report imposing restrictions on the retransfer of exported small arms and light weapons. In many cases these governments stipulate that exported weapons not be retransferred without their prior approval. Those imposing non-retransfer restrictions, either systematically or selectively, are Austria, Belgium, Canada, China, Germany, Italy, the UK, and the United States. US legislation stipulates that a non-retransfer clause be included in the contract between the exporter and the consignee (US, 2007, 123.9.a–b, d). Austria, Belgium, Canada, Germany, Italy, the UK, and the United States may (selectively) require the submission of a delivery verification certificate. In Belgium and Italy, delivery verification certificates are required, by law, for all small arms and light weapons exports (Belgium, 2003b, art. 7; Italy, 1990, art. 20.1.b).

States also differ in their employment of end-user and international import certificates. The decision to require one or the other is made on a case-by-case basis, at the discretion of export authorities in, for example, Austria and Brazil (Austria, 2006, p. 3; Dreyfus, Lessing, and Purcena, 2005, p. 57). In other states this is determined by national export policy. Germany requires an end-use certificate for all exports of 'military' small arms and light weapons, but an import certificate for all exports of 'non-military' small arms (Germany, n.d., sample forms 1–2). The Belgian and Italian governments require an end-use certificate for the export of all types of small arms and light weapons to non-EU or non-NATO countries and an import certificate for small arms and light weapons exports to EU or NATO states (Belgium, Walloon Government, 2006, p. 18; EU Council, 1998; Italy, 1990, arts. 11.3.c.2, 11.4). The United Kingdom generally requires an end-user undertaking for its small arms and light weapons exports. It uses import certificates only for the export of non- and semi-automatic small arms to EU member states (UK, 2005, p. 12).

Non-retransfer practices also show important variations. The Austrian and German governments, for example, waive the requirement that foreign importers obtain prior authorization if retransferring 'non-military' small arms to EU countries and certain other states (Austria, n.d.; Germany, n.d., sample form 2).

The United Kingdom and the United States are the only countries that report monitoring small arms and light weapons exports after delivery, albeit quite selectively in the UK case (O'Brien, 2003; USDoD, 2003, ch. 8). The United States, alone, indicates that it conducts physical inspections of end-user stockpiles following export of US-manufactured MANPADS. These inspections are stipulated in the associated export licence (see Box 5.3).

States differ in their employment of end-user and international import certificates.

Table 5.1 **End-user documentation required for small arms and light weapons exports**			
	Requirement for end-user certificates	**Requirement for international import certificates**	**Re-export and end-use restrictions**	**Requirement for delivery verification certificate**
Austria	Can be requested	Can be requested	Waived for re-export of non-military SALW to EU and certain other states	Can be requested
Belgium	For exports to non-EU/NATO states	For exports to EU/NATO states	For re-exports to non-EU/NATO states	Required for all exports
Brazil	Can be requested	Can be requested	Can be requested	Not known
Canada	Can be requested	Can be requested	Can be requested	Can be requested
China	Can be requested	Can be requested	Can be requested	Not known
Germany	For military SALW	For non-military SALW	Waived for re-export of non-military SALW to EU and certain other states	Can be requested
Italy	For exports to non-NATO/WEU states	For exports to NATO/WEU states	Can be requested when authorizing exports to non-NATO/WEU states	Required for all exports
Japan	No (ban on military exports)	Not known	Not known	Not known
UK	Can be requested	For export of non-military small arms to EU states	Can be requested	Can be requested
US	For military SALW	For non-military SALW	For all SALW	Can be requested

Notes: In their export control systems, some states distinguish between 'military' small arms and light weapons on the one hand, and 'non-military' small arms on the other. While there is no common definition of these categories, 'non-military' small arms usually denote non- and semi-automatic firearms,[15] whereas military small arms and light weapons typically refer to fully-automatic small arms (firearms) and all light weapons.

Overall, the legislative framework required to ensure 'effective control' over small arms and light weapons transfers (UNGA, 2001b, para. II.12) appears quite complete in nearly all of the leading exporting states. Yet this legislation tends to leave much to the discretion of export control officials, allowing them to decide, for example, when to require certain types of end-user documentation or impose retransfer or end-use restrictions on a particular end-user. It is unclear how such discretion is exercised in practice.

With rare exceptions, the ten countries reviewed in the chapter provided no information on the practical implementation of their transfer control systems. We do not know, in particular:

- what policies and practices states employ to assess diversion risks at the licensing stage (e.g. warning flags that trigger a denial of licence or a higher level of scrutiny);[26] nor
- the extent to which governments verify end-user documents and the information they contain before authorizing a transaction.

Future research, combined with greater transparency from governments, will, one hopes, lead to a better understanding of national practice. Each of the measures just mentioned is critical to an effective transfer controls (diversion prevention) system. No news is not, in this case, good news.

Despite the uncertainties that exist, this study of national practice has generated some clear findings. First, the world's leading small arms exporters employ a wide range of documents and procedures for purposes of certifying end-users. These vary, in particular, as a function of the type of material that is to be exported (especially whether military or non-military in nature) and the destination country. Second, looking past the licensing stage, the study has revealed that, while the ten principal exporters often require that the importing country confirm receipt of exported weapons by issuing a delivery verification certificate, this is not uniform practice.

Delivery verification is, in any case, no panacea. Many opportunities for diversion arise after weapons have been delivered to their intended destination; yet exporting states rarely conduct any checks beyond this point—the study's third major finding. Among the ten countries reviewed here, only two monitor the end use and retransfer of weapons that they export—specifically the United Kingdom (very selectively) and the United States (more often, but not consistently). While end-use monitoring may, in theory, figure in the control 'arsenals' of other leading exporters, it is not employed in practice. This finding echoes a study of national practice worldwide (BtB with IANSA, 2006. p. 162).

POLICY IMPLICATIONS

In its examination and assessment of national practice, the chapter has focused on the ten leading exporters of small arms and light weapons. What are the implications for the world as a whole? First, one should note that a high volume of exports does not necessarily translate into a more sophisticated end-user system. Examples of good practice situated outside the principal exporters' list include Swedish practices designed to prevent EUC forgery (discussed below), as well as Switzerland's use of selective end-use monitoring.[27] It seems likely, however, that gaps in control among the ten leading exporting countries are shared by many other states. Moreover, regulatory weaknesses anywhere in the world are cause for concern given the proven ability of arms traffickers to exploit them.[28]

Setting priorities

Transfer control systems have significant resource requirements. Necessary personnel must be recruited, trained, and paid. Systems for the acquisition, dissemination, and retention of crucial knowledge have to be established and maintained. Time is often in short supply. Resources for diversion prevention must compete with other pressing needs. States cannot eliminate the risk that the weapons they authorize for export will be diverted or misused. Yet careful priority-setting, coupled with the effective use of existing policy instruments such as end-user certification, can reduce this risk considerably at reasonable cost.

As the discussion of national practice has demonstrated, in tackling the problem of diversion states concentrate most of their efforts on the licensing stage. Interventions at this point are much easier for the exporting state (the weapons are still on its territory) and, as a rule, less costly (TRANSFER DIVERSION). And they have the important advantage of preventing diversion rather than discovering it after the fact. It is not surprising, then, that states like the UK, while retaining a role for end-use monitoring, emphasize the thorough assessment of diversion risks at the licensing stage.

Post-shipment controls present various complications. It may be politically difficult—even impossible—for the exporting country to intervene once the weapons have left its jurisdiction. The cooperation of the state of import will invariably be needed for reasons of sovereignty. Resources are also an issue. The exporting state may lack diplomatic

Exportin
rarely co
checks b
point of

representation in the recipient state. More often, existing diplomatic personnel may lack the time and/or expertise needed for routine end-use monitoring. For this reason, there is a temptation for states to rely on licensing alone to weed out diversion risks.

Post-shipment controls, including delivery verification and end-use monitoring, are, however, an indispensable component of the broader transfer controls (diversion prevention) package. Delivery verification can uncover and ultimately deter the diversion of weapons while en route to the importing state. End-use monitoring, where a condition of the export licence, can also exert a powerful deterrent effect on potential transgressors. By testing the reliability of the end-user, it also helps to reinforce and improve risk assessment at the time of licensing. If a state makes no attempt to verify possession and end use after export, there is a strong chance that any diversion that does occur will go undetected. Unless the diversion is revealed by other means, nothing prevents the state from approving further exports to the same end-user (Anders, 2007).

The resource arguments against end-use monitoring, though important, are less compelling than might first appear. The goal is not to monitor the end use of each and

A SWAT team provides back-up for police officers arresting a suspected illegal arms trafficker, near Yabucoa, Puerto Rico, September 2007. © Brennan Linsley/AP Photo

every export, but rather to deploy this measure periodically and selectively, paying special attention to cases presenting greater diversion risks. Developing countries may face capacity constraints, not only on post-shipment verification, but also on assessing diversion risks at the licensing stage. But these can be addressed in a variety of ways, most notably through the pooling of information and resources (GRIP et al., 2006).

The conclusion, then, is that while it may make sense to devote the lion's share of resources and attention to licensing, post-shipment verification—including some degree of end-use monitoring—is also essential to national efforts to combat diversion. Practice among the ten leading exporters, however, indicates that these measures are underutilized (delivery verification) or largely neglected (end-use monitoring).

Enhancing end-user certification

Although governments are devoting far greater attention to licensing and end-user certification than to post-shipment control measures, the quality of that attention is something of a question mark. On paper, it appears the norms, instruments, and systems needed to combat diversion are in place among the world's leading exporting states. Yet whether and how this framework translates into effective action remains unclear in the vast majority of cases.

As noted earlier, all of the principal exporters undertake some form of end-user certification when licensing small arms and light weapons exports, but the kinds of documents and procedures they use vary widely. This is not, in and of itself, a problem. Licensing decisions are, and are bound to remain, the prerogative of individual governments. The variation in end-user documents and procedures reflects differing national approaches to arms transfer licensing and, in particular, different perceptions of risk and acceptable risk. International instruments and best-practice guidelines, including those mentioned earlier, help raise standards across the board and ensure that certain minimum requirements are met when governments authorize small arms transfers. It is, however, neither helpful nor realistic to expect governments to use the same documents and procedures for end-user certification.

Certainly much more could be done to make the forgery of end-user documentation more difficult. Sweden, for example, prints the document it uses for state-to-state transfers ('Declaration by End User') on banknote paper precisely for this reason (Sweden ISP, 2005).[29] As for content, exporting states around the world could undoubtedly do more to ensure, pursuant to international best practice,[30] that end-user documents contain complete information, including details of the material to be transferred, destination country, end-user, and end use. Yet, whatever the form and content of end-user documents, they are worth little more than the paper they are written on if the documents themselves and the information they contain are not verified in advance of export.

Placing a phone call to an official who has signed an EUC is of little use if that individual has been bought off by an illicit trafficker (see above). Additional checks are needed. That said, a simple phone call can catch any forgery and any illicit EUC acquired from a government representative without 'follow-up service' (an official prepared to lie about a document's validity; see above). It is unclear, however, whether exporting states are systematically verifying end-user documents, even though this is vital to the exercise of 'effective control' over small arms transfers (UNGA, 2001b, para. II.12).

CONCLUSION

This chapter has reviewed national practices in the world's leading exporting states with a view to determining how well these countries meet their commitments, notably under the *UN Programme of Action*, to exert 'effective control' over small arms transfers (UNGA, 2001b, para. II.12). The best time to prevent the diversion of small arms and light weapons is obviously in advance of export, at the time of licensing. At this stage, diversion risks can be thoroughly assessed and end-users carefully vetted. Licensing alone, however, is insufficient. Post-shipment controls, including delivery verification and end-use monitoring, help detect (and deter) actual cases of diversion and ultimately reinforce licensing itself.

The challenges are clear, much less so the extent to which states are meeting them. The basic components of effective transfer control (diversion prevention) systems appear to be in place in the principal exporting countries; yet these systems leave much to the discretion of individual licensing officials, allowing them to decide when to increase or decrease the level of scrutiny required for a particular transaction. It is unclear, in particular, how thoroughly diversion risks are being assessed at the licensing stage, or how systematically end-user documentation is being verified.

It is quite clear, however, that post-shipment controls are being neglected. Many governments require that the delivery of weapons at destination be verified, but this is not uniform practice. Equally important, with rare exceptions verification stops at the time of delivery. As a rule, governments do not monitor the end use of exported weapons, not even selectively. They do not know, in other words, whether their decision to export weapons to a specific end-user was correct.

Rigorous licensing and end-user certification, coupled with targeted post-shipment controls, are obviously not the end of the story. These measures cannot eliminate diversion; yet, in concert with other policy instruments—such as the control of brokering and transport, plus systematic tracing—they would make it vastly more difficult. States have yet to demonstrate they are doing what is needed. ✍

LIST OF ABBREVIATIONS

EU	European Union	OAS	Organization of American States
EUC	End-user certificate	OSCE	Organization for Security and
LOA	Letter of Acceptance		Co-operation in Europe
MANPADS	Man-portable air defence system	SALW	Small arms and light weapons
NATO	North Atlantic Treaty Organization	WEU	Western European Union

ENDNOTES

1   See also UNGA (2007); Griffiths and Wilkinson (2007, secs. 6.2, 6.4, 6.5); Cattaneo (forthcoming).

2   Note that, in contrast to the *UN Programme of Action,* the *UN Firearms Protocol* is not an instrument of universal application as it binds only those states that have ratified, or otherwise adhered to, this treaty. For a list of States Parties to the *Firearms Protocol,* see <http://www.unodc.org/unodc/en/treaties/CTOC/countrylist-firearmsprotocol.html>

3   This section is partly based on Anders (2007).

4   Interviews by Holger Anders with arms export officials from various states, April–September 2007 (Anders, 2007).

5   The *UN Programme of Action* is exceptionally weak on the question of retransfer. It merely recommends that importing states notify the original exporting state before any retransfer (UNGA, 2001b, para. II.13).

6   Interviews by Holger Anders with arms export officials from various states, April–September 2007 (Anders, 2007).

7   Interviews by Holger Anders with arms export officials from various states, April–September 2007 (Anders, 2007).

8   This section is based on Anders (2007).

9   See also Chapter 3, Annexe 3.1, available online at <http://www.smallarmssurvey.org/files/sas/publications/yearb2007.html>

10 Telephone interview by Holger Anders with an Austrian arms export official, October 2007.

11 Telephone interview by Sarah Parker with an Austrian arms export official, February 2008.

12 Depending on the export, this could mean the Belgian federal government or the government of one of the three regions (Brussels, Flanders, Wallonia).

13 There is no fixed list of these additional states; Belgian licensing authorities have some discretion in this area. Telephone interview by Holger Anders with Walloon arms export official, October 2007.

14 Telephone interview by Holger Anders with Walloon arms export official, October 2007.

15 Note: this is different from the Excess Defense Articles (EDA) programme administered by the Defense Security Cooperation Agency, under which defence articles declared as excess by US military departments can be offered to foreign governments or international organizations in support of US national security and foreign policy objectives.

16 The categories of weapon requiring an export licence include items 2-1, 2-2, and 2-3 of the Canadian Export Control List, echoing items ML1, ML2, and ML3 of the Wassenaar Munitions List. See Canada (2006a, p. 49).

17 The White Paper refers, above all, to weapons of mass destruction. Chinese export authorities can, however, apply the same end-use controls to small arms and light weapons exports. Interview by Holger Anders with Chinese official, August 2007.

18 Interview by Holger Anders with German arms export official, July 2007.

19 As of October 2007, new EU members Romania and Bulgaria were not yet included on the list of countries benefiting from the waiver relating to the re-export of non-war weapons. Germany was, however, in the process of updating its regulations for this purpose. Interview by Holger Anders with German arms export official, October 2007.

20 Available at <http://www.berr.gov.uk/europeandtrade/strategic-export-control/legislation/export-control-act-2002/eca-2002-orders/index.html>

21 Interview by Holger Anders with British arms export official, August 2007 (Anders, 2007).

22 Interview by Holger Anders with US arms export official, August 2007.

23 'Blue Lantern checks are not conducted randomly, but are rather the result of a careful selection process to identify transactions that appear most at risk for diversion or misuse'; USDoS (2007b, p. 2).

24 This section is partly based on Anders (2007).

25 Some states define semi-automatic carbines and rifles as military weapons, however. See Austria (1977, art. 1).

26 For information on the US system, see Chapter 4 (TRANSFER DIVERSION).

27 In cases of concern, Switzerland verifies weapons exports post-delivery. It estimates that 'up to 5% of total exports (value)' undergo such verification. Written correspondence with Swiss export control authorities, February 2008.

28 See, for example, Griffiths and Wilkinson (2007).

29 See also Sweden ISP (n.d., 'Declaration by End User'; n.d., *National Practices*).

30 See EU Council (2007, sec. 2.1.2); *Nairobi Best Practice Guidelines* (2005, sec. 2.1.e); OSCE (2003, ch. V, sec. IV.6); OSCE (2004b); WA (2005).

BIBLIOGRAPHY

Anders, Holger. 2005. *Out of Sight, Out of Mind? Scope for Strengthened EU Standards on Delivery and Post-Delivery Controls for Military Equipment*. Note d'analyse. Groupe de recherche et d'information sur la paix et la sécurité (GRIP). 21 December.
<https://www.grip-publications.eu/bdg/g4591.html>

—. 2007. *The Role and Use of End Use Documentation among Major SALW Exporting States*. Unpublished background paper. Geneva: Small Arms Survey.

Austria. 1977. *Verordnung der Bundesregierung vom 22. November 1977 betreffend Kriegsmaterial (Kriegsmaterialverordnung; War Material Ordinance)*, BGBL. of 22 November 1977. <http://ris.bka.gv.at/taweb-cgi/taweb?x=d&o=d&v=bnd&d=BND&i=22233&p=10&q=und>

—. 2005a. *Bundesgesetz vom 18. Oktober 1977 über die Ein-, Aus- und Durchfuhr von Kriegsmaterial (Kriegsmaterialgesetz; War Material Act)*, BGBl. Nr. 540/1977 idF BGBl. I Nr. 50/2005. <http://www.bmi.gv.at/downloadarea/kunsttexte/Kriegsmaterialgesetz.pdf>

—. 2005b. *Bundesgesetz mit dem das Aussenhandelsgesetz 2005 – AussHG 2005 erlassen und das Kriegsmaterialgesetz geändert wird (Aussenhandelsgesetz; Foreign Trade Act)*, BGBL. of 9 June 2005.
<http://www.bmwa.gv.at/NR/rdonlyres/E61937F7-82AC-4BB6-AF03-F74B0872873D/0/AuHG.pdf>

—. 2006. National report on the implementation of the UN Small Arms Programme of Action.
<http://disarmament.un.org/cab/nationalreports/2006/austria.pdf>

—. n.d. *Statement of End Use by Ultimate Consignee and Purchaser* (sample end use statement).
<http://www.bmwa.gv.at/NR/rdonlyres/48FBD828-AD31-440E-836D-F3BF2DDE8B76/0/FormularCDmilgutendverblerklmlohnetechno.pdf>

Belgium. 2003a. *Loi relative à l'importation, à l'exportation, au transit et à la lutte contre le trafic d'armes, de munitions et de matériel devant servir spécialement à un usage militaire ou de maintien de l'ordre et de la technologie y afférente*. Adopted 5 August 1991. Amended July 2003.
<http://www.juridat.be/>

. 2003b. *Arrêté royal réglementant l'importation, l'exportation et le transit d'armes, de munitions et de matériel devant servir spécialement à un usage militaire ou de maintien de l'ordre et de la technologie y afférente*. Adopted 8 March 1993. Amended July 2003. <http://www.juridat.be/>

—. Walloon Government. 2006. *Rapport annuel 2005 au Parlement Wallon sur l'application de la Loi du 05 août 1991, modifiée par les Lois du 25 et du 26 mars 2003 relatives à l'importation, à l'exportation et au transit d'armes, de munitions et de matériel devant servir spécialement à un usage militaire et de la technologie y afférente*. <http://gov.wallonie.be/code/fr/rap_2005.pdf>

BtB (Biting the Bullet Project: International Alert, Saferworld, University of Bradford) with IANSA (International Action Network on Small Arms). 2006. *Reviewing Action on Small Arms 2006: Assessing the First Five Years of the UN Programme of Action*. London: Biting the Bullet.
<http://www.iansa.org/un/review2006/redbook2006/index.htm>

Brazil. 2000a. *Decreto no. 3.665 de 20 Novembreo de 2000 (Decreto no. 3.665; Decree no. 3.665)*.
<http://www.planalto.gov.br/ccivil_03/decreto/D3665.htm>

—. 2000b. *Certificado de Usuário Final* (sample end-user certificate). Annex XXXI to *Decreto no 3.665*.
<https://www.planalto.gov.br/ccivil_03/decreto/Anexos/D3665AnexoXXXI.htm>

—. 2005. National report on the implementation of the UN Small Arms Programme of Action.
<http://disarmament.un.org/cab/nationalreports/2005/brazil14.07.05.pdf>

Canada. 2006a. *A Guide to Canada's Export Controls*. June. <http://www.dfait-maeci.gc.ca/eicb/military/documents/exportcontrols2006-en.pdf>

—. 2006b. National report on the implementation of the UN Small Arms Programme of Action. 21 June.
<http://disarmament.un.org/cab/nationalreports/2006/Canada%20National%20Report%20-%20August%2010%202006.pdf>

—. 2007a. *Export and Import Permits Act* (R.S., 1985, c. E-19), as of August 2007. <http://laws.justice.gc.ca/en/ShowFullDoc/cs/E-19///en>

—. 2007b. *Export Permits Regulations* (SOR/97-204), as of August 2007. <http://laws.justice.gc.ca/en/ShowFullDoc/cr/SOR-97-204///en>

Cattaneo, Silvia. Forthcoming. *Illicit Brokering and Transportation Activities: Characteristics, Options, and Challenges in the Control of Transportation Agents*. Geneva: Small Arms Survey.

China. 2002. *Regulations of the People's Republic of China on Administration of Arms Export (Arms Export Regulations)*, as revised October 2002.
<http://www.gov.cn/english/laws/2005-07/25/content_16975.htm>

—. 2003a. National report on the implementation of the UN Small Arms Programme of Action.
<http://disarmament.un.org/cab/nationalreports/2002/china-e.PDF>

—. 2003b. *China's Non-Proliferation Policy and Measures*. White Paper published by State Council Information Office. December.
<http://www.china.org.cn/english/2003/Dec/81312.htm>

Dreyfus, Pablo, Benjamin Lessing, and Júlio César Purcena. 2005. 'The Brazilian Small Arms Industry: Legal Production and Trade.' In Rubem César Fernandes, ed. *Brazil: The Arms and the Victims*. Rio de Janeiro: 7 Letras/ISER.
<http://www.smallarmssurvey.org/files/portal/issueareas/transfers/transfers_pdf/2005_Dreyfus_et_al.pdf>

EU Council (Council of the European Union). 1998. *COARM Questionnaire on Transshipment, Re-Export and End User Statement*. 6 May.
<http://www.sipri.org/contents/expcon/coarm.html>

—. 2007. *User's Guide to the European Union Code of Conduct on Arms Exports*. Doc. 10684/1/07 REV 1 (en) of 3 July.
<http://register.consilium.europa.eu/pdf/en/07/st10/st10684-re01.en07.pdf>

Germany. 2000. *Politische Grundsätze der Bundesregierung für den Export von Kriegswaffen und sonstigen Rüstungsgütern vom 19 Januar 2000* (Political Principles of the Federal Government for the Export of War Weapons and other Military Equipment of 19 January 2000).
<http://www.ausfuhrkontrolle.info/ausfuhrkontrolle/de/krwaffkontrg/bekanntmachungen/grundsatz_politisch.pdf>

—. 2005. National report on the implementation of the UN Small Arms Programme of Action, 30 April.
<http://disarmament.un.org/cab/nationalreports/2005/Germany.pdf>

—. 2007a. *Aussenwirtschaftsgesetz* (Foreign Trade and Payments Act), 1961, as amended June 2007.
<http://bundesrecht.juris.de/bundesrecht/awg/gesamt.pdf>

—. 2007b. *Aussenwirtschaftsverordnung* (Foreign Trade and Payments Ordinance), 1986, as amended August 2007.
<http://bundesrecht.juris.de/bundesrecht/awv_1986/gesamt.pdf>

—. n.d. *End use certificate* (sample end-use certificates).
<http://www.ausfuhrkontrolle.info/ausfuhrkontrolle/de/antragstellung/endverbleibsdokumente/eve_muster.pdf>

Greene, Owen and Elizabeth Kirkham. 2007. *Small Arms and Light Weapons Transfer Controls to Prevent Diversion: Developing and Implementing Key Programme of Action Commitments*. Biting the Bullet Policy Report. London: Saferworld and University of Bradford. August.
<http://www.saferworld.co.uk/publications.php?id=275>

Griffiths, Hugh and Adrian Wilkinson. 2007. *Guns, Planes and Ships: Identification and Disruption of Clandestine Arms Transfers*. Belgrade: South Eastern and Eastern Europe Clearinghouse for the Control of Small Arms and Light Weapons. August. Abridged version available at <http://www.seesac.org/reports/EXTRACT%20Techniques.pdf>

GRIP (Groupe de recherche et d'information sur la paix et la sécurité), Oxfam GB, Saferworld, and University of Bradford. 2006. *NGO Submission on the Elaboration of Article 2, Criterion 7 of the Draft EU Common Position Defining Common Rules Governing the Control of Exports of Military Technology and Equipment*. April. <http://www.saferworld.org.uk/publications.php?id=184>

Italy. 1990. *Legge n° 185 de 9 luglio 1990 – Nuove norme sul controllo dell'esportazione, importazione e transito dei materiali di armamento* (*Legge n° 185; Law n° 185*), in Gazz. Uff., 14 luglio, n. 163. <http://www.italgiure.giustizia.it/nir/lexs/1990/lexs_310498.html>

—. 2003. National report on the implementation of the UN Small Arms Programme of Action.
<http://disarmament.un.org/cab/nationalreports/2002/italy.pdf>

Japan. 1997. *Foreign Exchange and Foreign Trade Control Law (Law no. 228 of December 1949)*, as amended 1997. Unofficial translation available at <http://www.japanlaw.info/forex/law/JS.htm>

—. 2006. *Export Trade Control Order* (*Order no. 378 of December 1949*, as amended by *Cabinet Order no. 304 of 2006*). Unofficial translation available at <http://www.asianlii.org/jp/legis/laws/etco1949con378od11949475/>

—. 2007. National report on the implementation of the UN Small Arms Programme of Action.
<http://disarmament.un.org/cab/nationalreports/2007/Japan.pdf>

Japan METI (Japan Ministry of Economy, Trade, and Industry). 2002a. *Japan's Policies on the Control of Arms Exports*.
<http://www.meti.go.jp/policy/anpo/kanri/top-page/top/japan's-policies-on.htm>

—. 2002b. *Security Export Control in Japan*. <http://www.meti.go.jp/policy/anpo/kanri/top-page/security-export-control.htm>

Johnson-Thomas, Brian. 2007. *End Use Certificates*. Unpublished background paper. Geneva: Small Arms Survey.

Nairobi Best Practice Guidelines (Best Practice Guidelines for the Implementation of the Nairobi Declaration and the Nairobi Protocol on Small Arms and Light Weapons). 2005. Approved by the Third Ministerial Review Conference of the Nairobi Declaration. Nairobi, June.
<http://www.recsasec.org/pdf/Best%20Practice%20Guidlines%20Book.pdf>

Nairobi Protocol (Nairobi Protocol for the Prevention, Control and Reduction of Small Arms and Light Weapons in the Great Lakes Region and the Horn of Africa). 2004. Adopted in Nairobi, Kenya, 21 April. Entered into force 5 May 2006.
<http://www.recsasec.org/pdf/Nairobi%20Protocol.pdf>

O'Brien, Mike. 2003. Written answer to parliamentary question 106074. House of Commons, UK. *Hansard of 7 April 2003*, column 14W.
<http://www.publications.parliament.uk/pa/cm200203/cmhansrd/vo030407/text/30407w04.htm#30407w04.html_sbhd5>

OAS (Organization of American States). 1997. *Inter-American Convention against the Illicit Manufacturing of and Trafficking in Firearms, Ammunition, Explosives, and Other Related Materials.* Adopted in Washington, DC on 14 November. Entered into force on 1 July 1998. UN doc. A/53/78 of 9 March 1998. <http://www.oas.org/juridico/english/treaties/a-63.html>

—. 1998. *Model Regulations for the Control of the International Movement of Firearms, Their Parts and Components and Ammunition.* 2 June. AG/RES. 1543 (XXVIII – O/98). <http://www.oas.org/juridico/english/cicad_inter_move.pdf>

—. 2003. *Report of the General Secretariat of the Organization of American States on the Diversion of Nicaraguan Arms to the United Defense Forces of Colombia.* OEA/Ser.G, CP/doc. 3687/03 of 29 January. <http://www.fas.org/asmp/campaigns/smallarms/OAS_Otterloo.htm>

—. 2005. *Denying MANPADS to Terrorists: Control and Security of Man-Portable Air Defense Systems (MANPADS).* 7 June. AG/RES. 2145 (XXXV-O/05). <http://cicte.oas.org/rev/cn/Documents/OASGA.asp>

OSCE (Organization for Security and Co-operation in Europe). Forum for Security Co-operation. 2000. *OSCE Document on Small Arms and Light Weapons.* FSC.DOC/1/00. Adopted 24 November. <http://www.osce.org/documents/fsc/2000/11/1873_en.pdf>

—. 2003. *Handbook of Best Practices on Small Arms and Light Weapons.* Vienna: OSCE. <http://www.osce.org/fsc/item_11_13550.html>

—. 2004a. *OSCE Principles for Export Controls of Man-Portable Air Defence Systems (MANPADS).* Decision No. 3/04. FSC.DEC/3/04 of 26 May. <http://www.osce.org/documents/fsc/2004/05/2965_en.pdf>

—. 2004b. *Standard Elements of End-User Certificates and Verification Procedures for SALW Exports.* Decision No. 5/04. FSC.DEC/5/04 of 17 November. <http://www.osce.org/documents/fsc/2004/11/3809_en.pdf>

Parker, Sarah. 2008. *Government-to-government transfers.* Unpublished background paper. Geneva: Small Arms Survey.

Small Arms Survey. 2005. *Small Arms Survey 2005: Weapons at War.* Oxford: Oxford University Press.

—. 2007. *Small Arms Survey 2007: Guns and the City.* Cambridge: Cambridge University Press.

Sweden ISP (Swedish Inspectorate of Strategic Products). 2005. *End-user certificate.* Updated 14 April. <http://www.isp.se/sa/node.asp?node=543>

—. n.d. 'Declaration by End User to the Government of Sweden.' <http://www.isp.se/documents/public/se/pdf/blanketter/DEU.pdf>

—. n.d. *National Practices for End Use Certificates – Sweden* Non-paper.

UK (United Kingdom). 2000. *The Consolidated EU and National Arms Export Licensing Criteria.* October. <http://www.fco.gov.uk/servlet/Front?pagename=OpenMarket/Xcelerate/ShowPage&c=Page&cid=1014918697565>

—. 2002. *Export Control Act 2002.* <http://www.opsi.gov.uk/acts/acts2002/20020028.htm>

—. 2005. National report on the implementation of the UN Small Arms Programme of Action. <http://disarmament.un.org/cab/nationalreports/2005/UNPoA-UK-Implementation%202003-%202005.pdf>

—. n.d. *End-User Undertaking* (sample end-user certificate). <http://www.berr.gov.uk/files/file13406.pdf>

UNGA (United Nations General Assembly). 2001a. *Protocol against the Illicit Manufacturing of and Trafficking in Firearms, Their Parts and Components and Ammunition, supplementing the United Nations Convention against Transnational Organized Crime ('UN Firearms Protocol').* Adopted 31 May. Entered into force 3 July 2005. A/RES/55/255 of 8 June. <http://www.undcp.org/pdf/crime/a_res_55/255e.pdf>

—. 2001b. *Programme of Action to Prevent, Combat and Eradicate the Illicit Trade in Small Arms and Light Weapons in All Its Aspects ('UN Programme of Action').* 20 July. A/CONF.192/15. <http://disarmament2.un.org/cab/poa.html>

—. 2007. *Report of the Group of Governmental Experts Established Pursuant to General Assembly Resolution 60/81 to Consider Further Steps to Enhance International Cooperation in Preventing, Combating and Eradicating Illicit Brokering in Small Arms and Light Weapons.* A/62/163 of 30 August 2007. <http://disarmament.un.org/cab/brokering/GGE%20brokering/GGEbrokering.htm>

UNSC (United Nations Security Council). 2000. *Final Report of the Monitoring Mechanism on Angola Sanctions.* S/2000/1225 of 21 December, enclosure.

—. 2003. *Report of the Panel of Experts on Somalia pursuant to Security Council Resolution 1425 (2002).* S/2003/223 of 25 March.

US (United States). 2005. *Arms Export Control Act* (AECA), Chapter 39 of the United States Code Title 22 – Foreign Relations and Intercourse, as amended in 2005. <http://www.access.gpo.gov/uscode/title22/chapter39_.html>

—. 2007. *International Traffic in Arms Regulations* (ITAR), consolidated version 2007. <http://www.pmddtc.state.gov/consolidated_itar.htm>

USDoD (US Department of Defense). 2003. 'End-Use Monitoring (EUM)', Chapter 8 in *Security Assistance Management Manual,* document DoD 5105.38-M. <http://www.dsca.osd.mil/samm/>

USDoS (US Department of State). 2005. *Guidelines for Completion of a Form DSP-5 Application /License for Permanent Export of Unclassified Defense Articles and Related Unclassified Technical Data* (DSP-5 guidelines). <http://pmddtc.state.gov/docs/d-trade/D-TradeDSP-5_Instructions.pdf>

—. 2007a. *Guidelines for Completing Applications for the Permanent Export, Temporary Export, and Temporary Import of Firearms and Ammunition* (Firearms export guidelines). July. <http://www.pmddtc.state.gov/docs/Firearms_Manual2007.doc>

—. 2007b. *End-use Monitoring of Defense Articles and Defense Services: Commercial Exports FY 2006* (End-Use Monitoring Report – FY 2006). <http://www.pmddtc.state.gov/docs%5CEnd_Use_FY2006.pdf>

—. n.d. *Instructions for DSP-83: Nontransfer and Use Certificate* (sample form with guidelines). <http://pmddtc.state.gov/docs/dsp83.pdf>

WA (Wassenaar Arrangement on Export Controls for Conventional Arms and Dual-Use Goods and Technologies). 2000. *Best Practices for Effective Enforcement.* 1 December. <http://www.wassenaar.org/publicdocuments/2000_effectiveenforcement.html>

—. 2002. *Best Practice Guidelines for Exports of Small Arms and Light Weapons (SALW).* 12 December. <http://www.wassenaar.org/docs/best_practice_salw.htm>

—. 2003a. *Elements for Export Controls of Man-Portable Air Defence Systems (MANPADS).* 12 December. <http://www.wassenaar.org/2003Plenary/MANPADS_2003.htm>

—. 2003b. *List of Advisory Questions for Industry.* 12 December. <http://www.wassenaar.org/publicdocuments/index.html>

—. 2005. *End-User Assurances Commonly Used: Consolidated Indicative List.* Agreed at the 1999 Plenary; amended at the 2005 Plenary. Reproduced in *Basic Documents,* compiled by the WA Secretariat. <http://www.wassenaar.org/publicdocuments/index.html>

ACKNOWLEDGEMENTS

Principal author

Glenn McDonald

Contributors

Holger Anders, Sahar Hasan, Brian Johnson-Thomas, Sarah Parker

The Meaning of Loss
FIREARMS DIVERSION IN SOUTH AFRICA

6

INTRODUCTION

On 18 October 2007 internationally acclaimed South African musician Lucky Dube was murdered in Johannesburg with an illegally owned handgun, allegedly during an attempted car hijacking. Directly following Dube's murder, South African president Thabo Mbeki called for the country to 'act together as a people to confront this terrible scourge of crime, which has taken the lives of too many of our people—and does so every day' (SAPA, 2007). As of January 2008 four male suspects were standing trial for Dube's murder, among other charges (SAPA, 2008).

Dube was one of about 20,000 murder victims in South Africa in 2007, a significant number of which were murdered with firearms. According to a 2006 study of reported firearm deaths in 112 countries, South Africa had the third-highest annual rate of firearm deaths (26.8 per 100,000 people), after Colombia and Venezuela. The overwhelming majority (97 per cent) of reported firearm deaths in South Africa are coded as homicides (Cukier and Sidel, 2006, p. 16, table 2.1). As with much armed crime and violence in South Africa, most gun homicides are reportedly committed with illegal firearms; researchers claim that these weapons have been diverted primarily from licensed civilian owners, state armouries, and state personnel (Chetty, 2000, p. 45; Gould and Lamb, 2004, pp. 133–266; Kirsten, 2007, p. 2).

The South African government has prioritized the combating of violent crime since the late 1990s. More comprehensive and stringent firearms control legislation covering private citizens, businesses, and state institutions was passed in 2000 and phased in from 2000 to 2004. The legal reform process aimed to promote more responsible firearm ownership and possession and reduce firearm diversions to criminals (Gould and Lamb, 2004, pp. 207–12). However, the new laws have not been uniformly welcomed. Pro-firearm groups and the main political opposition party, the Democratic Alliance (DA), in particular, have criticized the unequal implementation and enforcement of the Firearms Control Act (FCA) No. 60 of 2000 (South Africa, 2000), complaining that private citizens are punished when they fall foul of the new regulations, while public institutions that commit the same violations go unpunished (King, 2008; SAGA, 2007).

This chapter considers the following questions:

- What are the trends in firearm loss and theft from South African civilians, private security companies, and state institutions—especially the South African Police Service (SAPS) and the South African National Defence Force (SANDF)?
- What impact, if any, has the FCA had on reducing diversions from these sources?
- How well are state institutions safeguarding their firearms stocks?
- What obstacles stand in the way of more accurate assessments of firearm diversions in South Africa, and therefore better prevention of such diversion?

Among the chapter's key findings are the following:

- Civilians, state institutions, and private security companies have all contributed to diversions of firearms into the criminal sector, as all these entities have reported significant loss or thefts of firearms.
- Civilians have been the primary contributor to the pool of lost or stolen firearms in South Africa. Between 2000 and 2006 an average of 18,731 civilian firearms were reported lost or stolen each year.
- Though public data remains incomplete, it appears that the FCA has helped reduce firearm diversions from civilian stocks. Firearm crime and violence remain very high, however.
- Controls over state-held firearms have improved since 1994, but additional administrative action is required to further reduce firearm diversion.
- The lack of publicly available firearm crime and mortality data has hindered a more thorough examination of the FCA's effects.

The chapter proceeds by describing the recent history of firearms crime and violence in South Africa, and the legislative reform process that produced the FCA. It then focuses on the problem of diversion among civilians, private security companies, the police, the national defence force, and other official agencies. It concludes with some reflections on the impacts of the new legislation in preventing diversion from these various sources.

FIREARM CRIME AND THE LEGISLATIVE REFORM PROCESS

Violence in South Africa in the apartheid era was closely associated with political and social repression. In the five years preceding the arrival of democracy in 1994, however, the country began experiencing an upheaval as the old political system started to crumble. One aspect of this upheaval was a gradual widening of previously contained violence into the mainstream. As early as 1994, civil society organizations had identified firearms as a vector of violence

Reported crime in South Africa, 1994–2007*

	1994-95	1995-96	1996-97	1997-98	1998-99	1999-2000	2000-01	2001-02	2002-03	2003-04	2004-05	2005-06	2006-07
	25,965	26,877	25,470	24,486	25,127	22,604	21,758	21,405	21,553	19,824	18,793	18,545	19,202
	26,806	26,876	28,576	28,145	29,545	28,179	28,128	31,293	35,861	30,076	24,516	20,553	20,142
	**	**	12,912	13,052	15,773	15,172	14,930	15,846	14,691	13,793	12,434	12,825	13,599
	**	**	359	236	223	226	196	238	374	192	220	385	467
	10,999	12,336	12,750	13,386	14,714	15,387	14,770	15,494	15,839	16,839	15,497	13,453	14,354

n
s &
on

reporting runs from 1 April to 31 March.
lable.
.d.)

and criminality and had begun public campaigns, including a major firearms amnesty in 1994, to highlight their dangers (Kirsten, 2007, p. 2). Guns became a focus for politicians almost from the beginning of the democratic era.

In 1996 the Department of Safety and Security and the South African parliament, the National Assembly, moved to amend firearms control legislation and specifically to promote more responsible firearms ownership and use. This took place in the context of a concerted government effort to address crime in a more coordinated and focused manner through the National Crime Prevention Strategy (NCPS). The NCPS provided a more integrated and comprehensive policy approach, shifting the focus from crime control to crime prevention.

The NCPS focused on the role of handguns in crime, based on data showing their relative prevalence in crime compared to other types of firearms. In 1998, for example, handguns were used in 57.4 per cent of all firearm-related murders, compared to commercial rifles and shotguns (24.8 per cent together) (Chetty, 2000, p. 21). In the same year, handguns accounted for 80 per cent of total cases of attempted murder involving a firearm, while commercial rifles and shotguns accounted for 6 per cent (Chetty, 2000, p. 26).

In 2000 the National Crime Prevention Centre published disaggregated firearms data and analysis for the period 1994–98 in a booklet titled *Firearm Use and Distribution in South Africa* (Chetty, 2000). It reported an average of 25,743 murders each year over the four-year period, of which an average of 44.4 per cent involved firearms. Handguns (pistols and revolvers) were reportedly the most common firearms used to commit murder in 1998. There were an almost equal number of reported cases of attempted murder over the period, with an average of 27,979 per year, of which an average of 79.5 per cent involved firearms (Chetty, 2000, p. 26).

The reform of South Africa's firearm control laws was accompanied by a process of public consultation, which was initiated by the Secretariat for Safety and Security and the Parliamentary Portfolio Committee on Safety and Security in the late 1990s. In 1997 the minister of safety and security appointed a committee to carry out an '[i]nvestigation into a new Policy for the Control of Legal Firearms in South Africa'. Its brief was to 'produce progressive policy proposals which will contribute to a drastic reduction in the number of legal firearms in circulation

An armed policeman watches residents who set up a barricade of burning tyres during a protest against delivery of houses in the Oceanview area of Cape Town, where people still live in makeshift shacks. © Obed Zilwa/AP Photo

in South Africa' (Kirsten, 2004, p. 22). The committee fell under the policy unit of the national Secretariat for Safety and Security. It took another two years of research and intensive national and international consultation with various interest groups and foreign governments before the Department of Safety and Security completed the Firearms Control Bill (FCB), which was gazetted in December 1999, placing it in the public domain. As with other legislation in the new democratic South Africa, the FCB was subject to scrutiny by many interest groups, including weapons dealers and owners, as well as health professionals, women's anti-violence groups, human rights advocates, and community-based organizations.

Submissions from the public were invited, and both pro-gun and pro-gun control groups responded enthusiastically, submitting hundreds of documents, including letters, reports, and signed petitions. The FCB enjoyed high levels of public participation from a broad spectrum of society, enabling the department to produce a final piece of legislation that in many ways reflected the interests and concerns of those who had made oral presentations. Throughout this period there was intense public debate on the merits of the proposed law and its purpose. These discussions fostered a climate of greater public awareness and interest.[1]

The consultation process culminated in the formulation of the Firearms Control Act No. 60 of 2000, or FCA (South Africa, 2000), which replaced the Arms and Ammunition Act No. 75 of 1969 (AAA) (South Africa, 1969). The FCA introduced more stringent eligibility and competency requirements for legal firearm owners, both state and civilian. Chapter 5 of the FCA requires a successful civilian firearm licence applicant to be, among other things, a South African citizen or a permanent resident, 21 years or older (previously the minimum age had been 16), a 'fit and proper person', of a stable mental condition and not inclined towards violence, not addicted to drugs or alcohol, not convicted of a violent crime within the past five years, in possession of an appropriate firearm safe, and in possession of a competency certificate.

The competency certificate, which had not been a requirement of the AAA, is arguably the most innovative firearm control feature of the FCA. In order to be awarded a competency certificate, applicants are tested on their knowledge of the FCA, as well as whether they can demonstrate their ability to handle firearms safely. Testing may only be administered by a government-accredited service provider. Applicants also undergo an extensive background check, and this can entail interviews with intimate partners and/or neighbours by SAPS personnel. Other key reforms include the restriction of the number of firearms that individuals may possess (a maximum of four licences per individual, with a maximum of one licence for self-defence);[2] and the mandatory renewal of licences on a regular basis, depending on the type of firearm licence (five years for self-defence licences, ten years for sports shooting licences, ten years for private collection licences, two years for business licences, and ten years for hunting licences) (South Africa, 2000, ch. 6, sec. 27); and the inclusion of more comprehensive criteria for declaring a person unfit to possess a firearm (South Africa, 2000, ch. 12, secs. 102, 103).

The AAA permitted a firearm licence holder to lend his or her firearm to another person (who did not require a firearm licence) if the licence holder provided written permission. Drafters of the new law perceived this provision as contributing to firearm proliferation and misuse and closed this loophole in the FCA. A firearm owner is now only permitted to lend his or her firearm to a person (licensed or unlicensed) when the borrower is 'under his or her immediate supervision where it is safe to use the firearm and for a lawful purpose' (South Africa, 2000, ch. 6, sec. 22).[3]

Officially, the FCA came into full effect in July 2004, as it took close to four years to finalize the regulations and secure parliamentary approval. However, some elements of the Act, such as those mandating firearm-free zones (South Africa, 2000, ch. 20, sec. 140), were promulgated and came into effect as early as 2001. Furthermore, from

The competency certificate is the most innovative firearm control feature of the FCA.

the time the legislation was passed in 2000, the SAPS began to enforce existing measures more stringently, including some that had not previously been enforced—especially those related to background checks for licence applicants. At the same time, the public debate about firearms began to alter many people's behaviours. Thus, over the period 2000–04 it is possible to look for the initial effects of the new regulatory system, though available data is inconclusive.

CIVILIAN FIREARM DIVERSION AND ARMED VIOLENCE

From 2000 the Central Firearms Registry (CFR), which is an entity within the SAPS, and subject to the same rules and regulations as other SAPS divisions, began applying stricter criteria for civilian firearm licence applications.

For example (as indicated in Table 6.2), between 1994 and 1999 an annual average of 194,000 private civilian firearm licence applications were approved by the CFR, but for the years 2000 and 2001, the annual average of approvals decreased by 24 per cent to 146,500. By 2003 the number of total licensed firearms recorded on the SAPS Firearms Registry had fallen from 4.5 million in 1999 to 3.7 million. The SAPS appears reluctant to release updated Firearms Registry data, as it is currently implementing a relicensing process for civilian firearm licence holders, which will be completed by the end of March 2009.

In an independent 2003 study, gun dealers and gun shop owners confirmed a noticeable decline in completed gun sales due to the introduction of more lengthy and stringent licensing procedures by the SAPS (Gould and Lamb, 2004, pp. 212–27). The reduction in licence approvals appeared to track a dramatic reduction in the number of licensed gun dealers in South Africa. Of the 720 licensed gun dealers in the country in 2000, 'no more than 50' remained in 2006, a reduction of almost 90 per cent (Soutar, 2006). This reduction was the result of new licensing criteria for dealers, increased annual fees, and on-site safety requirements that many dealers were not prepared to adopt, as well as the decrease in demand for new firearms as a result of more stringent requirements for civilian owners and the limits on the number of guns that can now be owned under the new FCA.

The impact of the new licensing criteria on the diversion of firearms to the illegal market and on armed violence is difficult to determine. One major stumbling block is that from 2000 onwards, the South African government refrained

Table 6.2 **Annual total civilian firearm licences issued, 1994-2001**	
Year	**Number**
1994	242,911
1995	154,727
1996	199,365
1997	200,059
1998	179,523
1999	187,284
2000	131,489
2001	161,518

Source: Gould and Lamb (2004, p. 197)

from making disaggregated firearm crime data publicly available from 2000. Among the reasons for this regrettable reticence must be included the public and hostile nature of the debate around guns and gun control in South Africa, an increasing tendency to withhold information in general by the Mbeki administration on many matters, and a restructuring of government agencies that has had bureaucratic and resource consequences.[4] Consequently, after 2000 violence trends can only be estimated based on aggregate crime data, media reports, and public health injury surveillance reports, such those produced by the National Injury Mortuary Surveillance System (NIMSS) and Statistics South Africa (NIMSS, 2006; Statistics South Africa, 2006).

As reflected in Table 6.1, from 1 April 2002 to 31 March 2006 the SAPS reported an average of 19,583 murders per year, which is a 23.9 per cent decrease from the 1 April 1994–31 March 1998 yearly average. An NIMSS study (2006) revealed that firearm-related deaths in major urban areas decreased by approximately 50 per cent from 2001–02 to 2004–05. An unpublished assessment of media reporting on firearm violence in South African that was

undertaken by the Institute for Security Studies for 2005–07 suggests that handguns remain the firearms of choice for criminals (ISS, 2008).

From 1 April 2002 to 31 March 2006 the SAPS reported an average of 26,230 cases of attempted murder per year, a minor reduction (6.2 per cent) compared to the 1 April 1994–31 March 1998 period, but there is no disaggregated data available to determine changes in the rate of attempted murder with a firearm. As reflected in Table 6.1, from 1 April 2002 to 31 March 2006 there was an average of 15,196 cases of illegal possession of firearms and/or ammunition per year, which was an increase of 11 per cent compared to the period 1 April 1994–31 March 1998.

Figure 6.1 provides details on the number of firearms reported lost or stolen and the number of firearms recovered or confiscated from 1994–95 to 2006–07.[5] Between 2000–01 and 2006–07, an average of 18,731 civilian firearms were reported lost or stolen per year, a 5.8 per cent decrease compared to the period 1994–95–1998–99.[6] However, more importantly, from 2004–05 (when all of the provisions of the FCA came into effect) to 2006–07, an average of 15,054 civilian firearms were reported lost or stolen per year (a 24 per cent decrease). In the absence of data on the specific circumstances of these losses—and because of the lack of information about how many lost or stolen guns go unreported—it is not clear whether the reduction in the reported number of weapons lost or stolen is the result of increased penalties for failure to report loss, improved licensing and competency criteria (which require familiarity with all the FCA's provisions), or simply a reflection of the fact that, as a consequence of increased pressure on firearms commerce in South Africa since 2000, there are simply fewer weapons in circulation. All of these factors have probably had an influence.

Figure 6.1 **Civilian firearms reported lost/stolen and recovered/ confiscated, 1994-2007**

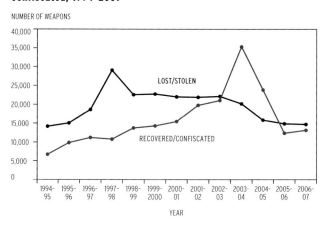

NUMBER OF WEAPONS

LOST/STOLEN

RECOVERED/CONFISCATED

YEAR

Figure 6.1 also shows that from 1994–95 to 2003–04 there was an annual increase in the number of firearms reported recovered or confiscated by the SAPS. In fact, by 2003–04 there had been an increase of 450 per cent compared to 1994–95. However, as Figure 6.1 reveals, there has been a gradual decline in the number of recoveries/confiscations since 2004–05, which is probably due to the gradual decline in loss/theft of firearms, the firearm amnesty process[7] (in which 100,066 firearms were collected) that was implemented in 2005, and the successful recoveries/confiscations of previous years.

It is important to note that not all the firearms that were recovered or confiscated by the SAPS during this period were necessarily those that were reported lost or stolen during the same period. Many of the weapons recovered or confiscated were likely reported lost or stolen prior to the year in which they were recovered. It is also likely that an unknown proportion of weapons recovered in any given year are former state weapons, have no marking to identify their origins, or originated from another country.

A man waits to hand in an inherited 1850s double-barrel shotgun at a police station in Pretoria in March 2005.© Leon Botha, Beeld/AP Photo

DIVERSION FROM PRIVATE SECURITY COMPANIES

The private security industry in South Africa has grown at rates of up to 30 per cent per year since the early 1990s. Valued at ZAR 1.2 billion (USD 500 million) in 1990, by March 2007 the industry had grown to an estimated ZAR 30 billion (USD 4.1 billion) (Reynolds, 2003, cited in Minnaar, 2007, p. 129). Approximately 25,000–30,000 newly trained security officers enter the market every year, but turnover is extremely high, and only one-third of all registered security officers are active (Minnaar, 2007, p. 130). By March 2007 there were approximately 900,000 registered security officers, of which only 301,584 were active (Badenhorst, 2007, cited in Minnaar, 2007, p. 130). Despite the low active-to-reserve ratio within the industry, there are more than twice as many active security officers as uniformed police officers in South Africa.

The rise in private security should be seen in the context not only of perceptions of increasing criminality in the years before and after apartheid was eclipsed, but also public frustration with the official police response, which was viewed as often insufficient or inappropriate.

The FCA introduced more stringent requirements for private security companies that utilize firearms to provide a service to either government or the public (South Africa, 2000, ch. 6, sec. 20). The requirements for business licences closely resemble those of private civilian licences. Each business firearm user must earn a competency certificate and be a 'fit and proper person', and the licence has to be renewed every five years. However, the firearm may only be used for business purposes (unless otherwise prescribed) and may be used by another person (if prescribed).

In practice, this means that security personnel are generally not permitted to carry their firearms when they are off duty. In addition, any business firearms may have multiple users. However, each user typically requires a competency certificate. The FCA

An bodyguard stands with her automatic weapon at the funeral service for seven of the National Congress supporters killed by unidentified gunmen in January 1999 in the hip outside Richmond. © Adil Bradlow/AP Photo

A robber l
after alleg
shot by a
security g
during a c
delivery r
a shoppin
in Johanne
September
© AP Phot

prohibits private security officers from using their own firearms on duty, as had previously been commonplace in the industry. To conform to this change, many private security companies that had previously relied on employees using their own firearms while on duty were obliged instead to acquire new 'company firearms'.[8]

Qualifying businesses are required to maintain accurate registers of the firearms and ammunition in their possession (which must be made available to the SAPS on request), as well as provide the required safe storage facilities. In addition, should the business cease to operate, the owners must safely store the firearms and/or surrender them to the SAPS. In practice, the owners of failed businesses are supposed to transfer their firearms and ammunition to the SAPS for safe storage, as they are not in a position to safely secure such weapons.

Data on the number of firearms held by security company employees is generally not publicly available. In 2003, however, the CFR reported that some 1,643 security companies possessed firearms and that the total number of firearms in their possession was 58,981 (CFR, 2003, cited in Gould and Lamb, 2004, p. 185). Armed response companies claim that the loss or theft of company firearms is rare. Guard companies also claim the same. By contrast, assets-in-transit (AIT) companies (which mainly transport cash) report firearms thefts on a regular basis. AIT officers are invariably armed while moving assets, they are attacked more frequently than any other private security company officers, and their attackers are almost always armed. For these reasons, AIT firearms are routinely stolen during successful heists.[9] In the absence of data on firearm diversion from the security industry overall, then, AIT heists provide an important indicator for firearms diversions from the private security industry.

Table 6.3 Cash-in-transit heists, 1 April 2001–31 March 2007						
Province	**2001–02**	**2002–03**	**2003–04**	**2004–05**	**2005–06**	**2006–07**
Eastern Cape	17	19	19	23	26	20
Free State	8	12	4	2	1	14
Gauteng	94	141	71	82	141	172
KwaZulu-Natal	41	85	35	22	66	121
Limpopo	15	23	12	12	44	23
Mpumalanga	16	51	26	32	19	18
Northern Cape	0	0	0	2	0	1
North West	33	29	14	25	33	20
Western Cape	14	14	11	20	53	78
Total	**238**	**374**	**192**	**220**	**383**	**467**

Source: SAPS (n.d.)

Since April 2003 there has been a significant increase in the number of reported cash-in-transit robberies. The SAPS reported 192 cash-in-transit robberies in 2003–04, 220 in 2004–05, 383 in 2005–06, and 467 in 2006–07 (see Table 6.3). This represented a 243 per cent increase in such robberies between 2003–04 and 2006–07. SAPS described many of these robberies as 'repeat offences committed by experienced perpetrators at the request of syndicate leaders' (see SAPS, 2007b, p. 19). There had been 374 heists in 2002–03 and 238 in 2001–02.

AIT companies estimate that their vehicles carry between two and three firearms on average. Assuming that each AIT vehicle attacked in 2006–07 carried 2.5 firearms, an average of 1,168 firearms would have been stolen in this way during the period (Gould and Lamb, 2004, p. 190). Figures providing total non-state firearm losses for this period had not been released at the time of writing. Using the same formula, however, it may be estimated that 958 firearms were lost/stolen through AIT heists in 2005–06, accounting for 6.5 per cent of the 14,842 civilian firearms reported lost/stolen that year (see Figure 6.1). It is important to note, however, that the primary objective of those groups that target AIT vehicles are the assets, which are predominantly cash.

In addition to AIT heists, firearms can also be diverted from private security companies when they lose their authorization and go out of business. In a presentation to the Parliamentary Portfolio Committee on Safety and Security in 2003, Eugene Vilakazi, director of the Private Security Industry Regulatory Authority (PSIRA), raised the concern that when security companies are deregistered their firearm licences are not automatically cancelled, as required by law, alleging that in some instances security companies register and then deregister simply to obtain licensed firearms to which they were not really entitled. According to Vilakazi, the PSIRA had no means of checking the status of private security companies' firearms after deregistration. When asked whether the PSIRA took stock of all the firearms possessed by a private security company before it withdrew its registration, Vilakazi said it did not, but that the process was 'being introduced' (Vilakazi, 2003, cited in Gould and Lamb, 2004, p. 187). Given this state of affairs, it has not been possible to determine accurately the nature and extent of firearm loss from defunct private security providers.

According to the FCA, when private security companies, or indeed any companies that have official firearms, cease to carry out their business, all their firearms and ammunition must be kept in safe storage (as indicated above). Asked by the same Portfolio Committee in November 2006 about the status of firearms of suspended or withdrawn private security providers, the PSIRA suggested that this remained a matter for the CFR alone (PSIRA, 2006b). The PSIRA, however, reported a 'working relationship' with the SAPS on the issue, but unlike in 2003 did not indicate that it was a matter about which it was particularly worried (South Africa, 2006b). The CFR too has not publicly expressed any concern on the issue.

FIREARMS DIVERSION FROM THE SOUTH AFRICAN POLICE SERVICE

Key provisions of the FCA attempted for the first time to comprehensively reduce the potential for the misuse and diversion of state-held firearms. Chapter 11 of the FCA (South Africa, 2000, secs. 95–101) requires employees of official institutions, which include state agencies such as the SAPS, the SANDF, and the Department of Correctional Services, to obtain an official permit to possess a firearm.[10] A permit can only be issued if the state employee is a 'fit and proper person', and has 'successfully completed the prescribed training and the prescribed test for the safe use of the firearm' (a competency test) (South Africa, 2000, sec. 98.8). If state employees are required to take their firearms home, then they are required by law to store them in an appropriate safe. Consequently, the SAPS has sought to provide those police personnel that are required to carry firearms with firearms safes. These provisions entailed a significant enhancement of firearm control processes and tools for official institutions. The improvements sought to bring police standards into line and improve public confidence.

In two ways, however, the provisions covering official institutions differ from those of civilians. Firstly, the issuance of permits to employees of official institutions is done by the head of each official body, not an independent organization (such as the CFR in the case of civilians) (South Africa, 2000, sec. 98.2). Secondly, any conditions attached to the permit relating to, for example, storage, transport, use, and disposal are completely at the discretion of the head of the official institution (South Africa, 2000, sec. 98.4). Although the FCA outlines standard practices for the carrying

Table 6.4 SAPS firearms losses, 1 April 2001–31 May 2007				
Year[1]	Stolen	Robbery[2]	Lost/misplaced	Total
2001–02	131	368	444	943
2002–03	239	487	195	921
2003–04	219	412	304	935
2004–05	179	289	267	735
2005–06	n/a[3]	n/a[3]	n/a[3]	2,297
2006–07	n/a[3]	n/a[3]	n/a[3]	3,856

[1] The SAPS statistical year runs 1 April-31 March.
[2] 'Robbery' entails the removal of the firearm from a person by force, while 'stolen' does not entail such force.
[3] Disaggregated data for 2005–06 and 2006–07 was not publicly available at the time of writing.
Source: Democratic Alliance[11]

and storage of official weapons, these may be superseded within certain boundaries by the head of the organization (South Africa, 2000, sec. 98.6).

In 1999 a Department of Safety and Security ministerial policy report on firearms control stated that over the previous nine years, 14,636 police firearms had been lost or stolen, an average of 1,626 per year (Department of Safety and Security, 1999, p. 4, cited in Gould and Lamb, 2004, p. 151). This figure fell to an annual average of 883.5 per year from 2001–02 to 2004–05 (see Table 6.4),[12] but in 2005–06 it began rising steeply, reaching a high of 3,865 lost or stolen firearms in 2006–07.

The apparent increased disappearance of police firearms has been extremely embarrassing to the SAPS, which is tasked with enforcing more responsible firearm possession and use among civilians. One possible explanation for the increased loss is inadequate implementation of firearm control processes and measures within the SAPS. For example, in the SAPS *Annual Report 2004/05,* the auditor general indicated that in many cases firearms and ammu-

ican police
his weapon
s a vehicle
hind him in
)5, outside
ville police
n the south
Joao Silva/
AP Photo

nition from officials who had left the service were not returned to the SAPS, and that weaknesses existed regarding the safe storage of firearms by SAPS members (SAPS, 2005). In the following year, the auditor general further found that SAPS firearm control registers were not properly maintained and that the required number of weapons inspections had not been undertaken (SAPS, 2006).

In January 2007 SAPS national commissioner Jackie Selebi appeared before the National Assembly's Standing Committee on Public Accounts (SCOPA) to respond to questions by members of parliament about the dramatic increase in the loss/theft of SAPS firearms. Selebi told the committee that police personnel were being provided with safes to store their firearms at home, and that the

SAPS has introduced a more effective firearm marking system (South Africa, 2007). The September 2007 SAPS *Annual Report* (covering 2006–07) implies that there was been some improvement in the internal firearm control measures: firearm registers were being appropriately maintained in three provinces, and inspections of SAPS firearms holdings had improved. Nevertheless, the number of lost or stolen SAPS firearms had increased to 3,856 (a 68 per cent hike from the previous year) (SAPS, 2007).

The opposition DA was highly critical of the increase in SAPS losses/thefts of firearms, claiming that the national police commissioner had reneged on his promises to SCOPA (DA, 2007b). However, CFR director Jaco Bothma defended the SAPS, indicating that the police were fully compliant with the FCA. Bothma also suggested the apparent increase may be the result of better bookkeeping: that many of the SAPS firearms reported lost or stolen in 2006–07 had in reality been lost or stolen in earlier years, but had been reported due to improved SAPS firearms stock taking, as required by the FCA.[13]

Table 6.5 **Attacks on and murders of SAPS officers, 1 April 2001–31 March 2007**		
Year	**Total attacks**	**Murders***
2001–02	737	139
2002–03	906	150
2003–04	717	108
2004–05	721	94
2005–06	1,274	95
2006–07	769	108

* Murders are a portion of attacks.
Source: SAPS (2007b, tables 33 and 34, p. 54)

Meanwhile, a disturbing 2006 report by the SAPS Independent Complaints Directorate (ICD) about the Durban Metro Police Service (DMPS; a municipal police force established by but independent of the SAPS) gave an indication of problematic reporting dynamics of lost/stolen police firearms between policing structures in South Africa. The DMPS has its own firearm stocks and its members are subject to the same firearm control measures as SAPS personnel. The ICD investigated after it was informed of discrepancies in the reports of firearms alleged to be in the custody of the DMPS, or reported to the latter as lost or stolen, and that some of the case numbers supplied to the ICD did not match DMPS records or were non-existent. The ICD found that there were serious discrepancies between the DPMS firearms records, what the SAPS CFR had on record, and actual events as determined by ICD investigators. The ICD concluded that the DMPS did not effectively implement the FCA provisions on the control of police firearms (ICD, 2006).

South African police officers have some of the highest rates of homicide victimization of police in the world. One possible explanation for this is that they are targeted for their firearms. From 2001 to 2006, 694 SAPS officers were fatally wounded in a total of 5,124 attacks (see Table 6.5).

The SAPS has suggested that most police killings occurred during hot pursuit of suspects or while making arrests, and that there is no evidence that police officers are mainly killed for their guns (SAPS, 2007b, p. 54). However, as with other firearm-related violent crime, the SAPS has not publicly revealed how many firearms its officers have had stolen from them annually as a result of murders and attacks. Yet the fact remains that police officers are regularly attacked and murdered, and it is likely that in at least some cases their firearms are stolen.

FIREARMS DIVERSION FROM THE SOUTH AFRICAN NATIONAL DEFENCE FORCE

Like the SAPS, the FCA also requires South African National Defence Force (SANDF) personnel to obtain a firearm permit, which entails a competency certificate. However, as indicated above, SANDF personnel are exempted from this requirement 'while performing official duties under military command' and 'if they have in their possession a written order, instruction or route form specifying the duty to be performed and the nature and type of firearm they are authorised to carry' (South Africa, 2000, ch. 11, sec. 98). Like all official institutions, the SANDF is required to maintain an accurate register of its firearm holdings.

Historically, South Africa's apartheid state, particularly the military (then called the South African Defence Force, or SADF[14]), facilitated the transfer of arms and military equipment to a number of insurgent groups in Southern Africa, in particular the União Nacional para a Independência Total de Angola (better known as UNITA) in Angola and Resistência Nacionaal Moçambique (RENAMO) in Mozambique (Seegers, 1996, pp. 210–40). Weapons diverted to these insurgent groups were allocated the same SADF administrative code as those earmarked for disposal. Further cryptic sub-categories were added by the SADF in the 1980s referring to weapons sent to Namibia and those sold to the South African Police[15] (Gould and Lamb, 2004, p. 157).

The SADF's records of the thousands of weapons it diverted to homeland[16] defence forces (which were often commanded by SADF officers) and the Inkatha Freedom Party (IFP) were for the most part destroyed. The IFP was also supplied with weaponry by the South African Police, and used it to wage war against the African National Congress (ANC) in KwaZulu-Natal, particularly in the late 1980s and early 1990s (Batchelor, 1997, p. 108). As indicated in Gould and Lamb (2004, pp. 161–84), each homeland's firearm registers were incomplete, and there is evidence of substantial weapon diversions from homelands' military and police stockpiles. In addition, thousands of firearms from homeland defence forces were reintegrated into the SANDF stockpile after 1994, but to date the exact number of missing firearms from former homeland militaries has not been established.

An audit in 2000 revealed that many weapons could not be accounted for, but in 2003 the SANDF indicated that 2,547 firearms had been lost or stolen since 1994 and 788 recovered, leaving a balance of 1,759. This relatively low number, however, did not include weapons still in possession of the SANDF commando units,[17] 'donated' to neighbouring countries, or given to former homeland governments (Gould and Lamb, 2004, pp. 161–63).

In a written answer to a parliamentary question from the DA in November 2005, Minister of Defence Mosiuoa Lekota stated that between 1 January 2000 and 31 August 2005, 479 firearms were stolen or lost from the SANDF, and that during the same period 2,898 weapons were recovered, which Lekota attributed to the successful implementation of the FCA (Van Dyk, 2007).

The auditor general's annual reports on the SANDF provide a less rosy picture. The *2006 Report* of the auditor general complained of the SANDF's 'lack of monitoring compliance with policies and procedures relating to stock and equipment' and also stated that 'stock takes were either not performed or certificates could not be provided at all units'. In addition, the audit found that firearm registers were not appropriately maintained (South Africa, 2006a, pp. 97–99).

One problematic area that the audit identified was the lack of policy and oversight of firearms and other SANDF equipment in foreign operations (such as the one in Burundi). In October 2006 the *Star* newspaper published a story in which it claimed that some SANDF weapons from the latter's Burundi peace support operation had been acquired by the rebel Parti pour la libération du peuple

s remove a Zulu Inkatha Freedom Party (IFP) supporter who tried to enforce a strike call by stopping hannesburg in March 1996. About 7,000 armed Zulus staged a protest in Johannesburg to commemorate e Massacre', during which eight IFP supporters were gunned down in 1994. © Adil Bradlow/AP Photo

hutu–Forces nationales pour la libération. The *Star* identified the missing SANDF arms in Burundi as 40 mortar bombs, 54 R4 rifles, 4 R5 rifles, a sniper rifle, 2 12-gauge shotguns, 8 machine guns, 8 pistols, and 27 grenade launchers (Maughan, 2006).

The government's decision in 2006 to disband commando units presented the SANDF with a major firearms management challenge. These units had been struggling since 1994 to shake off their apartheid-era associations, and remained mistrusted by the ANC, despite commando units' appeals to government that they were necessary to combat rural crime. The disbanding began in 2006 and final unit closures are scheduled for mid-2008. In 2003 the SANDF had already expressed concern about firearm management within commando units, indicating that it suspected that many of the automatic rifles that had been issued to them would prove, upon inspection, to be missing (Gould and Lamb, 2004, pp. 160–61).

The issue was picked up by the DA, which condemned the SANDF's lack of control over commando firearms for 'allowing weapons to fall into the hands of unknown persons' (DA, 2007a). The SANDF responded by indicating that the FCA has improved firearms management standards in the SANDF, enabling it to control its stockpile better and trace disappearances and losses (Maughan, 2007a). This was also the perspective of the CFR, whose director reported that the SANDF is 'fully compliant' with the FCA.[18]

However, the official SANDF position has been challenged by Major General B. S. Mmono, the SANDF's head of legal services. In April 2007 Mmono wrote a brief for the military council expressing a range of concerns about firearms management. The brief, which was later leaked to the *Star,* alleged that the SANDF had no system in place by which it can immediately report thefts and losses of arms and ammunition to the police, the SANDF lacked a register for the particulars of all firearms less than 20 mm in calibre, and there was no system in place to deal with SANDF members who are declared unfit to possess a firearm by a military court (Maughan, 2007b).

In Mmono's view, existing SANDF policy and procedures for the control of firearms and ammunition still required review by 'relevant role players' to bring them into line with the FCA. Mmono also wrote of his concern that the SANDF could be faced with civil lawsuits from members of the public injured or killed by firearms in the hands of unfit soldiers (Maughan, 2007b). The concerns and criticisms appear to have been taken into consideration by the South African Department of Defence (DoD). In the Report of the accounting officer (dated 31 August 2007), which is included in the DoD's *Annual Report FY 2006–2007* (DoD, 2007), the concerns of the auditor general are presented in conjunction with the DoD's proposed remedial action with respect to asset management. For example: 'asset management' units and teams have been established, and reform measures and milestones are in the process of being implemented to convert the current SANDF asset management system to a system that is prescribed by the National Treasury (DoD, 2007, pp. 181–88). While these developments show the distance that state institutions must go to reform, it appears that the FCA has created an institutional dynamic for weapons management reform within the SANDF.

OTHER STATE FIREARMS DIVERSIONS

The Department of Correctional Services (prisons) possesses firearm holdings, and has the same obligations as the SAPS under the FCA in terms of firearm permits, testing, record keeping, and safe keeping. Firearms and armaments held by the Department of Correctional Services were valued at ZAR 2.95 million (USD 420,000) in 2006, according to the department's *Annual Report 2006* (Department of Correctional Services, 2006, p. 55).

In the auditor general's section of this annual report, no specific mention is made of deficiencies in weapons management. However, the auditor general did observe in general terms that there was 'insufficient capturing of assets . . . which resulted in the fixed asset register not being adequately maintained or updated'. The auditor general noted a number of problems, including the fact that Correctional Services has been using three different computer programmes to manage its inventory and fixed assets, but that no reconciliation has been performed among the three systems. The auditor general discovered that a large number of purchased assets that showed up on one of the systems did not show up on another. Because of the confusion, the auditor general stated that he was 'unable to verify the accuracy and completeness of the asset register'. This judgement includes the Correctional Services armoury and implies that the department is not yet fully FCA-compliant, since a core requirement of the FCA for official institutions like Correctional Services is that they maintain accurate weapons registers. The auditor general noted in the *Annual Report 2006* that Correctional Services management had undertaken 'to introduce manual reconciliation procedures to overcome the interface problems for the following year' (Department of Correctional Services, 2006, p. 62). This will have been a huge and daunting operation; it remains to be seen to what extent it was indeed carried out.

In answer to a written question from the DA in the National Assembly in 2005, the minister for safety and security revealed that South African municipalities owned 15,843 registered firearms. The minister continued that under the terms of the FCA, municipalities had to apply for accreditation to possess firearms, and that the firearm safe facilities that municipalities made use of had to comply with the requirements of the South African Bureau of Standards. The minister said that municipalities could not receive firearms accreditation until their safes had been inspected to ensure that they did indeed comply with this standard. The minister said that according to the records of the CFR, 1,945 municipality firearms had been reported lost or stolen since 1993, giving an average annual firearms loss for municipalities of 163 (Jankielsohn, 2005). This is a low number compared to the total number of firearms lost or stolen in South Africa overall, but it still means that municipalities have been losing 1 per cent of their licensed firearms per annum, a worryingly high percentage that raises the question of whether municipalities are in fact FCA-compliant.

CONCLUSION

Along with Australia and Canada, South Africa has taken bold initiatives in recent years to revise its national laws covering both civilian and state firearm holdings. The initiative was based on an evidence base and an open, public dialogue. This in and of itself is a major accomplishment.

Unfortunately, almost simultaneous with the passage of the new law, the flow of disaggregated firearm mortality and morbidity data abruptly stopped. Six years later, the ability of researchers, policy-makers, and others to measure the effectiveness of this major public policy intervention remains extremely limited. That situation is improving, but is a stark reminder of the sensitivities that surround the development of firearms policy in many countries.

Despite the data gaps, it appears that the vast majority of licensed firearms in South Africa remain in private civilian hands, and that most lost or stolen firearms—those that form the pool of diverted weapons—originate from private civilians. Under these circumstances, the FCA's primary focus on civilian firearm ownership is appropriate. There is some indication that the new administrative and competency requirements have contributed to reductions in firearm loss and theft from private citizens, as well as in firearm homicides, though this remains to be proven.

At the same time, the FCA and associated regulations properly seek to stem diversion from state institutions as well, especially the police and the military. There is clear evidence that mismanagement, poor enforcement of safety and storage requirements, and other problems continue to plague these agencies and contribute to ongoing firearm diversions. Further improvements, especially administrative measures, are required to enhance firearms control within these institutions.

Further investigation of firearm diversion in South Africa is required in order to institute more targeted measures to this problem. However, this is not possible in the absence of publicly available, detailed, and timely information on the nature of firearm crime and violence in South Africa. ▰

LIST OF ABBREVIATIONS

AAA	Arms and Ammunition Act No. 75 of 1969	NCPS	National Crime Prevention Strategy
AIT	assets-in-transit	NIMSS	National Injury Mortuary Surveillance
ANC	African National Congress		System
CFR	Central Firearms Registry	PSIRA	Private Security Industry Regulatory
DA	Democratic Alliance		Authority
DMPS	Durban Metro Police Service	SADF	South African Defence Force
DoD	Department of Defence (South Africa)	SANDF	South African National Defence Force
FCA	Firearms Control Act	SAPS	South African Police Service
FCB	Firearms Control Bill	SCOPA	Standing Committee on Public Accounts
ICD	Independent Complaints Directorate	USD	United States dollar
IFP	Inkatha Freedom Party	ZAR	South African rand

ENDNOTES

1   A more detailed analysis of the formulation of this legislation appears in King, Proudlock, and Michelson (2006).

2   The FCA allows for the issuing of additional licences to professional hunters and sport shooters. However, the number of additional licences is determined by the registrar of firearms on a case-by-case basis.

3   The motivation behind this provision was primarily to allow for firearm training for and firearm use by hunters under the age of 21.

4   In April 2007 the minister of safety and security announced that crime data would be released more than once a year. More regular crime reports have been published since then, but major gaps still remain in our understanding of mortality over the period 2000–06.

5   SAPS data does not distinguish between guns that are unintentionally lost and those that are stolen; or between those that have been recovered and returned to their owners and those that have been confiscated (presumably because either the guns are illegal or the owners are prohibited from owning firearms).

6   Data relating to the loss and theft of firearms is combined by the SAPS, and often firearms that have in reality been lost (hence through negligence) are often reported as being stolen, as the penalties for losing a firearm can be severe.

7   A firearm amnesty process was initiated in 2005 to collect unlicensed firearms. The key motivation was that the SAPS suspected that there were significant numbers of unlicensed firearms in existence due to the reduction in the maximum number of licensed firearms for civilians (as permitted by the FCA) and that numerous firearms had been inherited without being licensed. Owners of unlicensed firearms were encouraged to surrender these firearms to the SAPS with the commitment from the authorities that no legal action would be taken against such individuals so long as the firearm had not been used in the commission of a crime (ballistic testing of surrendered firearms was carried out). No financial compensation for these firearms was provided. See Kirsten (2007) for more details.

8   Interviews with private security companies, Johannesburg, Pretoria, Durban, and Cape Town, 2003.

9   Interviews with private security companies and the Private Security Industry Regulatory Authority. The findings are discussed at greater length in Gould et al. (2004).

10   As the FCA provides, SANDF personnel are exempted from the permit requirement while they are 'performing official duties under military command' and 'if they have in their possession a written order, instruction or route form specifying the duty to be performed and the nature

and type of firearm they are authorised to carry'. The reason for the provision is that the SANDF makes use of firearms that other users and institutions are prohibited from possessing, such as automatic firearms. In addition, the military's role is to engage in armed combat when required. SANDF personnel, however, are not permitted to carry their official firearms when off duty, and if they wish to acquire a private firearm licence, then the normal civilian licensing procedures apply.

11   Figures for 2001–05 derived from a transcript of the answer to a DA question in the National Assembly, 28 June 2005; figures for 2005–07 from a telephone interview with Dianne Kohler-Barnard, DA spokesperson, 20 September 2007.

12   Democratic Alliance figures make a distinction between 'stolen' and 'robbery', although it is not immediately clear what this might be.

13   Telephone interview with Jaco Bothma, CFR director, 21 September 2007.

14   In 1994, following the democratic election in that year, the SANDF was created, an amalgamation of the SADF, the liberation armed factions, and the homeland militaries (for 'homeland', see endnote 16).

15   Apartheid-era precursor of the SAPS.

16   Homelands were so-called black 'independent states' created by the apartheid government as a logical (if unworkable) extension of the apartheid system, which aimed at the complete physical separation of black and white people.

17   Commando units were units primarily consisting of rural, white civilians who received training in the SADF, were issued with firearms, and performed intelligence-gathering and counter-insurgency activities and fought crime.

18   Telephone interview with Jaco Bothma, CFR director, 21 September 2007.

BIBLIOGRAPHY

Altbeker, Antony. 2001. *The Police and Firearms: What Do They Think?* Johannesburg: Gun Free South Africa.

Badenhorst, P. 2007. 'The Role of the Private Security Industry in Preventing and Combating Crime in South Africa.' Presentation at the South African Human Rights Commission Conference on Crime and Its Impact on Human Rights: Ten Years of the Bill of Rights, Sandton, 22–23 March.

Batchelor, Peter. 1997. 'Intra-State Conflict, Political Violence and Small Arms Proliferation in Africa.' In V. Gamba, ed. *Society under Siege: Crime, Violence and Illegal Weapons, Vol. 1.* Halfway House: Institute for Security Studies. <http://www.issafrica.org/dynamic/administration/file_manager/file_links/SBATCHELOR.PDF?link_id=19&slink_id=4873&link_type=12&slink_type=13&tmpl_id=3>

CFR (Central Firearms Registry). 2003. 'Presentation to the Parliamentary Portfolio Committee on Safety and Security.' September.

Chetty, Robert, ed. 2000. *Firearm Use and Distribution in South Africa.* Pretoria: National Crime Prevention Centre.

Crime, Violence and Injury Lead Programme, UNISA (University of South Africa). 2005. *Fatal Violence in South Africa: The Role of Firearms.* Pretoria: UNISA.

Cukier, Wendy and Victor Sidel. 2006. *The Global Gun Epidemic: From Saturday Night Specials to AK-47s.* Westport and London: Praeger Security International.

DA (Democratic Alliance). 2007a. 'Lack of Weapons Control a Disgrace.' Press release. 20 July. <http://www.gunownerssa.org/forum/viewtopic.php?p=1558>

——. 2007b. 'Selebi Fails to Keep Promises to Scopa.' Press release. 20 September.

Department of Correctional Services. 2006. *Annual Report 2006.* Pretoria: Department of Correctional Services. <http://www-dcs.pwv.gov.za/Publications/Annual%20Reports/DCS%20Annual%20Report%202006.pdf>

Department of Safety and Security. 1999. *Report to the Minister for Safety and Security: Proposed Ministerial Policy on the Control of Firearms in South Africa.* September.

DoD (Department of Defence). 2007. *Annual Report FY 2006–2007.* Pretoria: DoD.

Gould, Chandré, et al. 2004. 'Country Study: South Africa.' In Chandré Gould and Guy Lamb, pp. 132–266. <http://www.iss.co.za/dynamic/administration/file_manager/file_links/HIDESOUTHAFRICA.PDF?link_id=3&slink_id=1633&link_type=12&slink_type=13&tmpl_id=3>

Gould, Chandré and Guy Lamb, eds. 2004. *Hide and Seek: Taking Account of Small Arms in Southern Africa.* Pretoria: ISS. <http://www.iss.co.za/pubs/Books/Hide+Seek/Contents.htm>

ICD (Independent Complaints Directorate). 2006. *Report on the Investigation into the Missing Firearms and Related Matters at Durban Metro Police.* Pretoria: ICD. <http://www.icd.gov.za/reports/2006/firearms_rpt.pdf>

ISS (Institute for Security Studies). 2008. *An Assessment of Media Reporting on Firearm Crime and Violence in South Africa, 2005–2007.* Unpublished report. Pretoria: ISS.

Jankielsohn, R. 2005. 'Internal Question Paper No. 7/25.' Cape Town: National Assembly.

King, Maylene, Paula Proudlock, and Lori Michelson. 2006. 'From Fieldwork to Facts to Firearms Control: Research and Advocacy towards Stricter Firearms Control Legislation in South Africa.' *African Security Review,* Vol. 15, No. 2, pp. 2–15. Pretoria: Institute for Security Studies. <http://www.iss.co.za/index.php?link_id=3&slink_id=3625&link_type=12&slink_type=12&tmpl_id=3%20>

King, Ryno. 2008. '425% Increase in Lost and Stolen SAPS Firearms since 2004.' DA media statement. 21 February. <http://www.da.org.za/da/Site/Eng/News/Article.asp?ID=8678>

Kirsten, Adéle. 2004. *The Role of Social Movements in Gun Control: An International Comparison between South Africa, Brazil and Australia.* Centre for Civil Society Research Report No. 21. Durban: Centre for Civil Society Research, pp. 1–36.

——. 2007. *Simpler, Better, Faster: Review of the 2005 Firearms Amnesty.* ISS Occasional Paper No. 134. April. Pretoria: Institute for Security Studies. <http://www.iss.co.za/dynamic/administration/file_manager/file_links/PAPER134.PDF?link_id=19&slink_id=4353&link_type=12&slink_type=23&tmpl_id=3>

——. 2008. *A Nation without Guns? The Story of Gun Free South Africa.* Scottsville: University of KwaZulu-Natal Press.

Maughan, Karyn. 2006. 'Burundi Bungle Leaves SANDF Chiefs Red-faced.' *Star* (Johannesburg). 31 October. <http://www.int.iol.co.za/index.php?set_id=1&click_id=15&art_id=vn20061031034304313C570808>

——. 2007a. 'Hundreds of SANDF Weapons Misplaced.' *Star* (Johannesburg). 16 July.

——. 2007b. 'SANDF Chief Fingered on Shoddy Control of Weapons.' *Star* (Johannesburg). 20 July.

Minnaar, Antony. 2007. 'Oversight and Monitoring of Non-State/Private Policing: The Private Security Practitioners in South Africa.' In S. Gumedze, ed. *Private Security in Africa.* ISS Monograph Series No. 139. Pretoria: Institute for Security Studies, pp. 127–49. <http://www.iss.co.za/dynamic/administration/file_manager/file_links/M139CHAP8.PDF?link_id=30&slink_id=5355&link_type=12&slink_type=13&tmpl_id=3>

NIMSS (National Injury Mortality Surveillance System). 2006. *Fatal Violence in South Africa: The Role of Firearms.* Pretoria: NIMSS.

PSIRA (Private Security Industry Regulatory Authority). 2006a. *Annual Report 2005/06.* Pretoria: PSIRA.

——. 2006b. 'PowerPoint presentation to the Parliamentary Portfolio Committee on Safety and Security.' November.

Reynolds, T. 2003. 'South Africa's Security Business Is Booming.' *Pretoria News.* 24 July.

SAGA (South African Gun Owners Association). 2007. *SAGA Submission on Draft Regulations.* 19 February. <http://www.saga.org.za/Act&Regs.htm#Draft%20FCA%20Amend%20Regs%20Oct07>

SAPA (South African Press Association). 2007. 'Dube Murder: Mbeki Calls for Action.' 19 October. <http://www.iol.co.za/index.php?set_id=1&click_id=3045&art_id=nw20071019112703541C136372>

——. 2008. 'Men Appear in Court for Dube Murder.' 18 January. <http://www.iol.co.za/index.php?set_id=1&click_id=15&art_id=nw20080118122438354C186387>

SAPS (South African Police Service). 1997. *Annual Report 1996/97.* Pretoria: SAPS.

——. 1998. *Annual Report 1997/98.* Pretoria: SAPS.

——. 1999. *Annual Report 1998/99.* Pretoria: SAPS.

——. 2000. *Annual Report 1999/2000.* Pretoria: SAPS.

——. 2001. *Annual Report 2000/01.* Pretoria: SAPS.

——. 2002. *Annual Report 2001/02.* Pretoria: SAPS.

——. 2003. *Annual Report 2002/03.* Pretoria: SAPS. <http://www.saps.gov.za/saps_profile/strategic_framework/annual_report/index.htm>

——. 2004. *Annual Report 2003/04.* Pretoria: SAPS. <http://www.saps.gov.za/saps_profile/strategic_framework/annual_report/index.htm>

——. 2005. *Annual Report 2004/05.* Pretoria: SAPS. <http://www.saps.gov.za/saps_profile/strategic_framework/annual_report/index.htm>

——. 2006. *Annual Report 2005/06.* Pretoria: SAPS. <http://www.saps.gov.za/saps_profile/strategic_framework/annual_report/index.htm>

——. 2007a. *Annual Report 2006/07.* Pretoria: SAPS. <http://www.saps.gov.za/saps_profile/strategic_framework/annual_report/index.htm>

——. 2007b. *Crime Situation 2007.* <http://www.saps.gov.za/statistics/reports/crimestats/2007/_pdf/crime_situation1.pdf>

——. n.d. SAPS Web site. <http://www.saps.gov.za>

Seegers, Annette. 1996. *The Military and the Making of Modern South Africa.* London: Tauris.

Smit, I. 2003. 'South African's Guarding Industry: Challenging Future Ahead.' *Security Focus,* Vol. 21, No. 1, p. 10.

Soutar, Andrew. 2006. 'South African Arms and Ammunitions Dealers Association, Oral Submission to Parliament on the Firearms Control Amendment Bill.' B12-2006. 16 August.

South Africa. 1969. Arms and Ammunition Act No. 75. Pretoria: Government Printer.

——. 2000. Firearms Control Act No. 60. *Government Gazette,* Vol. 430. Pretoria. <http://www.info.gov.za/gazette/acts/2000/a60 00.pdf>

——. 2003. Firearms Control Amendment Act 2003. *Government Gazette,* Vol. 462. Pretoria. <http://www.info.gov.za/gazette/acts/2003/a43-03.pdf>

——. 2004. Firearms Control Act: Regulations. *Government Gazette,* Vol. 465. Pretoria. <http://www.info.gov.za/regulations/2004/26156/index.html>

——. Auditor General. 2006a. *2006 Report.* Pretoria: Auditor General.

——. Parliamentary Portfolio Committee on Safety and Security. 2006b. 'Minutes of PSIRA Presentation.' November.

——. Standing Committee on Public Accounts. 2007. 'Minutes of Standing Committee on Public Accounts (SCOPA) Meeting.' 26 January. <http://www.pmg.org.za/minutes/20070125-south-african-police-service-independent-complaints-directorate-interrogation-audit>

Statistics South Africa. 2006. *Adult Mortality (Age 15–64) Based on Death Notification Data in South Africa: 1997–2004.* Pretoria: Statistics South Africa.

Van Dyk, S. 2007. 'Internal Question Paper No. 36-2005.' 28 November. Cape Town: National Assembly.

Vilakazi, Eugene. 2003. 'Briefing by PSIRA to the Parliamentary Portfolio Committee on Safety and Security.' September.

ACKNOWLEDGEMENTS

Principal authors

Gregory Mthembu-Salter and Guy Lamb

ADVENTURES OF A WOULD-BE ARMS DEALER

BASED ON A TRUE STORY

Robert Butler 2008

AS I FLEW INTO KIGALI, MY THOUGHTS FLOATED BACK TO THE HORRORS OF 1994.

I HAD TAKEN REFUGE IN KIGALI'S STADIUM—THE UN'S HEADQUARTERS DURING THE RWANDAN GENOCIDE.

I HAD BEEN AMONG THE PRIVILEGED FEW... BUT NOW I WAS BACK ON A SPECIAL MISSION.

I HAD BEEN HIRED TO ORGANIZE AN ILLICIT ARMS DEAL AS A WAY OF TESTING THE STRENGTH OF EXPORT CONTROL SYSTEMS.

HEY, BABY!

MY FIRST TASK WAS TO MEET CHARLES—AN OLD CONTACT WHOSE PICKUP I HAD RENTED IN '94. I WAITED IN THE BACK OF A BAR.

WHERE IS HE?

SORRY I'M LATE, RED. MY WIFE... SHE'S THREATENING TO LEAVE ME. I DON'T KNOW WHAT TO DO. I NEED A DRINK!

SHE SAYS MY DEFENCE MINISTRY SALARY IS A DISGRACE, THAT I'M A DRUNK, THAT SHE WANTS NEW CLOTHES...

NOW, NOW...

I NEED ANOTHER BEER, RED.

AFTER HE HAD PRODUCED A MOUNTAIN OF EMPTIES, I MADE MY MOVE...

TAKE THIS, CHARLES.

YOU CAN HAVE THREE MORE OF THESE IF YOU BRING ME A BLANK, SIGNED END-USER CERTIFICATE TOMORROW NIGHT.

CHARLES BLINKED AND THEN NODDED. IF HE DECIDED TO RAT ON ME, I WOULD ARGUE THAT HE'D BEEN SO DRUNK HE MISUNDERSTOOD ME.

MY NEXT BEER RUN PROVED FUTILE. CHARLES HAD ALREADY PASSED OUT.

I'LL GET YOU A CAB, BUDDY.

I SPENT THE NEXT DAY ANXIOUSLY PACING AROUND MY HOTEL ROOM.

WHEN I ARRIVED AT THE BAR THAT EVENING, CHARLES WAS ALREADY THERE.

AS I BROUGHT OVER THE RITUAL BEERS, CHARLES PLACED AN ENVELOPE ON THE UPTURNED CRATE NEXT TO MY STOOL.

INSIDE THE ENVELOPE WAS THE EUC AS I HAD REQUESTED IT: ON MINISTRY OF DEFENCE LETTERHEAD, SIGNED...

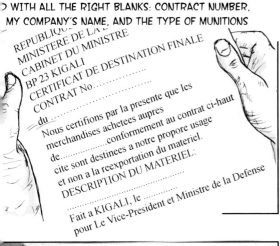

...D WITH ALL THE RIGHT BLANKS: CONTRACT NUMBER,
MY COMPANY'S NAME, AND THE TYPE OF MUNITIONS

REPUBLIQUE...
MINISTERE DE LA...
CABINET DU MINISTRE
BP 23 KIGALI
CERTIFICAT DE DESTINATION FINALE
CONTRAT No................
du................
Nous certifions par la presente que les
merchandises achetees aupres
de................conformement au contrat ci-haut
cite sont destinees a notre propore usage
et non a la reexportation du materiel.
DESCRIPTION DU MATERIEL:
....
Fait a KIGALI, le ....
pour Le Vice-President et Ministre de la Defense

WITH THE EUC TUCKED SAFELY IN MY INSIDE POCKET, I HANDED CHARLES THE PROMISED CASH.

I BOUGHT ANOTHER ROUND FOR CHARLES AND THE BARTENDER AND KEPT A DISCREET EYE ON THE TIME.

THEN I CAUGHT THE LAST PLANE TO CYPRUS. PHASE II COULD BEGIN.

THE NEXT DAY—ON MY HOTEL BALCONY IN CYPRUS—I BEGAN TO FILL IN THE EUC BLANKS.

WITH THE EUC, I COULD PRETEND THAT THE RWANDAN ARMED FORCES HAD HIRED ME TO SOURCE MUNITIONS FOR THEM. WHY NOT 2 MILLION ROUNDS OF AMMUNITION?

...ease advise availability, price, and packaging for 2,000,000 rounds of 7.62 x 39 mm ex. Bulgarian port.

I have an EUC made out to my company from the Government of Rwanda

A speedy respon...
time sche...

I KNEW THAT AMPRO, A BULGARIAN AMMUNITION PRODUCER, HAD SUPPLIED RWANDA IN THE PAST. I SENT A FAX REQUESTING A QUOTE.

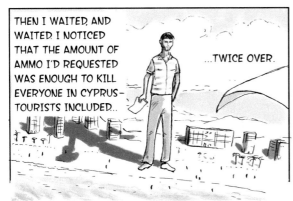

THEN I WAITED, AND WAITED. I NOTICED THAT THE AMOUNT OF AMMO I'D REQUESTED WAS ENOUGH TO KILL EVERYONE IN CYPRUS—TOURISTS INCLUDED...

...TWICE OVER.

AMPRO'S REPLY CAME THAT SAME EVENING.

Further to your request, please find below the required data:

7.62 x 39 mm rounds
Quantity: 2,000,000 rounds
Year of manufacture: 1978
Price: USD 64/1,000 pcs FOB Bulgarian port
Packing: 2 metal boxes x 700 = 1,400 pcs in one wooden case
Case dimensions 480 x 360 x 160 mm
Gross weight 30 kg
Volume 0.028 m³
Total: 1,429 cases

AMPRO PRICED A SINGLE BULLET AT

USD 0.064.

WHY SO CHEAP?

WAS IT BECAUSE THEY WERE MANUFACTURED IN 1978 AND THUS GETTING A BIT OLD AND LESS RELIABLE?

AND WHY DIDN'T AMPRO'S FAX SPECIFY THAT THE ORDER WOULD BE EXPORT LICENSABLE ONLY IF IT MET EU CODE OF CONDUCT CRITERIA?

CRITERION FOUR
Preservation of regional peace, security and stability
Member States will not issue an export licence if there is a clear risk that the intended recipient would use the proposed export aggressively against another country or to assert by force a territorial claim.
When considering these risks, EU Member States will take into account inter alia:
) the existence or likelihood of armed conflict between the cipient and another country;

BOSS, THERE'S ONLY ONE WAY TO FIND OUT WHETHER AMPRO IS WILLING TO TURN A BLIND EYE –I NEED TO PAY A DEPOSIT ...TYPICALLY 20%.

THE ANSWER IS NO, RED. NO.

NO?

?!%€*!!?...

NO!

THIS WASN'T THE END OF MY ADVENTURE, HOWEVER. IT WAS TIME FOR PHASE III. NEXT STOP: GUERNSEY, CHANNEL ISLANDS - GENTEEL TOURIST RESORT...

... AND HOME TO A LOT OF REMARKABLY ANONYMOUS FRONT COMPANIES, SOME OF THEM OPERATED BY THE WORLD'S MOST NOTORIOUS GUNRUNNERS.

FROM GUERNSEY, I WOULD HAVE A PLAUSIBLE AREA CODE WHEN TRYING TO ARRANGE A SHADY SHIPMENT DEAL.

+44 1841 123 456

I WASTED NO TIME. I CALLED MAXIM SAMOLETOV, A RUSSIAN AIRPLANE OWNER BASED IN DUBAI, UAE.

MR. SAMOLETOV?

YES.

SAMOLETOV HAD BEEN ON THE UN SANCTIONS COMMITTEE'S RADAR SCREEN FOR OPERATING AN OLD ANTONOV AN-8 WITH CONNECTIONS TO KNOWN ARMS DEALERS.

SIR, MY PRINCIPALS HAVE ASKED ME TO FIND AN AIRCRAFT TO FLY FROM YEMEN TO GPS COORDINATES IN CENTRAL SOUTHERN SOMALIA...

... AND THEN PARACHUTE-DROP AMMUNITION FROM THE AIRCRAFT.

HE'LL NEVER BUY THIS!

WE NEED TO DROP ABOUT FOUR METRIC TONS OF AMMUNITION AND THE FLIGHT OVER SOMALIA WILL NOT BE DECLARED. WE WOULD ALSO NEED YOU TO SOURCE CARGO PARACHUTES.

AND MR. SAMOLETOV, SINCE THERE IS NO SURVEILLANCE OF AIRCRAFT IN THE REGION, WE EXPECT THIS WILL NOT BE A PROBLEM FOR YOU...

SEND ME YOUR REQUEST BY FAX, PLEASE.

SAMOLETOV PROMISED TO RESPOND TO MY FAX THE NEXT MORNING. IT WAS ABUNDANTLY CLEAR THAT THE ILLEGAL NATURE OF THE DEAL WAS IRRELEVANT TO HIM.

SURELY SAMOLETOV KNEW THAT A UN ARMS EMBARGO PROHIBITS THE SUPPLY OF ARMS TO ANY SOMALI GROUP, INCLUDING THE TRANSITIONAL GOVERNMENT.

AND HE DEFINITELY WASN'T GOING TO APPLY TO THE UN SANCTIONS COMMITTEE FOR AN EXEMPTION.

I SENT HIM A FAX WITH QUANTITIES, VOLUMES AND WEIGHTS, AND A DESIRED DELIVERY SCHEDULE.

Dear Mr. Samoletov,

As discussed earlier today, I confirm that my principals are interested in a charter of your aircraft for two flights from an airstrip in western Yemen to GPS coordinates in central southern Somalia, such flights to be undertaken in approximately three weeks' time.

I need to know th
flight. W

AFTER A LONG, MEDITATIVE STROLL, I WOUND UP IN A GOURMET RESTAURANT—BUT I COULDN'T TASTE A THING.

THE NEXT MORNING I NOTICED THAT A FAX HAD BEEN SLIPPED UNDER THE DOOR.

Dear Sir,

We need to know distance between point of departure and destination to determine alternate airport. We would like to receive in advance total amount $200,000 for aircraft positioning.

The cost of each flight will be $50,000 plus ground expenses and fuel required Await your reply

Regards,
Maxim Samoletov

to know distance between point of d
n to **determine alternate airport**. We
n advance total amount $200,000 for
ng.
of each flight will be $50,000 plus g
and fuel required. Await your reply.

SAMOLETOV WAS PLANNING TO DECLARE ANOTHER DESTINATION BUT NEEDED IT TO BE THE SAME DISTANCE FROM THE YEMEN PORT.

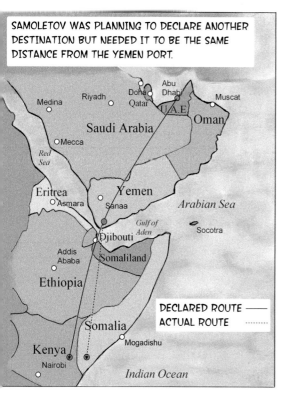

NO DOUBT SAMOLETOV'S PLANES WERE REGISTERED UNDER FLAGS OF CONVENIENCE–PERHAPS UNDER SÃO TOMÉ'S...

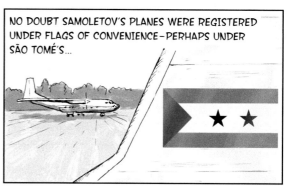

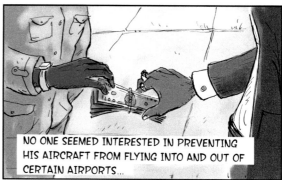

NO ONE SEEMED INTERESTED IN PREVENTING HIS AIRCRAFT FROM FLYING INTO AND OUT OF CERTAIN AIRPORTS...

SO WHAT KIND OF A PROFIT WERE WE TALKING ABOUT?

MY INVESTMENT INVOLVED PAYING POOR CHARLES A MEASLY USD 200.

man killed in a shootout among gangs
w street typical of the Spanish Quarter
ly © Francesco Cito/Panos Pictures

Reducing Armed Violence
THE PUBLIC HEALTH APPROACH

7

INTRODUCTION

In 1985 the US Surgeon General, C. Everett Koop, convened a landmark workshop on violence and public health. At the time, many viewed violence as a criminal problem. This conference 'signaled public health's entry into the field of violence prevention' (Mercy et al., 1993, p. 7), and set the stage for a proliferation of research and action on violence prevention. In 2002 the World Health Organization (WHO) released its *World Report on Violence and Health*, bringing the issue of violence, its effects on population health, and the role of the public health community in prevention efforts to the attention of the international community. Since the release of the report, efforts to use the public health approach to address the problem of violence have grown worldwide.

The public health approach has made a number of contributions to the understanding of violence. First and foremost, public health practitioners have highlighted and emphasized the preventable nature of violence. This shifts attention away from punishing those who have already committed violent crimes and towards intervening to prevent violence from occurring in the first place. Although perhaps an obvious contention, many approaches to violence perceive it as a common occurrence, and therefore something to be managed rather than prevented. As such, the public health approach presents a dramatically different way of thinking about the problem.

The second major contribution includes the identification of risk factors for violence. In 2002 the WHO developed a now widely used ecological model to identify potential risk factors, which offers a novel heuristic device for understanding what influences the likelihood of violence in a given situation. The ecological model underlines the embedded nature of the individual in his/her environment by identifying the various levels and types of factors that influence the individual, including an individual's family, community, and society. This model has become a prominent reference point for understanding the complexity of armed violence and identifying key risk factors that elevate an individual's propensity to become a perpetrator or a victim. A better understanding of risk factors in turn provides the basis for designing interventions targeting these factors.

This chapter considers the following questions:

- What is already known about armed violence, and how can the public health approach contribute to a better understanding of the problem?
- What is the public health approach to armed violence prevention?
- How does the social context influence armed violent behaviour?
- How does armed violence alter the social context and thereby contribute to further violence?
- How can the public health approach contribute to designing interventions to prevent armed violence?
- What does this approach add to the toolbox of policy-makers? And how can further research and refinement improve these tools?

The chapter is divided into six sections. The first section provides a definition of armed violence and discusses several types of armed violence. The second section presents a discussion of the scope and magnitude of armed violence at the global and regional levels. The third section discusses current approaches to understanding and addressing armed violence. The fourth section lays out the public health approach, explaining what it is and how it works. The fifth section focuses the discussion on how community factors influence the risk of violence in a given setting and the impact of violence on community characteristics and the possibility of future violence. The chapter finishes with an assessment of the public health approach, identifying its contributions to, as well as some of its limitations in, addressing armed violence.

The main conclusions include the following:

• The public health approach offers an additional lens for understanding the complexity of armed violence, thereby contributing to a more comprehensive approach to the problem and to possible solutions. It provides the backbone for a robust, evidence-based approach to understanding the complex, multi-causal phenomenon of armed violence and designing multifaceted and multi-level interventions to reduce the prevalence and negative impact of violent events.

• Understanding and preventing armed violence require better information about violent incidents. At present, current methods of obtaining data about armed violence are insufficient. The scope and magnitude of violence is likely to be underestimated in many parts of the world, especially in areas where the national capacity for data collection and analysis remains very limited. In these areas where national surveillance is not possible, efforts should be made to boost data collection through other methods, including surveys, and by collating information obtained by government and non-governmental agencies on various aspects of armed violence.

• Context matters. The prevention of armed violence depends upon a general understanding of armed violence combined with local knowledge of the community in which the violence takes place. Effective interventions require more than just data on how many people are killed with small arms. Contextual data on who perpetrates violence, how, when, where, and against whom, is important in order to tailor interventions to community dynamics.

• While many armed violence reduction programmes are community-based, they are not focused on the community. Instead, these programmes often focus on the individual and address factors that contribute to an individual becoming a perpetrator or victim. While such programmes are necessary and important in reducing armed violence, community approaches are also necessary, wherein programmes target community relations and community-level factors, and rely on community action to address the problem of armed violence.

• While the public health approach can make positive contributions to violence prevention, solutions cannot be found using this approach alone. Public health is not an alternative to criminal justice, education, poverty reduction, or any other programme targeting violence. Instead, it offers a framework for the coordination of efforts based on evidence, analysis, and action.

—lic health offers an —al lens for —nding the of armed violence.

ARMED VIOLENCE: DEFINITIONS AND TYPOLOGIES

While there is no universally accepted definition of violence, WHO, at the forefront of the public health approach to preventing and reducing violence, provides a useful first cut at defining the problem. It defines violence as:

The intentional use of physical force or power, threatened or actual, against oneself, another person, or against a group or community, that either results in or has a high likelihood of resulting in injury, death, psychological harm, maldevelopment or deprivation (Krug et al., 2002, p. 5).

This definition covers a broad range of acts, numerous actors, and a spectrum of outcomes. As a general definition, it suits the purposes of being inclusive and generating a rough understanding of what is meant by violence. As a definition to be used for the study of the phenomenon, it lacks the specificity required to operationalize the concept and ensure consistency across studies (Krauss, 2006, pp. 11–13). The definition simply covers too many acts, actors, and outcomes. It includes acts of suicide, child abuse, gender-based violence, crime, community clashes, and civil wars. The perpetrators and victims of these acts include young men; criminals; children; women; the elderly; communities; groups defined by their religion, ethnicity, or political party; or simply unlucky individuals. The outcomes range from minor bodily injury to grave bodily harm and death, from psychological scarring to impaired daily functioning, from economic hardship to economic devastation, and from disruption of daily life to disruption of a government's capacity to govern. While all of these acts, actors, and outcomes are important when considering the scope and magnitude of violence, they are difficult to study as a single phenomenon—violence. Instead, what becomes necessary to better understand these various violent acts and design interventions to prevent them is the delineation of these acts according to a typology of violence.

WHO has begun this process by identifying three main categories of violence: self-directed, interpersonal, and collective. Self-directed violence is any violent act an individual commits against himself or herself, and includes mutilation and suicide. Interpersonal violence is any violent act committed by an individual or small group of individuals against another individual or small group of individuals, and includes child abuse, rape, spousal abuse, fist fights, random acts of assault, and homicide. Collective violence is any organized act of violence committed by one group against another, and includes state-sponsored human rights abuses, terrorism, and civil wars. Figure 7.1 is a diagram designed by WHO to depict this typology of violence.

Figure 7.1 **WHO typology of violence**

Source: Krug et al. (2002, p. 7)

This delineation assists in understanding which actors might be involved and the scale at which the violence is taking place, i.e. directed at the individual, between individuals or small groups, or between large groups or countries, but does not aid in understanding or identifying the method, the context, or the nature of the violence—characteristics crucial to designing effective prevention strategies.

One important defining characteristic of violence is the method used to commit the violent act. It is important to distinguish between unarmed and armed violence. The importance of the tool used lies in the fact that different tools impart different levels of violence and costs of that violence. For example, a fist fight will impart costs on those involved in the fight, but these costs are often low and confined to the participants. A knife fight by contrast can produce more serious wounds that require medical attention and potentially produce long-term disabling effects, though again these effects are often confined to those involved in the incident. An exchange of gunfire, however, can produce severe and life-threatening injuries that require extensive medical attention and impose long-term costs on the victims, who can be far greater in number and include innocent bystanders, not just those engaged in the violent exchange. While various instruments have been used to injure and kill individuals and groups of people, small arms and light weapons have been responsible worldwide for a disproportionate amount of this violence, with some 63 per cent of homicides in 2000 being committed with firearms (WHO, 2001, p. 4).

Armed violence is the use of an instrument or tool to commit an act of violence. This instrument can be a knife, a stick, a broken bottle, a firearm, or any of a range of items used to intentionally inflict harm on another individual or oneself. Since a large percentage of armed violence in the world is committed with firearms, this chapter focuses where possible on small arms-related violence. The phrase 'small arms' is used to refer broadly to all types of military and commercial, hand-held, man-portable, explosively, or chemically propelled or detonated devices. This includes firearms. 'Firearms' is a term more commonly used in discussions of crime and non-conflict situations and encompasses handguns, shotguns, and assault rifles.

Guns line a wall of the firearms reference collection at the Metropolitan Police Department headquarters in Washington, DC, September 2007. Most of the guns were seized during crimes.© Jacquelyn Martin/AP Photo

Table 7.1 **Violence by context**	
General context	**Common types of violence[1]**
In the home	Self-directed, suicide Domestic violence: intimate partner violence, family violence, child maltreatment, elder abuse Sexual violence
In a community	Sexual violence Interpersonal violence Youth violence, school violence Gang violence Violent crime, organized crime
Between communities	Sexual violence Gang violence Violent political/economic/social conflict Armed conflict Terrorism
In a country	Civil war, armed conflict Violent political/economic/social conflict Terrorism Organized crime Gang violence State-perpetrated violence
Between countries or across borders	War, armed conflict Violent political/economic/social conflict Terrorism Organized crime

Previous editions of the *Small Arms Survey* have explored urban armed violence (2007), the costs of small arms violence (2006), the role of small arms in conflict (2005) and in crime (2004), and the impact of armed violence on humanitarian assistance (2002) and development (2003). This theme chapter explores armed violence and violence prevention using a public health framework. This framework emphasizes the context within which individuals interact and within which violence takes place, and the risk factors that exist in these environments. Table 7.1 provides a categorization of violence according to general context.

While understanding the context serves to identify risk factors, potential violent offenders, and possible victims, it also suggests the level at which interventions should be targeted: family, group, community, city, etc. It also indicates the level at which data should be collected about the phenomenon, or the level at which national data should be disaggregated. National crime rates offer only marginal insight into the prevalence of violence in any given community or the distribution of different types of violence across a country. For example, the homicide rate for Caracas, Venezuela was 60 per 100,000 members of the population in 1995, but the national average was only 20.5, and was heavily influenced by the high rate in Caracas (IADB, 1999a, p. 5). At the local level (see Box 7.1), data collection about violence generates more detailed information about a specific context and the risk factors contributing to the environment of violence.

Box 7.1 Mapping violence

Communities facing problems of violence must answer at least three important questions before engaging in violence prevention and reduction strategies: Does violence exist in the community? What kind of violence exists? And, what is the distribution
of violence–by type and frequency–in the community? Answers to these questions produce a detailed map of violence 'hot
spots' and the sources of violence, e.g. knives or firearms, residents or outsiders. This information in turn enables the design
of targeted intervention strategies and aids in their implementation. School violence offers one clear example where violence
mapping has provided important local information on the nature, scope, and frequency of the problem and enabled the
implementation of safety strategies to reduce the risk of violence to students.

   Schools have mapped violence successfully in Europe, Australia, and Israel by asking students a series of questions about
their experiences, their knowledge of violence, and their fears about violence in school. Schools have used this information to
determine whether metal detectors are necessary to identify students carrying weapons, or monitors are needed in certain
hallways or other areas at particular times, or bus stops need to be moved to ensure that students do not face risks while
waiting for the bus or getting on or off one. Importantly, this process empowers school administrations and students to
respond to violence in a public, collective, and targeted manner, rather than administrators ignoring the problem and students avoiding certain hallways at lunchtime.

Source: Based on Astor, Benbenishty, and Meyer (2004); Astor and Benbenishty (2006)

THE SCOPE AND MAGNITUDE OF ARMED VIOLENCE

Irrespective of the approach taken to armed violence reduction, e.g. education, crime prevention, or public health,
understanding the nature, scope, and magnitude of armed violence is important for designing effective strategies
and interventions to reduce armed violence and for targeting these interventions appropriately. Unfortunately, the
availability of information about armed violence remains extremely limited and patchy across the globe.

   While national homicide rates, a commonly used estimate of violence, are available for many countries, not all
countries possess the capacity to collect this information systematically. In many parts of the world, especially low-
income countries, mechanisms such as civil registration systems do not exist to record and report the births and
deaths of citizens. Under-reporting poses a large challenge to data collection. A number of factors influence reporting, including the type of crime committed, police capacity to respond, corruption, and public trust in government
(Soares, 2004).

   The case is even graver for recording and reporting incidents of violence. Most countries do not routinely collect
reliable data on violent deaths or the circumstances of these deaths (Rosenberg et al., 2006, p. 756), with only one-third
of the countries outside of North America and Europe possessing the capacity to collect and utilize mortality statistics
(Setel et al., 2007, p. 1569). This means that these governments do not know the extent or distribution of armed
violence in their countries and cannot develop armed violence reduction strategies based on credible information.

   Even in areas of the world where such civil registration mechanisms function and violence reporting exists, the
resulting data is incomplete and suffers from problems of under-reporting, making cross-national comparisons difficult.
The lack of data on armed violence, especially from low-income countries, has compounded this problem of data
inaccuracy. Dependence on data from high-income countries to extrapolate to broader regional and global trends is
cause for concern about misrepresentation of regional and global trends in armed violence. The result is a limited
understanding of the full extent of armed violence in many countries and regions.

Given the difficulties in obtaining reliable and valid data on incidents of violence at the national, regional, and global levels, the current data must be viewed with caution. As methods for collecting data improve and more data becomes available, new assessments of the national, regional, and global burdens of armed violence may vary significantly and substantially from current figures. For example, the Latin America and Caribbean region is often cited as the region with the highest level of armed violence, particularly homicide. However, this assessment could be the result of better data reporting rather than higher rates of violence. The Americas region has proven much better at reporting cause of death data to WHO (33 of 35 countries have useable data) than the African region (4 of 46 have useable data) (Mathers et al., 2005, p. 173). Imbalanced reporting across regions can distort the overall picture of the distribution of violence regionally and globally. This also has implications for where donors focus their funding and whether regional factors can be taken into consideration in designing interventions.

With these caveats in mind, global and regional trends can be identified in the current data, with the understanding that these generalizations are based on an imperfect, limited dataset. These trends in armed violence are discussed here not as a definitive measure of the problem of armed violence, but as an illustration of the scope and widespread costs of armed violence, and the need for additional attention to preventive and curative measures to reduce these negative effects and high costs.

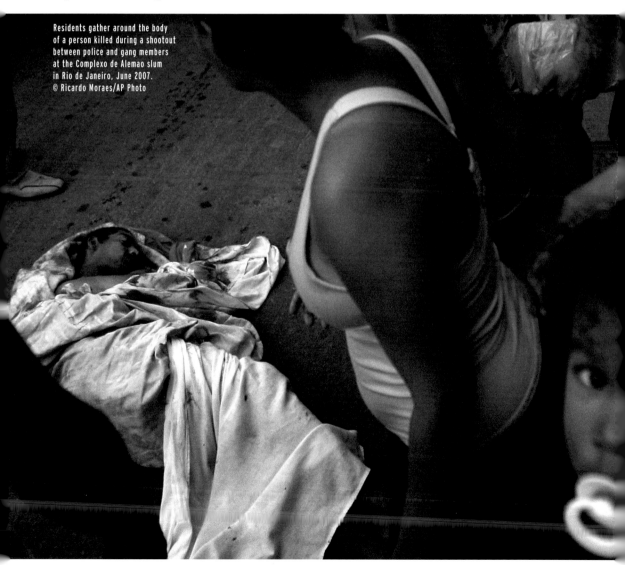

Residents gather around the body of a person killed during a shootout between police and gang members at the Complexo de Alemao slum in Rio de Janeiro, June 2007.
© Ricardo Moraes/AP Photo

Global burden of armed violence

Although many violent events never make it to the nightly news, and few incidents result in large numbers of deaths, cumulatively armed violence has a tremendous impact on the health of national populations around the globe each year. In some countries considered 'at peace' the death and damage wreaked by armed violence surpasses that taking place in countries in conflict. The death tolls are significant. An estimated 196,000–270,000 non-conflict deaths result each year from armed violence, and many more are wounded as a result of this violence.[2] Estimates of conflict-related deaths and non-fatal injuries from conflict and non-conflict violence are even more difficult to develop with any confidence, though there is some evidence that the former are on the decline (Human Security Centre, 2006, p. 8).

Non-conflict deaths result from homicide, suicide, accidents, and incidents of unknown intent. The vast majority of deaths result from homicide or suicide. Globally, suicide outnumbers homicide by a rate of three to two (Krug et al., 2002, p. 10). However, if only events involving firearms are included, the ratio shifts substantially to a rate of four homicides to one suicide, with firearms being 'used in approximately six per cent of suicides worldwide and in almost 40 per cent of homicides' (Small Arms Survey, 2004, p. 175).

Despite the lack of information to generate exact estimates, many would agree that 'by any measure, violence is a major contributor to premature death, disability and injury' (Mercy et al., 1993, p. 8) in many parts of the world. Despite this grave—and valid—claim, violence should not be viewed as homogenous across countries or even within countries. Violence is 'disproportionately felt by low and middle income countries' (Rutherford et al., 2007b, p. 764). 'The estimated rate of violent deaths in [low- and middle-income countries] was 32.1 per 100,000 in 2000, compared with 14.4 per 100,000 in high-income countries' (Rosenberg et al., 2006, p. 755). This means that violence is most prevalent in those countries and populations least able to respond to the threat, pay the costs, and manage the short- and long-term impacts of violence. Even within high-violence regions and countries, wide variance exists in terms of the types of violence prevalent; the frequency of violence; and where violence is concentrated in certain countries, areas, and cities (see Box 7.2). These characteristics have a significant impact on devising strategies to reduce violence.

Regional distribution of armed violence

The difficulty in collecting reliable and regular data on armed violence and violent deaths results in an uneven understanding of the regional distribution of violence. Data is more widely available in certain regions, such as North America and Europe, followed by Latin America and the Caribbean, because there are systems in place in these regions

Box 7.2 Violence in Sri Lanka

In Sri Lanka, where a civil war has raged for several decades, a surprising mix of violence and peace exists within the country. Social relationships and economic vitality are not depressed nationwide. Instead, the levels of social cohesion and the strength of the local economy are largely dependent on the location of any given village. Villages that sit squarely in either government- or rebel-controlled territory experience far more stability than villages that sit on the borderlands between the two fighting factions. This is largely the result of the monopoly of power held by one faction, resulting in lower levels of actual fighting, and the mono-ethnic nature of the communities, producing more trust among neighbours. The low levels of insecurity enable wider mobility and opportunities for economic engagement. The planting of crops, for example, becomes possible due to more certainty about the future. By contrast, in the border areas between fighting factions, social cohesion is low and economic opportunities are extremely limited. Insecurity reduces mobility and economic activities, while frequent displacement reduces interest in investing in the future, such as by the planting of crops.

Source: Goodhand, Hulme, and Lewer (2000)

Table 7.2   Regional armed violence rates, estimated per 100,000 people, 2004

Region	Firearm homicide	Firearm suicide
Latin America and the Caribbean	15.47	1.12
Africa	5.90	0.59
North America	3.50	5.52
Central and Eastern Europe	3.09	1.41
Middle East	1.89	0.06
South-east Asia	1.45	0.10
Asia-Pacific	0.54	0.39
Western Europe	0.35	1.66
Worldwide	3.14	0.81

Note: These estimates are the upper threshold estimates. Additional details on the regional divisions, the derivation of these estimates, and the datasets used can be found in Small Arms Survey (2004, Appendix 6.1, 6.2, 6.3, pp. 199-204).
Source: Small Arms Survey (2004, pp. 199-200)

to collect this information. In other regions, data is collected, if at all, on a more ad hoc and unsystematic basis. There are efforts to improve the collection of information in hospitals and through crime victim surveys, but these remain in their early stages (Rosenberg et al., 2006, pp. 756–57).[3] In addition, more is known about certain types of violence, e.g. homicide, than other types, e.g. domestic violence. To date, most efforts to collect data still provide snapshots of the situation in any given location, not reliable longitudinal data that can depict clear trends over time or map the various types, frequencies, and impacts of armed violence across a region. Despite the limitations imposed by gaps in existing knowledge, some regional trends can be identified using the currently available data.

The proportion of deaths resulting from firearm homicide versus firearm suicide varies by region and country (see Table 7.2). Firearm homicides are more common in Latin America, the Caribbean, and Africa, whereas firearm suicides significantly outnumber homicides in North America and Western Europe. The rest of the world falls below the estimated average global rate of firearm homicide, 3.14 homicides per 100,000 people, with significantly lower rates in Asia and Western Europe. However, it is important to note that religious and cultural beliefs that suicide is an unacceptable practice contribute to the under-reporting of suicides in many regions.

Firearms are used in an estimated 60 per cent of all homicides in Latin America, the Caribbean, and North America, and an estimated 30 per cent of all homicides in the Middle East, Western Europe, and South-east Asia (Small Arms Survey, 2004, pp. 199–200). This suggests that firearms are a common tool of armed violence and therefore a significant concern for many countries.

Common factors contributing to armed violence

Current information on armed violence in a number of countries and settings suggests a number of common risk factors that heighten the probability of armed violence. These include age; gender; geographical location; level of economic inequality; density of population; the presence of gangs; and the availability of alcohol, drugs, and weapons.

Demographically, young men aged 15–29 are the primary perpetrators and victims of violence worldwide. Moreover, young men, more than any other group, use firearms when carrying out a crime (Small Arms Survey, 2006,

p. 297). For every young man killed through violence, there are an estimated 20–40 more young men who are injured and treated in hospitals (Sethi et al., 2006, p. 31). The homicide rates among young men are substantially higher than those among young women.

Low-income countries experience higher death rates due to violence than high-income countries. The risk of violent death for young men in low-income countries is 11.3 times greater than the risk for young men living in high-income countries (Sethi et al., 2006, p. 31).

Although no direct link between urbanization and armed violence exists, evidence suggests that the larger the city, in general, the higher the rate of armed violence (see Table 7.3). Factors that contribute to this urban–rural divide include population density, higher levels of economic inequality in urban areas, the prevalence of slum areas, and the presence of gangs.

The presence of firearms, drugs, and alcohol increases the likelihood of violence. While firearm ownership cannot be equated with firearm violence in a simple manner, the availability of firearms is a contributing factor to armed

Gang members with a 9 mm pistol in the hallway of a public housing project in Brooklyn, New York, December 2003. © Boogie

Table 7.3 **US homicide rates by city population per 100,000 people, 1985–2004**	
City population	**20-year mean rate**
1 million +	19.04
500,000–999,999	13.86
250,000–499,999	11.31
100,000–249,999	7.21
United States overall	7.57

Source: Wilkinson and Bell (2006)

violence. In particular, firearms contribute to higher lethality rates when used in crimes (Dahlberg, 1998, p. 265). The use of alcohol and drugs by individuals also increases the risk of violence. Excessive use of alcohol contributes to higher rates of all types of violence, with a number of studies revealing high levels of alcohol consumption by both perpetrators and victims of homicide (IADB, 1999d, p. 8).

Understanding the context through better data

The lack of a comprehensive global map of armed violence is the result of problems relating to obtaining data, the quality of data produced, and the incomparability of different datasets.[4] While important to understand the global burden of violence for policy and funding reasons, a global map of armed violence, depending on its detail, may not prove particularly useful for designing national or local-level interventions. Context-specific data becomes equally important to a global map, and thus collecting this data should be a priority for armed violence reduction.

Violence data can be drawn from a variety of sources, including civil registration systems, which record births and deaths; vital statistics records; medical examiners' reports; hospital records; police crime statistics; court records; population surveys; demographic surveillance sites; population censuses; sample registration systems; victim surveys; and interviews, among others.[5] Various actors collect data, including hospital workers, non-governmental organizations, journalists, scholars, police and customs officials, and a variety of other government agencies and local organizations. The collection of data can be driven by the interests of these actors and their financial and political constraints, leading to biases in the type of data collected, how it is collected, and how it is reported. Information from these various sources adds to an overall—yet necessarily imperfect—picture of the burden of armed violence in a given area, country, or region.

Yet even with statistics on who has died and how (i.e. murder, natural causes, accident), what is missing, but is needed for designing interventions, is contextual data. Contextual data moves beyond these basic statistics to address the questions of when, where, how (e.g. knife, gun), and by whom armed violence is committed. This data contributes to a better understanding of which factors are important to armed violence in a given setting (RISK AND RESILIENCE). These factors include the demographics of the population, environmental characteristics (e.g. the presence of street lighting, use of public space), common behavioural patterns of community and non-community members (e.g. cohesive community, transitory population), the presence of high-risk materials (e.g. weapons, drugs), and the presence of high-risk groups (e.g. gangs, youth, organized crime). The identification of existing risk factors contributes to targeting violence prevention efforts at the most significant problems within a given context.

TACKLING ARMED VIOLENCE: APPROACHES TO PREVENTION

It is not only the magnitude and scope of armed violence that argue in favour of enhanced prevention and reduction efforts, but also its preventable nature. There is no simple solution or single measure that can address the complexity of armed violence. Given the fact that such violence takes place in a wide variety of contexts, strategies to address it need to be tailored to fit the situation—politically, economically, socially, and culturally. These strategies need to be multifaceted in nature and require a cross-sectoral approach.

A current challenge to effective armed violence reduction efforts is the wide range of groups and sectors (e.g. police, health, education) working on the problem, but not working together. Instead, 'each of the groups working in violence prevention has their own culture, concepts, theory, language, methods and priorities' (Rutherford et al., 2007b, p. 767), which leads to each group focusing on its own aspect of the problem. This piecemeal and ad hoc approach leads at times to misunderstandings and misinterpretation of efforts, as well as to conflicts among groups who should be working together; exacerbates the scarcity of resources; and misses opportunities for sharing information and collaborating on violence reduction initiatives.

There is no simple solution for reducing armed violence. Given the wide variation in the nature of such violence, no single approach is likely to address all types equally. Widely used approaches include mental health, safety education, conflict prevention, criminal justice, and public health, among others. Each approach has its strengths and weaknesses, and some may be used better for addressing specific types of violence or particular target audiences. The question remains one of how to promote collaboration across approaches rather than singling out the best approach. Many approaches have contributed, and will continue to contribute, to understanding armed violence and working to reduce its scope and magnitude. What is needed is a comprehensive, collaborative approach—one that looks at perpetrators and victims, violent incidents and the effects of that violence, deterrence and prevention, punishment, and treatment—in order to ensure an efficient use of resources, information, and skills, and ultimately to have the greatest impact on reducing armed violence in response to the circumstances of a specific locality.

The publi⬛
approach⬛
risks to t⬛
of a spec
populatio⬛
them, an⬛
measure⬛
them.

THE PUBLIC HEALTH APPROACH

Understanding what is meant by a public health approach is important. Public health focuses on promoting the health of a population as a whole. Rather than focusing on any specific individual, public health identifies the risks of injury and disease for a population with the intent to prevent the spread of disease or reduce the propensity to injury through interventions at the individual, family, community, and societal levels. In a nutshell, the public health approach identifies risks to the health of a specified population, assesses the identified risk, and then takes measures to reduce this risk.

The field of public health originally developed as a response to the problem of communicable diseases and the dramatic impact these had on populations. Following the improved ability to prevent epidemics of disease through vaccinations, sanitation, and medical treatment, and therefore greatly reduce the burden of disease, public health practitioners expanded their efforts to include other problems that negatively affect population health. Initially, public health practitioners turned their attention to trying to reduce the burden of unintentional injury and death. Successes in this area suggested that the public health approach could be extended further to other public health concerns.

Public health officials have only shifted their focus to violence over the past two decades. In the United States, the Centers for Disease Control and Prevention identified violence as a leading public health priority in the mid-1980s (CDC, 2008), followed by the recognition by the World Health Assembly in 1996 that 'violence is a leading worldwide public health problem' (WHO, 1996) and the publication of WHO's first report on violence and health in 2002. Prior to this time, public health officials were far more concerned with communicable diseases and preventing unintentional injuries. As evidence increasingly demonstrated the widespread impact of armed violence on the health of the public (Prothrow-Stith, 2004, pp. 82–83), as opposed to viewing its impact more narrowly as the burden of the victim, public health officials have increasingly recognized the importance of addressing violence in order to promote the health of populations.

Starting in the 1980s, members of the public health community began focusing their attention on the problem of intentional violence. Using lessons learnt from successful efforts in reducing the burden of disease and reducing the prevalence of unintentional injury and death in other areas, public health practitioners suggested that a similar approach could reduce the burden of intentional violence and the harmful effects of small arms. Public health efforts have contributed to eradicating smallpox, making automobiles safer, and reducing the harmful health effects of consumer products such as cigarettes and alcohol (Hemenway, 2001; Mercy et al., 1993). In the case of automobiles, public health measures focused on improving the environment (e.g. roads), the product (e.g. seatbelts in cars), and the response (e.g. improved emergency medical care) drastically reduced the fatalities due to automobile accidents (Hemenway, 2001, p. 384). These measures did not stop the accidents from happening (prevention), but rather reduced the harm caused by the accidents (harm reduction). In addressing armed violence, both preventive and harm reduction measures will be important to reducing the burden of violence.

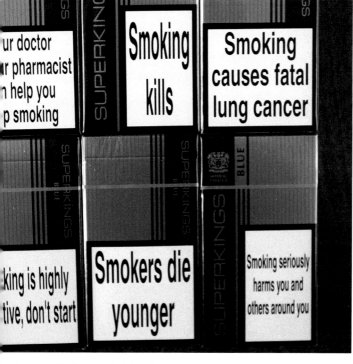

arnings required by law on packs of cigarettes.
n/AP Photo

The public health approach emphasizes the scientific nature of its methods for gathering and analysing data, which are based in epidemiology. Epidemiology is the study of the incidence and distribution of disease to identify risk factors in order to control the disease. One of the primary tools of epidemiology is surveillance: 'the systematic gathering, analyzing and interpreting of specific data to be used in the planning, execution and evaluation of programs' to deal with a specific problem (IADB, 1999b, p. 1). In trying to understand armed violence, this approach views the act of violence as the result of the influence of a complex set of factors at the individual, familial, community, and societal levels rather than simply the will or choice of a single individual. As such, surveillance aims to identify those factors

Figure 7.2 **The four-step public health approach**

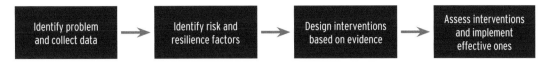

that increase or reduce the risk of an individual becoming a perpetrator or victim of violence in order to design interventions that target high-risk groups.

The public health approach involves a four-step process of: identification, evaluation, treatment, and assessment (see Figure 7.2). The first step is to identify the problem clearly and collect valid and reliable data on its scope and magnitude. The second step entails an analysis of the data in order to identify prominent risk and resilience factors. The third step is to design interventions based on this analysis of patterned risk and resilience. The fourth step is to assess implemented interventions to determine which work, and then implement those that are most effective.

Identifying the problem clearly and in a manner enabling study and data collection is the first step in the public health model. As part of the identification process, and in preparation for collecting data, a clear definition of the problem needs to be established. This definition sets the parameters for the type of data to be collected. Data is then collected in a systematic way, often through surveillance systems in hospitals or crime victim surveys. Other methods include population surveys, media reports, and other case study research on the topic.

After data is collected, the second step is to analyse the data for patterns of identifiable risk and resilience factors (RISK AND RESILIENCE). Importantly, this step identifies commonalities among actors, instruments, and situations of violence (i.e. location, time of day) in order to produce a map of violence.

One example of using data for generating violence prevention strategies comes from the study of gang violence among teenagers in the United States. This study revealed significant differences between teenage gang members and at-risk youth (youth at risk of joining a gang). Gang members proved more likely to assault rivals (72.3 per cent), commit homicide (15.2 per cent), carry weapons in school (40.4 per cent), and sell drugs outside of school (61.7 per cent) than their non-gang teenage counterparts (16.3, 0.0, 10.2, and 16.7 per cent, respectively) (IADB, 1999c, p. 6).

Box 7.3 **Identifying violence in the home**

The public health approach has proved particularly good at identifying domestic violence, as injuries from this type of violence more often display themselves in the emergency rooms of medical facilities than in police stations (Moore, 1993, p. 36; Rosenberg et al., 2006, p. 756). This places public health officials in the best position to identify this violence and to provide the evidence to convince governments and donors that more attention should be paid to the problem.

Violence against women and girls is a major public health problem in many countries, but it remains a largely invisible problem. Governments have failed to respond. A common response of governments has been 'show us the data'. Yet data tends to reflect only reported cases, offering a descriptive, not definitive, assessment of the problem, and often underestimating the level of violence and its wide-reaching effects.

Recent research has highlighted the problem in stark detail. In a study in two counties of post-conflict Liberia, 'domestic violence affected about 55 percent of women' (Shiner, 2007). In Niger, rape is not illegal and domestic violence is increasingly common. In one study, 70 per cent of female respondents found it normal that men regularly beat, raped, and humiliated women. The government has not acted on the problem of domestic violence in Niger because the health care community does not collect statistics on injuries resulting from violence, and authorities deny that the problem exists.

Sources: Based on Shiner (2007); IRIN (2007b)

Figure 7.3 **The WHO ecological model**

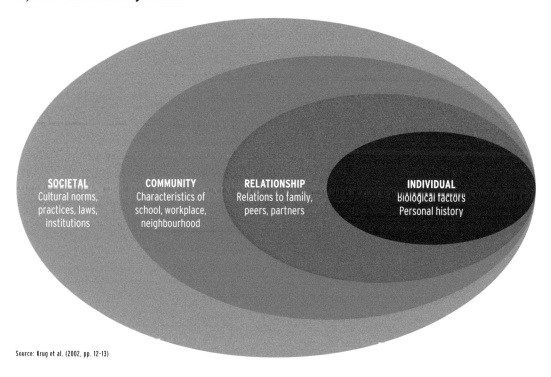

SOCIETAL
Cultural norms,
practices, laws,
institutions

COMMUNITY
Characteristics of
school, workplace,
neighbourhood

RELATIONSHIP
Relations to family,
peers, partners

INDIVIDUAL
Biological factors
Personal history

Source: Krug et al. (2002, pp. 12–13)

Understanding these differences can aid in developing universal strategies to protect everyone at risk, e.g. deploying metal detectors in schools, and targeting strategies at gangs, e.g. hot spot policing.

A widely used model for categorizing risk factors is the ecological model put forward by WHO in its 2002 report (see Figure 7.3). This model recognizes the complexity of violence, the embedded nature of individuals in complex social networks, and the role of a wide range of factors at various levels—from the individual to the societal—that influence individual risk, resilience, and behaviour (Rosenberg et al., 2006, p. 761).

The ecological model aids in understanding the multifaceted nature of violence by acknowledging the myriad influences on behaviour at several levels. This contextual knowledge of particular communities is crucial to designing effective harm reduction and violence prevention strategies. One-size-fits-all strategies will not work. Each set of circumstances requires modifying effective interventions to fit the context.

Once patterns are identified, including clusters of risk factors and high-risk groups, the next step is to design interventions that target these risk factors or groups (RISK AND RESILIENCE). The public health approach commonly talks about three levels of intervention. At the primary level, the focus is on prevention. At the secondary level, interventions address the immediate effects of violence and seek to limit mortality. At the tertiary level, interventions aim to provide care to address the long-term effects of violence. Table 7.4 illustrates how interventions can be designed to reduce the prevalence and impact of firearm injury according to the level of intervention.

The fourth step in the public health model requires evaluating existing interventions to determine which ones are effective in preventing or reducing violence (INTERVENTIONS). This requires a detailed and scientific evaluation of the intervention. The purpose of the evaluation is to determine whether the intervention should be replicated on

Table 7.4 Reducing firearm injury

Level of prevention	Intent	Examples of interventions
Primary prevention (pre-injury or pre-event phase)	Prevent the initial creation of the risk	• Require background checks before gun purchase • Prohibit manufacture of certain types of firearms
	Reduce the amount of risk created	• Encourage police to use less lethal weapons • Prohibit manufacture of specific types of ammunition
	Reduce the prevalence of a risk that already exists	• Store firearms in locked boxes • Incarcerate firearm offenders
Secondary prevention (injury or event phase)	Modify the prevalence or spatial distribution of the risk	• Require registration of firearms • Improve gun tracing through better firearm labelling
	Separate, in time or space, the risk from persons to be protected	• Require waiting periods for firearm purchases • Install weapons detectors in some stadiums, high schools
	Interpose a barrier between the risk and the person to be protected	• Provide bulletproof vests for police • Offer bulletproof barriers for convenience store clerks, taxi drivers
	Modify contact surfaces and structures to reduce injury	• Redesign bullets to reduce injury severity • Redesign firearms to reduce rate of fire, muzzle velocity
	Strengthen the resistance of persons who might be injured	• Provide training and counselling for persons suffering repeated victimizations • Train people in non-lethal means of self-defence
Tertiary prevention (post-injury or post-event phase)	Rapidly detect and limit the damage	• Improve emergency medical and law enforcement response • Assure prompt incarceration of firearm offenders
	Initiate immediate and long-term reparative actions	• Improve physical rehabilitation • Improve counselling for victims of violence

Source: Adapted from Hemenway (2004, p. 13)

a regional, national, or international scale. Unfortunately, such reviews are rarely done, making it difficult to determine which interventions have been effective, which have not, and therefore which ones should be used more broadly. Most interventions continue to be developed based on fads or best guesses rather than scientific study (Waller and Sansfaçon, 2000, p. 6).

The public health approach brings a number of advantages to studying armed violence. The scientific epidemiological approach to assessing risk factors provides a rigorous method for better understanding the scope and magnitude of armed violence, as well as the primary risk factors that contribute to heightened vulnerability. This provides a baseline for understanding armed violence within a specified context, enabling both the designation of appropriate interventions and a means by which to assess those interventions. The population-based approach and the ecological model's inclusion of community- and social-level factors provide a means by which to better study and understand how social contexts, or environmental factors, affect the risk of armed violence, as well as its social impact.

ARMED VIOLENCE IN COMMUNITIES

Armed violence has been called an epidemic. The widespread impacts of such violence, both direct and indirect, are costly and far-reaching. The gravity of the situation has prompted greater efforts to identify the causes of armed violence and the factors that contribute to its prevalence, and greater attention to preventive efforts.

One of the contributions of the public health approach's ecological model is its emphasis on the multiple, and multi-level, influences on risk, resilience, and behaviour. This model recognizes that community- and societal-level factors play an important role in constituting the environments in which people live, and therefore influence the prospects for violence within these different contexts. Unfortunately, knowledge of these contextual factors and how they influence the risk of violence remains insufficient (RISK AND RESILIENCE).

Community characteristics both offer protective measures against violence and generate conditions conducive to violent behaviour. The nature of this influence on

A Jamaica Defense Force soldier carries out a search on a resident of West Kingston, where special police squads were on the lookout for gang activity and violent crime in December 2002. © Collin Reid/AP Photo

violence depends largely on the characteristics of a population and the nature of the relationships among community members: their strength, their inclusive or exclusive nature, and the purpose for which groups organize and mobilize.

Just as community characteristics can influence the potential for violence, armed violence can alter community dynamics in important ways. Armed violence can negatively affect communities. Such negative effects include the breakdown of social networks, community disintegration, loss of social capital,[6] the dissolution of family ties, population dislocation, the generation of new forms of social organization based on violence, and the resort to self-help policies of procuring firearms or vigilantism. These changes contribute to decreasing the ability of a community to respond collectively and effectively to violence. In some situations, armed violence can generate the opposite outcome: a positive, collective community response to addressing violence, thereby reducing the impact and costs of violence on the community. Understanding these dynamics is essential to designing interventions at the community level. The following sections discuss, first, the characteristics of communities in terms of risk and resilience; second, the impact of armed violence on communities and their responses to violence; and, third, what these dynamics mean for designing armed violence reduction measures.

Risk and resilience: the permissive and protective nature of communities

It is clear that certain characteristics of communities enable violence in some situations and contribute to the defence against violence in other contexts (RISK AND RESILIENCE). The question is which characteristics contribute to risk and resilience, respectively. It is important to identify these characteristics and examine their relationship to the potential for violence in order to determine the targets of violence reduction strategies.

It would be impossible to identify all community characteristics that influence individual or group risk of experiencing armed violence. A number of community characteristics have been identified as risk and resilience factors (see Table 7.5). Risk factors are generally seen as negative community characteristics and equated with low levels

Table 7.5 **Community risk and resilience factors**	
Risk factors	**Resilience factors**
• Social, political, and economic inequality • Discrimination • History of violence and/or crime • Existence of gangs • Ineffective social institutions • Poor rule of law • Lack of access to social services • Social isolation • Heterogeneity • Cultural norms enabling violence • High residential mobility • High unemployment • Lack of economic opportunities • High population density • Proximity to drug trade, weapons • Strong cultural or ethnic identity	• High levels of social, political, and economic equality • Strong rule of law • Effective policing • Strong ties between the community and the police • Existence of inclusive community groups • High levels of participation in community associations • Availability of social services • Strong ties among groups • High levels of interaction among groups • Cultural norms against violence • Economic opportunities • High levels of school attendance • Low levels of unemployment

Sources: Based on Buvinic, Morrison, and Shifter (1999); Rosenberg et al. (2006)

of community capacity to act collectively. For example, high levels of inequality, discrimination, unemployment, and access to small arms are widely believed to be associated with higher levels of risk for violence. In contrast, resilience factors are generally viewed as positive, protective factors that deter violence and heighten the potential for collective action. For example, the rule of law, school attendance, and access to social services are associated with resilience, and therefore a decreased likelihood of violence.

The factors listed in Table 7.5 suggest commonalities within high-risk and low-risk (e.g. high-resilience) communities. On the permissive side, these risk factors suggest a lack of overall community, divisions between individuals and groups leading to an inability or lack of desire to work together, economic desperation, the lack of any safety net or external source of security, and group ties based on narrow interests. On the protective side, these factors suggest a broader sense of cooperation among individuals and groups, a shared sense of community, and the availability of assistance for anyone in need, whether for security or economic reasons.

Although a number of factors fit into either the risk or resilience category, it is important to remember that a single factor cannot determine the likelihood of violence. No direct link can be drawn between any one risk factor and any given individual or group committing a crime or engaging in communal violence. Armed violence and the deterrence of such violence are both the result of a combination of risk and resilience factors in any given community.

Unfortunately, to date, there is no standard means of definitively calculating the probability of violence in a community based on any given combination of community characteristics. While, by definition, risk factors contribute to an environment more conducive to or permissive of violence, whereas resilience factors contribute to an environment that is less enabling of violence or provide a buffer against violence, where the balance tips to favour violence is unclear (RISK AND RESILIENCE). Those communities with more risk factors than protective (resilience) factors are more likely to experience violence, while the opposite should hold true for those communities with higher levels of protective factors. However, these assumptions are only generally indicative and cannot predict the likelihood of violence in any given community at a given time.

The impact of armed violence on communities

The previous discussion suggests that the characteristics of a community influence the risk of violence in that community. There is also the flip side: how armed violence affects a community, alters its characteristics, and changes its social dynamics. The impact of armed violence depends on the characteristics of the given community, the level of violence experienced, the nature of the violence, and the geographic spread of the violence. In short, there is no easy answer. The social characteristics of a community are a combination of risk and resilience factors. As such, no community can be easily defined as good or bad, safe or unsafe.

Instead of viewing the impact of armed violence as good or bad, a better approach is to ask how armed violence impacts a community, what effects it has on social organization, how it increases or decreases levels of risk and resilience, and whether the altered nature of the affected community is protective against or permissive of future violence.

Armed violence is likely to have a larger impact on a community the more intense the violence, the longer the violence lasts, and the wider it is felt across the community. Communities that possess high levels of resilience, strong intra- and inter-community relationships, and a good relationship with security officials will be better able to cope with the damaging effects of armed violence. They can also utilize their pre-existing relationships and networks to mobilize in order to address the problem and prevent future violence. Communities that lack these strong bonds, display low levels of interaction, and have poor ties to security forces are likely to experience an even greater

unity can
efined as
d, safe or
unsafe.

decrease in any resilience factors that do exist, further reducing the ability to respond to violent attacks or engage in violence prevention efforts and increasing the atomization of the community.

Armed violence can produce at least three identifiable effects in community organization and social support (see Figure 7.4). First, armed violence can have a broad detrimental effect on social organization and community collective action. Second, despite a widespread negative effect on community cohesion, violence can increase social organization and community mobilization among certain segments of the population. In these cases, this cohesive effect is narrowly felt and results in more violence. Third, violence can provoke a broad collective response to defend against future violence, thereby increasing social organization and mobilization, with the positive outcome of decreasing levels of violence. The following provides a more detailed discussion of these dynamics.

First, armed violence can result in sharp reductions in community organization and cohesion (see A in Figure 7.4). These effects are felt by the community at large and include increased levels of fear and insecurity among community members, a decline in trust in neighbours and the state apparatus, a reduction in interactions with neighbours and outsiders, a change in behaviour in terms of outdoor activities, departure from the neighbourhood, or a turn to self-help methods for protection from violence (see Box 7.4).[7] These changes in the community reduce the ability of the community to organize and respond to the violence, thereby increasing the prospects for future violence.

Figure 7.4 **The dynamics of armed violence**

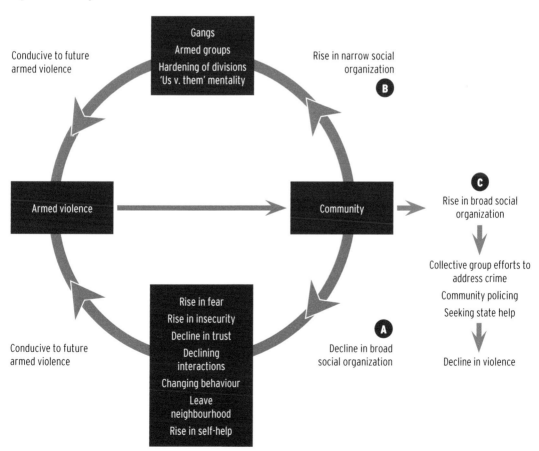

Box 7.4   Rising fear and violence in Afghanistan

Insecurity and violence reached record levels in Afghanistan in 2007 (see Table 7.6), with 2008 looking to be an equally violent year. On 17 February 2008 Kandahar experienced one of the most deadly suicide attacks since 2001, with a suicide bomb killing at least 80 people. This attack topped the November 2007 attack in Baghlan province that killed 79 people, most of whom were school children.

The negative trend of increased violence began in 2005 as the Taliban relaunched its insurgency. Bombings in 2006 were nearly double those in 2005. Suicide attacks increased six-fold between 2005 and 2006, with these attacks killing eight times as many civilians and combatants. The Taliban increased its use of suicide attacks as part of its offensive strategy. While many of these attacks targeted 'hard' targets, e.g. the police and the military, many civilians were caught in the violence. The number of conflict-related deaths doubled from 2005 to 2007.

This set the stage for 2007 to be a 'year of record violence'. The average number of violent incidents per month increased from 425 in 2006 to 550 in 2007. Although widespread across the country, violence is concentrated in the southern and eastern regions. Certain provinces, such as Kabul, Kandahar, Khost, Kunar and Nangarhar, experienced exceptionally high numbers of security incidents in 2007 (see Figure 7.5). These are areas where the Taliban presence is strong, borders are weak, and opium production continues unabated.

Violence against students and teachers remains a significant problem, especially in the south of the country, where there is a substantial Taliban presence. The Taliban increased its attacks on schools, educators, and students three-fold in 2007. The Taliban's strategy focuses on preventing students from attending non-religious schools and encouraging these students to join the Taliban. This strategy has produced higher levels of insecurity and led to the closure of numerous schools and a number of students staying home from school to avoid the violence. Although fearful, many youths are still seeking opportunities for education, but in many cases this requires them leaving their hometowns for school in larger cities where the Taliban has less power and the youths do not have to fear being recognized and having their families reported to the Taliban back home.

Violence has also moved from the provinces into the capital city, Kabul. Residents of Kabul are now experiencing the everyday insecurity that has engulfed most of the country, and it has led to changes in behaviour. Violence threatens to reverse progress made on improving education and literacy levels in the country. Parents are keeping their children home from school or threatening to do so if the violence continues. At least 237 school children have died from violence in Afghanistan in the past three years. Officials believe this number is actually much higher, but lack the capacity to investigate and monitor events. Shops are increasingly empty and streets that once bustled with life are deserted. Citizens attempt to continue a normal life, but much has changed, and even routine shopping has become a hazard under the threat of more suicide bombings. By November 2007 violence had killed an estimated 1,400 Afghan civilians. Fear of violence has risen despite the growing police presence on the streets. Some are blaming the government, while many are simply staying at home waiting for the situation to improve.

Sources: Afghanistan Conflict Monitor (2008); Amani (2007); BBC (2007; 2008); Chandrashekhar (2007); HRW (2007a; 2007b); IRIN (2007a); Shiner (2007); Straziuso (2008); Zwak (2007)

An Afghan boy stands near a drawing of a gun on the wall of his family's run-down home in the outskirts of Kabul, August 2006. © Saurabh Das/AP Photo

Table 7.6 **Selected violent incidents in Afghanistan by type, 2007**

Type of violent incident	Number of incidents
Armed criminality	429
Assassination	248
Complex attack	1,180
Hand grenade	52
Improvised explosive device (IED)	775
IED attempt	681
Kidnapping	165
Local dispute/clash	460
Military operation	555
Mine	142
Police operation	267
Rocket/mortar	489
Rocket-propelled grenade	140
Small arms fire	652
School attack	52

Figure 7.5 **Selected violent incidents in Afghanistan by province, 2007**

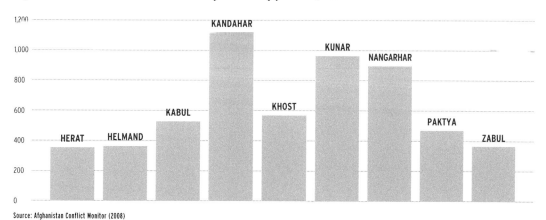

Source: Afghanistan Conflict Monitor (2008)

Second, armed violence can mobilize narrow sections of the community to organize (see B in Figure 7.4). This tends to produce a positive effect for those involved in the resulting organized group, but a negative effect for the community at large. This narrow increase in community organization tends to take the form of gangs, armed groups, or militias, which profit from and thrive on the existence of violence. These groups, often exclusionary and insular, can become more attractive to community members as violence increases and options for escape diminish. These groups can offer protection, possibilities for economic gain, and opportunities for attaining positions of power—things not easily gained in the community. As these groups grow in strength through recruitment, ethnic or religious rhetoric to mobilize the population, the procurement of small arms, and the expansion of territorial control, the prospects for future violence increase.

Third, armed violence can contribute to strengthening community organization, and cohesion comes through widespread community mobilization in the face of violence (see C in Figure 7.4). This outcome, which seems less

---

Box 7.5   Community efforts to reduce violence

In Stockton, California, a former gang member created Mothers Against Gang Warfare (MAGW) in 1991 to respond to the high levels of gang violence in the community. MAGW strives to coordinate the efforts of groups throughout the San Joaquin county to curb gang violence. One of the primary activities of MAWG is public education about gang life, gang violence, and alternatives to gang membership. MAGW works with other community organizations, such as the Boys and Girls Club, to provide children and youth with a safe environment to spend their free time, thereby keeping them off the streets and away from gang territory. MAGW works not only to prevent youth from joining gangs, but also to convince gang members to leave their gangs. The latter requires providing gang members with opportunities outside of gang life. MAGW seeks to provide youth and former gang members with job training and opportunities, peer-to-peer counselling, and recreational activities that create positive options for youths

Source: MAGW (2008)

Children and adults from nearly two dozen organizations take part in a march against violence in June 2001 in South Central Los Angeles. © Lee Celano/AP Photo

In Manchester, United Kingdom, a group of citizens came together in 2002 to take a stand against the rising gang violence in their neighbourhood. Under the motto 'it's time to take back our community', this group works to bring alternative opportunities to youths in the surrounding neighbourhoods to discourage them from joining gangs and engaging in a violent life. Carisma (Community Alliance for Renewal) provides an umbrella for this community movement by working on a variety of fronts to combat violence through public information campaigns, peace workshops, encouraging partnerships among community organizations, and lobbying politicians for changes in gun control laws and for improving violence reduction strategies. Carisma aims to ensure that youngsters and their families can access education, health care, and housing in order to provide youth with a positive outlook and future life opportunities away from gang life.

Source: Carisma (2007)

common in violent communities, is likely the result of a high level of pre-existing sense of community prior to the violent event, enabling the community to join together to devise strategies to counter violence in an inclusive manner. This sense of community cohesion provides a network for group mobilization, for reaching out to other groups and communities in similar situations and exchanging lessons learnt, and for working collaboratively with state security forces to bring their presence to bear on the problem of violence (see Box 7.5).

Developing community interventions

'The uniqueness of communities precludes a blanket prescription for all locales' (Mercy et al., 1993, p. 21). While true, such a statement does not require reinventing the wheel for each intervention. Instead, it points to the importance of context, and the need to adopt context-specific strategies. Interventions cannot follow a simple, standardized approach, but this does not preclude the creation of a core foundation for interventions, which can then be modified according to community characteristics. How a community is defined will determine the pattern and level of risk to community members. The risk pattern of a particular city will look different from the risk pattern of a neighbourhood within that city or the risk pattern of the country as a whole. Different maps of violence will suggest different strategies for violence reduction and prevention. For example, a neighbourhood in South Central Los Angeles, well known for its gangs, will exhibit a different pattern of risk factors from Los Angeles county as a whole, suggesting gang violence reduction strategies would be appropriate in the former, but might be less appropriate or make up only one element of a strategy for addressing violence concerns in the latter.

In addition to understanding the map of violence and the risk factors of a given community, the design of interventions also depends on the level of violence and the level of community action in response to this violence (see Figure 7.6). The level of violence and the level of community action suggest what types of interventions will have the most chance of success.

Community-based action may be more difficult to achieve in communities with high levels of violence but low levels of community action (see cell 4 in Figure 7.6). In these cases, targeted policing might be a first step towards

Figure 7.6 **Community action and armed violence**

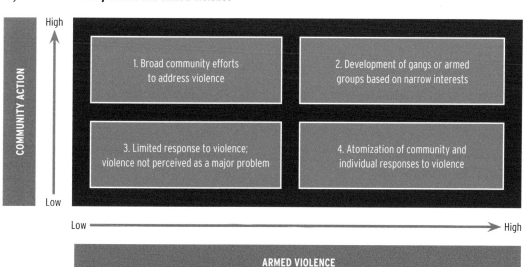

reining in the violence and providing a basis for community action. In areas with high levels of community action (see cell 1 in Figure 7.6), support to these community initiatives and coordination between these initiatives and police-based interventions should be considered. In communities with high levels of crime and gang violence (see cell 2 in Figure 7.6), efforts targeting these groups and aiming to reduce their capacity and incentives to commit crimes can produce positive results. Prevention remains a key element to reducing violence. An important part of any prevention strategy is convincing the community that there is a problem that deserves attention (Calonge, 2005, p. 4) (see cell 3 in Figure 7.6).

ASSESSING THE PUBLIC HEALTH APPROACH

Approaching armed violence reduction from an injury prevention perspective offers a new lens for understanding the factors that contribute to violence and for designing effective harm reduction and violence prevention interventions (INTERVENTIONS). The emphasis on prevention shifts the focus from punishing perpetrators to preventing the violent event from happening in the first place. By utilizing data on violent events and their circumstances, injury prevention introduces an evidence-based method for addressing the problem. Despite progress made on developing this approach and putting it into practice, it remains a relatively new approach to violence reduction.

Contributions to understanding armed violence

The public health approach contributes to the study of armed violence by broadening the view of violence from an individual, criminal experience to a social phenomenon. By expanding the lens used for understanding violence, public health presents an alternative to a sole focus on criminality and incarceration as a primarily reactive response to violence. Instead, the public health approach suggests a complementary approach to that of the criminal justice system; one that focuses on prevention over response, and the community over the individual. Importantly, the public health approach recognizes violence as a social phenomenon that can be prevented, and underlines the need for targeted preventive strategies.

As part of viewing violence as a social phenomenon, the public health approach

A former Crips gang member chats with his old high school teacher at Compton High School, one of several sites where he counsels students. California, November 2005. © Ric Francis/AP Photo

emphasizes the need to understand the context within which individuals live and make choices. This includes the recognition that multiple factors influence the decisions and behaviours of individuals. The public health approach uses the ecological model to identify these different levels of influence and the risk and resilience factors that might fit into each level. In particular, the public health approach emphasizes the importance of looking beyond the individual to an understanding of community- and societal-level factors.

The third contribution of the public health approach is its scientific methods for data collection and analysis. The approach emphasizes the need for systematic data collection to understand the nature, scope, and magnitude of armed violence. This data forms an integral part of understanding the problem of armed violence in a given population and designing violence prevention and reduction strategies to address it. Data collection also provides the best basis for assessing the effectiveness of interventions. While to date most programmes have not been rigorously reviewed, the public health approach continues to offer this possibility.

Finally, the public health approach emphasizes the need for collaboration across various government sectors, non-governmental organizations, and the citizens of affected communities. Understanding the multifaceted nature of violence underscores the need for multi-level, multivariate approaches to violence prevention (Krauss, 2006, p. 15). Public health could act as the backbone of a comprehensive approach by generating important data on violence, collating data from multiple sources, and presenting a more complete picture of violence in communities that can be used by a wide range of agencies, organizations, and communities to prevent and respond to violence.

Moving forward and looking ahead

Although the public health approach has made significant contributions, it is important to understand some of the difficulties in implementing this approach. One area requiring additional development is the data-to-policy nexus. Currently, public health practitioners have difficulty in translating their knowledge into convincing arguments for policy-makers to take action. Important in advancing the role of public health in designing interventions is the ability to determine which risk factors are most important to address in a given context. While the ecological model offers a useful heuristic device for thinking about the range of influences on violent behaviour and for identifying risk factors, moving the approach forward requires developing a better understanding of how and why these factors contribute to risk. Some argue that determining causality is not necessary and that it is sufficient to identify common risk factors for populations (Powell et al., 1999), but such an approach can lead to the identification of an unmanageable number of risk factors, thus overwhelming policy-makers, who then face the challenge of addressing multiple risk factors with limited funds. Designing targeted interventions requires an understanding of which factors are most significant in a given context.

While the public health approach highlights the importance of community-level factors to understanding the risks of violence in a given population, many studies and interventions continue to focus on the individual. Community factors are not often captured in epidemiological surveillance (Lomas, 1998, p. 1181; Leung, Yen, and Minkler, 2004). Even when they are, there are methodological problems of trying to understand how these community factors influence levels of violence (Harpham, Grant, and Thomas, 2002, p. 110; Hawe and Shiell, 2000, p. 878), and which level, e.g. individual or community, is most appropriate for understanding the dynamics of violence (Lochner, Kawachi, and Kennedy, 1999, p. 269). More thought

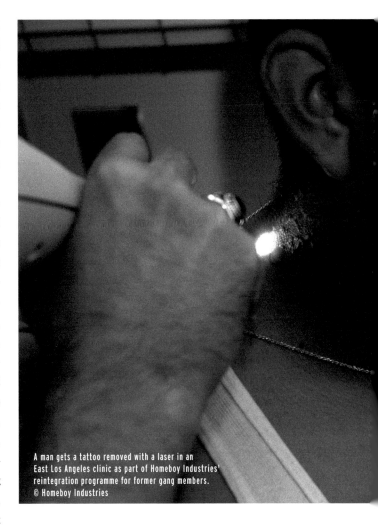

A man gets a tattoo removed with a laser in an East Los Angeles clinic as part of Homeboy Industries' reintegration programme for former gang members.
© Homeboy Industries

should be given to how to incorporate community-level factors into inquiries into violence trends, such as victimization surveys, epidemiological surveillance, and focus groups.

Although many public health interventions are community-based, and this is a specific intent of the public health approach to devise community-generated and community-supported interventions (Krauss, 2006, p. 8), the actual target of the interventions remains the individual. These interventions continue to address primarily individual-level risk factors, and very few address community- or societal-level risk factors. While there is a recognized need to move beyond a focus on high-risk groups to include interventions that also address the 'underlying social forces that give rise to a high incidence of violence in the population' (Kennedy et al., 1998, p. 15), few interventions have achieved this in practice. This is an area for future action.

Public health practitioners and those utilizing the public health approach should realize, acknowledge, and accept the political role they play. While public health practitioners are in a unique position to advocate for changes in policies, an increase in resources allocated to violence prevention, and improved means of protection and response (Rutherford et al., 2007b, p. 769), such advocacy is intensely political and in some societies divisive, especially when it leads to restrictions on individual freedoms, e.g. through the creation of laws restricting firearms possession.

Redesigning the ways communities function suggests social engineering, which remains an unpalatable idea in much of the world (Lomas, 1998, p. 1184), e.g. efforts to alter cultural practices, such as female genital mutilation, or long-held beliefs, such as domestic violence not being a crime. In some cases, public health interventions can provide 'scientific' cover for conservative and unacceptable social policies (Hawe and Shiell, 2000, p. 881). The individual-based approach is preferred, targeting the behaviours of individuals, rather than the community structures, such as social inequalities, discrimination, and poverty, that influence individual behaviour.

The public health approach should recognize more fully the role of individual choice, or agency, in both coping with violence and inflicting violent harm on others. Despite the existence of violence in a community, 'individual and community capacities exist' to cope with the effects of violence (Rutherford et al., 2007b, p. 767) and to design strategies to prevent further violence. The challenge is how to empower these capacities and how to enable individuals to choose to support violence prevention efforts, especially when confronted by violence on a daily basis. Acknowledging agency is also integral to understanding violent acts and the choice made in committing those acts. While critiques of the criminal justice approach to violence prevention argue against a focus on the perpetrator and assessing blame, moving too far away from agency removes an important part of the violence equation. Collaboration between the criminal justice approach and the public health approach could reinsert agency back into the equation and contribute to understanding why under similar circumstances individuals choose different means of responding to insecurity.

CONCLUSION

The public health approach provides a clear model for research, evaluation, and the design of interventions to address armed violence. This model offers a method for collecting data systematically and utilizing this data to design more effective interventions. The model is not limited to public health officials, but can also be utilized by medical officials, police officers, judiciary officials, and any researcher of armed violence. It is a basic model of the social and natural sciences: collect data, evaluate, and respond.

While clearly a useful model, it has not been widely adopted. There have been some promising steps forward in local and national public health systems endeavouring to collect data on armed violence, but such efforts remain limited. Some police forces are also collecting data on crime and using it for developing more effective and targeted policing strategies. But still more needs to be done.

One of the largest obstacles to promoting the public health approach is the inability of public health practitioners to demonstrate clearly the value added in implementing a time- and labour-intensive and expensive approach. Although evaluation is a key part of this approach, evaluations of programmes have not been conducted in a systematic or rigorous fashion. Instead, many programmes continue to be implemented without evidence to support them and without evaluation of their impact. This leaves little in the way of persuasive evidence to convince politicians that a heavy investment in public health surveillance is warranted.

The future of the public health approach lies in the ability of practitioners to demonstrate the collaborative and comprehensive nature claimed for it by its proponents. The approach asserts the need for multifaceted, multi-level, and collaborative interventions to prevent violence. Yet there is continuing evidence of an ongoing divide between the public health and criminal justice approaches in particular, as well as a number of individual approaches being taken by the various sectors involved in violence prevention. In practice, although there has been improvement in some areas, broad cooperation across sectors remains difficult, and sectors continue to fight over turf and who has the right approach. Effective armed violence reduction will require the broad collaboration of all sectors.

This cooperation should extend to involving affected communities. Violence is a community problem, not an individual or government problem. Community context matters for designing effective interventions, but community participation and support of interventions determines whether these interventions succeed. Ignoring community input; de-emphasizing community participation; and taking a top-down, law enforcement-heavy approach are likely to reduce the effectiveness of interventions, and ultimately fail to reduce armed violence. Collaborative partnerships should exist horizontally across all sectors of government, as well as vertically between government actors and community members. ◾

LIST OF ABBREVIATIONS

Carisma	Community Alliance for Renewal	MAGW	Mothers Against Gang Warfare
IED	Improvised explosive device	WHO	World Health Organization

ENDNOTES

1   For a list of definitions of these different types of violence, see Rutherford et al. (2007a).

2   There is no agreed upon estimate for the global burden of armed violence. This range comes from discussions in two publications: Richmond, Cheney, and Schwab (2005, pp. 348–52) and Small Arms Survey (2004, ch. 6, pp. 174–75).

3   For example, International Physicians for the Prevention of Nuclear War launched its Aiming for Prevention programme in 2001. One aspect of this programme is to improve national capacity for public health research, and includes efforts to create hospital surveillance mechanisms in a

number of African, Latin American, and South Asian countries. For more details, see <http://www.ippnw.org/Programs/AFP/index.html>. The UN Office on Drugs and Crime launched a Data for Africa programme in 2005 aimed at improving data collection on drug and crime problems in African countries. See <http://www.unodc.org/unodc/en/data-and-analysis/Data-for-Africa.html>.

4   The Small Arms Survey is undertaking a global mapping of armed violence as part of the 'measurability' objectives of the Geneva Declaration on Armed Violence and Development. Preliminary findings should be available by mid-2008. For additional information, see <http://www.geneva declaration.org>.

5   See Rosenberg et al. (2006) and Hill et al. (2007) for a discussion of some of these methods.

6   'Social capital' remains poorly defined, highly contested, and therefore difficult to use in studying armed violence. For a discussion of social capital, see Adler and Kwon (2002); Harpham, Grant, and Thomas (2002); Lederman, Loayza, and Menendez (2002); and Portes (1998).

7   For a more detailed discussion of the social impacts of small arms availability, proliferation, and use, see Lederman, Loayza, and Menendez (2002); Louise (1995); and Rosenfeld, Messner, and Baumer (2001).

BIBLIOGRAPHY

Adler, Paul and Seok-Woo Kwon. 2002. 'Social Capital: Prospects for a New Concept.' *Academy of Management Review*, Vol. 27, No. 1, pp. 17–40.

Afghanistan Conflict Monitor. 2008. Web site. Accessed 18 February 2008. <http://www.afghanconflictmonitor.org/>

Amani, Wahidullah. 2007. *Kabul: The City of Fear*. Institute for War and Peace Reporting, Afghan Recovery Report No. 267. 5 October. <http://iwpr.net/?p=arr&s=f&o=339635&apc_state=heniarr200710>

Astor, Ron and Rami Benbenishty. 2006. *Zero Tolerance for Zero Knowledge: Empowering Schools and Communities with Data and Democracy*. Urban Initiative Public Policy Brief. University of Southern California.

Astor, Ron, Rami Benbenishty, and Heather Meyer. 2004. 'Monitoring and Mapping Student Victimization in Schools.' *Theory into Practice*, Vol. 43, No. 1. Winter, pp. 39–49.

BBC (British Broadcasting Corporation). 2007. 'Children Killed in Afghan Bombing.' 24 November. <http://news.bbc.co.uk/2/hi/south_asia/7110593.stm>
——. 2008. 'Scores Killed in Afghan Bombing.' 17 February. <http://news.bbc.co.uk/2/hi/south_asia/7249138.stm>

Buvinic, Mayra, Andrew Morrison, and Michael Shifter. 1999. *Violence in Latin America and the Caribbean: A Framework for Action*. Unpublished technical study. Sustainable Development Department, Inter-American Development Bank. March. <http://www.iadb.org/publications/search.cfm?language=English&COUNTRIES=&KEYWORDS=inequality&RESCATEGORY=&TOPICS=SC>

Calonge, Ned. 2005. 'Community Interventions to Prevent Violence: Translation into Public Health Practice.' *American Journal of Preventive Medicine*, Vol. 28, pp. 4–5.

Carisma. 2007. Web site. Accessed 9 October 2007. <http://www.carisma.me.uk/>

CDC (Centers for Disease Control and Prevention). 2008. *Violence Prevention at CDC*. Accessed 6 March 2008. <http://www.cdc.gov/ncipc/dvp/prevention_at_CDC.htm>

Chandrashekhar, Vaishnavi. 2007. 'Afghan Suicide Bombing Targets Local Police.' *Christian Science Monitor* (Boston). 4 October.

Dahlberg, Linda. 1998. 'Youth Violence in the United States: Major Trends, Risk Factors, and Prevention Approaches.' *American Journal of Preventive Medicine*, Vol. 14, pp. 259–72.

Goodhand, Jonathan, David Hulme, and Nick Lewer. 2000. 'Social Capital and the Political Economy of Violence: A Case Study of Sri Lanka.' *Disasters*, Vol. 24, No. 4, pp. 390–406.

Harpham, Trudy, Emma Grant, and Elizabeth Thomas. 2002. 'Measuring Social Capital within Health Surveys: Key Issues.' *Health Policy and Planning*, Vol. 17, No. 1, pp. 106–11.

Hawe, Penelope and Alan Shiell. 2000. 'Social Capital and Health Promotion: A Review.' *Social Sciences and Medicine*, Vol. 51, pp. 871–85.

Hemenway, David. 2001. 'The Public Health Approach to Motor Vehicles, Tobacco, and Alcohol, with Applications to Firearms Policy.' *Journal of Public Health Policy*, Vol. 22, No. 4, pp. 381–402.
——. 2004. *Private Guns, Public Health*. Ann Arbor: University of Michigan Press.

Hill, Kenneth, et al. 2007. 'Interim Measures for Meeting Needs for Health Sector Data: Births, Deaths, and Causes of Death.' Who Counts? Series, No. 3. *Lancet*, Vol. 370. 17 November, pp. 1726–35.

HRW (Human Rights Watch). 2007a. 'Afghanistan: Civilians Bear Cost of Escalating Insurgent Attacks.' Press Release. 16 April.
——. 2007b. *The Human Cost: The Consequences of Insurgent Attacks in Afghanistan*. HRW Report, Vol. 19, No. 6C. April. <http://www.hrw.org/english/docs/2007/04/16/afghan15688.htm>

Human Security Centre. 2006. *Human Security Brief 2006*. Vancouver: University of British Columbia.

IADB (Inter-American Development Bank). 1999a. *How is Violence Measured?* Violence Prevention Technical Note 2. July.

——. 1999b. *Preventing Violence*. Violence Prevention Technical Note 5. July.

——. 1999c. *Controlling Violence*. Violence Prevention Technical Note 6. July.

——. 1999d. *Violence Control at the Municipal Level*. Violence Prevention Technical Note 8. July.

IRIN (Integrated Regional Information Networks). 2007a. 'Afghanistan: Children Increasingly Affected by Conflict.' 27 November.
    <http://www.irinnews.org/Report.aspx?ReportId=75530>

——. 2007b. 'Niger: Rape and Beatings of Women Seen as "Normal".' 6 December. <http://www.irinnews.org/Report.aspx?ReportId=75720>

Kennedy, Bruce, et al. 1998. 'Social Capital, Income Inequality, and Firearm Violent Crime.' *Social Science and Medicine*, Vol. 47, No. 1. July, pp. 7–17.

Krauss, Herbert. 2006. 'Perspectives on Violence.' *Annals of the New York Academy of Science*, Vol. 1087, pp. 4–21.

Krug, E. G., et al., eds. 2002. *World Report on Violence and Health*. Geneva: World Health Organization.

Lederman, Daniel, Norman Loayza, and Ana Menendez. 2002. 'Violent Crime: Does Social Capital Matter?' *Economic Development and Cultural Change*,
    Vol. 50, No. 3. April, pp. 509–39.

Leung, Margaret, Irene Yen, and Meredith Minkler. 2004. 'Community-based Participatory Research: A Promising Approach for Increasing Epidemiology's
    Relevance in the 21st Century.' *International Journal of Epidemiology*, Vol. 33, pp. 499–506.

Lochner, Kimberly, Ichiro Kawachi, and Bruce Kennedy. 1999. 'Social Capital: A Guide to Its Measurement.' *Health and Place*, Vol. 5, pp. 259–70.

Lomas, Jonathan. 1998. 'Social Capital and Health: Implications for Public Health and Epidemiology.' *Social Sciences and Medicine*, Vol. 47, No. 9, pp. 1181–88.

Louise, Christopher. 1995. *The Social Impacts of Light Weapons Availability and Proliferation*. UN Research Institute for Social Development Discussion
    Paper DP59. March. <http://www.unrisd.org/unrisd/website/document.nsf/d2a23ad2d50cb2a280256eb300385855/50aa0457c9ef4d2c80256b670
    05b6718/$FILE/dp59.pdf>

MAGW (Mothers Against Gang Wars). 2008. Web site. Accessed 18 February 2008. <http://home.inreach.com/gangbang/magw.htm>

Mathers, Colin, et al. 2005. 'Counting the Dead and What They Died From: An Assessment of the Global Status of Cause of Death Data.' *Bulletin of
    the World Health Organization*, Vol. 3, No. 83, pp. 171–77.

Mercy, James, et al. 1993. 'Public Health Policy for Preventing Violence.' *Health Affairs*, Vol. 12, No. 4. Winter, pp. 7–29.

Moore, Mark. 1993. 'Violence Prevention: Criminal Justice or Public Health?' *Health Affairs*, Vol. 12, No. 4, pp. 34–45.
    <http://content.healthaffairs.org/cgi/reprint/12/4/34.pdf>

OECD–DAC (Organisation for Economic Co-operation and Development–Development Assistance Committee). 2009 (forthcoming). *Guidance
    on Armed Violence Reduction and Development*. Paris: OECD–DAC.

Portes, Alejandro. 1998. 'Social Capital: Its Origins and Applications in Modern Sociology.' *Annual Review of Sociology*, Vol. 24, pp. 1–24.

Powell, K. E., et al. 1999. 'Public Health Models of Violence Prevention.' In Lester Kurtz and Jennifer Turpin, eds. *Encyclopedia of Violence, Peace and
    Conflict, Vol. 3*. San Diego: Academic Press, pp. 175–87.

Prothrow-Stith, Deborah. 2004. 'Strengthening the Collaboration between Public Health and Criminal Justice to Prevent Violence.' *Journal of Law,
    Medicine and Ethics*, Vol. 32, pp. 82–88.

Richmond, T. S., R. Cheney, and C. W. Schwab. 2005. 'The Global Burden of Non-conflict Related Firearm Mortality.' *Injury Prevention*, Vol. 11,
    pp. 348–52.

Rosenberg, Mark, et al. 2006. 'Interpersonal Violence.' In Dean Jamison et al., eds. *Disease Control Priorities in Developing Countries*, 2nd ed. New York:
    Oxford University Press, ch. 40. April.

Rosenfeld, Richard, Steven Messner, and Eric Baumer. 2001. 'Social Capital and Homicide.' *Social Forces*, Vol. 80, No. 1, pp. 283–309.

Rutherford, Alison, et al. 2007a. 'Violence: A Glossary.' *Journal of Epidemiology and Community Health*, Vol. 61, pp. 676–80.

——. 2007b. 'Violence: A Priority for Public Health? Part 2.' *Journal of Epidemiology and Community Health*, Vol. 61, pp. 764–70.

Setel, Philip, et al. 2007. 'A Scandal of Invisibility: Making Everyone Count by Counting Everyone.' Who Counts? Series, No. 1. *The Lancet*, Vol. 370.
    3 November, pp. 1569–77. <http://www.alphagalileo.org/nontextfiles/WhoCounts1.pdf>

Sethi, Dinesh, et al. 2006. *Injuries and Violence in Europe: Why They Matter and What can Be Done*. Geneva: World Health Organization.

Shiner, Cindy. 2007. 'New Study Spotlights Sexual Violence.' AllAfrica.com NEWS. 5 December.

Small Arms Survey. 2002. *Small Arms Survey 2002: Counting the Human Cost*. Oxford: Oxford University Press.

——. 2003. *Small Arms Survey 2003: Development Denied*. Oxford: Oxford University Press.

——. 2004. *Small Arms Survey 2004: Rights at Risk*. Oxford: Oxford University Press.

——. 2005. *Small Arms Survey 2005: Weapons at War*. Oxford: Oxford University Press.

——. 2006. *Small Arms Survey 2006: Unfinished Business*. Oxford: Oxford University Press.

——. 2007. *Small Arms Survey 2007: Guns and the City*. Cambridge: Cambridge University Press.

Soares, Rodrigo. 2004. 'Crime Reporting as a Measure of Institutional Development.' *Economic Development and Cultural Change,* Vol. 52, No. 4. July, pp. 851–71.

Straziuso, Jason. 2008. 'Attacks on Afghan Students up Sharply.' Associated Press. 23 January.

Waller, Irvin and Daniel Sansfaçon. 2000. *Investing Wisely in Crime Prevention: International Experiences.* Washington, DC: US Department of Justice, Bureau of Justice Assistance. September.

Wilkinson, Deanna and Kerryn Bell. 2006. *Urban Gun Homicide and Youth Violence: Perspectives from Trends in the United States and Violent NYC Youth.* Unpublished background paper. Geneva: Small Arms Survey.

WHO (World Health Organization). 1996. *Prevention of Violence: A Public Health Priority.* WHA49.25. Resolution of the World Health Assembly, 49th session, 25 May. <http://www.who.int/violence_injury_prevention/resources/publications/en/WHA4925_eng.pdf>

——. 2001. *Small Arms and Global Health.* Geneva: WHO.

Zwak, Samar. 2007. 'Suicide Bomber Kills 9 Afghans and Italian Soldier.' Reuters. 24 November.

ACKNOWLEDGEMENTS

Principal author

Jennifer M. Hazen

This video still shows two armed Columbine High School students in the cafeteria during their shooting rampage in April 1999 in Littleton, Colorado.
© Jefferson County Sheriff's Department/AP Photo

Risk and Resilience

UNDERSTANDING THE POTENTIAL FOR VIOLENCE

8

INTRODUCTION

Prevention is at the core of the public health approach to reducing violence. Prevention depends on understanding why violence occurs, who commits violent acts, and who is at risk of victimization. Identifying these parameters requires both a general knowledge of violence and a specific knowledge of the context in which violence occurs. These factors paint a picture of perpetrators, victims, means, and types of violence in a community, which in turn enables communities to design interventions to target those committing violence and to protect those most vulnerable.

At the centre of this targeting approach is the identification of risk and resilience factors. These are factors—whether at the individual, family, community, or societal level—that contribute to increasing the likelihood that an individual will commit a violent act or become a victim of a violent attack, or that aid individuals in adverse circumstances to overcome adversity and avoid violence.

The study of risk and resilience since the 1980s has led to a better understanding of these concepts and of how risk and resilience factors can influence individual behaviour, but experts remain far from creating perfect checklists for identifying future perpetrators. The key challenge to utilizing this approach to prevention is that while identifying risk and resilience factors can assist in defining high-risk groups, it cannot single out which individuals specifically will actually commit acts of violence in the future. This does not reduce the effectiveness of the approach, but it does constrain how it can be used, and poses important questions about how best to use known risk and resilience factors to develop effective violence reduction programmes.

This chapter considers the following questions:

- How are risk and resilience defined?
- What is known about risk and resilience?
- How do risk and resilience factors affect the probability of individuals becoming perpetrators or victims?
- Which risk and resilience factors are important to reducing violence?
- How are risk and resilience factors identified in practice?
- How can an understanding of risk and resilience contribute to the development of effective violence reduction programming?

The chapter is divided into four sections. The first section provides definitions of key terms used in the public health approach, including violence, risk, and resilience. This is followed by a discussion of how risk and resilience factors can be identified in practice. The second section provides an overview of important findings about risk and resilience. It highlights important identified risk factors and points to the key risk factors identified for different types of violence. The third section explains how risk and resilience factors can be used to develop violence reduction programmes and provides an overview of various types of intervention. The fourth section looks at the prospects for moving forward with public health research to improve knowledge about risk and resilience and to use this knowledge to design more effective interventions in the future.

The main conclusions of this chapter include:

- The more risk factors that exist, and the more domains they involve, the higher is the risk of an individual engaging in violence or becoming a victim of violence. Despite this reality, many individuals in high-risk groups will never commit violent acts, and it remains impossible to predict whether or when a particular individual will commit an act of violence.

- Important risk factors for violence change over the course of an individual's lifetime. Individual and family factors are important in early childhood, while peers, school, and family factors are important during adolescence. In early adulthood social skills, relationships, and employment become important factors. Throughout, substance abuse is an important risk factor for violence.

- The availability of firearms, the lack of regulation of firearm possession and use, the carrying of firearms in public places, the presence of guns in the home, and improper storage of these firearms are all important factors increasing the risk of gun violence.

- Resilience factors play an important role in mediating the negative impacts of risk factors and enabling an individual to avoid or overcome violence. Resilience factors are most effective when there is a high number of resilience factors and low risk, but can be overwhelmed in situations of high risk.

- Diverse settings represent different combinations of risk factors. A general understanding of violence aids in identifying important risk and resilience factors across contexts, while community-specific knowledge indicates the presence of specific factors and provides guidelines for targeting interventions.

e factors
mportant
ating the
mpacts of
k factors.

UNDERSTANDING RISK AND RESILIENCE

Understanding violence requires understanding the terms used in defining, studying, measuring, and predicting violence. This section first provides a brief overview of key concepts—violence, risk, and resilience—which forms the basis for the ensuing discussion of how to identify risk and resilience factors in practice.

Defining risk and resilience

The World Health Organization defines violence as 'the intentional use of physical force or power, threatened or actual, against oneself, another person, or against a group or community, that either results in or has a high likelihood of resulting in injury, death, psychological harm, maldevelopment or deprivation' (Krug et al., 2002, p. 5). Many of the known risk and resilience factors stem from investigations into delinquency and violence, generally speaking. These are discussed in this chapter. In addition, this chapter also strives to address the risk and resilience factors associated with *armed* violence, when possible. Armed violence is defined here as the use of an instrument or tool to commit an act of violence. This instrument can be a knife, a stick, a broken bottle, a firearm, or any item used to intentionally inflict harm on another individual or oneself (PUBLIC HEALTH APPROACH). This definition incorporates a number of types of armed violence including interpersonal violence, communal clashes, and gang warfare.

For the purposes of this chapter, a risk factor is defined as *any factor that contributes to the increased likelihood of a person engaging in a violent act or becoming a victim of violence.* Risk factors can contribute to violence in three ways. First, a risk factor can contribute to the likelihood of an individual engaging in a violent act. Here the focus is on the risk of someone becoming a perpetrator. Examples of risk factors for perpetration include substance abuse, previous aggressive or violent behaviour, and prior experience of abuse. Second, a risk factor can contribute to an individual's vulnerability to attack. Here the focus is on the risk of an individual becoming a victim. Examples of risk factors for victimization include living in a gang-beset neighbourhood, working in a dangerous job (e.g. as a security guard), or associating with delinquent peers. Third, a risk factor can contribute to the degree of harm inflicted by a violent act. For example, the use of a gun instead of a knife during the perpetration of a violent crime increases the likelihood of numerous and serious injuries.

In identifying risk factors attention has often focused on offenders rather than victims. While this chapter focuses mainly on offenders, the importance of studying victimization to identifying those factors that place an individual at higher risk of becoming a victim should also be noted. For example, a study of child victimization in Turkey suggests that violent physical victimization is common and that victims share common characteristics (Deveci, Acik, and Ayar, 2007). Male children are more likely to suffer violent victimization than female children. Violent victimization is higher for older than for younger children. Violence is higher in families with lower household incomes, with lower levels of education, and where the father is unemployed. Alcohol, unlike in many other places (PUBLIC HEALTH APPROACH), is not a risk factor in Turkey. This is likely the result of the influence of Turkish culture and the Islamic religion and related views on alcohol consumption (Deveci, Acik, and Ayar, 2007, p. 30). Turkish culture also plays a strong role in the high rate of violent victimization of children, including the belief that 'physical punishment of children' is 'culturally and legally' acceptable and only 'excessive punishment' is prohibited (Deveci, Acik, and Ayar, 2007, p. 30). These identified risk factors for both violence perpetration (by the father) and violent victimization (by male children) could be used to design violence reduction initiatives directed at fathers and protective programmes directed at children.

Defining resilience is more complex. For the purposes of this chapter, a resilience factor is defined as *any factor that enables an individual to manage adversity and respond to risk in a positive fashion.* The lack of a common definition and usage of the term 'resilience' has caused confusion (Stouthamer-Loeber et al., 2002, p. 112). Part of the challenge of defining resilience is that it is often used alongside or interchangeably with the terms 'protective', 'moderating', 'buffer', and 'promotive'. Resilience, especially in early studies, was presumed to be simply the opposite of risk. For example, living in a disadvantaged neighbourhood increases one's risk of violence, whereas living in a decent neighbourhood reduces one's risk. However, risk and resilience may not be absolute categories into

Turkish children, some of them holding toy guns, play in Sirnak, near the Iraqi border, in February 2008. © Burhan Ozbilici/AP Photo

which different factors can be neatly separated. Instead, it may be that risk factors have diverse effects on individuals, or that individuals respond to similar situations in different ways. For example, men and women tend to respond differently to risk even when faced with similar circumstances (Dahlberg and Potter, 2001, p. 10).

Important to understanding resilience is the interaction between risk and resilience factors. Resilience requires adversity to present itself (Luthar, Cicchetti, and Becker, 2000a, p. 543), and in the absence of adversity resilience is unlikely to be demonstrated, even though resilience factors might exist. Resilience factors enable an individual to positively adapt in the face of significant adversity (Luthar, Cicchetti, and Becker, 2000a, p. 546), where adversity is represented here as high risk of violence. Resilience factors can also be viewed as contributing to a positive outcome rather than simply negating risk. In this case, resilience is more than just evading violence, but also involves 'doing well' in adverse conditions and maintaining a positive developmental trajectory (Luthar, Cicchetti, and Becker, 2000b, p. 574). This suggests that resilience factors play a major role in explaining why certain individuals who are at high risk of violence never engage in a violent act but instead stay in school, find jobs, and lead productive lives.

An assessment of risk and resilience factors aids in understanding why violence occurs in some circumstances and not in others. However, risk and resilience factors do not cause violence. Instead they influence the beliefs and behaviour of individuals and the decision to commit an act of violence. This distinction is important. It remains necessary to acknowledge the agency involved in committing acts of violence. For example, two male teenagers living in a gang-controlled neighbourhood in single-parent homes still decide which path to take, resulting in one young man joining a gang and the other young man continuing in school, going to college, and moving out of the neighbourhood. While an improved understanding of resilience is expected to provide insight into the success cases that 'shouldn't have been', there are still no clear explanations as to why individuals facing the same circumstances choose different paths.

Box 8.1 Guiding theories

A number of theories guide the understanding of armed violence. These theories 'provide appropriate starting points for examining' why an individual engages in violence (Saner and Ellickson, 1996, p. 95).

Social bonding theory posits that young people are particularly influenced by the relationships they have with their families and their peers during adolescence (Dahlberg and Potter, 2001, p. 8). Based on this theory, an assessment of risk and resilience begins with identifying characteristics of family life, school life, and relationships with peers. These characteristics help to identify risk and resilience factors that can be used to generate profiles of high-risk groups, and the individuals that fit these profiles.

Social learning theory recognizes the role of peers, mentors, and adults in the formation of youth attitudes, beliefs, and behaviours (Moore, 2001, p. 2910). Youths look to those around them for role models and learn behaviour by adopting their practices (Bearinger et al., 2005, p. 275). Who these role models are, how they behave, and their attitudes towards violence in turn help to influence how youths develop. Accordingly, youths who have positive family role models, associate with non-violent and non-delinquent peers, and are presented with strong anti-violence norms are at far less risk of engaging in violence than youths whose main role models are violent.

Problem behaviour theory highlights the role of past deviant behaviour and attitudes supportive of violence in contributing to future violence (Saner and Ellickson, 1996, p. 95). This theory focuses mainly on the characteristics and past actions of the individual as predictors of violence. For example, youths with histories of serious violence are more likely to display violence later in life (Brook, Brook, and Whiteman, 2007; Loeber and Stouthamer-Loeber, 1998). Youths who possess the attitude that violence is a normal and accepted means of resolving conflicts are also more likely to display violent tendencies or to resort to violence when confronted with adversity. In contrast, youths who have no history of violence and who abhor violence as a tool of conflict resolution are less likely to engage in violent means to resolve conflicts or respond to adversity.

Identifying risk and resilience factors

Various approaches exist for identifying risk and resilience factors. They include theories of violence (see Box 8.1) and empirical studies of violent incidents (see Box 8.2). This section discusses two approaches in particular and in detail: the ecological model and the pathways model. The former emphasizes the identification of risk factors across various domains at a given time, while the latter focuses on how the risk factors individuals face change as they pass through different stages of development. Both of these models emphasize the need to understand the multiple influences on individual behaviour.

Box 8.2 Empirical studies

Theories and general knowledge about violence provide the basis for deductively identifying risk factors. Inductive methods can also identify risk factors through empirical studies. Examples include interviews, focus group discussions, survey questionnaires, analysis of media reports, correlation analysis, time-series studies, and case-control studies. The purpose of inductive studies is to collect data that can be used to generate broader generalizations about risk factors.

Survey questionnaires pose a series of questions on a range of issues, from 'social, contextual, and demographic information' to 'values, cultural identity, relationship, decision-making skills' (Bearinger et al., 2005, p. 271), attitudes about violence and the use of violence to resolve problems, and measuring how often an individual engages in a range of problematic behaviours (e.g. substance abuse) and violent acts. These questionnaires can elicit 'the most salient risk and protective factors for violence perpetration' in a given community or group of individuals (Bearinger et al., 2005, p. 270). For example, one study of violence among urban Native American youth was able to identify salient risk (e.g. substance abuse and suicidal thoughts and behaviour) and resilience (e.g. strong positive family role models, positive peer groups, positive affect, and connectedness to school) factors (Bearinger et al., 2005, p. 275). With the presence of three protective factors (positive peer groups, positive affect, and connectedness to school), the risk of violence was ten per cent (Bearinger et al., 2005, p. 273). When the two risk factors (substance abuse and suicidal thoughts and behaviour) were added, but the three protective factors maintained, the risk of violence increased to 36 per cent (p. 273). When the number of protective factors decreased to two while the two risk factors remained constant, the risk of violence ranged from 51 to 62 per cent (p. 273).

Longitudinal studies measure changes over time. These studies involve the selection of a group for study and follow the development of these individuals through interviews or questionnaires conducted at regular intervals. Conducting this type of study allows for a number of useful measures: how levels of violence increase, decrease, or persist over time; how risk and resilience factors associated with different developmental stages play roles in violent outcomes; and commonalities among persistent, intermittent, and non-offenders. A two-year study of adolescents in the cities of Bogotá, Medellín, and Barranquilla in Colombia provides insight into a number of risk factors in various domains that contribute to high levels of delinquency and violence (Brook, Brook, and Whiteman, 2007, p. 83). A key presumption in this study is that early develop-

mental experiences influence future rates of violence, and that individuals who behave violently during childhood tend to continue to act violently during adolescence and adulthood (p. 84). The study concluded that previous violence indeed predicted future violence, while also noting a number of factors that influenced the likelihood of violence over time, including the use of illicit drugs by parents, the use of illicit drugs by the individual, peer delinquency and drug use, and acts of violence in the home. These factors contributed to continued violence over time due to presumed learning and modelling of behaviour on peers and family as the adolescent ages (pp. 89–92).

After years of substance abuse and jail time for battery, this man—seen with his daughters at a Sioux reservation in South Dakota—is now a counsellor in a domestic violence programme. May 2006. © Katja Heinemann/Aurora/Getty Images

The ecological model

The ecological model is a useful heuristic device for considering the various factors that can influence risk and resilience patterns and the various domains, or levels, at which these factors operate (PUBLIC HEALTH APPROACH). This model can be thought of as a set of concentric circles around the individual (see Figure 8.1). Each circle is a level, or domain, at which various factors influence the individual. In this model, the individual is situated within a set of environments including the family, school, the community, and society. Each of these domains plays an important role in shaping the context in which the individual lives and how the individual thinks and acts.

As an example of the ecological model, take the situation of a male teenager living in a poor neighbourhood where there are gangs, many single-parent homes, little police presence, high exposure to violence, little supervision of teenagers during their free time, limited neighbourhood cohesion, crowded schools where achievement is not rewarded or positively promoted, bullying with impunity in schools, few options to leave the neighbourhood, and violence is seen as an acceptable form of resolving conflicts. Each of these factors can be placed in its respective domain (see Figure 8.1). By dissecting the different domains of risk, and the various factors that influence youth development and behaviour, a more complete picture emerges of the risk of the individual engaging in a violent act.

The strength of the ecological model is that it recognizes the complexity of violence, the embedded nature of individuals in complex social networks, and the role of a wide range of factors at various levels—from the individual

Figure 8.1 **Ecological model**

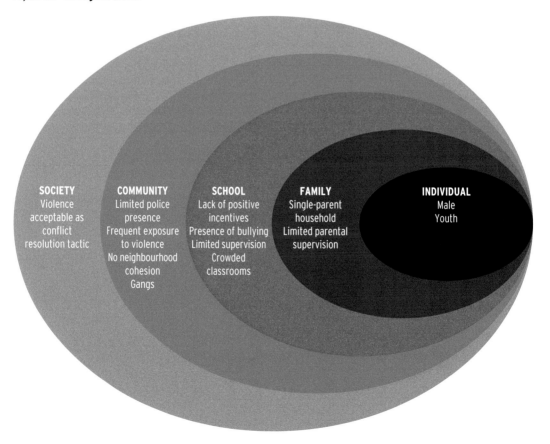

to the societal—that influence individual risk, resilience, and behaviour (Rosenberg et al., 2006, p. 761). The eco-logical framework for studying risk factors within various domains has been used in a number of studies,[1] all of which attempt to answer the question of what influences an individual's decision to engage in violence.

Pathways model

An important evolution of the work on risk factors for violence is the contention that risk factors do not remain constant over a person's lifetime. Certain risk factors are more dominant at the different stages in a person's develop-ment: infancy and childhood, adolescence, and early, middle, and late adulthood (Dahlberg and Potter, 2001, p. 7). At each stage, an individual faces a variety of biological (physical and mental) and social changes and challenges. Different relationships at each stage—familial during childhood, peer-related during adolescence, and marital during adulthood—pose unique challenges to the individual. In addition, as one ages it is common to experience a number of changes in one's environment, neighbourhood, and employment opportunities. Different patterns of risk suggest the need for targeted violence reduction strategies that take into account these life stages.

There are three common patterns of offending: persistent offending that increases in gravity over time, intermit-tent or limited offending that is non-continuous and often desists over time, and late-onset violence that occurs in adulthood without a prior history of violence (Dahlberg and Potter, 2001, p. 6; Loeber and Stouthamer-Loeber, 1998, pp. 245–46). This suggests different risk factors contribute to the onset of violence and to the desistance from vio-lence, and therefore violence cannot necessarily be viewed as something that begins during childhood and continues through adulthood. However, those who begin on a delinquent-violent trajectory early in life account for the largest proportion of violent adults (Loeber and Stouthamer-Loeber, 1998, p. 245).

> Risk factors remain constant over a person's lifetime.

While long-term offenders represent only a small percentage of the offending population, they commit the major-ity of violent offences (Brook, Brook, and Whiteman, 2007, p. 82; Dahlberg and Potter, 2001, p. 6; Moore, 2001, p. 2911). This offers good reason to focus on the most serious and most frequent offenders (Stouthamer-Loeber et al., 2002, p. 111), but it also suggests the need to focus on early offenders in order to prevent them from becoming chronic offenders.

Lifetime chronic offenders pass through a series of stages of increased delinquency over time, eventually leading to violence (Moore, 2001, p. 2911; Verlinden, Hersen, and Thomas, 2000, p. 18). This passage through stages of problem behaviour has been described as a 'developmental pathway'. There are three common developmental pathways to violence: overt, early authority conflict, and covert (Loeber and Stouthamer-Loeber, 1998, pp. 247–48). The overt pathway involves the progression of delinquency from minor aggression to physical fighting and then to extreme violence. The early authority conflict pathway consists of less extreme behaviour involving mainly defiance of authority. The covert pathway entails a sequence of escalating behaviours from petty theft to vandalism and then to serious theft.

Individuals can follow different pathways, each of which leads to a distinct outcome in terms of the nature and severity of the delinquency and violence involved (see Figure 8.2). These three pathways are not necessarily inde-pendent of one another. Individuals can follow more than one pathway at the same time, or shift from one pathway to another. Individuals can also stop at any step along the pathway, and do not necessarily proceed to the pinnacle of extreme violence and crime. In fact, relatively few individuals make it to the top of the scale of delinquency and violence.

Box 8.3 Risk factors along the life course

Following an individual's life course is instructive for understanding how risk factors evolve with age. In infancy and early childhood, individual biological factors and family factors play the strongest role in influencing the development of the child, including the child's risk of engaging in or being a victim of violence. Biological factors include any genetic defects, early trauma while in the womb or during birth, personality traits, and cognitive functioning. Family factors include the type of parenting (e.g. level of contact with and stimulation by parents) and the family environment (e.g. whether there is violence or substance abuse in the home). Children learn their behaviours by mimicking those around them, making family life an important setting for learning and a strong contributor to attitudes towards violence and violent behaviour.

Table 8.1 Important risk factors and domains in life stages

Childhood	Adolescence	Early adulthood
Biology	Peers	Substance abuse
Family	School	Social skills
Parenting	Parenting	Relationships
	Social skills	Employment
	Substance abuse	

As children move into adolescence they face numerous social, psychological, and emotional challenges. School becomes an important domain for learning at this stage, and social skills play an important role in navigating this new environment. The ability of an individual to interact socially and in a positive fashion contributes to emotional stability, maturity, and integration into school life. Peers serve as strong role models for the development of individual attitudes and behaviours. Interacting with peers who engage in delinquent and violent behaviour increases the likelihood of the individual engaging in this same negative behaviour. The family domain remains important, in particular with respect to family management, parental supervision and support, and the conflict resolution skills of the parents to handle their own challenges as well as to assist a teenager in managing life's growing pains.

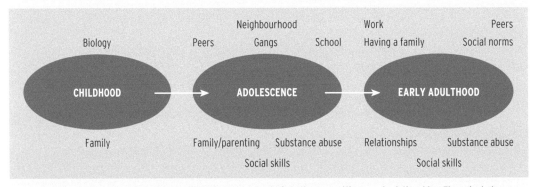

In early adulthood, an individual once again faces a new set of challenges, settings, and relationships. These include assuming independence, facing the challenges of finding a job and making a living, and the responsibilities of relationships, marriage, and family. Key risk factors identified at this stage of life include unemployment, relationship difficulties, and substance abuse. After the age of 44, the rate of homicide drops significantly, and in the United States it falls out of the top ten causes of death for both men and women.

Although the level of risk increases as the number of risk factors accumulates, risk is not necessarily cumulative over the course of an individual's life. However, a study of children and adolescents suggests that the accumulation of risk factors during this stage of development is possible. In the study, the older youth exhibited far more risk factors than the children, but the children exhibited a subset of the important risk factors identified for the adolescent group, suggesting at least some carry-over from childhood to adolescence and the accumulation of risk factors with age (Stouthamer-Loeber et al., 2002, p. 120). A key question to be answered is which factors are likely to persist throughout an individual's life and contribute to future potential for violence (e.g. a history of violence, being victimized as a child) and which factors are likely to decline or disappear as an individual ages.

Sources: CDC (2008b); CDC WISQARS (2008); Dahlberg (1998); Dahlberg and Potter (2001); Loeber and Stouthamer-Loeber (1998); Wasserman, Miller, and Cothern (2000)

Figure 8.2 **Three pathways to boys' delinquency and violence**

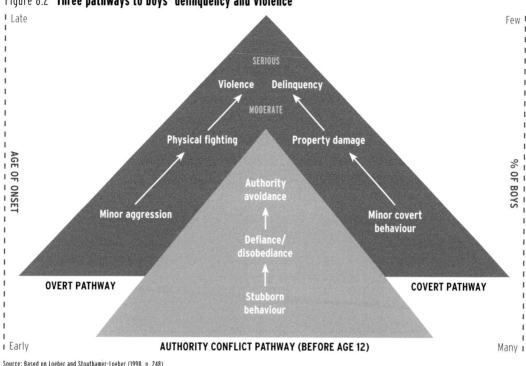

Source: Based on Loeber and Stouthamer-Loeber (1998, p. 248)

Many violent offenders desist from delinquency and violence as they transition from adolescence to adulthood (Stouthamer-Loeber et al., 2004, p. 913). In a study of youths aged 13–25 in Pittsburgh, nearly 40 per cent of those studied desisted from severe violence, though half of these individuals continued with some form of minor delinquency while the other half desisted completely (Stouthamer-Loeber et al., 2004, p. 907). Serious offenders stop committing violent acts as a result of maturity through aging, rational choice to desist enabled by improved cognitive skills for decision making, the formation of social bonds and informal social controls, as well as a number of other 'biological, sociological and psychological' factors (p. 898). While most of these explanations 'assume that there are key changes taking place in individuals, relationships, contexts, or opportunities that are related in some way to the transition to adulthood', few of these explanations possess the empirical data to confirm their claims (p. 898). The probability of desistance is not the same for all offenders. The most deviant offenders have the lowest prospects for desistance (Loeber and Stouthamer-Loeber, 1998, p. 244). A better understanding of why individuals choose to stop offending could contribute to the design of programmes that encourage such choices.

IMPORTANT FINDINGS

Research into risk and resilience has produced a number of findings important to advancing the understanding of these factors and their influence on violence. For example, no single risk factor can explain violence. Multiple factors play a role in raising risk levels across various domains. Risk factors are indicators of the potential for violence, not predictors of actual violent events. Context matters, and community and societal level factors can be as important as individual and family level factors. Attention has focused far more on risk than resilience, leading to greater advances in knowledge about risk factors. This section focuses on these advances.

A wide range of factors contribute to delinquency, poor behaviours, and violence. The difficulty is determining which factors are most important, or most influential in determining a poor outcome, and whether there are some key configurations of factors that lead to violence. It is widely accepted that no one risk factor and no single configuration of risk factors can explain all violence. In fact, it appears that some risk factors may contribute directly to a specific type of bad behaviour or subset of behaviours, while other risk factors can contribute to a wide range of bad behaviours (see Table 8.2), indicating the need to identify clusters of risk factors and clusters of behavioural problems that are interrelated.

Violence cannot be predicted by a single risk factor. Any one risk factor is unlikely to significantly increase the risk that an individual will engage in violence. For example, while the mentally ill have often received blame for violent behaviour, studies suggest that it is not mental illness alone that causes an individual to become violent, but rather a combination of risk factors that create an environment in which mentally ill individuals are more likely to act in a violent manner (see Box 8.4). Risk increases as an individual accumulates risk factors: the more risk factors an individual faces, the higher is the probability that that individual will engage in violent behaviour (Stouthamer-Loeber et al., 2002, p. 111). Risk is thus related to the number of risk factors present, rather than the existence of any specific

Table 8.2 Risk factors for behaviour problems

Risk factors	Substance abuse	Delinquency	Teenage pregnancy	School dropout	Violence
Community					
Availability of drugs	X				
Low neighbourhood attachment	X	X			X
Extreme economic deprivation	X	X	X	X	X
Family					
Family management problems	X	X	X	X	X
School					
Early and persistent anti-social behaviour	X	X	X	X	X
Lack of commitment to school	X	X	X	X	
Individual/peer					
Rebelliousness	X	X		X	
Friends who engage in problem behaviour	X	X	X	X	X

Source: Based on Bownes and Ingersoll (1997, p. 3)

Box 8.4 Identifying violence in the home

'Most seriously mentally ill persons in the public mental health system do not commit violence' (Arehart-Treichel, 2002). Whether mentally ill individuals are predisposed to violence remains a highly controversial topic of research and discussion. While popular images of the mentally ill or the criminally insane have presumed a direct link between mental illness and violence, the evidence to date is inconclusive. Violence rates among the mentally ill vary widely depending on the study conducted, and numerous risk factors have been cited to explain violence by the mentally ill (Arehart-Treichel, 2002). These studies suggest that, while severe mental illness is a risk factor for violence, it is not alone sufficient to cause violence. In other words, other risk factors must be involved as well.

A study at Duke University makes the case that other risk factors play an important role in compounding risk and making 'violence more probable' among those with severe mental illness. The lead author of the study claims that 'acts of violence by people with mental illness are rare' and that 'those with severe mental illness were no more likely to engage in violent behaviours than people in the general population without a psychiatric disorder' (Duke University, 2002). Instead, this study found that certain risk factors in combination with mental illness drastically increased the probability of violence. These factors include childhood violent victimization, current exposure to violence, and substance abuse. The study found that those who possessed none or one of these factors had a predicted probability of violence of two per cent, similar to the rate for the general population without mental illness. However, the addition of other risk factors significantly increased the probability of violence. The addition of a second factor doubled the probability of violence, while the presence of all three risk factors raised the probability to 30 per cent (Swanson et al., 2002, p. 1529).

These findings suggest that a focus on the mental health of the individual is insufficient for violence prevention. Instead, violence prevention efforts should also address the factors that increase the risk of mentally ill persons committing violent acts through safe housing, substance abuse treatment, and clinical support for patients who have experienced physical and sexual victimization as children.[2]

factor or group of factors (Saner and Ellickson, 1996, p. 102; US Surgeon General Report, 2001, ch. 4). Similarly with resilience: the more resilience factors present, the greater is the likelihood that an individual can avoid violence. This raises a number of difficult questions about risk and resilience factors. For example, how many risk factors are necessary before an individual becomes violent? How many risk factors compared with resilience factors are needed to tip the balance towards violence? It remains unclear whether any such thresholds exist (Stouthamer-Loeber et al., 2002, pp. 111–12).

While it is important to consider multiple risk factors, it is also important to understand that these risk factors exist within multiple *domains* (e.g. individual, family, and community) of an individual's environment. Research suggests that the greater the number of domains affected by risk factors, the higher is the probability of violence (Saner and Ellickson, 1996). Effective prevention, therefore, requires programming that addresses multiple risk factors across multiple domains and settings (Bownes and Ingersoll, 1997, p. 2; Moore, 2001, p. 2912; Stouthamer-Loeber et al., 2002, p. 121). Such multidimensional programmes are especially important given that it remains unclear which factors and domains are most influential (Luthar, Cicchetti, and Becker, 2000a, p. 548); such knowledge would provide some indication of how to narrow interventions to target those factors and domains that are most important.

Risk factors are *indicators* of the potential for violence in a given individual or group in the population, though they are much better at indicating the probability of violence in an individual than in the population at large. Risk factors are not perfect predictors of violence. Instead, they indicate a higher likelihood of violence in those who posses numerous risk factors. Thus, while it is possible to identify those at risk of violence given identified risk factors, it remains impossible to predict which individuals specifically will actually become violent offenders. In fact, most *at-risk* youths never become violent (US Surgeon General Report, 2001, ch. 4; O'Toole, 2002, p. 3). Most identified risk factors come from the study of offending youth, which produces a profile of offenders but does not indicate how they differ from non-offending youth (Saner and Ellickson, 1996, p. 94), or which factors contribute to the small percentage of at-risk youths who do commit violent acts. This raises questions about how known risk factors should be used to design violence reduction initiatives.

If risk factors do not cause violence, then the question remains: what sparks violence in a person at risk of committing violence? One answer is the existence of *triggers* or *stressors* that when activated serve to push a predisposed person into committing an act of violence. These triggers are often 'the straw that broke the camel's back', the immediate spark to spontaneous violence. There are different triggers depending on the context and type of violence. In a gang setting, showing disrespect for a member of another gang might suffice to instigate a fight. In domestic violence there are well-known triggers including disobeying one's husband, not having dinner ready on time, refusing sex, or questioning a husband's activities (Heise, Ellsberg, and Gottmoeller, 2002, p. S8). While studies have identified common triggers, removing these triggers may be more difficult than addressing risk factors due to the speed at which triggers can appear and lead to violent outcomes.

…an push a
…ed person
…an act of
violence.

An understanding of the interaction of risk and resilience factors across domains is important. For example, youths who live in abusive households have been found to demonstrate academic success despite their high-risk family life, but these same youths did not demonstrate high levels of social competence, such as the ability to interact easily and well with other students (Luthar, Cicchetti, and Becker, 2000a, p. 548). Individual difference could account for these varying successes and failures across domains. Community context could also play a role. Great variation exists in terms of levels of violence among neighbourhoods (Hawkins, Van Horn, and Arthur, 2004) and this variation is likely based on community characteristics (Stouthamer-Loeber et al., 2002, p. 111). This suggests the need for different approaches in different settings (see Box 8.5). It also indicates that an assessment of individual risk factors must be considered alongside community level factors, but that individual risk factors are likely to have more influence when they are numerous. For example, while youths in high-risk neighbourhoods tend to offend more than those in the general population, young males with high levels of risk (i.e. many individual risk factors) offend at the same rate regardless of their neighbourhood environment (Stouthamer-Loeber et al., 2002, p. 121), suggesting that there is a tipping point at which individual risk factors dominate.

The study of the interaction of risk and resilience factors has provided important insights into how individuals overcome adversity or succumb to violence (Roosa, 2000, p. 567). First, the interaction of risk and resilience factors can elicit a 'protective-stabilizing role' for resilience factors (Li, Nussbaum, and Richards, 2007, p. 22). In this situation, resilience factors mediate the negative impacts of risk factors, thereby protecting the individual from the risk factor and enabling the individual either to avoid or to overcome that risk. This effect is most frequently found when there is a high number of resilience factors and low risk (Li, Nussbaum, and Richards, 2007, p. 22). This has also been called a 'protective but reactive' response, indicating the low level of advantage or protection offered when an individual faces high levels of risk (Luthar, Cicchetti, and Becker, 2000a, p. 547).

Second, resilience may simply prove insufficient to overcome extant risk factors. In this situation of 'overwhelming risk', the high number of risk factors outweighs the beneficial and protective nature of resilience factors leading to adverse outcomes (Li, Nussbaum, and Richards, 2007, p. 22). One study of Chicago youth found that '*none* of the minority adolescent males' who lived in high-stress families, faced high levels of risk, and lived in highly dangerous settings exhibited any evidence of resilience (Garbarino, 2001, p. 364). The constant high level of risk simply overwhelmed any ability of the individual to cope with the situation. Similar findings came from a study of combat

Box 8.5 **The urban-rural divide**

In general, firearm injury is more common in urban settings than in rural ones. Intentional injury with a firearm is more common in an urban setting. Homicides involving firearms are more common in urban contexts, and tend to cluster in specific neighbourhoods. Gun violence in urban areas often involves the use of handguns, as opposed to other types of firearms. A number of longitudinal studies provide evidence to support this: in urban Milwaukee, 85 per cent of gunshot wounds came from handguns; and in urban Philadelphia 90 per cent of homicides were committed with handguns.

However, rural areas also demonstrate both high levels of firearm access and high levels of firearm mortality. The difference between rural and urban settings appears to be more one of intent and weapon type than levels of firearm injury. In rural areas, while homicides are less common, accidents and suicides pose a big problem in terms of firearm injury. A second difference is that these injuries often result from the use of rifles and shotguns rather than handguns. For example, in a study of rural Wisconsin 60 per cent of gunshot wounds were from shotguns or rifles, while 20 per cent came from handguns.

While these general findings suggest important differences between urban and rural settings, such generalizations should not be overstated. A study of gun deaths in Washington State in the United States revealed that, although differences between rural and urban gun deaths did exist, there were also distinct similarities between them. The differences between rural and urban areas mimicked those discussed above. However, two findings on the similarities between rural and urban areas of Washington State are of particular interest: handguns were the most common type of gun involved in both rural and urban gun deaths, and suicides were the most common form of gun death in both settings. The findings of this study continue to support the common knowledge about the urban-rural divide, but they also point to the need to consider local conditions rather than an unquestioning reliance on generalized findings when designing gun violence prevention strategies.

Source: Based on Dresang (2001)

veterans who had experienced combat conditions for a sustained period, with 98 per cent of those studied exhibiting severe psychiatric problems (Garbarino, 2001, p. 364). In situations of overwhelming risk, it might be difficult to implement strategies to decrease significant risk factors. In these situations, emphasis should be placed on strategies to increase existing resilience factors in an effort to balance out the risk–resilience equation (Stouthamer-Loeber et al., 2002, p. 121) and reduce the negative effects of extremely high levels of risk. Reducing violence is not merely a matter of reducing risk, but also involves bolstering resilience factors.

Important risk factors

One key question is what the risk factors for predicting violence are; another is what the most important risk factors are. While it is evident that multiple risk factors increase risk, it is still unknown whether some risk factors can contribute more significantly to increasing risk than others, or should be given greater consideration in designing interventions. Ideally it would be best to have not only a list of relevant risk factors in a given context, but also a ranking of these risk factors from most to least important. This would enable a prioritization of risks to be managed when designing interventions. In an ideal world, interventions would be designed to cover all pertinent

An armed 18-year-old drug trafficker stands by shacks in a Rio favela
© Ian Teh/Panos Pictures

risk factors, but the reality is that resources often do not exist for such comprehensive programming. Thus, resources could be better used if primary risk factors could be identified. To date this is not possible.[3] However, it is possible to identify significant indicators of violence, important risk factors for certain types of violence, and the nature of these factors in terms of their potential for modification through intervention.

In terms of intervention, there are three types of risk factor: non-changeable, changeable in the short term, and potentially changeable over the long term. A number of risk factors can potentially be mitigated in the short term (see Table 8.3). The majority of these factors fall within the individual, family, peer, and school domains. They include addressing substance abuse, keeping youths in school, family management training to improve parenting, and social skills training for youth to enable them to integrate better and to handle conflicts in a non-violent fashion. Interventions tend to focus on the individual or the familial level because factors in these domains are easier to target, the targets are more concrete, the scope of programming is more manageable (e.g. an individual or a handful of individuals rather than a community or society), and the scale of programming is smaller (i.e. these programmes can be implemented at the neighbourhood level and do not require national programming).

Key community- and society-level risk factors (see Table 8.2) have proven far more challenging to address. While potentially modifiable, changing these risk factors is difficult and is likely to take a long time, from years to generations, to achieve. These factors include economic inequality, poverty, low economic opportunity, low community participation, disorganized or socially non-cohesive neighbourhoods, the presence of gangs, and cultural norms supportive of at least some forms of violence. Interventions at the community level often entail community watches, hot-spot policing, or gang-reduction initiatives. Interventions at the societal level do take place, but in many cases these tend to be targeted less at violence prevention than at economic and social issues such as inequality, employment, and poverty.

Two important indicators of risk are age and gender. This holds true across the globe: young men are the primary perpetrators and victims of firearms violence.[4] Males are at higher risk than females of engaging in violence. In 2004 homicide ranked among the top six causes of death for both males and females aged 1–34 in the United States, although the percentage of deaths was significantly higher for males than females (CDC, 2008b; CDC WISQARS, 2008). Youth (defined as those individuals between the ages of 15 and 24) are at higher risk than children and adults of engaging in violence. Homicide falls out of the top ten causes of death after the age of 44 for both males and

Table 8.3 General risk factors for violence

Individual	Family	Peer	Community	Society
• Birth defects • Personality disorders • Early aggressive behaviour • Low academic achievement • Attitudes and beliefs supportive or tolerant of violence	• Weak family bonds • Violence in the home • Poor parental supervision • High levels of stress in the home	• Poor social or interaction skills • Anti-social behaviour • Involvement with delinquent peer groups	• Presence of gangs • Presence of drugs • Presence of arms • Community disorganization • High unemployment • Lack of economic opportunities	• High levels of inequality • High levels of poverty • Social norms supportive or tolerant of violence

Source: Adopted from IVPA (n.d.)

females in the United States (CDC, 2008b; CDC WISQARS, 2008). Violence and homicide rates vary across the globe, and the lack of cross-national research makes it difficult to compare a country such as the United States, where data is more abundant, with other countries. Studies, however, do suggest that the rates of youth homicide 'in many low- and middle-income countries greatly exceed those in the United States' and that these rates are at least three times greater than youth homicide rates in high-income countries (Mercy and Dahlberg, 2004, p. 592).

A third important indicator of risk that has received much attention in the United States is race. Studies suggest that blacks are at a higher risk of violence than other groups (Dahlberg, 1998; Jagers et al., 2007; Loeber et al., 2005). In 1998 homicide rates for blacks were twice the rate for Hispanics and 13 times the rate for non-Hispanic Caucasians (Dahlberg and Potter, 2001, p. 4). In 2004 homicide ranked among the top ten causes of death for black, Native American, Asian, and Hispanic men in the United States, ranking fifth and sixth for blacks and Hispanics, respectively, while not making the top ten for white men (CDC WISQARS, 2008). Homicide has been the predominant cause of death among *young* black men in the United States since the 1990s (Dahlberg, 1998, p. 259; Loeber et al., 2005, p. 1074). Whether this is unique to the United States or whether it is the characteristics and living situation of certain ethnic or racial groups that explain better why the risk is higher for these groups remains unclear. It will be important to broaden research to include other countries to determine whether race and ethnicity are in fact risk factors in other places.

Although age, gender, and race are important indicators of risk, they are not risk factors. Instead, these demographic categories tend to indicate underlying conditions or the presence of significant risk factors. For example, research indicates that statistically in the United States young black males are commonly involved in crime, but none of these three factors (age, race, or gender) causes crime. Instead they indicate other biological, social, and environmental processes and conditions prevalent in the young, male, and in some cases black, population (Ellickson and McGuigan, 2000, p. 571). This suggests that profiling in terms of race, gender, or age may not be especially helpful in reducing violent crime rates as this would require implementing violence reduction programming across entire segments of the population without being able to target the interventions any more specifically than to large demographic categories. While such universal programming is used, there is ongoing debate as to whether this is a cost-effective approach to reducing violence, or whether it makes more sense to focus attention on those groups and individuals deemed to be at the highest risk of engaging in violence. While race, age, and gender can be used to indicate important sub-populations, a better understanding of additional risk factors can help to narrow the focus to high-risk groups within these populations.

Risk factors for different types of violence

While the presence of these general risk factors increases the likelihood of violence, the type of violence also matters. While similar sets of risk factors have been identified for similar violent behaviour, such as the link between delinquency and violence (see Table 8.2), there are also indications that certain risk factors might be influential in contributing to specific types of violence. If true, then identifying what is unique to different types of violence in terms of risk and resilience factors could enable the development of more targeted interventions. The following discussion of four types of violence suggests that such 'profiling' of types of violence might be possible, and could contribute to identifying key risk factors in these and other types of violence across the spectrum from interpersonal to collective violence.

Demogra
categorie
age, gen
race–can
the prese
risk factc

Domestic violence

A number of risk factors have been identified for domestic violence, but they mainly pertain to the person perpetrating the violence. They include a history of domestic violence, a history of threatening the partner, unemployment, access to guns, and substance abuse (Campbell et al., 2003). Although the risk factors for a person committing domestic violence may be similar to risk factors for a person committing other types of violence (i.e. they exhibit many general characteristics of high-risk individuals), there are certain important differences in the situation of gender-based violence, and in particular domestic violence that occurs within the confines of the home. Two differences in particular pose higher risks for domestic violence as well as affecting the ability of practitioners to identify domestic violence and intervene to prevent it, namely, the monitoring capacity of the community in which the domestic violence takes place and a community norm that recognizes partner violence as deviant (Browning, 2002, p. 834).

Domestic violence remains a 'hidden' form of violence in many communities and in many countries. This often means there are few witnesses to the actual event, or the witnesses are children or other family members who may be unwilling to report the violence to the police or other authorities. While the effects of such violence might appear

in hospital emergency rooms, there is often a limited capacity to respond to this violence apart from providing proper medical care. The lack of a preventive response results from a number of circumstances: the lack of specific training of medical professionals to either identify victims of abuse or provide support in seeking help, the reluctance of an abused spouse to admit openly what has taken place, and extant cultural beliefs that such marital activities remain a private matter. In these situations, external interventions are less likely to be forthcoming as such interventions would be seen as intrusions into the private lives of individuals.

A second important risk factor involves community norms towards domestic violence. Communities are less likely to provide a check on domestic violence when the norms of the community tolerate the use of violence within marriage or in punishing children or when there is weak informal social control over community member behaviour. If domestic violence is not viewed as deviant behaviour, then community members are likely to have limited influence over it (Browning, 2002, p. 835). The ability to act collectively is effective in discouraging domestic violence only when community tolerance for such violence is extremely low and social organization is high (p. 838).

f domestic
tands by a
ure repre-
victim who
a result of
violence in
nce, Rhode
May 2001.
ia Arocho/
AP Photo

This suggests that community values towards domestic violence and levels of social organization are important factors explaining the prevalence of domestic violence. In communities and countries where partner abuse is tolerated, or in some cases encouraged as a form of 'training' one's wife, domestic violence is considered a private matter, women and children are viewed as a husband's possessions, and where women have a low social status the likelihood of gender-based violence is higher. The lack of a strong social support network and the lack of viable 'exits' from abusive relationships increase the likelihood that domestic violence will continue (Browning, 2002, p. 848).

Gang violence

Interest in gangs has increased since the 1980s, given the prevalence of gangs and gang violence in a number of cities around the globe. A number of common characteristics of gang violence and gang members have been identified. Gang violence, in particular homicide, is not a random event. Incidents tend to occur between known gangs, and gang members, and often result from battles over 'turf, status, and revenge' (VPC, 2002). While gang violence also affects innocent bystanders who get caught in the crossfire, gang violence remains largely targeted. For example, a study of drive-by shootings in Los Angeles in 1991 found that the vast majority of those committing drive-by shootings were gang members, and that nearly three-quarters (71 per cent) of those injured in these incidents were also gang members (Hutson, Anglin, and Pratts, 1994). In 2001 gangs accounted for 51 per cent of all homicides in Los Angeles County, and the majority of these killings were perpetrated with handguns (VPC, 2002). Gangs exist within a range of communities. Although typically considered an inner-city problem, gangs exist in the inner cities, in suburbs, as well as in smaller communities and rural areas (Esbensen, 2000, p. 1; Hixon, 1999). Gangs are clearly a community problem, and one which requires a multifaceted approach to prevention and violence reduction.

Typically, gang members have been portrayed as young, male, inner-city boys from racial and ethnic minorities living in impoverished conditions who are gang members for life (Esbensen, 2000, p. 3). The situation has changed, but whether as the result of better research, or actual changes in gang membership, or both of these, is not entirely clear. Gangs are increasingly cropping up in non-urban areas. Girls are contributing to larger percentages of gang membership. One study found females accounted for at least one-third of gang members (Esbensen, 2000, p. 3). Gang membership is not restricted to minority groups, and in fact research suggests that previous estimates of extremely high percentages of gang members in the United States being either Hispanic or black might have distorted the reality of the situation (p. 3). In addition, studies have found that not all gang members are members for life. Instead, nearly one-half to two-thirds of gang members are members for one year or less (p. 4).

The key risk factors for youths joining gangs are similar to those for youth violence more generally. Risk factors include delinquency, substance abuse, interaction with anti-social or deviant peers, low commitment to school, poverty, unemployment, and social disorganization, among others. However, research suggests that there are significant differences between gang members and non-gang members, and that gang membership is actually a self-selecting process with most youth avoiding gang membership (Esbensen, 2000, pp. 4–5). If this is the case, then factors must exist that provide the extra influence or incentive to join. The presence of gangs in the neighbourhood and having an older sibling who is in a gang are likely important predictors of gang membership (Hixon, 1999; Kaplan, Valdez, and Cepeda, 2008). Other factors might include feeling unsafe in school or in the neighbourhood and seeking safety through gang membership, or seeking gang membership as one of the few opportunities for economic gain in an economically disadvantaged situation (Kaplan, Valdez, and Cepeda, 2008). Even if these factors persuade individuals to join gangs, there is no clear answer as to why so many individuals do not remain gang members for long. Given that any of the aforementioned risk factors would be highly unlikely to abate within one year, other factors must contribute to desistance.

There are important differences between at-risk youth and youth gang members. Youth gang members are more extensively involved in criminal behaviour than at-risk but non-gang youth. 'Gang members are more likely to commit certain crimes, such as auto theft; theft; assaulting rivals; carrying concealed weapons to school; using, selling, and stealing drugs; intimidating or assaulting victims and witnesses; and participating in drive-by shootings and homicides than non-gang youth, even though the latter may have grown up under similar circumstances' (Huff, 1998, p. 4). There are also significant differences in gun possession between gang youth and non-gang youth. In one study, three-quarters of gang member respondents claimed that their fellow gang members owned guns, and that they favoured larger calibre guns; while only 25–50 per cent of non-gang youth stated that their friends owned guns (Huff, 1998, p. 5). In another study, 68 per cent of gang member respondents stated they owned a firearm, 56 per cent claimed they had carried it publicly in the previous 30 days, and 82 per cent claimed they had used a firearm in a gang-related fight (Kaplan, Valdez, and Cepeda, 2008).

Youth violence

Violence rates among youth remain at high levels in many countries. This suggests that youth face similar challenges, and similar sets of risk factors, across the globe. Youth will of course face culturally specific and context specific factors, which must be taken into account, but a profile of youth violence is emerging as consensus gels around common risk factors in various domains (see Table 8.4).

These lists of risk factors suggest numerous entry points for designing interventions. They also suggest factors that could play a larger role in early life (e.g. in the family and peer domains) as well as the importance of viewing the school environment as not only a positive learning experience but also a potentially damaging one depending on the performance of the individual as well as the nature of the school. This suggests the need for early life-cycle interventions as well as an emphasis on school-based interventions to address not only individuals but also the contextual characteristics of the school itself (see Box 8.6).

Gun violence

Gun violence is not necessarily a distinct type of violence, but instead refers to the use of firearms during the perpetration of a violent act. Gun violence can include armed robbery, assault, homicide, rape, domestic violence, and drive-by shootings. Violence, in general, is much more common than gun violence, raising the important question of why some individuals opt to use firearms while many others do not.

Civilian possession could offer one explanation, but it is likely to be only one of several factors influencing the risk of firearm violence. For example, even though Australia, Canada, and New Zealand have high rates of gun ownership, they have far lower rates of firearm homicide than the United States, in large part because these 'countries

Table 8.4 Youth violence risk factors

Individual	Family	Peer	School
• Attention deficit • History of early aggression • Substance abuse • Low cognitive skills	• Exposure to violence in the family • History of victimization • Poor parenting • Severe or erratic punishment • Poor family functioning • Parental substance abuse • Poor supervision	• Associating with delinquent peers • Peer substance abuse • Involvement in gangs • Social rejection by peers	• Lack of involvement in school extracurricular activities • Poor academic performance • Low commitment to school • Poor school environment • School bullying

Sources: CDC (2007); Christie, Jolivette, and Nelson (2001); HAY (2008); Loeber et al. (2005)

do a much better job of regulating their guns' (Hemenway, 2004, pp. 2–3). This suggests that who can access firearms and how the possession and use of firearms is regulated might be more important than simply counting who is licensed to own a firearm.

The availability of firearms is an important risk factor for firearm violence. Availability involves both civilian legal possession and the ability to obtain a weapon both legally and illegally. Suicide rates are higher in homes where guns are present (Hemenway, 2004, pp. 41–44). There is a strong correlation between gun availability and homicide rates (pp. 49–53). Homicides are facilitated by easy access to firearms. Gun possession also contributes to the escalation of violence during arguments, assaults, and robberies. Most criminals never intend to use their firearms during the commission of a crime, but the carrying of weapons during crimes increases the risk that they will be used (p. 46). 'More people are murdered during arguments with someone they know than during the commission of a robbery' (p. 47).

How firearms are stored in the home is another risk factor for both unintentional and intentional shootings. Improper storage of firearms in the home provides the opportunity for misuse by unsupervised juveniles. Accidental firearm shootings occur when young people find improperly stored firearms and play with them. 'Most shootings of younger children involve firearms belonging to parents or grandparents' (Hemenway, 2004, p. 33). Domestic disputes are more likely to result in death when a firearm is available (pp. 47, 122–23).

Many risk factors for violence in general are cited as risk factors for gun violence; the only difference between violence with a firearm and violence without one is the possession of the firearm (Cukier and Sidel, 2006, p. 49). Yet possession alone does not appear to explain all firearm violence. Countries with similar levels of firearm possession face different levels of homicide. Even within countries, for example the United States, homicide rates vary (INTERVENTIONS). This suggests the need to identify additional risk factors that influence the rate of firearm violence. Some of these potential risk factors have been identified, and include feelings of insecurity, presence of gangs, presence of organized crime and drug trafficking, social norms, and cultural practices (Cukier and Sidel, 2006, pp. 50–51). These factors pertain mainly to demand for firearms, and may not explain their use. An important advance in understanding firearm violence will be identifying whether the mere presence of firearms explains firearm violence, or whether additional factors need to be considered, identified, and addressed via violence reduction programming.

INTERVENTIONS: USING RISK FACTORS TO REDUCE VIOLENCE

The primary reason for identifying risk factors is to provide a reliable basis for designing violence prevention and reduction programming. This poses key questions about what a practitioner does when faced with a list of risk factors. How can a list of risk factors be turned into a viable programme? While it is essential to ascertain all pertinent risk factors that influence violent outcomes, it is equally imperative to pinpoint those factors amenable to change. Not all risk factors are equally amenable to change, and some factors are unchangeable. This section first discusses how to utilize risk assessments, or lists of risk factors, to design intervention strategies, and then identifies a range of approaches to intervention design.

From lists to interventions

Ideally, given a list of risk factors for violence, practitioners would design comprehensive interventions to address all risk factors. Practically, for a variety of financial, resource, political, and institutional reasons, this remains impossible to achieve. The second approach, then, would be to focus interventions on those risk factors that are most important or most influential to an individual becoming violent. This, too, is a herculean task at present given the current inability to rank risk factors according to their degree of importance to the potential for violence.[1] As a result of these challenges, attention has focused on identifying which risk factors are potentially modifiable, what it would take to modify these factors, and then designing interventions targeting these factors.

Determining which risk factors are amenable to change is itself a formidable challenge. Ease of change can be measured by asking a series of questions. Which factors require individual behavioural changes? Which factors require individual attitudinal changes? Which factors require familial or community behaviour changes? Which factors require changes to societal norms or practices? Which factors can be altered by changing the circumstances surrounding individual action (e.g. laws reducing availability of firearms or restrictions on access to alcohol)? The public health approach is based on the premise that effective prevention will require changes to attitudes, behaviours, norms, and circumstances. Yet many practitioners believe that it is easier to change the context within which an individual lives than to change an individual's, or a community's, beliefs and behaviour. For example, efforts to reduce access to alcohol during certain times or restrictions on carrying weapons in public have had a positive impact on reducing armed violence (Aguirre et al., 2005). Greater efforts at behavioural and attitudinal change will also be required to prevent violence, despite the immense challenges this poses at the community and societal levels. Programming at the individual and family levels has already demonstrated positive effect through providing individuals with training in social skills, conflict resolution training, and conducting home visits and training in parenting skills (INTERVENTIONS).

It is important to understand that lists of identified risk factors cannot be used as checklists for violence prevention. Currently, when used as screening mechanisms, lists of risk factors produce too many false positives, that is, identifying individuals as offenders who would never actually offend in the future, to be reliable measures for pinpointing future perpetrators (Ellickson and McGuigan, 2000; Loeber et al., 2005, p. 1087; Moore, 2001, p. 2913). In effect, using such lists cannot reliably distinguish perpetrators from non-offenders: 'when the incidence of any form of violence is very low and a very large number of people have identifiable risk factors, there is no reliable way to pick out from that large group the very few who will actually commit the violent act' (O'Toole, 2002, p. 3). This suggests that additional risk factors must be identified that can distinguish between offenders and non-offenders.

The use of lists of risk factors as screening mechanisms can also prove detrimental to individuals (see Box 8.6). This type of profiling can lead to the unfair labelling of at-risk individuals as *dangerous* individuals (O'Toole, 2002, p. 2), which can impose undue stress and harm on these individuals, lead to the singling out of these individuals as troublemakers even though they might not be, and generate unhealthy or fearful family, school, and work environments. In other words, marking individuals as dangerous might actually produce a self-fulfilling prophecy by creating conditions in which the individuals have few opportunities but to act in a violent fashion.

Lists of identified risk factors cannot be used as checklists for violence prevention.

Box 8.6 School shootings

Several high-profile cases of students shooting students and others in the presumed safety of their school have shocked communities across the United States. The 1999 shooting at Columbine High School killed 15 and wounded 23, making it the largest school shooting in US history until 2007, when a shooting at Virginia Tech left 33 dead and 15 wounded (ANS, 2007; CNN, n.d). These incidents, and many others (see Table 8.5), have led many federal investigators and school administrators to try to determine what makes a student a school shooter, and how school shootings can be prevented.

Table 8.5 **Selected school shootings**

Date	Location	Outcome
December 1997	Kentucky, USA	Teenage student killed three students
March 1998	Arkansas, USA	Two young students killed four students and a teacher
April 1999	Columbine, Colorado, USA	Two students killed 12 students, 2 teachers, and themselves
December 1999	Veghel, Netherlands	Teenage student wounded one teacher and three students
March 2000	Branneburg, Germany	Student killed teacher and himself
April 2002	Erfurt, Germany	Former student killed 14 teachers, 2 students, one policeman, and himself
September 2003	Minnesota, USA	Student killed 2 students
September 2004	Carmen de Patagones, Argentina	Student killed 3 students and wounded 6 others
March 2005	Minnesota, USA	Student killed 9 students and himself
November 2005	Tennessee, USA	Student killed assistant principal and wounded 2 school administrators
April 2007	Virginia, USA	University student killed 32 and himself, and wounded 15 others
October 2007	Ohio, USA	Teenage student injured two students and two teachers and killed himself
November 2007	Tuusula, Finland	Student killed 7 students, the principal, and himself, and wounded 10 others
February 2008	Illinois, USA	Former graduate student killed 7 students and himself, and wounded 15 others

Sources: Based on BBC (2002; 2007); Infoplease (2007)

While the phenomenon has made the headlines most often in the United States, other countries are not devoid of school violence or school shootings (see Table 8.5). Nevertheless, news reporting in the United States would suggest that the occurrence of school shootings is commonplace. It is not. A study of US school shootings between 1992 and 2004 reports that school-related homicide is extremely rare, representing 'approximately 1% of homicides that occur among school-age youths' (CDC, 2008a). Despite these statistics, 'there is a great deal of pressure to compile a list of red flags or characteristics to identify kids that may be school shooters,' but unfortunately such a list 'simply doesn't exist' (Kupersanin, 2002).

Risk factors for school violence are much the same as those for youth violence (see Table 8.3). This does not help much in narrowing the list of potential candidates for school shootings. Youths who exhibit high levels of social isolation and experience high levels of social rejection are more likely to act aggressively (Verlinden, Hersen, and Thomas, 2000, p. 13). Students involved in school shootings have often exhibited problematic behaviour prior to the shooting, though they did not threaten anyone specifically (US Secret Service, 2002, p. 17). In addition to a focus on the individual, studies have suggested that schools that experience school shootings have a number of characteristics in common. These include overcrowding, poor supervision, school disciplinary policies, lack of a caring attitude among school administrators and teachers, chaotic environments in classrooms, and lack of security (or feeling of security) in the school environment (Verlinden, Hersen, and Thomas, 2000, p. 13). Identifying these characteristics in students and in schools could provide an indication of where to target interventions, but interventions will remain broad in scope. Under these conditions, interventions can concentrate on at-risk groups of students and at-risk schools, but cannot be more specific than this.

Caution should be used in declaring students and schools as 'at-risk' (exhibiting some risk factors) or 'high-risk' (exhibiting many risk factors), especially in the current climate of fear over student shootings. 'Fear generated by the media coverage of the multiple-victim events has been used to justify actions against students by schools that would previously have been viewed as excessive', including the expulsion of students for minor offences (Verlinden, Hersen, and Thomas, 2000, p. 4). Such extreme disciplinary actions can be harmful to students already facing difficult circumstances. The labelling of students as 'high-risk' can also produce adverse effects by leading to these youths being ostracized, encouraging bad behaviour or association with delinquent peers, and reducing the incentives to engage positively in school activities. In extreme cases it could lead to actions being taken against labelled students, including violence, even when these students have never demonstrated an intention to harm.

While producing screening mechanisms for at-risk youths could provide a useful targeting mechanism for interventions, such a mechanism needs to be used with great care so as not to cause more harm than it prevents. This calls for better screening mechanisms because at present they produce far too many false positives. In one study, the false-positive rate was 86.6 per cent for youths with a high number of risk factors for homicide, suggesting the severe limitations of the use of risk-screening at its current level of accuracy (Loeber et al., 2005, p. 1087). It also demands additional means for identifying those who are most likely to commit violence. One proposed identification tool is the utilization of threat assessment methods after a student has made a threat (US Secret Service, 2002). In this situation, the threat is analysed to determine the seriousness of the threat and the risk that the student will carry out the threat. This approach is based on the presumption that not all threats are equal and that 'once a threat is made, having a fair, rational, and standardized method of evaluating and responding to threats is critically important' to responding appropriately to the situation at hand (O'Toole, 2002, p. 1).

A number of programming solutions have been advocated to reduce the number of school shootings and other school violence. These include fostering cultures of respect and safety, fostering relationships between students and teachers, discouraging a 'code of silence' among students that prevents students from informing school officials about students with problems, and actively preventing bullying and punishing bullying when it does occur (US Secret Service, 2002). In cases where guns or other weapons are brought to school, metal detectors can provide a means of detecting these weapons (Astor and Benbenishty, 2006, p. 6). Many schools have 'unowned' areas, such as hallways, playgrounds, and cafeterias, for which no one assumes responsibility, making them prime areas for violent incidents and suggesting the need for school officials to reclaim these areas through the use of monitors to provide supervision and decrease the attractiveness of these areas for violence (Astor, Benbenishty, and Meyer, 2004, p. 45).

A student goes through a metal detector to enter a high school in Philadelphia, Pennsylvania, in October 1999, one day after a school shooting incident.
© Dan Loh/Pool/AP Photo

Designing interventions

Once the relevant risk factors are identified, the next step is to design interventions to address them. There are a number of options. Interventions can focus on a single risk factor or on multiple risk factors. They can focus on a single domain or across domains. Single-factor interventions can be coordinated across domains in order to address multiple risk factors simultaneously. Alternatively, interventions can be designed in a sequential fashion to target one risk factor after another over time. In addition to identifying the risk factors of interest, it is also necessary to identify the target population of the intervention. Different types of interventions will be discussed briefly in this section to provide an overview of the options for programming. Which option is selected will depend on a wide range of financial, personnel, political, and bureaucratic considerations (INTERVENTIONS).

The majority of interventions in the United States focus on changing individual behaviours, attitudes, or beliefs (Dahlberg, 1998, p. 267). These efforts often focus on single traits: building cognitive skills, developing social skills, reducing substance abuse, or modifying an identified undesirable behaviour. Interventions, although less common, also exist at the peer and family levels. At the peer level, efforts are made to improve peer-group interactions, or to persuade individuals to avoid negative peer influences. At the family level, attention focuses on family management, parent training, and developing conflict resolution skills among family members. Community and societal level interventions are far less common. Some interventions at the community level include neighbourhood watch schemes, efforts to improve social organization, as well as targeted policing. Common to all of these interventions is their targeting of single risk factors.

Table 8.6 Multi-factor interventions

Type of intervention	Description	Advantages	Disadvantages
Coordinated single-factor interventions	Interventions are coordinated bilaterally by intervening agencies or hierarchically by a central agency	Enables targeted focus on specific risk factors Enables best-positioned agency to conduct intervention Targets multiple risk factors	Difficult to coordinate and manage Requires effective coordination of multiple interventions Requires high levels of coordination among agencies that may not normally work together
Sequenced single-factor interventions	Interventions are staged in a particular sequence to address single factors longitudinally	Enables targeted focus on specific risk factors Enables best-positioned agency to conduct intervention	Difficult to coordinate and manage Question of whether addressing risk factors sequentially rather than simultaneously achieves same effect
Multi-factor interventions	Interventions address multiple risk factors simultaneously in the same programme	Comprehensive Can address numerous factors that raise the risk of particular types of violence Increases likelihood of success Targets multiple risk factors simultaneously	Can produce 'shotgun' approach that covers too many factors in a superficial manner Difficult to coordinate and manage Expensive and complex to implement

Sources: Dahlberg (1998); Dahlberg and Potter (2001); Saner and Ellickson (1996)

Table 8.7 **Targets of interventions**			
Type of intervention	**Target of intervention**	**Level of risk and need for prevention**	**Purpose**
Universal	Entire community or population	Average	Reduce risk of violent behaviour
Selected	Identified high-risk groups	Elevated	Reduce risk and prevent occurrence of violent behaviour
Indicated	Individuals who have already exhibited violent tendencies or behaviour	High	Prevent recurrence of violent behaviour

Approaching violence reduction one risk factor at a time has its benefits. It enables a targeted focus on a specific risk factor. It also makes the intervention easier to design and implement. In some cases, it might be the only option available given existing resources. On the downside, single-factor interventions address only a fraction of the risk of any individual or group. If the commonly held assumption is true that high risk is the result of an accumulation of risk factors, then addressing only one of these factors will prove insufficient to address risk, and might have only minimal effect on reducing violence (Wasserman, Miller, and Cothern, 2000, p. 9). It is increasingly accepted and widely believed that interventions that address multiple risk factors are more effective in reducing risk and lowering levels of actual violence (INTERVENTIONS).

There are three options for designing interventions that address multiple risk factors (see Table 8.6). These include single-factor interventions coordinated through partnerships between implementing agencies; sequenced interventions that address single risk factors one after the other in a coordinated sequence; and multi-factor interventions that address multiple factors in a single intervention. As Table 8.6 suggests, each type of multi-factor intervention has its advantages and disadvantages. The selection of intervention type should be related to the targeted risk factors, but

Table 8.8 **WHO identifies 'top ten' violence prevention strategies**
Increase safe, stable, and nurturing relationships between children and their parents and caretakers
Reduce availability and misuse of alcohol
Reduce access to lethal means
Improve life skills and enhance opportunities for children and youth
Promote gender equality and empower women
Change cultural norms that support violence
Improve criminal justice systems
Improve social welfare systems
Reduce social distance between conflicting groups
Reduce economic inequality and concentrated poverty

Source: WHO (2008, p. 27)

CARRYING A GUN CAN GET YOU INTO THE COOLEST PLACES.
Call Crimestoppers anonymously 0800 555 111.

TRIDENT

METROPOLITAN POLICE | Working together for a safer London

selection should also realistically acknowledge the available resources, administrative capacity, political commitment, and community support. In some communities, comprehensive multi-factor interventions cannot be implemented for a variety of reasons (Wyrick and Howell, 2004), and in these contexts other options have to be considered.

In addition to selecting the risk factors to address, the target population of the intervention must also be identified. The target population is often divided into three categories: universal, selective, and indicated (see Table 8.7). Universal interventions target an entire population. Selected interventions target high-risk groups. Indicated interventions focus specifically on problem individuals who have already demonstrated a tendency towards, or actual, violent behaviour (Wasserman, Miller, and Cothern, 2000, p. 2).

Which population is targeted will depend on the intent of the intervention in terms of both purpose and the risk factors addressed. This decision will also depend on available resources. Universal interventions are potentially more expensive and more difficult to implement because they address large populations. However, standard programming might be possible in these cases due to the more general nature of these interventions. Selected and indicated interventions target smaller groups of individuals, but arguably individuals who possess characteristics and behaviours that are more difficult to address. While universal interventions are attractive in that they offer the potential to prevent violence, and thereby reduce the need for more targeted interventions, their effectiveness remains unclear. Selected and indicated interventions target those who are most likely to commit violent acts in the future, and therefore could be perceived as being more cost effective if they are successful. Assessments of existing interventions can indicate which types of interventions work best (see Table 8.8) and provide guidance for future violence reduction efforts (INTERVENTIONS).

MOVING FORWARD

While research on risk and resilience factors has improved general knowledge about factors that contribute to violence, there is still much work to be done. This section highlights the need for a shared understanding of concepts to improve both research and practice, identifies some areas in which additional research should be undertaken, and suggests concrete goals for future research in order to enhance the effectiveness of interventions and the ability of practitioners to intervene.

Research has identified common risk factors for violence, and for some sub-types of violence. The first step is to improve upon this knowledge, especially in the area of gun violence. The next step is to determine how best to use this knowledge. One goal is to demarcate clearly the differences between offenders and non-offenders in order to better predict the likelihood of violence. This will require expanding studies to include not only known offenders but also those in the general population.

While numerous risk factors for violence have been identified, and statistics on violent acts are more common today, there is far less understanding of why violent offenders stop offending (Stouthamer-Loeber et al., 2004). Key questions include: what factors influence the decisions of individuals to stop committing violent acts? Is it the decline in risk factors or the rise in resilience factors that accounts for desistance? Do individuals simply outgrow the desire or need to commit violence? Are other factors at play? Are any of these factors amenable to external influence through interventions?

More attention needs to be paid to the concept of resilience, to factors that provide resilience, and to programmes that might prove effective in boosting resilience. An important question is which factors aid individuals in maintaining a positive developmental trajectory in the face of extreme adversity. In addition, research should move beyond trying to understand how individuals manage adversity and avoid violence to answer the question of how individuals overcome adversity and actually flourish and 'do well'.

An important aspect of future research will be generating local knowledge about risk and resilience factors for designing community-based interventions. Targeting interventions to local circumstances is essential to avoid basing programming on common stereotypes and media images of violence that can be sensational and misleading, if not outright inaccurate. For example, in the 1980s and 1990s the United States witnessed a resurgence of gang activity alongside the crack cocaine epidemic, which produced predictions of 'a new cohort of superpredators (young, ruthless, violent offenders with casual attitudes about violence)' who would be responsible for a rising number of homicides as well as the stereotype of the 'drug-crazed, drug-dealing, gang-banging gang member' that depicted all gang members, inaccurately, as 'marauding, drug-dealing murderers' (Esbensen, 2000, p. 2). Basing interventions on such stereotypes leads to poor policy and ineffective programming.

An important step forward would entail research aimed at ranking risk factors and risk domains. Currently, the large number of important risk factors and domains identified in violence research makes it difficult to design interventions that comprehensively address all relevant factors and domains. A better understanding of the degree of influence of each risk factor and domain could contribute to improving the targeting of interventions towards those factors that are most important in increasing risk and most cost effective to change. If the most important risk factors can be identified, then practitioners will know where to focus their attention, efforts, and resources. ◢

ENDNOTES

1   Bownes and Ingersoll (1997); Brook, Brook, and Whiteman (2007); Dahlberg (1998); Dahlberg and Potter (2001); Saner and Ellickson (1996); and US Surgeon General Report (2001).

2   For a complete discussion of this study and its findings, see Swanson et al. (2002).

3   Cicchetti and Curtis (2007, p. 628); Luthar, Cicchetti, and Becker (2000a; 2000b, pp. 573–74); Moore (2001, p. 2913).

4   For a more detailed discussion, see Small Arms Survey (2006, ch. 12).

5   Luthar, Cicchetti, and Becker (2000a; 2000b, pp. 573–74); Cicchetti and Curtis (2007, p. 628); Moore (2001, p. 2913).

BIBLIOGRAPHY

Aguirre, Katherine et al. 2005. 'Assessing the Effect of Policy Interventions on Small Arms Demand in Bogotá, Colombia.' Background paper (unpublished). Centro de Recursos para el Análisis de Conflictos (CERAC), Bogotá. Geneva: Small Arms Survey. 29 October.

ANS (ASSIST News Services). 2007. 'School Shooting at Virginia Tech Leaves 33 Dead.' 16 April.
    <http://www.assistnews.net/STORIES/2007/s07040074.htm>

Arehart-Treichel, Joan. 2002. 'Experts Narrow List of Violence Risk Factors.' *Psychiatric News*, Vol. 37, No. 19. 4 October, p. 24.
    <http://pn.psychiatryonline.org/cgi/content/full/37/19/24>

Astor, Ron Avi, and Rami Benbenishty. 2006. *Zero Tolerance for Zero Knowledge: Empower Schools and Communities with Data and Democracy.* Urban Initiative Public Policy Briefing. Los Angeles: University of Southern California.
    <http://urban.usc.edu/main_doc/downloads/Zero_Tolerance_for_Zero_Knowledge.pdf>

—, and Heather Ann Meyer. 2004. 'Monitoring and Mapping Student Victimization in Schools.' *Theory into Practice*, Vol. 43, No. 1. Winter, pp. 39–49.

BBC (British Broadcasting Corporation). 2002. '18 Dead in German School Shooting.' 26 April. <http://news.bbc.co.uk/2/hi/europe/1952869.stm>

—. 2007. 'Timeline: US School Shootings.' 10 October. <http://news.bbc.co.uk/2/hi/americas/4371403.stm>

Bearinger, Linda H., et al. 2005. 'Violence Perpetration among Urban American Indian Youth.' *Archives of Pediatrics and Adolescent Medicine*, Vol. 159. March, pp. 270–77.

Bownes, Donna and Sarah Ingersoll. 1997. 'Mobilizing Communities to Prevent Juvenile Crime.' *Juvenile Justice Bulletin*. U.S. Department of Justice, July. <http://www.ncjrs.gov/pdffiles1/165928.pdf>

Brook, Judith S., David W. Brook, and Martin Whiteman. 2007. 'Growing Up in a Violent Society: Longitudinal Predictors of Violence in Colombian Adolescents.' *American Journal of Community Psychology*, Vol. 40, pp. 82–95.

Browning, Christopher R. 2002. 'The Span of Collective Efficacy: Extending Social Disorganization Theory to Partner Violence.' *Journal of Marriage and Family*, Vol. 64. November, pp. 833–50.

Campbell, Jacquelyn C., et al. 2003. 'Risk Factors for Femicide in Abusive Relationships: Results from a Multisite Case Control Study.' *American Journal of Public Health*, Vol. 93, No. 7. July, pp. 1089–97.

CDC (Centers for Disease Control and Prevention). 2007. 'Youth Violence: Fact Sheet.' Webpage last modified 19 April 2007; accessed 29 March 2008.
    <http://www.cdc.gov/ncipc/factsheets/yvfacts.htm>

—. 2008a. 'School-Associated Student Homicides – United States, 1992–2006.' *Morbidity and Mortality Weekly Report*, Vol. 57, No. 2. 18 January, pp. 33–36. <http://www.cdc.gov/mmwr/preview/mmwrhtml/mm5702a1.htm>

—. 2008b. '10 Leading Causes of Death by Age Group, United States – 2004.' <http://www.cdc.gov/ncipc/osp/charts.htm>

CDC WISQARS (CDC Web-based Injury Statistics Query and Reporting System). 2008. <http://www.cdc.gov/ncipc/wisqars/default.htm>

Christle, Christine A., Kristine Jolivette, and C. Michael Nelson. 2001. 'Youth Aggression and Violence: Risk, Resilience, and Prevention.' ERIC Digest. <http://www.ericdigests.org/2001-4/youth.html>

Cicchetti, Dante and W. John Curtis. 2007. 'Multilevel Perspectives on Pathways to Resilient Functioning.' *Development and Psychopathology*, Vol. 19, pp. 627–29.

CNN. n.d. 'Are U.S. Schools Safe?' <http://edition.cnn.com/SPECIALS/1998/schools/>

Cukier, Wendy and Victor W. Sidel. 2006. *The Global Gun Epidemic: From Saturday Night Specials to AK-47s.* Westport, Connecticut: Praeger Security International.

Dahlberg, Linda L. 1998. 'Youth Violence in the United States: Major Trends, Risk Factors, and Prevention Approaches.' *American Journal of Preventive Medicine*, Vol. 14, pp. 259–72.

— and Lloyd B. Potter. 2001. 'Youth Violence: Developmental Pathways and Prevention Challenges.' *American Journal of Preventive Medicine*, Vol. 20, pp. 3–14.

Deveci, S. E., Yasemin Acik, and A. Ayar. 2007. 'A Survey of Rate of Victimization and Attitudes towards Physical Violence among School-Aged Children in Turkey.' *Child: Care, Health and Development*, Vol. 34, No. 1, pp. 25–31.

Dresang, Lee T. 2001. 'Gun Deaths in Rural and Urban Settings: Recommendations for Prevention.' *Journal of the American Board of Family Medicine*, Vol. 14, No. 2. March–April, pp. 107–15.

Duke University. 2002. 'Three Risk Factors Cited in Violent Behaviour among People with Severe Mental Illness.' Press release. 30 August. <http://www.dukemednews.com/news/article.php?id=5806>

Ellickson, Phyllis L. and Kimberly A. McGuigan. 2000. 'Early Predictors of Adolescent Violence.' *American Journal of Public Health*, Vol. 90, No. 4. April, pp. 566–72.

Esbensen, Finn-Aage. 2000. 'Preventing Adolescent Gang Involvement.' *Juvenile Justice Bulletin*. Washington, DC: U.S. Department of Justice. September. <http://www.ncjrs.gov/pdffiles1/ojjdp/182210.pdf>

Garbarino, James. 2001. 'An Ecological Perspective on the Effects of Violence on Children.' *Journal of Community Psychology*, Vol. 29, No. 3, pp. 361–78.

Hawkins, J. David, M. Lee Van Horn, and Michael W. Arthur. 2004. 'Community Variation in Risk and Protective Factors and Substance Abuse Outcomes.' *Prevention Science*, Vol. 5, No. 4. December, pp. 213–20.

HAY (Helping America's Youth). 2008. 'Introduction to Risk Factors and Protective Factors.' Fact sheet. Accessed 11 February 2008. <http://guide.helpingamericasyouth.gov/programtool-factors.cfm>

Heise, L., M. Ellsberg, and M. Gottmoeller. 2002. 'A Global Overview of Gender-Based Violence.' *International Journal of Gynecology and Obstetrics*, Vol. 78, Suppl. 1, pp. S5–S14.

Hemenway, David. 2004. *Private Guns, Public Health*. Ann Arbor: University of Michigan Press.

Hixon, Allen L. 1999. 'Preventing Street Gang Violence.' *American Family Physician*. 15 April. <http://www.aafp.org/afp/990415ap/medicine.html>

Huff, C. Ronald. 1998. 'Comparing the Criminal Behavior of Youth Gangs and At-Risk Youth.' Research in Brief. Washington, DC: National Institute of Justice. October. <http://www.ncjrs.gov/pdffiles/172852.pdf>

Hutson, H. Range, Deirdre Anglin, and Michael J. Pratts. 1994. 'Adolescents and Children Injured or Killed in Drive-by Shootings in Los Angeles.' *New England Journal of Medicine*, Vol. 330, pp. 324–27.

Infoplease. 2007. 'A Time Line of Recent Worldwide School Shootings.' Accessed 3 March 2008. <http://www.infoplease.com/ipa/A0777958.html>

IVPA (Illinois Violence Prevention Authority). n.d. 'Risk and Protective Factors for Violence.' Fact sheet No. 3. Chicago: IVPA.

Jagers, Robert J., et al. 2007. 'Protective Factors Associated with Preadolescent Violence: Preliminary Work on a Cultural Model.' *American Journal of Community Psychology*, Vol. 40, pp. 138–45.

Kaplan, Charles D., Avelardo Valdez, and Alice Cepeda. 2008. *Risk and Resilience for Gang Membership and Firearms Violence*. Background paper. Geneva: Small Arms Survey.

Krug, Etienne G. et al., eds. 2002. *World Report on Violence and Health*. Geneva: World Health Organization. <http://www.who.int/violence_injury_prevention/violence/world_report/en/>

Kupersanin, Eve. 2002. 'FBI Expert Says School Shooters Always Give Hints About Plans.' *Psychiatric News*, Vol. 37, No. 12. 21 June, p. 2. <http://pn.psychiatryonline.org/cgi/content/full/37/12/2>

Li, Susan Tinsley, Karin M. Nussbaum, and Maryse H. Richards. 2007. 'Risk and Protective Factors for Urban African-American Youth.' *American Journal of Community Psychology*, Vol. 39, pp. 21–35.

Loeber, Rolf and Magda Stouthamer-Loeber. 1998. 'Development of Juvenile Aggression and Violence: Some Common Misperceptions and Controversies.' *American Psychologist*, Vol. 53, No. 2. February, pp. 242–59.

Loeber, Rolf, et al. 2005. 'The Prediction of Violence and Homicide in Young Men.' *Journal of Consulting and Clinical Psychology*, Vol. 73, No. 6, pp. 1074–88.

Luthar, Suniya S., Dante Cicchetti, and Bronwyn Becker. 2000a. 'The Construct of Resilience: A Critical Evaluation and Guidelines for Future Work.' *Child Development*, Vol. 71, No. 3. May–June, pp. 543–62.

—. 2000b. 'Research on Resilience: Response to Commentaries.' *Child Development*, Vol. 71, No. 3. May–June, pp. 573–75.

Mercy, James A. and Linda L. Dahlberg. 2004. 'Adolescent Violence: Is It the Same Everywhere?' *Archives of Pediatrics and Adolescent Medicine*, Vol. 158, pp. 592–94.

Moore, K. J. 2001. 'Crime and Delinquency, Prevention of.' In N. J. Smelser and P. B. Baltes, eds. *International Encyclopedia of the Social and Behavioral Sciences*. Oxford: Pergamon Press, pp. 2910–14.

O'Toole, Mary Ellen. 2002. *The School Shooter: A Threat Assessment Perspective*. Washington, DC: National Center for the Analysis of Violent Crime, US Federal Bureau of Investigation. <http://www.fbi.gov/publications/school/school2.pdf>

Roosa, Mark W. 2000. 'Some Thoughts about Resilience versus Positive Development, Main Effects versus Interactions, and the Value of Resilience.' *Child Development*, Vol. 71, No. 3. May–June, pp. 567–69.

Rosenberg, Mark L., et al. 2006. 'Interpersonal Violence.' In Dean T. Jamison et al., eds. *Disease Control Priorities in Developing Countries,* 2nd edn. New York: Oxford University Press, ch. 40.

Saner, Hilary and Phyllis Ellickson. 1996. 'Concurrent Risk Factors for Adolescent Violence.' *Journal of Adolescent Health,* Vol. 19, pp. 94–103.

Small Arms Survey. 2006. *Small Arms Survey 2006: Unfinished Business.* Oxford: Oxford University Press.

Stouthamer-Loeber, Magda, et al. 2002. 'Risk and Promotive Effects in the Explanation of Persistent Serious Delinquency in Boys.' *Journal of Consulting and Clinical Psychology,* Vol. 70, No. 1, pp. 111–23.

—. 2004. 'Desistance from Persistent Serious Delinquency in the Transition to Adulthood.' *Development and Psychopathology,* Vol. 16, pp. 897–918.

Swanson, Jeffrey W., et al. 2002. 'The Social-environmental Context of Violent Behaviour in Persons Treated for Severe Mental Illness.' *American Journal of Public Health,* Vol. 92, No. 9. September, pp. 1523–31.

US Secret Service and US Department of Education. 2002. *Threat Assessment in Schools: A Guide to Managing Threatening Situations and to Creating Safe School Climates.* Washington, DC. <http://www.secretservice.gov/ntac/ssi_guide.pdf>

US Surgeon General Report. 2001. *Youth Violence: A Report of the Surgeon General.* Washington, DC: US Department of Health and Human Services. <http://www.surgeongeneral.gov/library/youthviolence/>

Verlinden, Stephanie, Michel Hersen, and Jay Thomas. 2000. 'Risk Factors in School Shootings.' *Clinical Psychology Review,* Vol. 20, No. 1, pp. 3–56.

VPC (Violence Prevention Coalition of Greater Los Angeles). 2002. 'Fact Sheet: Gang Violence in Los Angeles County.' Webpage last updated September 2007; accessed 29 March 2008. <http://www.vpcla.org/factGang.htm>

Wasserman, Gail A., Laurie S. Miller, and Lynn Cothern. 2000. 'Prevention of Serious and Violent Juvenile Offending.' *Juvenile Justice Bulletin.* Washington, DC: US Department of Justice. May. <http://www.ncjrs.gov/html/ojjdp/jjbul2000_04_1/contents.html>

WHO (World Health Organization). 2008. *Preventing Violence and Reducing Its Impact: How Development Agencies Can Help.* Geneva: WHO.

Wyrick, Phelan A. and James C. Howell. 2004. 'Strategic Risk-based Response to Youth Gangs.' *Juvenile Justice Journal,* Vol. 9, No. 1. September. <http://www.ncjrs.gov/html/ojjdp/203555/jj3.html>

ACKNOWLEDGEMENTS

Principal author

Jennifer M. Hazen

Contributors

Charles D. Kaplan, Avelardo Valdez, and Alice Cepeda; Sharon Lund; Ananda Millard

s hold up gang signs in a police precinct cell in San Salvador
They were arrested as part of the Super Mano Duro plan to
g violence. © Luis Romero/AP Photo

Targeting Armed Violence
PUBLIC HEALTH INTERVENTIONS

9

INTRODUCTION

Armed violence is a widespread social problem that affects communities around the globe. Growing recognition of the detrimental effects of armed violence on the health of populations, the economies of countries, and the ability of governments to ensure the security of their citizens has prompted calls for action to prevent future violence. A number of international initiatives—the Geneva Declaration, the World Health Organization's Violence Prevention Alliance, the Inter-American Development Bank's Violence Prevention programme, the UN Development Programme's Violence Prevention and Small Arms Control programmes, and the Oslo Ministerial Declaration—indicate mounting political support for armed violence prevention programming.

This international recognition of the threat of armed violence has not yet been followed by widespread serious action, commitment of resources, and long-term strategies at the national level. While the situation has improved, violence remains a public health concern, and armed violence prevention measures are still needed to further reduce the burden of violence and to prevent violence from occurring.

A number of armed violence reduction strategies and programmes have been implemented around the globe. In Colombia, the government has increased the police presence in the cities and the military presence outside the cities to deter crime and violence and improve law and order, while also engaging the youth through social outreach programmes aimed at reducing the country's culture of violence (Ceaser, 2007, p. 1601). Several countries in Latin America have implemented alcohol bans during elections or other large public events or holidays, reduced opening hours of bars, or changed drinking laws in order to reduce the high incidence of violence related to alcohol abuse (Ceaser, 2007, p. 1602). In Jamaica and Burundi, governmental and non-governmental agencies collaborate in the running of crime observatories, which collect and collate information about armed violence in order to better inform and guide prevention strategies. In Mozambique, the government has established a national commission for violence and injury prevention, while in Johannesburg, South Africa, violence prevention has been integrated into the city's human development agenda (WHO, 2007b).

An important question needs to be answered: what is an effective intervention to prevent armed violence or reduce the harmful effects of armed violence? Currently, while a number of programmes show promise in preventing violence or reducing its negative impacts, no clear answer exists about what works best. In part this inability to answer the question results from a lack of necessary data on the problem of armed violence and from the scarcity of rigorous evaluations of existing and past interventions. In addition, information pertinent to understanding armed violence comes largely from high-income countries and the interventions implemented in these countries. Far less information has come from low- and middle-income countries about the kinds of armed violence prevention interventions being implemented there and the impact of these programmes. To date, armed violence prevention programmes that do not work or have not been evaluated are more widely used than those shown to be effective, because of the lack of clear evidence of what works and what does not. What practitioners need is a guide for armed violence reduction programming and implementation.[1]

This chapter considers the following questions:

- What is a 'public health' intervention?
- What types of interventions are available?
- Which interventions have demonstrated positive results?
- What lessons have been learnt?
- What steps need to be taken to improve interventions?

This chapter is divided into three sections. The first section defines what is meant by a 'public health intervention', followed by a discussion of a range of available interventions developed to counter armed violence. The second section provides two cases studies, one in a high-income country, and the other in a developing country. The first case study provides an overview of the problem of armed violence in the United States, a pioneer in the public health approach to armed violence prevention, and then discusses two promising programmes in detail. The second case study focuses on El Salvador and the ways in which this country has tried to control the rising burden of armed violence. The third section identifies a number of lessons learnt from these case studies, as well as from various other studies since the late 1980s.

The main conclusions include the following:

- No single intervention can address the complex, multi-causal problem of armed violence. Instead, intervention strategies must address multiple risk factors by combining the strengths and capabilities of a wide range of actors, from police and judicial officials to local government officials, local organizations, neighbourhoods, and families, and incorporating a range of interventions targeting specific contexts and risk factors.
- A criminal justice approach to reducing crime through targeted policing, arrests, and prosecution can be effective, but it is insufficient alone to produce widespread violence prevention results. Programming tailored to communities, families, and individuals provides an appropriate complement to law and order tactics, and has shown promising results in preventing violent crime.
- Effective strategies target three important elements of the overall violence equation: the actor who commits acts of violence, the instrument used in perpetrating an act of violence, and the environment in which violence takes place.
- Characteristics of successful intervention strategies include being evidence-based, credible, cooperative, tailored to the community and its context, targeted at both the supply and the demand of firearms, and publicly, politically, and financially supported at all levels.
- While many armed violence prevention programmes exist in the United States, they also exist in many other countries. However, to date much more is known about programming in the United States than in these other countries. It remains unclear whether successful interventions in the United States can be replicated elsewhere. Efforts should be made to broaden knowledge about various existing prevention programmes, to develop means by which countries can share lessons learnt, and to replicate successful interventions in other communities and countries in order to generate a shared understanding of what works, where, and why.

No single
ntion can
dress the
x, multi-
oblem of
violence.

UNDERSTANDING PUBLIC HEALTH INTERVENTIONS

A public health intervention is any programme designed to prevent or to reduce the actual level of armed violence or the perception of violence in a given population (Lab, 2008, p. 234). For the purposes of this chapter, violence is defined as 'the intentional use of physical force or power, threatened or actual, against oneself, another person, or against a group or community, that either results in or has a high likelihood of resulting in injury, death, psychological harm, maldevelopment or deprivation' (Krug et al., 2002, p. 5). Armed violence, more specifically, is the use of an instrument or tool to commit an act of violence. This instrument can be a knife, a stick, a broken bottle, a firearm, or any range of items used to intentionally inflict harm on another individual or oneself. Since a large percentage of armed violence in the world is committed with firearms, this chapter focuses where possible on small arms-related violence (PUBLIC HEALTH APPROACH).

Public health interventions are based on a four-step process that includes problem identification, data gathering and analysis, programme development based on data analysis, and assessments of implemented programmes (PUBLIC HEALTH APPROACH). Many other social and natural science disciplines use a similar problem-solving approach. However, the public health approach possesses some unique characteristics worth noting. First, the public health approach focuses on problems that affect community (or population) health. These range from communicable and non-communicable diseases to unintentional injuries to intentional injuries and armed violence. Second, public health data is collected in a scientific fashion, often through epidemiological surveillance, crime statistics, or victimization surveys. Third, the public health approach seeks to identify risk and resilience factors for populations. In other words, the approach does not necessarily seek to understand the root causes of violence, but instead focuses on identifying those factors that raise the risk of violence for individuals or for a given population. Fourth, when public health interventions are designed they typically focus on preventive efforts aimed at high-risk groups within the population, though they also include broader programmes for the population as a whole.

Public health interventions include measures to reduce the risks of individuals engaging in violence and increase the resilience of individuals and communities to violence. Some interventions focus on preventing armed violence, others on reducing the rate of armed violence, and still others on reducing the harm caused by armed violence. Some target the instrument of violence—firearms—while others target the behaviour of individuals. It is important to note that the public health approach, while supporting efforts to change individual behaviour, often focuses on changing the environment (whether social or physical) in which people act on the presumption that it is easier to alter the environment, and therefore the risks of violence, than it is to change behaviour (Hardy, 2002; Hemenway, 2001). An example, seen from the public health and criminal justice perspectives, respectively, should illustrate the difference in approach. A study of injuries resulting from fights in bars indicated that the majority of wounds resulted from the use of bar mugs as weapons during the fight. From the public health perspective, a solution could be to substitute plastic cups for the heavy bar mugs (Moore, 1995, p. 245). From a criminal justice perspective, a solution could be either to hire more security personnel on nights identified as more problematic or to arrest those who engage in fights.

The public health approach incorporates a wide range of possible interventions, which can be categorized in a number of ways. These typologies can be based on the level of intervention: primary, secondary, and tertiary (Krug et al., 2002); the target population: universal, selected, indicated (Wasserman, Miller, and Cothern, 2000) (see Table 9.1); the sector involved in implementing the intervention: police, judiciary, health, education; or the level at which the intervention is aimed: individual, family, community, society (Krug et al., 2002). These typologies are more generic in nature and could be used to address a broad range of public health issues, not just armed violence.

The public health approach seeks to identify risk and resilience factors for populations.

Table 9.1 **Targeting interventions**

Type of intervention	Target of intervention	Strategies for reducing violence*
Universal	Entire at-risk community	• Poverty reduction strategies • Job creation programmes • Social services availability
Selected	High-risk group with the potential to commit violence	• Incentives to finish school • Social skills training • Conflict resolution education
Indicated	High-risk group that has already committed violence	• Targeted policing • Tracing firearms used in crimes

Examples added by author
Source: Wasserman, Miller, and Cothern (2000)

When addressing armed violence in particular, the framework for thinking about prevention and harm-reduction should include an explicit recognition of the weapon used to commit acts of violence, i.e. small arms.[2] One promising strategy is to design interventions focused on controlling the instrument itself (see Table 9.2). Under this strategy, interventions address how firearms are used, who can possess them, the level of lethality of firearms, and the number of firearms in circulation (Sheppard, 1999; Mercy et al., 1993; Powell, Sheehan, and Christoffel, 1996). For example, legal measures imposed to restrict the types of firearms available can reduce the harm caused by firearm injury, e.g. a pistol

Table 9.2 **Interventions targeting firearms**

Type of intervention	Examples of interventions
Change how firearms are used	Restrictions on where guns can be carried Restrictions on concealed weapons Safety education Personalized weapons to prevent unauthorized use Consistent and credible punishment for misuse Metal detectors in schools and other public places
Affect who has firearms	Licensing and registration policies Age restrictions on ownership Mandatory background checks Waiting periods Interdiction of illegal firearm trafficking Targeted policing of gangs
Reduce lethality of firearms	Protective clothing (e.g. bullet-proof vests) Restrictions on the types of weapons/ammunition available for purchase Restrictions on size of magazines Bans on particularly harmful firearms and ammunition
Reduce number of firearms	Restrictions on licensing Bans on civilian ownership Increased taxes on firearms Incentives for disarmament Reductions in demand (e.g. improve security)

Sources: Based on Mercy et al. (1993); Powell, Sheehan, and Christoffel (1996)

carries fewer rounds of ammunition than an assault rifle, therefore its scope of injury is less than that of an assault rifle, and likewise the injury caused by the bullet of a pistol is far less than that caused by a round from an assault rifle. Another example comes from prevention, rather than harm reduction. The use of child-safe locks on guns could prevent the occurrence of shooting accidents by children playing with unsecured firearms in the home (Teret and Culross, 2002).

Another promising strategy comes from looking at the interaction of the agent, instrument, and environment (see Table 9.3).[3] This strategy not only targets the instrument of violence and the individuals using firearms, but also seeks to reduce the opportunities for armed violence and to alter the contexts in which individuals would need or choose to use firearms.

Table 9.3 **A three-pronged strategy for addressing intentional armed violence**		
Target of intervention	**Intent of intervention**	**Examples of possible interventions**
Actor	Keeping weapons out of the hands of criminals or unlawful users	Laws on possession of firearms Laws on the legal use of firearms Targeted and hot-spot policing
	Reducing the propensity of actors to turn violent	Reducing drug and alcohol availability Programmes to help high-risk youths finish school Alternatives to gang membership
	Taking chronic offenders off the streets	Targeting chronic offenders
Instrument	Preventing illegal access and criminal misuse	Personalized guns Tracing arms used in crimes Registration of firearms
	Detecting illegal weapons	Metal detectors in schools Regulatory inspections Police targeting of suspected illegal gun dealers Enforcement of laws prohibiting straw purchases
	Reducing negative effects of injury with weapons	Restrictions on specific types of weapons and ammunition Laws on safety requirements
Environment	Reducing incentives and opportunities to use firearms	Targeted and hot-spot policing Zero-tolerance policy for gang violence backed by punishing violence when it occurs ('pulling levers strategy') Increasing probability of prosecution for gun crimes Public information campaigns
	Addressing community risk factors	Reduce number of gangs De-concentration of poverty Equal access to social support services Changing cultural norms about violence

Source: Author, based on OECD-DAC Guidance discussions

INTERVENTIONS IN CONTEXT

What is known about armed violence prevention programming is largely based on programmes implemented in high-income countries, with a great deal of these programmes and assessments coming from the United States. Limited knowledge exists about programming in low- and middle-income countries in terms of the types of programmes that are being implemented, the contexts of violence, capacity to manage and respond to violence, and the programmes that have proven effective.

Some tentative conclusions can be drawn from previously implemented and evaluated programmes. Such assessments form the basis for the implementation of armed violence prevention programmes in other contexts. However, programme effectiveness and success depend on the context, resources, and capacity available in any given community. Successful programmes in one context might not produce the same results in another context. A future step is to start to identify whether successful programmes in one context can be translated into successes elsewhere. The first step is to better understand what works, and the next step is to see whether positive results can be replicated in other communities and in other countries.

The following presents a discussion of armed violence prevention programming in two different contexts: the United States and El Salvador. The United States provides the opportunity to investigate the best-case scenario: good data on crime and violence, a number of interventions implemented, and at least some rigorous reviews of interven-

Map 9.1 **Homicide rates by state (per 100,000), United States, 2006**

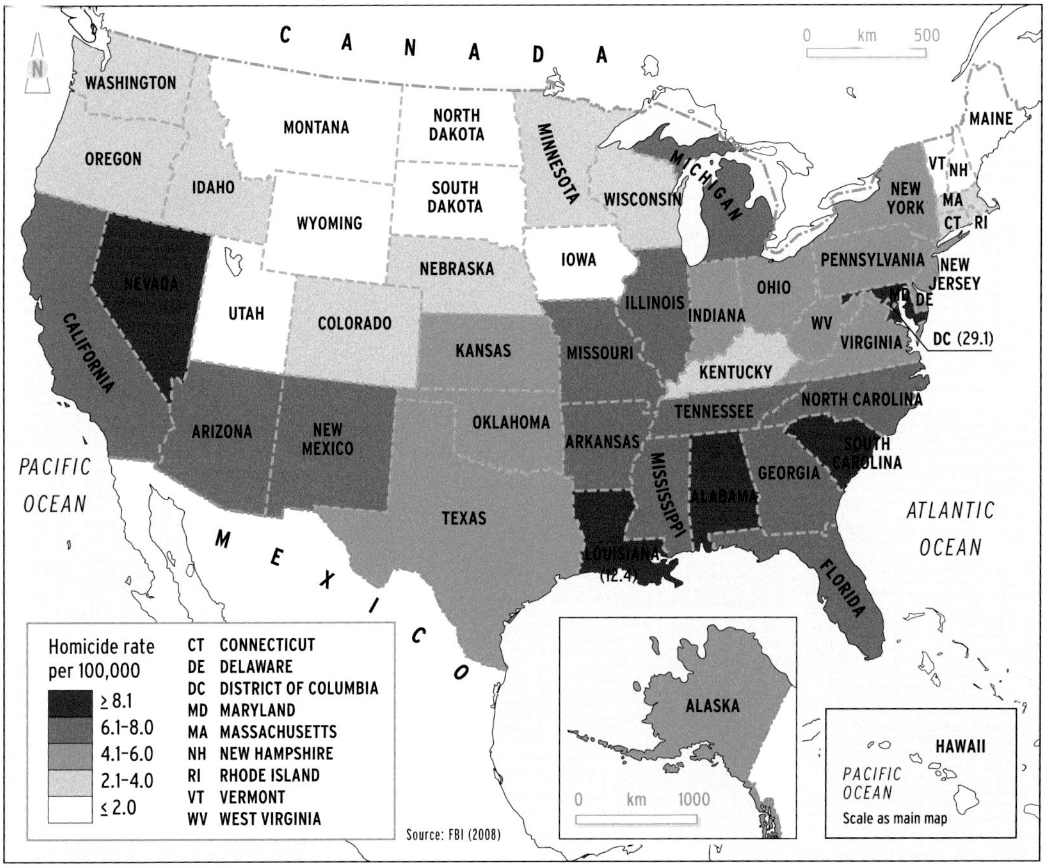

Source: FBI (2008)

tions. This case highlights the difficulties of addressing armed violence even under good circumstances, and offers some insights into programmes that could be adopted elsewhere. El Salvador provides a more typical scenario facing many countries with high levels of armed violence—low levels of income, weak law and order, and great social inequality—and highlights many of the challenges of addressing armed violence, while also offering some insights into what has worked. Each study beings with a discussion of the nature of the armed violence problem in the country followed by examples of current armed violence prevention programmes and evidence of the success of these programmes in reducing the rates of violence crime and armed violence.

The United States

Since the mid 1980s, violence—and the resulting mortality and morbidity—has been recognized as a pressing public health concern in the United States (PUBLIC HEALTH APPROACH). This recognition led to a more concerted effort to understand the causes, risks, and consequences of violence as well as subsequent efforts to reduce the burden of violence through armed violence prevention programming across a number of sectors. While many point to tougher laws and harsher sentencing as the reason behind the decline in violence levels since the late 1990s, other factors, such as a growing economy, better employment opportunities, and violence reduction strategies, are likely to have played a role as well (Sniffen, 2000). Despite the overall decline in reported violent crime, violence continues to exact a heavy toll in the United States (see Map 9.1), with high homicide rates in a number of states, and extremely high rates in Louisiana and DC.

According to the US Bureau of Justice, the level of violent crime in the country fell to its lowest level in 2005 since the early 1970s (see Figure 9.1). Violent crime includes rape, robbery, assault, and homicide.

While this assessment offers some good news, a closer look at homicides, and more specifically homicides involving firearms, paints a more cautious picture of the situation. After a significant rise in the 1960s, the homicide rate in the United States has followed a number of peaks and valleys (see Figure 9.2).

Figure 9.1 **US violent crime rates (per 100,000), 1973–2005**

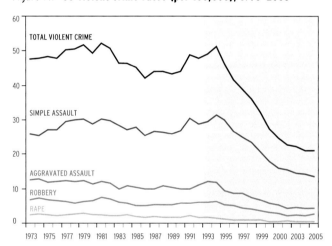

Notes: Murder is not shown because the 0.1 rate found through the survey fell below the threshold of the diagram.
The Department of Justice redesigned the National Crime Victimization Survey in 1993. The data before 1993 has been adjusted to make it comparable with data collected since 1993.
Source: USDoJ (2007)

Figure 9.2 **US homicide rate (for all weapons) (per 100,000), 1950–2005**

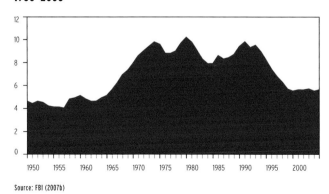

Source: FBI (2007b)

Figure 9.3 **US firearm homicide rate (firearms only) (per 100,000), 1999-2005**

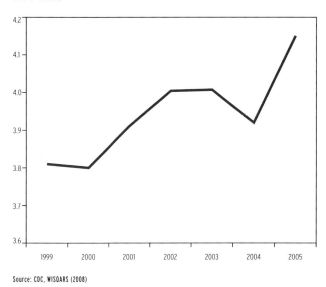

Source: CDC, WISQARS (2008)

The homicide rate hit its highest peak in 1980 at a rate of 10.2 per 100,000, and then nearly reached this rate again in the early 1990s. After 1994 the rate of homicides fell to just over 5 per 100,000 in 2000, and stabilized at this rate for the following five years.

Although the homicide rate (ratio of homicides to population size) and the number of homicides (raw number of homicides committed) follow roughly the same pattern, it is important to note that, while the homicide rate remained relatively stable between 2000 and 2005, the number of homicide victims has been gradually increasing since 1999 (FBI, 2007b). The number of homicides remains well below the peaks of 1980 and 1991, though still significantly higher than in the 1960s. Just as the number of overall homicides has begun to edge slowly upward, so too did the number of homicides committed with firearms until 2004 (see Figure 9.3). However, in 2005 the rate of violent crimes committed with a firearm increased once again from 1.4 to 2.0 victims per 1,000 persons (Catalano, 2006, p. 10). While these increases have not been dramatic, they do give cause for concern, especially if these upward trends continue.

An important part of understanding this violence, particularly from a public health perspective, is identifying the primary offenders and victims of violence and their respective risk and resilience profiles (RISK AND RESILIENCE). In the United States 'males represent 77 per cent of homicide victims and nearly 90 per cent of offenders' (FBI, 2007a). Violence is an important problem among young males. The majority (59 per cent) of violent incidents and homicides in 2000 involved males aged 15 to 44 years (Corso et al., 2007, p. 476, table 1). In 2004 'homicide was the second leading cause of death for young people ages 10–24' with an average of 15 young people being murdered each day (CDC, 2007). Firearms were used in 81 per cent of homicide deaths in this age group (CDC, 2007), and in 70 per cent of all homicide deaths (Catalano, 2006, p. 2). Violent crime is more common among those of black or Hispanic origin than those of white or other origin (Catalano, 2006, p. 6). Violence rates are higher among the low-income population than the high-income population, with the rate declining as average household income increases (Catalano, 2006, p. 6). These national statistics provide insight into the overall picture of violence in the United States, and can be used to guide national legislation and national approaches to reducing armed violence. They also suggest factors that should be considered at the sub-national, community, and neighbourhood levels when designing intervention strategies.

The majority of armed violence prevention programmes in the United States are not rigorously evaluated for their ability to prevent or reduce violence. A number of factors contribute to the lack of evaluations and the difficulty in implementing them. Evaluations are expensive to conduct. They require baseline data against which interventions can be compared. This baseline often does not exist. Even where it does exist, the lack of control case studies as well as the numerous factors that contribute to violence make it difficult to assess the impact of a single programme. In places with numerous interventions it becomes more difficult to determine which programmes have a positive effect. Given these difficulties, evaluations often entail assessments of the process of implementing a programme, rather than judging the impact of the programme on reducing armed violence.

A number of studies suggest that a large percentage of implemented programmes that are evaluated are ineffective. The Centre for the Study and Prevention of Violence conducted a study of more than 600 programmes, finding 11 to be 'model' programmes and 18 to be 'promising' (CSPV, 1996). The US Department of Justice reviewed 400 programmes, identifying 89 as 'promising' or 'innovative' (Sheppard, 1999). Another report found that of more than 50 programmes identified, fewer than half had received formal, rigorous evaluations, and

A police officer and ATF special agent knock on doors to announce a 'Stop Gun Violence' programme in New Orleans in October 2006. © Alex Brandon/AP Photo

of these only eight programmes had proven effective in reducing violence (Rosenberg et al., 2006, pp. 762–63). While there must be some method of trial and error in designing and implementing programmes, since otherwise innovation and knowledge advancement would cease, these studies suggest that more needs to be done in the way of

Box 9.1 'Consent-to-Search' programme

The overall homicide rate in St. Louis increased in the late 1980s and early 1990s. In particular, homicide rates among young black males reached astonishing levels at 380 per 100,000 for the 15-19 years range and 600 per 100,000 for the 20-24 years range. At least 97 per cent of these deaths resulted from firearms. One response to the problem came in the form of the Consent-to-Search programme initiated in 1994. Under this programme, police identified high-risk youths with the help of community members, and then visited their homes and asked parents' permission to search the house for illegal weapons. The community supported the programme as a result of the involvement of the community, the response of the police to a problem identified by the community, and the promise not to prosecute youths for weapons found in homes. Although seen as effective by the community and the police units carrying it out, the programme did not receive support throughout the police department. The police did not think the programme worked and wanted to take a tougher stance against crime. Without any structured assessments of the programme, little evidence existed to demonstrate that it worked. As a result, the police changed tactics in 1996 to a more aggressive approach that included arrests and prosecutions and relied very little on community information or support. This approach failed to produce positive results. Although the police changed their approach again in 1998 with an effort to return to some of the positive aspects of the first programme, the strategy failed to produce results and was terminated in late 1999. A review of the three phases of this strategy suggests that the first phase demonstrated the largest effect, with police seizing 510 weapons in 18 months, compared with the seizure of 31 and 29 weapons in the two subsequent phases, each 9 months in duration.

Source: Based on NIJ (2004)

evaluating programmes and implementing those deemed most promising. Definitive proof need not be the threshold at which programmes are selected for implementation. Programmes should be implemented that demonstrate promising or positive effect, but, equally, further work should be done to provide a guide to what is effective and in which contexts. Sometimes perceptions of effectiveness are inaccurate and can lead to the cancellation of effective programmes or the promotion of ineffective ones (see Box 9.1).

It is well known that criminal violence tends to be concentrated within specific individuals, groups, and neighbourhoods (Kennedy, 1997, p. 449). In response to this, many armed violence prevention strategies focus on these areas of concentration by either targeting 'hot-spot' neighbourhoods that exhibit high levels of crime and violence or concentrating on high-risk individuals, such as chronic offenders, and high-risk groups, such as street gangs. The following discusses two initiatives that have been implemented in the United States to reduce armed violence. These initiatives target high-risk offenders in different ways. The first initiative aims to prevent high-risk offenders from gaining access to firearms. The second initiative aims to reduce the rate of violence committed by high-risk groups through targeted policing, arrests, and interdicting the movement of illegal weapons.

Reducing criminal access[4]

One promising strategy based on the public health model to reduce armed violence is to reduce criminal access to firearms (Webster, Vernick, and Hepburn, 2002; Webster, Vernick, and Teret, 2006). Reducing criminal access refers to efforts to prevent high-risk individuals from gaining access to firearms. Such high-risk individuals include convicted felons, certain persons convicted of domestic violence misdemeanours, those deemed insane or having been committed previously to a mental institution, and minors, especially those involved in gangs. While federal laws prevent the sale of firearms to these individuals by arms dealers, there is no national firearms registration database to track firearm ownership, and high-risk individuals can access firearms in a number of ways, including second-hand sales and 'straw purchases'.

Second-hand sales involve the sale of a previously owned firearm to a new owner. The majority of US states do not require owners to report the private sale of their firearm to another individual. In most states, individuals and unlicensed vendors can also buy and sell firearms at gun shows with relatively few restrictions, regulations, or reporting requirements (Wintemute, 2007,

This Colorado gun dealer alerted federal authorities when four young people in black trench coats attempted to purchase a machine gun several weeks before the shooting rampage at Columbine High School. © Jeff Mitchell/Reuters

Box 9.2 Mayors Against Illegal Guns

New York City Mayor Michael Bloomberg, famous for promoting a strategy of addressing illegal guns through sting operations on firearms dealers identified as the source of a high percentage of firearms used in crimes, launched Mayors Against Illegal Guns in April 2006 with 14 other mayors in an effort to tackle illegal gun crime.

Several key principles form the basis for the work of the coalition: punish criminals involved with illegal guns; target and hold accountable irresponsible gun dealers; oppose federal efforts to restrict access to and use and sharing of crime gun trace data; work to enable the detection and tracing of illegal guns; and support all local state and federal legislation that targets illegal guns (Mayors Against Illegal Guns, 2007). By late 2006 more than 50 mayors had joined the effort. This initiative aims to share knowledge, tactics, and skills among cities in order to remove illegal guns from circulation. This initiative has grown significantly and now includes more than 250 mayors in more than 40 states. These public officials work in partnership with law-enforcement and public-health officials to reduce armed violence and the circulation of illegal firearms (Mayors Against Illegal Guns, 2007). Public-health scholars are assisting the campaign by highlighting a number of promising strategies based on research on firearm trafficking (Webster, Vernick, and Teret, 2006).

Sources: Mayors Against Illegal Guns (2007); Webster, Vernick, and Teret (2006)

p. 150). In the United States alone about 270 million civilian-owned firearms were in circulation in 2007 (Small Arms Survey, 2007, p. 47). The second-hand market thus provides a large market for easily purchased firearms with little in the way of paper trails to follow should the firearms be used to commit crimes. However, despite this availability, there is evidence that criminals prefer new firearms. Interviews with convicted felons and data from firearms traced to crimes suggest that many young criminals prefer new firearms to second-hand ones (Webster et al., 2002, p. 66).

All sales of new firearms must take place through federally licensed gun dealers in accordance with federal and state laws, which include background checks of applicants. However, these dealers are not always required to register the firearm purchase with a state database; this depends on state law. This provides a loophole for purchasers to sell the firearm, without restriction, to another private individual. If this sale is intended to provide a weapon to an individual who is ineligible to purchase one, this is called a 'straw purchase'. While some states do have strong laws against straw purchases, these laws are often undermined by the weak laws in neighbouring states (Webster, Vernick, and Hepburn, 2001, p. 188). This suggests that, while laws are important, and their enforcement equally important, additional interventions will be needed to address the problem of criminal access to firearms.

One strategy that has gathered support is police sting operations against firearms dealers (see Box 9.2). In the 1990s a number of police departments conducted sting operations on firearms dealers identified as having sold a high proportion of guns used in criminal acts. The sting operations involved police officers posing as potential buyers who were clearly purchasing firearms for other individuals who were not eligible to own a firearm. Studies suggest that these operations—or the threat of them—led to changes in dealer practices that have produced positive effects in Chicago (Webster et al., 2006), Milwaukee (Webster, Vernick, and Bulzacchelli, 2006), and New York City (Cardwell, 2006). These successes have encouraged other cities to adopt similar approaches to reducing armed violence.

A review of the tracing of firearms used in crimes indicates that a little more than one per cent of firearm dealers are responsible for more than 50 per cent of the firearms recovered from crimes (ATF, 2000a, p. 2). Public health research suggests that this finding cannot be explained by the location of the stores alone and that sales practices and 'local gun tracing policy' are likely to account for at least part of this trend (Wintemute, Cook and Wright, 2005, p. 361). However, there is no agreement on this. Some suggest that the store's proximity to high-crime areas might be more important to this finding (Ludwig, 2005, p. 688) than the sales practices of any given store. Furthermore, it remains unclear how widespread straw purchase practices are for obtaining firearms used in crimes.

The US Bureau of Alcohol, Tobacco and Firearms (ATF) found that from July 1996 to August 1998 nearly one-third of illegally diverted firearms came from straw purchases, though it remains unclear what percentage of these were used in crimes (ATF, 2000b, p. 18). More research is needed in this area. For those firearms that are bought with criminal intent, there is evidence to suggest that sting operations have contributed to the reduction of firearm availability for criminals.

The ATF is responsible for the federal regulation of firearms. In 1997 the ATF established the National Tracing Center (NTC), which traces guns used in crimes. The oversight role of the ATF is limited by modest resources and legal restrictions on its scope of operations. Federal legislation has further reduced the ability of the ATF to perform its oversight function. For example, in 1986 the federal Firearm Owners Protection Act significantly weakened the ability of the federal ATF to prevent diversions by limiting its capacity to conduct routine, on-site inspections of gun dealers to no more than one per year (actual inspections are much less common), imposing a higher standard of proof for certain violations, and weakening penalties for violators.

In 2003 Congressional Representative Todd Tiahrt introduced an amendment to the 2004 Commerce, Justice and State appropriations bill, known now as the Tiahrt Amendment, which significantly reduced the ATF's ability to share gun-tracing data from crimes, including preventing the ATF from publicly publishing its trace data. The Tiahrt Amendment has remained a part of this spending bill since this time, although it has undergone important changes. In 2005 and 2006 the provisions of the amendment further restricted access to crime gun data by imposing constraints on sharing information across geographical jurisdictions, preventing the use of such data in civil court cases, and adding criminal liability for law-enforcement officers who violated these conditions. In August 2007, for the first time in several years the ATF published the tracing data on firearms used to commit crimes in 2006.[5] This change in policy was followed by a change in the Tiahrt Amendment in December 2007. The modified amendment eliminates both the threat of prosecution of police officers who utilize this data to map illegal gun trafficking and the geographic restrictions on access to data, while also enabling both the ATF to publish yearly summary statistics of gun-tracing data

---

Box 9.3   The Boston Gun Project: Operation Ceasefire

In 1995 city officials in Boston began the development of the Boston Gun Project, leading to the implementation of the Operation Ceasefire intervention in 1996. The project aimed to reduce youth homicide and youth firearms violence in Boston. This project, based on a problem-solving approach, focused on the use of strategic policing to target the source of the youth violence: illegal guns and gangs. Strategic policing involves 'problem identification, analysis, response, evaluation, and adjustment of the response' (Braga et al., 2001, p. 4): a process very close to the public health approach.

Research showed that 'youth homicide was concentrated among a small number of chronically offending gang-involved youth' (Braga et al., 2001, p. 5). Based on this, officials designed a two-prong strategy of law enforcement directed at illegal firearms traffickers and a strong deterrent aimed at gang violence. The former involves tracing firearms used in crimes and focusing policing on those traffickers used by gangs and whose weapons have the shortest time period from purchase to crime. The latter involved a 'pulling levers' strategy (Kennedy, 1997) of communicating with gang members, a clear zero-tolerance message, and backing this up by using all legal means to punish violence when it occurred. This programme was not designed to eliminate gangs or all gang behaviour, but instead 'to control and deter serious violence' by gangs (Braga et al., 2001, p. 8).

The Boston Gun Project has been widely viewed as successful. One evaluation of the project indicated that the project resulted in a 63 per cent decline in youth homicide (Braga et al., 2001, p. 17). This project has since served as a model for interventions aimed at reducing youth armed violence, in particular gang violence. A number of cities developed programmes based on this framework, including Baltimore, Indianapolis, Los Angeles, and Minneapolis; and these programmes showed early positive results (Braga et al., 2001, p. 27). This project also served as the foundation for the US Department of Justice's Project Safe Neighbourhoods initiative (Decker et al., 2007, p. 2).

and federal-law enforcement officials to share gun-tracing data for criminal investigations and prosecutions and for national security and intelligence purposes (Mayors Against Illegal Guns, 2008). Although these changes improve the prospects for information sharing, they do not remove all of the constraints introduced by the original Tiahrt Amendment.

Addressing gun violence

In 2001 US President George W. Bush 'made the reduction of gun crime one of the top priorities of the U.S. Department of Justice' (McGarrell et al., 2007, p. i). The primary vehicle for this policy was Project Safe Neighborhoods (PSN). This project incorporated five strategic tactics learnt from past successful initiatives: 'partnerships, strategic planning, training, outreach, and accountability' (McGarrell et al., 2007, p. i). The strategic planning element of this strategy put forward, though not explicitly, a public health approach to tackling gun crime: 'Strategic problem-solving involves the use of data and research to isolate the key factors driving gun crime at the local level, suggest intervention strategies, and provide feedback and evaluation to the task force' (McGarrell et al., 2007, p. i). Each PSN project was tailored to the local community in which it was implemented. The following provides a more detailed description of one of these projects.

US Attorne
John Ashc
announces
580 new p
nationwid
gun crime
spread the
administra
message t
crime mea
time'. Jan
© Lou Kra

In the Middle District of the state of Alabama, Project Safe Neighborhoods maintained a heavy emphasis on utilizing a criminal justice approach, as captured in the consistent message of '*Gun Crime – Hard Time*' (McGarrell et al., 2007, p. 3). While emphasizing the need for strong policing, the project also put forward a multifaceted programme for addressing high levels of gun crime in the district. The development of the programme, although not explicitly expressed in public health terms, represents an example of utilizing a data-based approach for designing effective strategic interventions that utilize a combination of 'suppression, intervention, and prevention strategies' (McGarrell et al., 2007, p. 12). This suggests an area in which public health practitioners and law enforcement officials can collaborate on violence reduction strategies.

This billboard is part of the 'Hard Time for Gun Crime' gun violence prevention awareness campaign of the US Attorney's Office in the Southern District of West Virginia. © Progressity, Inc,

A key element of the Project Safe Neighborhoods programme is an analysis of the problem of violence in a given community based on research conducted by community partners. This analysis of 'the nature and distribution of gun crime across the district' provides the basis for identifying hot spots in the community, high-risk groups, and high-risk individuals, which could then be targeted by interventions (McGarrell et al., 2007, p. 10). The perception of police officials was that gun crime was largely the result of 'chronic offenders who chose to illegally carry and use guns,' and this assessment was largely supported by the findings of the research partners (McGarrell et al., 2007, p. 11). In addition, the research indicated the concentration of crime in one city in the district, Montgomery, and attributed the lack of a deterrent for gang violence to the absence of credible sanctions at either state or federal level due to prison overcrowding in the former and a lack of federal prosecutions in the latter (McGarrell et al., 2007, p. 11).

This analysis led to the development of a tripartite strategy, including elements of suppression, intervention, and prevention. The suppression strategy focused on increasing federal prosecution for gun crimes as a means of removing chronic offenders from the streets and deterring potential offenders from committing gun crimes. The intervention strategy emphasized a community-wide dissemination of the key theme of 'gun crime equals hard time' with the intent of rebuilding the deterrent value of sanctions by emphasizing their impact under the new suppression strategy. The prevention strategy targeted youths through programming in schools to address the problem of students found with firearms, to provide alternatives to violence during the summer months, and to introduce incentives for staying in school.

These research partners also conducted analyses to determine whether the PSN task force strategies were targeting 'the sources of the gun problem' and then collaborated with Michigan State University to assess the impact of the PSN initiative (McGarrell et al., 2007, p. 10). This assessment demonstrated positive, though not conclusive, results, suggesting the promise of this strategy. The number of federal prosecutions of gun crime offences increased significantly, arguably adding to the deterrent effect by making sanctions more credible (McGarrell et al., 2007, p. 16). The programme successfully targeted chronic offenders, removing them from the streets for an average of six years and three months (McGarrell et al., 2007, p. 16). The effect on reducing gun crime was harder to determine. While the review study suggests the programme did have an effect on reducing gun crime, this effect was not consistently large or significant. The programme appeared to reduce the number of gun assaults and homicides by small percentages, but did not seem to affect the rate of armed robbery. A similar review was not conducted on the prevention strategy.

The idea behind PSN is for law-enforcement officials to design innovative strategies for tackling tough crime problems that have eluded traditional criminal justice approaches. While the emphasis is on the enforcement of firearms laws, the strategy also aims to link 'federal, state, and local law enforcement, prosecutors, and community leaders' in a multifaceted approach to deter and punish gun crime (PSN, 2007). The Bush administration provided significant support for this initiative. In addition to expanding the programme geographically, the administration also committed significant funding to projects under the PSN umbrella. The Bush administration provided more than USD 1.5 billion for PSN projects between 2001 and 2008 (PSN, 2007), and a number of case study reviews of PSN projects suggest the promise of these programmes in making progress on reducing the rate of gun crime and access to firearms by chronic offenders.[6]

El Salvador[7]

The current situation in El Salvador has been called an epidemic of violence (BBC, 2004). El Salvador had become one of the most violent countries in the world by the late 1990s, and has one of the highest homicide rates in Latin America. The national homicide rate rose 25 per cent between 2004 and 2005 (USDoS, 2007b) and by 2006 El

[margin note:] e current tion in El has been epidemic violence.

Figure 9.4 **National homicide rate (per 100,000), El Salvador, 1999-2005**

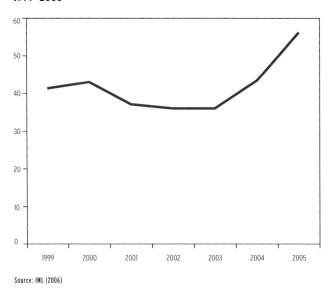

Source: IML (2006)

Salvador registered 56.2 homicides for every 100,000 inhabitants[8] (Comisión Nacional, 2007, p. 25).

The majority of the recorded homicides and injuries in El Salvador are caused by small arms and light weapons. Firearms are used in 80 out of every 100 murders (UNDP–El Salvador, 2006, p. 5), and an estimated half-million firearms are in circulation in the country, although only 211,577 have been registered nationally.[9] Evidence suggests that violence and insecurity have plagued the country since the 1990s[10] despite stringent government measures, such as the national plans *Mano Dura* (Operation Hard Hand) and *Super Mano Dura* (see Box 9.6), put in place to limit the civilian use of firearms (Ávila, 2006, p. 77).

Homicide rates remained steady from 1999 to 2003, with a slight decline between 2001 and 2003 (see Figure 9.4). Since 2003 homicides have consistently increased each year. As in many other parts of the world, violence and homicide pose a particularly large problem for persons under the age of 40. According to the El Salvador National

Map 9.2 **Homicide rates by department (per 100,000), El Salvador, 2006**

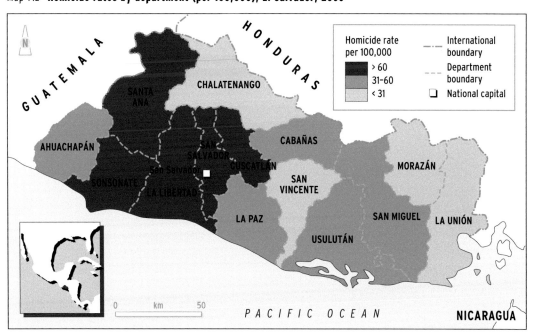

Sources: Comisión Nacional (2007, p. 26); IML (2007)

Box 9.4 Deportation policies adding to gang problems

Gangs, known as *maras* in Central America, contribute to the increasing rate of violence and destabilization in the region (Comisión Nacional, 2007, pp. 39–40). Part of the regional epicenter with Guatemala and Honduras, El Salvador is home to some of the largest and most violent gangs. Two such gangs include the Mara Salvatrucha (or MS-13) and the Eighteenth Street Gang (or M-18). Both are believed to have originated in Los Angeles, California. A conservative estimate in 2006 suggested that at least 100,000 gang members operate in Central America and are involved in violent crimes, including murder, rape, human and drug trafficking, smuggling, extortion, and kidnapping (Lakshmanan, 2006).

Today, maras have links to an estimated 8,000–10,000 gang members across the United States. Major gangs, in particular MS-13 and M-18, have formed alliances with prison officials located in the United States and Central America and with cross-national traffickers. Members of these gangs are notorious for beheadings, mutilations, and torture-killings of rival gang members and those believed to be informants. Given their sophisticated methods and their involvement in violent crime and illegal trafficking, maras are increasingly posing a threat that reaches across national borders (Lakshmanan, 2006).

The transnational nature of gangs today is the result of several factors: a lack of services and opportunities, migration, and deportation trends (USAID, 2006, p. 21). The Washington Office on Latin America reports that the US deportation policy embodied in the Illegal Immigration Reform and Immigration Responsibility Act of 1995 has affected gang evolution in Central America. This act enables the deportation of individuals convicted of a crime after they serve their jail sentences (WOLA, 2006, p. 4). From 1994 to 1997, the United States deported more than 150,000 people back to their countries, leaving these deportees without social networks, local language skills, or family upon their return, which has increased their proclivity to join existing local gangs (WOLA, 2006, p. 4). In 2006, 2,179 criminal aliens were deported to their home countries through Operation Return to Sender, of which 370 were assumed to be MS-13 members (WOLA, 2006, p. 4).

Many of the youth deported are believed to have originally become involved in gang activities while living in the United States, and then joined gangs in their countries of origin upon involuntary return. US deportation policies are not the only reason for the increase in the number of gangs and gang membership in Central America (USAID, 2006, p. 21), but deportation policies and practices are believed to contribute to the problem and to encourage the transnational nature of gangs through member exchange. The United States is proposing more aggressive policies and practices, such as the Alien Gang Removal Act and Operation Community Shield, which attempt to identify and deport gang members based on immigration violations. There are concerns that this could increase gang violence in Central America as well as strengthen the links between US and Central American gang members (WOLA, 2006, p. 4).

Until recently, gangs and related violence were dealt with on a national basis. Central American governments have earmarked between 5 and 25 per cent of their gross national products and received international aid for security purposes, most of which has been dedicated to gang control (VOA, 2007). Within Central America various 'tough' laws have been tried, but these have often overwhelmed the national judicial system rather than reducing the violence. For example, more than 16,000 gang suspects were arrested between 2004 and 2006 under the El Salvadoran Super Mano Dura (Super Hard Hand) plan, which targeted youth suspects with tattoos or gang-style clothing, but only one out of four of these suspects ended up in jail. The barrage of deportees from the United States has further challenged local law enforcement, leading to a blatant disregard for authority by maras. As a result, in El Salvador, Guatemala, and Honduras, soldiers have taken on the role of conducting anti-gang operations (Lakshmanan, 2006).

The growing threat of transnational gang violence combined with limited success at the national level in responding to gang violence has forced the United States, Central American countries, and Mexico to rethink their approaches. These countries are now responding through multinational coordinated efforts, based on a combination of violence prevention, rehabilitation, and prosecution. Regional cooperation includes a series of measures: the improvement of the US deportation process to help deportees become productive community members in their home countries; the enhancement of law-enforcement capabilities; and collaboration among regional police and justice officials to track gang members through joint law-enforcement activities. One such activity involves a fingerprinting strategy under the new Transnational Anti-Gang Unit in El Salvador. This unit is generating a computer database of known offenders to aid in identifying criminals who cross partner country borders (USDoS, 2007a). Additional joint efforts include programmes to keep children out of gangs, community policing, community gang reduction projects, information sharing, and training programmes. Persistent high levels of gang violence in Central America and the United States raise questions about whether the coordinated efforts are working.

Commission for Citizen Security and Social Peace (Comisión Nacional), the vast majority of homicide victims (80.4 per cent) are males between 15 and 39 years of age. However, there was a 50 per cent increase in female homicides from 1999 to 2006 (Comisión Nacional, 2007, pp. 25–26).

Violence is a particularly urban phenomenon in El Salvador. Armed violence is concentrated in the larger cities, with suburbs that have high poverty rates and marginal communities (Comisión Nacional, 2007, p. 12). In 2006 five of the 14 administrative areas ('departments') in the country had extremely high levels of homicide, more than 60 per 100,000, while only two administrative areas reported homicide rates of fewer than 20 per 100,000 (see Map 9.2).

Reported factors that contribute to violence in El Salvador include income inequality, marginalized communities, unemployed youth, US immigration policies (see Box 9.4), and high national poverty levels (Comisión Nacional, 2007, pp. 12–13). The widespread circulation and proliferation of firearms in the civilian population (UNDP, 2005, p. 27), organized crime, and narco-trafficking contribute further to the growing violence. Violence manifests itself in a variety of ways, including homicide, intentional injuries, crime, robbery, physical and sexual aggression and violation, intra-familial violence, child abuse, psychological trauma, extortion, and gang violence.

The cost of violence in El Salvador is estimated at 11.7 per cent of the national gross domestic product (UNDP–El Salvador, 2006, p. 9). According to a 2007 national poll, 44.5 per cent of respondents reported that violence and delinquency were the main problems in the country, 43.8 per cent reported having been victims of crime in public places or on the street, 76.9 per cent reported feeling insecure on buses, while others reported insecurity in markets, plazas, parks, and their communities, and more than 40 per cent indicated a change in their chosen marketplaces and recreational sites in response to the insecurity (Comisión Nacional, 2007, p. 32).

In El Salv
female h
increaseo
per cent
1999 and

Armed violence awareness

Since the late 1990s El Salvador shifted its focus to the prevention of armed violence. Despite political polarization that led to stalemates on nearly every issue, armed violence reduction proved the only issue that has recently received unanimous support among politicians and civil society alike.[11] Within this context, the office of the United Nations Development Programme (UNDP office in San Salvador (UNDP–El Salvador)), in collaboration with its local partners, was instrumental in laying the foundation for armed violence prevention efforts.

In 1998, UNDP–El Salvador sought advice from local and international experts on the problem of armed violence and how to address it. In 2000, UNDP–El Salvador and the National Council for Public Security commissioned research to document the scope, magnitude, and cost of armed violence in El Salvador. This study provided information on the causes of violence, key actors, important risk factors, the health and social costs of violence, and a review of related existing legislation. It also provided a baseline for understanding the problem and developing programmes to reduce armed violence, and resulted in a number of actions taken by a variety of actors. These included efforts to unify relevant data and national sources, the computerization of police crime and hospital entry reports, additional research into armed violence, and the integration of new actors into armed violence prevention efforts (Appiolaza and Godnick, 2003, p. 48). Finally, it laid the framework for ongoing advocacy with government and party representatives on the need to reduce national armed violence.

El Salvador used some of the successful experiences of Colombia to guide its own understanding of armed violence prevention programmes[12]. Interventions implemented in Colombia, including regulations and programmes focused on organized crime, urban violence, and arms control, gained international and regional attention in the 1990s (Small Arms Survey, 2006; Aguirre et al., 2005). Armed violence research provided the basis for the adoption of a number of national and municipal level interventions to counter the high homicide rate and widespread percep-

Box 9.5   Medellín Plan Desarme–a local disarmament plan

In 1991 homicide rates peaked in Medellín, Colombia, at 381 homicides per 100,000 people[13]. This rate dramatically declined in the following decade, from 224 homicides per 100,000 inhabitants in 1995 to 160 in 2000 and 57 in 2004 (Alcadía de Medellín, 2008). In 2007 the homicide rate dropped to 26.3 per 100,000[14]. Contributing to this reduction in homicide rates are the various national regulations, municipal-level action plans, private and civil society sector initiatives, and disarmament, demobilization, and reintegration programmes in the country. The Medellín Plan Desarme has furthered the reduction of homicides. Plan Desarme is a municipal-level intervention implemented in 2004 by UNDP-Colombia in partnership with the Medellín Mayor's Office and the Metropolitan Area of the Aburra Valley. The main objective of the plan is to contribute to the prevention and reduction of violent deaths and injuries of civilians by firearms through a cultural change to confront the problem of violence, strengthen the social fabric of the community, and develop conflict resolution mechanisms within the community.[15]

Plan Desarme emphasizes increased dialogue, public awareness, legislative reform, restrictions on civilians carrying weapons, coordination among actors, and a reorientation of social attitudes towards the censorship of violence and aggressive behaviour. The plan involves various activities, including public debates, education, youth events, symbolic use of public spaces, a public awareness campaign, coordinated research, arms destruction and arms control programmes, and encouragement of voluntary disarmament.

Medellín's Plan Desarme has demonstrated important results. These include the widespread participation of more than 100 organizations, government investment, the destruction of 80,000 weapons in 2005, the collection of an additional 41,000 weapons in 2006 and 2007, of which 28,763 were firearms, the collection of 4,049 toy weapons in 2006 and 2007, the creation of eight participatory youth groups, and the development of new public spaces for community use. Overall an estimated 420,000 people have benefited from the plan through the above and related measures to reduce violence.[16]

tion of insecurity in the country. These programmes, particularly in Bogota, included efforts to make public spaces safer, restrictions on the carrying of weapons, enhanced police enforcement, and curfews on selling alcohol (Aguirre et al., 2005). Many of these programmes showed promising results, serving as a model for other municipalities in Colombia (see Box 9.5), as well as in other countries.

Society without Violence coalition

The original UNDP-led effort and resulting data on national armed violence costs and figures provided the basis for the creation of an inclusive coalition under the name Society without Violence (Sociedad sin Violencia). This unprecedented network linked civil society, the business community, academia, public health and medical practitioners, government representatives, and personally affected civilians in a participatory and comprehensive process aimed at reducing armed violence. Funded by UNDP, the coalition aimed to reach its objective of reducing violence by limiting the number of weapons carried by civilians through judicial reforms. The coalition put forward a strategy and public awareness campaign comprising research, dialogue, capacity building, and advocacy.[17] This campaign generated additional initiatives, including an emphasis on judicial and political reforms, as well as the incorporation of social, medical, and academic perspectives on addressing violence. Although largely inactive today, Society without Violence served as a basic institutional reference point for many subsequent small arms control activities (UNDP, 2005, p. 27), including the World Health Organization's Armed Violence Prevention Programme from January 2004 to December 2007 (WHO, 2007a), the International Physicians for the Prevention of Nuclear War's Aiming for Prevention Programme (IPPNW, 2007), and the Arms-free Municipalities Project, among others (see Box 9.6).

Arms-free Municipalities Project

The Arms-free Municipalities Project (AFMP), launched in 2005, was aimed at imposing local restrictions on civilians carrying weapons. The initial pilot project, implemented at the municipal level, endeavoured to reduce violence

Box 9.6 Additional government efforts to reduce armed violence

The Government of El Salvador has responded to the evidence disseminated in the joint UNDP and National Council report regarding the costs and impacts of armed violence and resulting targeted campaigns. The El Salvador government has agreed to basic reforms of existing laws, which led to some amendments by the Legislative Assembly, including a change in legal weapon-carrying age from 18 to 21, a limit on the number of guns a household can legally own per year, and an extension of the existing temporal prohibition to carry weapons in public spaces to parks, plazas, and gas stations (UNDP-El Salvador, 2006, p. 16).

The government also took measures against gang violence. In October 2003, Decree 158, the Anti-Maras Act, was adopted. In 2003-04 the government enacted strict anti-gang reforms, firearms controls, and penalties through Plans *Mano Dura* (Operation Hard Hand) in July 2003 and *Super Mano Dura* in July 2004. None of these initiatives has helped reduce violence in the country (Ávila, 2006, p. 77); instead they have resulted in increased organization of local and transnational gangs (WOLA, 2006, p. 5).

A tax on firearms was incorporated into the existing taxation law on alcohol and tobacco in December 2005. This taxation, charged at the time of weapon registration, is earmarked for the Fondo Solidario para la Salud (FOSALUD, Health Solidarity Fund). Managed and implemented by the Ministry of Health for public services, the increase in funds is used to expand health service coverage, including through clinics and hospitals in rural areas and night provisions. FOSALUD includes normal health services provided by the Ministry of Health, other than mental health assistance and violence prevention.[18]

The National Commission on Citizen Security and Social Peace was created on 1 November 2006, tasked with seeking a consensus on overcoming the problems of violence, delinquency, and insecurity, which resulted in the articulation of a series of short-, medium-, and long-term proposals encompassing prevention, rehabilitation, reinsertion, and countering crime (Comisión Nacional, 2007, p. 5).

In December 2006, Decree 176 was adopted. This decree enables municipalities to prohibit civilians from carrying weapons within a given municipality for a specified time period. Under the decree, any municipality has the right to apply to the Ministry of Security to impose this prohibition for a 90-day period. The criteria for gaining permission to do so include an increased rate of violence, a high number of violent incidents, an increase in firearms in circulation, the negative impact of armed violence on people, and the presence of gang delinquents. Only one of these criteria, demonstrated by police and medical records or national polls, is necessary to obtain approval. To date no application has been denied. Two municipalities are expected to maintain a consistent prohibition: San Salvador since 29 March 2007, and Soyapango since 14 August 2007.

through local restriction. UNDP–El Salvador and the National Council on Public Security, in coordination with the National Civilian Police, the Metropolitan Police Corps, and two municipalities near the capital city, namely, San Martín and Ilopango, joined efforts to implement the pilot phase of this project. The pilot phase produced mixed results and provided a model for other municipalities to follow.

According to UNDP–El Salvador (2006, p. 12), the AFMP interventions aimed to achieve six goals. These goals included: municipal-level laws restricting the carrying of arms in all public places; an increase in policing capacity to enforce this prohibition; a mass publicity campaign on the dangers of firearms and the new regulations on carrying weapons; the voluntary surrender and collection of firearms; evaluative research on the impact of the project components; and an analysis of the overall experience in order to inform legislative debate and serve as a model for other municipalities.

In the case of San Martín, many aspects of the programme could be considered successful. The project was implemented in a timely fashion beginning in August 2005. San Martín experienced a reduction in its homicide rate (UNDP–El Salvador, 2006, p. 43). Local people were active in the project implementation, including the governing mayor. The local leadership change in March 2006 did not affect the level of political support for the project. Campaign visibility was widespread, with announcements on radio stations and materials posted on billboards and buses, and in bars and restaurants (UNDP–El Salvador, 2006, p. 19). The programme also provided benefits through a number of workshops, the provision of new equipment and hiring of new officers in the security offices, and the

creation of a computer program for mapping criminal incidents in the municipality. The municipality successfully implemented a prohibition on carrying firearms in October 2006. Overall, the project involved cooperation among the project committees, coordination units, and local actors.

In Ilopango the programme reported fewer successes and experienced more challenges in implementation. The challenges resulted largely from disputes among political parties and the poor relations between these parties. Disagreement among the implementing partners delayed the start of the programme. The local mayor's office was not supportive in the early implementation stages, and the project was subjected to allegations of political manoeuvring (UNDP–El

▶ran police) enter the suspected ber during operation no Dura in ober 2004. a/Reuters

Salvador, 2006, p. 22). During the elections all activities stopped. Despite these difficulties, the programme in Ilopango did make some progress with the training of security officials, the provision of new equipment to these forces, and the hiring of new officers. In addition, following the elections the newly elected officials restarted the programme.

One of the major difficulties the project faced was the divisive politics of the country. The poor relations between the two major political parties generated a number of roadblocks to implementation. The local leadership of San Martín came from the ruling party, whereas Ilopango represented the main opposition party. Local leaders of Ilopango saw the AFMP as a national government platform (UNDP–El Salvador, 2006, p. 21), even through the programme was based on local perspectives and balanced political representation. Support for the programme declined in the early stages due to eroding political support for the ruling party at the local and national levels, as well as political manoeuvres by the opposition party to depict the programme as a threat to civilian rights to own firearms. This led to criticisms of the AFMP agenda and strategy. With the integration of disarmament measures into the political platform of the opposition party, critics pointed to the increased politicization of the programme. Although the project recovered some of its momentum through hours of diplomacy and lobbying by UNDP and supporting local partners, doubts remained about levels of support from some members of government (UNDP–El Salvador, 2006, p. 21). While several national and local government institutions proved to be cooperative in the process, many local government leaders consistently resisted the programme, which reduced the participation of local leaders.

Despite various difficulties, the project did report the following successes in reducing armed violence in the municipalities during 2005 and early 2006 (Jiménez, González, and Ramírez Landaverde, 2006, p. 87): in total, 64 arms-free spaces were identified and created in the two municipalities, sustained by local police vigilance; in San Martín, firearms crimes were reduced by 29 per cent and the homicide rate declined by 47 per cent; and, despite an early delay in initiating the programme in Ilopango, the municipality experienced a 24 per cent reduction in crime

Figure 9.5 **Monthly firearm homicide rates in Ilopango and San Martín municipalities (smoothed average), January 2004–August 2006**

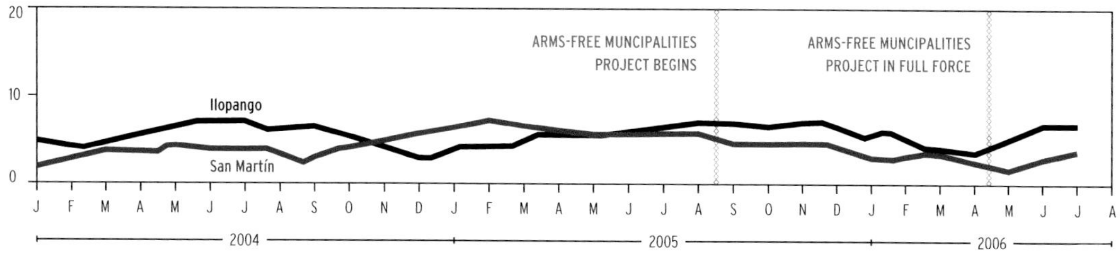

Source: UNDP-El Salvador (2006, p. 42)

and a 47 per cent reduction in homicides. However, by April 2006, when UNDP considered the programme to be in full effect, evidence suggested that the rate of homicide had begun to stabilize or even increase once again in these municipalities (UNDP–El Salvador, 2006, p. 41), suggesting an end to the positive downward trend (see Figure 9.5). At the end of 2006, Ilopango witnessed an increase in the municipality's homicide rate (UNDP–El Salvador, 2006, p. 41).

UNDP–El Salvador (2006, pp. 55–61) reported a number of conclusions from the pilot project. The AFMP programme successfully implemented the majority of its planned activities and is considered a model for extension to other municipalities. A number of involved institutions demonstrated an ability to coordinate actions and data collection. The policing of firearms violations improved, and a database for registering and mapping crimes was established. AFMP contributed to the ongoing national debate on firearms and the means to address their devastating effects.

The project also faced a number of challenges. The implementation of the project was delayed on several occasions for a variety of administrative and political reasons. The motives of politicians supporting the programme were called into question, reducing support for the initiative. It was not possible to complete a full evaluation of the project due to data limitations. Finally, it was not possible to confirm whether the project resulted in a reduction in the number of firearms purchased during the implementation period.

El Salvador is currently experiencing a snowball effect in its armed violence prevention efforts. Early activities have led to new violence prevention programmes and legislative reforms initiated by actors at all levels, increasing the momentum behind legal reform and violence reduction in the country. Project evaluations and public opinion polls are starting to record a slight decline in the level of armed violence in intervention sites, as well as a small increase in popular perceptions of security in the country[19]. The National Commission has recommended to the president specific actions to reduce violence, including an expansion of the AFMP. The sustainability of these efforts and their continued positive impact on reducing homicide rates is unknown. The challenge will be maintaining the momentum at the municipal and national levels and learning how to adequately confront other forms of violence, such as gang violence and organized crime.

LESSONS LEARNT FROM PAST INTERVENTIONS

The number of evaluations of armed violence prevention programmes, while still limited, has grown. 'The uniqueness of communities precludes a blanket prescription for all locales' (Mercy et al., 1993, p. 21). While each intervention generates lessons learnt from its own design and implementation, these insights are largely contextual to the com-

Table 9.4 Promising interventions for preventing youth from engaging in crime

Intervention	Effectiveness	Reason for success
Parenting classes	Effective	Reduces violence in the home and improves supervision and parenting
Home visits to high-risk homes	Effective	Reduces violence in the home and improves supervision and parenting
Incentives to finish school	Promising	Provides basis for employment
Conflict resolution training	Promising	Provides skills for handling conflicts through non-violent means
Life skills training programmes	Promising	Provides employment opportunities and alternatives to criminal activity

Sources: Buvinic and Morrison (1999); Wasserman, Miller, and Cothern (2000)

munity at hand, and therefore must be considered carefully when trying to replicate the intervention under different circumstances. Despite these limitations, a number of general lessons emerge from these assessments.

Interventions since the late 1980s demonstrate that early interventions work best and that long-term programming is better than short-term or one-off interventions (Rutherford et al., 2007, p. 768; Rosenberg et al., 2006, p. 761). This suggests that primary prevention efforts should be targeting infants and children, and their parents, before problems arise. Addressing violent behaviour once it begins is far more difficult than preventing its onset.

Sustained long-term interventions over a number of years are likely to be more effective than short-term or one-time interventions (Rutherford et al., 2007, p. 768). Those interventions that show promise in preventing violence and crime include home visitation, parent training, social skills training for youth, conflict resolution skills training, job skills training, and incentives for youths to finish their education (Mercy et al., 1993, p. 14; Rosenberg et al., 2006, p. 762). The success of these programmes stems in part from their long-term nature and the fact that these programmes provide the necessary training and skill sets for individuals of various ages to enter into productive lives and to resolve conflicts through non-violent means.

A number of interventions target one risk factor or one type of individual. These are unlikely to achieve a great deal of success alone. Single-focus interventions are not likely to succeed due to the complexity of factors that influ-

Table 9.5 Interventions demonstrating limited success

Intervention	Reason for lack of effectiveness
Gun safety training	Focuses on changing behaviour that is difficult to alter
Gun buy-back programmes	Do not address supply of weapons or reasons for demand
Disarmament programmes	Do not address supply of weapons or reasons for demand
Peer-based counselling	Interaction with negative peers can encourage delinquency
Shock programmes, 'Scared straight'	Often short-term or one-time programmes aimed at scaring youths by introducing them to jails and prisoners

Sources: Hardy (2002); Marsh (2007); Sherman et al. (1997)

Box 9.7   Jamaica's Crime Observatory

While Jamaica is a popular tourist destination, it has one of the highest homicide rates in the world and is home to gang warfare and a bustling drug trade. These illicit activities contributed to Jamaica's high homicide rate of 50 per 100,000 in 2004 and 63 per 100,000 in 2005. In response to rising homicide and crime levels, the country's Violence Prevention Alliance created the Crime Observatory in 2006. Various stakeholders participate in the Crime Observatory, including government agencies and departments, non-governmental organizations, community associations, and members of the private sector. The primary purpose of the Observatory is to collect data on crime and violence in communities from a wide variety of sources—the police, the health department, churches, and NGOs—in order to understand the nature of the problem, inform violence prevention strategies, and measure the impact of these strategies. The Crime Observatory contributes to reducing violence by identifying 'hot spots', or communities with high rates of crime and violence, which can be targeted with context-specific programming.

Sources: Economist (2005); VPA Jamaica (2006; 2007)

ence risk and resilience (Wasserman, Miller, and Cothern, 2000, p. 10). The ecological model presumes that 'violence is the product of multiple and overlapping levels of influence on behaviour' (Rosenberg et al., 2006, p. 761). If this premise is valid, then interventions should either target multiple risk factors within a single programme or combine several single-focus programmes into a coherent whole.

If armed violence prevention programmes require a multifaceted approach, or the coordination of multiple concurrent programmes, then successful implementation will depend upon the collaborative efforts of a wide range of organizations. Comprehensive understanding of the violence problem will come only from shared knowledge and collaborative efforts. An important role for public health is to establish effective working relationships among the sectors involved in violence prevention efforts, including 'education, labour, public housing, media, business, medicine, and criminal justice' (Mercy et al., 1993, p. 16). Each of these sectors can target a specific aspect of the violence problem. What is needed is collaboration and cooperation across these sectors in order to share information, economize on resources, build efficiencies, and improve the capacity to address multiple risk factors at the same time (see Box 9.7). One way of encouraging cooperation is the development of national action plans for armed violence prevention that provide an organizing structure, indicate political support, and incorporate the actions of non-state actors (Rosenberg et al., 2006, p. 766).

Table 9.6   Effectiveness of national interventions

Intervention	Effectiveness
Reducing access to weapons by high-risk individuals	Promising
Reducing availability of alcohol at events or during volatile periods of time	Promising, evidence of effectiveness
Child Access Prevention (CAP) laws	Ineffective in preventing child access to weapons or improving safety behaviour of parents
Grip safety	Potential to reduce unintentional injury; no effect on intentional injury
Loaded chamber indicator	Potential to reduce unintentional injury; no effect on intentional injury
Magazine disconnect device	Potential to reduce unintentional injury; no effect on intentional injury
Personalized guns	Potential to reduce unintentional and intentional injury

Sources: Ceaser (2007); Hardy (2002); Teret and Culross (2002)

Table 9.7 **Community interventions**	
Intervention	**Effectiveness**
Community policing	Helps to reduce fear of crime Little evidence that it actually reduces crime
Hot-spot policing	Promising
Targeted policing	Promising
Street lighting	Helps to reduce fear of crime Unclear whether it actually reduces crime levels

Sources: Braga et al. (2001); Waller and Sansfaçon (2000)

A number of countries have implemented nationally based interventions, such as federal regulations or laws on gun ownership, product safety features, and the right to carry. These measures have produced mixed results (see Table 9.6).

Many armed violence prevention programmes are implemented at the community level. Data collection on the nature and scope of violence and the environment in which violence occurs should drive intervention design. Interventions should be tailored to community conditions, to the causes of violence, and to those at risk of committing violent offences. In designing interventions, 'we must listen to the communities that are affected and understand what they consider to be the best approaches to preventing violence among their residents' (Mercy et al., 1993, p. 25). The effectiveness of these community programmes will depend largely on the level of community commitment to addressing the problem and community involvement in implementing programmes targeting violence and violent offenders.

This discussion of interventions suggests there is no simple means of preventing armed violence. The distinction between unintentional and intentional injury with firearms is important to the design of interventions. Unintentional injury is easier to address with changes to the product, while intentional injury requires both environmental and behavioural changes. A number of programmes show promise for reducing armed violence. These programmes require additional implementation in a variety of settings to determine their applicability across communities as well as more rigorous assessment of their impact on reducing armed violence.

CONCLUSION

Due to numerous local, national, and international initiatives since the late 1980s, much more is known about the causes of violence, the risk and resilience factors that influence exposure to violence, and the various programmes available to prevent armed violence. Although no silver bullet exists for ending armed violence, assessments of interventions suggest programmes that are promising and those that are ineffective in addressing violence. Analysis of past efforts points to a number of key ingredients for successful interventions: they should be science-based, community developed and implemented, multifaceted, and financially, publicly, and politically supported.

The inability of the public health sector to demonstrate clearly which interventions are effective in preventing armed violence, as well as being cost-effective, reduces the attractiveness of these interventions. Improving armed violence prevention programming will require investing in research and data collection, analysing collected data, designing interventions based on data, implementing interventions with clear goals and timelines and in such a fashion as to enable assessment, and assessing these interventions in a rigorous fashion that produces a better understanding of what works, what does not, and why. The lessons can then be used to replicate successful interventions in other communities and countries. They can provide the means for low- and middle-income countries to learn from lessons elsewhere, although these countries must also experiment within their own community contexts to determine what works best for them. Improving armed violence prevention efforts will depend heavily on persuading developing countries that violence prevention is a priority, not a luxury.

Public health professionals are in a unique position to demonstrate the importance of doing more to reduce armed violence in a scientific fashion. They can promote armed violence prevention as a public good aimed at increasing security and improving public health. This shift from security as a private concern to security as a community good can contribute to clearing away the political roadblocks to using a variety of means to address armed violence rather than relying on a criminal justice approach alone. It can also lessen the perceptions that paint armed violence prevention as an attack on personal freedoms rather than an effort to promote public health. ◤

LIST OF ABBREVIATIONS

AFMP	Arms-free Municipalities Project	PSN	Project Safe Neighborhoods
CDC	Center for Disease Control	OECD–DAC	Organisation for Economic Co-operation
FOSALUD	Health Solidarity Fund, El Salvador		and Development–Development
M-18	Eighteenth Street Gang		Assistance Committee
MS-13	Mara Salvatrucha	UNDP	UN Development Programme
NCVS	National Crime Victimization Survey		

ENDNOTES

1   The Small Arms Survey is currently contributing to the development of the OECD–DAC *Guidance on Armed Violence Reduction and Development,* which should be publicly available in 2009.

2   For additional examples of different approaches to various types of violence, see Decker et al. (2007); Krug et al. (2002); Moser and Shrader (1999).

3   This discussion draws on the work of the Small Arms Survey on the OECD–DAC *Guidance on Armed Violence Reduction and Development* (OECD–DAC, 2009).

4   This section is based in part on LeBrun (2007).

5   This data can be found at <http://www.atf.gov/firearms/trace_data/index.htm>

6   Case study reports and other documentation of the PSN programme can be found at <http://www.psn.gov/pubs/index.aspx>

7   Chris Stevenson conducted field research in El Salvador in August 2007 in support of the OECD–DAC Guidance (2009) and this chapter.

8   The Government of El Salvador completed a national census in late 2007. According to preliminary results, the estimated population *increased* from 6.5 million to 7.1 million habitants. Using this new estimate, and on the assumption that the number of homicides remains constant, the national homicide rate would be 68 per 100,000. The census is to be published in 2008. For more details, see <http://www.elpais.com/articulo/internacional/Violencia/guerra/Salvador/elpepuintlat/20070827elpepuint_2/Tes>

9   Interview with Inspector Carlos Cornejos, Weapons Division, National Civilian Police, San Salvador, 16 August 2007.

10   El Salvador has seen a flux in homicide rates since the signing of the Peace Agreement in 1992. Immediately afterwards the violence decreased, but only briefly. By the mid-1990s, the homicide rate had reached nearly 150 deaths per 100,000 inhabitants, and was 80 deaths per 100,000 inhabitants in 1998. See UNDP (2005) and Paniagua et al. (2005).

11   Interview with Dr. José Mauricio Loucel, Rector, Coordinator of Comisión Nacional para la Seguridad Ciudadana y la Paz Social, Universidad Tecnológica, San Salvador, 17 August 2007. This was reiterated in several other interviews.

12   Interview with Marcela Smutt, UNDP, San Salvador, 17 August 2007.

13   Presentation by Carlos Morales, Coordinator of Plan Desarme, UN Habitat State of Cities Conference, Monterrey, Mexico, 3 October 2007.

14   See note 13.

15   See note 13.

16   See note 13.

17   SAS interview with Marcela Smutt, UNDP, San Salvador, 17 August 2007.

18   Interview and subsequent discussions with Dr. Emperatriz Crespín, Director, Latin American Public Health Network of IANSA and IPPNW, and independent consultant, PAHO El Salvador. San Salvador, 14 August 2007.

19   Interviews and subsequent discussions with various respondents in San Salvador, August 2007. See also UNDP (2006) and Comisión Nacional (2007).

BIBLIOGRAPHY

Aguirre, Katherine et al. 2005. 'Assessing the Effect of Policy Interventions on Small Arms Demand in Bogotá, Colombia.' Unpublished background paper. Centro de Recursos para el Análisis de Conflictos (CERAC), Bogotá. Geneva: Small Arms Survey. 29 October.

Alcaldía de Medellín (Medellín Mayor's Office). 2008. *Medellín en Cifras*. Centro Administrativo Municipal. Accessed 5 March 2008.
    <http://urbanismosocialmedellin.universia.net.co/downloads/articulos/medellin_cifras.pdf>

Appioloza, Martín and William Godnick. 2003. *Armas. . . ni de juguete: Una iniciativa para el control de armas pequeñas en El Salvador*. San Salvador: UNDP.

ATF (Bureau of Alcohol, Tobacco and Firearms). 2000a. *Commerce in Firearms in the United States*. Washington, DC: US Department of the Treasury. February.

—. 2000b. *Following the Gun: Enforcing Federal Laws against Firearms Traffickers*. Washington, DC: US Department of the Treasury. June.

Ávila, Rodrigo. 2006. 'Armed Violence Control and Prevention in El Salvador.' In *Regional Forum for the Exchange of Experiences in the Prevention and Control of Armed Violence*. San Salvador: UNDP, pp. 76–80.

BBC (British Broadcasting Corporation). 2004. 'Combating El Salvador's Gangs.' 20 March. Accessed 20 October 2007.
    <http://news.bbc.co.uk/2/hi/americas/3553529.stm>

Braga, Anthony A., et al. 2001. 'Problem-Oriented Policing, Deterrence, and Youth Violence: An Evaluation of Boston's Operation Ceasefire.' Draft paper, 1 March. Published in *Journal of Research in Crime and Delinquency*, Vol. 38, No. 3. August, pp. 195–225.

Buvinic, Mayra and Andrew Morrison. 1999. *Preventing Violence*. Violence Prevention Technical Note 5. Washington, DC: Inter-American Development Bank. July.

Calonge, Ned. 2005. 'Community Interventions to Prevent Violence: Translation into Public Health Practice.' *American Journal of Preventive Medicine*, Vol. 28, pp. 4–5.

Cardwell, D. 2006. 'Two Gun Dealers Settle Lawsuit with the City.' *New York Times*. 1 August.

Catalano, Shannan M. 2006. 'National Crime Victimization Survey: Criminal Victimization, 2005.' *US Bureau of Justice Statistics Bulletin NCJ 214644*. Washington, DC: USDoJ, Office of Justice Programs. September.

CDC (Centers for Disease Control and Prevention). 2007. 'Youth Violence.' *Facts At A Glance*. Summer.

—. WISQARS (US Centers for Disease Control and Prevention Web-based Injury Statistics Query and Reporting System). 2008. Accessed 6 March 2008.
    <http://webappa.cdc.gov/sasweb/ncipc/mortrate.html> For general information about WISQARS see <http://www.cdc.gov/ncipc/wisqars/>

Ceaser, Mike. 2007. 'Colombia Continues to Struggle with Violence.' *Lancet*, Vol. 370, No. 10, pp. 1601–02.

Comisión Nacional para la Seguridad Ciudadana y Paz Social. 2007. *Seguridad y Paz, un reto de país: Recomendaciones para una política de Seguridad Ciudadana en El Salvador*. San Salvador: Secretaría Técnica. <http://www.pnud.org.sv/2007/content/view/27/83?id_publ=14>

Corso, Phaedra S., et al. 2007. 'Medical Costs and Productivity Losses Due to Interpersonal and Self-Directed Violence in the United States.' *American Journal of Preventive Medicine*, Vol. 32, No. 6, pp. 474–82.

CSPV (Centre for the Study and Prevention of Violence). 1996. 'Blueprints for Violence Prevention Overview.' <http://www.colorado.edu/cspv/blueprints>

Dalton, Juan José. 2007. 'Violencia de guerra en El Salvador: Las tasas de homicidios en el país más pequeño de la América continental se acercan peligrosamente a los índices que se registran durante los conflictos armados.' *El País* (San Salvador). 28 August.

Decker, Scott H., et al. 2007. *Project Safe Neighborhoods: Strategic Interventions. Strategic Problem-Solving Responses to Gang Crime and Gang Problems: Case Study 8*. Washington, DC: USDoJ. February.

Economist. 2005. 'Calling Scotland Yard.' 11 August.

FBI (Federal Bureau of Investigations). 2007a. Supplementary Homicide Reports, 1976–2005. Accessed 19 October 2007.
    <http://www.ojp.usdoj.gov/bjs/homicide/hmrt.htm>

—. 2007b. Uniform Crime Reports, 1950–2005. Accessed 19 October 2007. <http://www.ojp.usdoj.gov/bjs/homicide/hmrt.htm>

—. 2008. Crime in the United States. Accessed 18 February 2008. <http://www.fbi.gov/ucr/cius2006/data/table_04.html>

Geneva Declaration (Geneva Declaration on Armed Violence and Development). 2006. 7 June.
<http://www.genevadeclaration.org/geneva-declaration.html>

Gonzalez, Alberto R. 2006. Transcript of Attorney General Alberto R. Gonzales' One-Year Anniversary Speech. Washington, DC. 15 February.

Hardy, Marjorie S. 2002. 'Behavior-Oriented Approaches to Reducing Youth Gun Violence.' *The Future of Children*, Vol. 12, No. 2 (Autumn), pp. 100–117.

Hemenway, David. 2001. 'The Public Health Approach to Motor Vehicles, Tobacco, and Alcohol, with Applications to Firearms Policy.' *Journal of Public Health Policy*, Vol. 22, No. 4, pp. 381–402.

IML (Instituto de Medicina Legal). 2006. *Boletín Sobre Homicidios*. Corte Suprema de Justicia, Instituto de Medicina Legal Dr. Roberto Masferrer Unidad de Estadísticas Forenses, Año 2, No. 1, January. <http://www.csj.gob.sv/iml/docs/IML_BOLETIN_HOMIC_0201.pdf>

—. 2007. *Anuario Estadístico 'Defunciones Por Homicidios en El Salvador': Período Enero-Diciembre 2005*. Dr. Roberto Masferrer Unidad de Estadísticas Forenses, Corte de Suprema de Justicia. July.

IPPNW (International Physicians for the Prevention of Nuclear War). 2007. *Aiming for Prevention*. <http://www.ippnw.org/Programs/AFP/index.html>

Jiménez, Armando, Mario González, and Mauricio Ramírez Landaverde. 2006. 'Municipalities Free of Arms Project.' In *Regional Forum for the Exchange of Experiences in the Prevention and Control of Armed Violence*. San Salvador: UNDP, pp. 84–88.

Kennedy, David M. 1997. 'Pulling Levers: Chronic Offenders, High-Crime Settings, and a Theory of Prevention.' *Valparaiso University Law Review*, Vol. 31, No. 2. Spring, pp. 449–84.

—. 1998. 'Pulling Levers: Getting Deterrence Right.' *National Institute of Justice Journal*, No. 236. July, pp. 2–8.

Kerezsi, Klara and Daniel Sansfaçon. 1999. *Prevention of Crime: Harnessing What Works. Synthesis Report on the Montreal International Conference*. Montreal: International Centre for the Prevention of Crime.

Krug, Etienne G., et al., eds. 2002. *World Report on Violence and Health*. Geneva: World Health Organization.

Lab, Steven P. 2008. 'Crime Prevention.' In Shlomo Giora Shohan, Ori Beck, and Martin Kett, eds. *International Handbook of Penology and Criminal Justice*. Boca Raton, Florida: CRC Press, pp. 231–93.

Lakshmanan, Indira A.R. 2006. 'Gangs Roil in Central America: Troubles Linked to US Deportees'. *Boston Globe*. 17 April.
<http://www.boston.com/news/world/latinamerica/articles/2006/04/17/gangs_roil_central_america/>

LeBrun, Emile. 2007. *Recent Innovative Approaches to Preventing Criminal Access to Firearms in the United States*. Unpublished background paper. Geneva: Small Arms Survey.

Ludwig, Jens. 2005. 'Better Gun Enforcement, Less Crime.' *Criminology and Public Policy*, Vol. 4, No. 4, pp. 667–716.

Marsh, Nicholas. 2007. 'Taming the Tools of Violence.' *Journal of Public Health Policy*, Vol. 28, pp. 401–09.

Mayors Against Illegal Guns. 2007. Accessed 17 December 2007.
<http://www.mayorsagainstillegalguns.org/html/about/about.shtml>

—. 2008. Accessed 18 February 2008. <http://www.mayorsagainstillegalguns.org/html/federal/tiahrt.shtml>

McDevitt, Jack, Anthony A. Braga, and Shea Cronin. 2007. *Project Safe Neighborhoods: Strategic Interventions. Lowell, District of Massachusetts: Case Study 6*. Washington, DC: USDoJ. February

McGarrell, Edmund F., et al. 2007. *Project Safe Neighborhoods: Strategic Interventions. Middle District of Alabama: Case Study 5*. Washington, DC: USDoJ. February.

Mercy, James A., et al. 1993. 'Public Health Policy for Preventing Violence.' *Health Affairs*, Vol. 12, No. 4. Winter, pp. 7–29.

Moore, Mark H. 1995. 'Public Health and Criminal Justice Approaches to Prevention.' *Crime and Justice*, Vol. 19, pp. 237–62.

Moser, Caroline and Elizabeth Shrader. 1999. *A Conceptual Framework for Violence Reduction*. Latin America and Caribbean Region, Sustainable Development Working Paper No. 2. Washington, DC: World Bank. August.

Muggah, Robert and Keith Krause. 2007. Room Document B. 'Framing Contexts and Responses to Armed Violence: Perspectives from Latin America and the Caribbean.' The DAC Network on Conflict, Peace, and Development Co-Operation (CPDC). Security and Development Task Team Meeting. Paris, May.

NIJ (National Institute of Justice). 2004. *Research Report: Reducing Gun Violence. The St. Louis Consent-to-Search Program*. Washington, DC: USDoJ, Office of Justice Programs. November.

OECD–DAC (Organisation for Economic Co-operation and Development–Development Assistance Committee). 2009 (forthcoming). *Guidance on Armed Violence Reduction and Development*. Paris: OECD–DAC.

Paniagua, Igacio, Emperatriz Crespin, Ademar Guardado, and Ana Mauricio. 2005. 'Wounds Caused by Firearms in El Salvador, 2003–2004: Epidemiological Issues.' *Medicine, Conflict and Survival*, Vol. 21, No. 3, pp. 191–98.

Powell, Elizabeth C., Karen M. Sheehan, and Katherine Kaufer Christoffel. 1996. 'Firearm Violence Among Youth: Public Health Strategies for Prevention.' *Annals of Emergency Medicine*, Vol. 28, No. 2. August, pp. 204–12.

PSN (Project Safe Neighborhoods). 2007. *Making America's Communities Safer*. <http://www.psn.gov/about/execsumm.html>

Rosenberg, Mark L., et al. 2006. 'Interpersonal Violence.' In Dean T Jamison et al., eds. *Disease Control Priorities in Developing Countries*, 2nd edn. New York: Oxford University Press, ch. 40.

Rutherford, Alison, et al. 2007. 'Violence: A Priority for Public Health? (part 2).' *Journal of Epidemiology and Community Health*, Vol. 61, pp. 764–70.

Sheppard, David. 1999. 'Strategies to Reduce Gun Violence.' OJJDP Fact Sheet No. 93. Washington, DC: USDoJ. February.

Sherman, Lawrence W., et al. 1997. *Preventing Crime: What Works, What Doesn't, What's Promising*. Report to the United States Congress, Prepared for the National Institute of Justice. A summary of the findings can be found at <http://www.ncjrs.gov/pdffiles/171676.pdf>

Small Arms Survey. 2006. *Small Arms Survey 2006: Unfinished Business*. Oxford: Oxford University Press.

—. 2007. *Small Arms Survey 2007: Guns and the City*. Cambridge: Cambridge University Press.

Sniffen, Michael J. 2000. 'Violent Crime Plummets in U.S.' *Chicago Sun Times*. 28 August.

Store, Jonas Gahr, et al. 2007. 'Oslo Ministerial Declaration – Global Health: A Pressing Foreign Policy Issue of Our Time.' *Lancet*, Vol. 369, No. 9570. 21 April, pp. 1373–78.

Teret, Stephen P. and Patti L. Culcross. 2002. 'Product-Oriented Approaches to Reducing Youth Gun Violence'. *Future of Children*, Vol. 12, No. 2. Summer/Fall, pp. 119–31.

UNDP (United Nations Development Programme). 2005. *Securing Development: UNDP's Support for Addressing Small Arms Issues*. New York: UNDP.

UNDP–El Salvador. 2006. *Living without Arms? Evaluation of the Arms-free Municipalities Project: An Experience in Risk-Taking in a Risky Context*. San Salvador: UNDP.

USAID (US Agency for International Development). 2006. *Central America and Mexico Gang Assessment*. <http://www.usaid.gov/locations/latin_america_caribbean/democracy/gangs_cam.pdf>

USDoJ (US Department of Justice). Bureau of Justice Statistics. 2007. Accessed 19 October 2007. <http://www.ojp.usdoj.gov/bjs/glance/viort.htm>

USDoS (US Department of State). 2007a. 'U.S.–Central American Cooperation Focuses on Fighting Gangs. Stopping gang violence part of U.S. security plan for region.' America.gov. 24 July. <http://www.america.gov/st/foraid-english/2007/July/200707241205091xeneerg0.4201471.html>

—. 2007b. Consular Information Sheet: El Salvador. 3 October. <http://travel.state.gov/travel/cis_pa_tw/cis/cis_1109.html>

VOA (Voice of America). 2007. 'Gang Violence Spreads Across US, Central American Borders.' 30 November. <http://www.voanews.com/english/archive/2007-11/2007-11-30-voa32.cfm?CFID=18795617&CFTOKEN=72066332>

VPA (Violence Prevention Alliance) Jamaica. 2006. *Crime Observatory Newsletter*. Vol. 1, No. 1 (November).

—. 2007. *Crime Observatory Newsletter*. Vol. 2, No. 1 (April).

Waller, Irvin and Daniel Sansfaçon. 2000. *Investing Wisely in Crime Prevention: International Experiences*. Washington, DC: USDoJ, Bureau of Justice Assistance. September.

Wasserman, Gail A., Laurie S. Miller, and Lynn Cothern. 2000. 'Prevention of Serious and Violent Juvenile Offending.' *Juvenile Justice Bulletin*. Washington, DC: USDoJ. May.

Webster, Daniel, Jon Vernick, and Lisa Hepburn. 2001. 'Relationship Between Licensing, Registration and Other State Gun Sales Laws and the Source State of Crime Guns.' *Injury Prevention*, Vol. 7, No. 3, pp. 184–89.

Webster, Daniel, Jon Vernick, and Maria Bulzacchelli. 2006. 'Effects of a Gun Dealer's Change in Sales Practices on the Supply of Guns to Criminals.' *Journal of Urban Health*. Vol. 83, No. 5, pp. 778–87.

Webster, Daniel, Jon Vernick and Stephen Teret. 2006. 'How Cities Can Combat Illegal Guns and Gun Violence.' Johns Hopkins Center for Gun Policy and Research. Baltimore: Johns Hopkins Bloomberg School of Public Health, October.

Webster, Daniel, et al. 2002. 'How Delinquent Youths Acquire Guns: Initial Versus Most Recent Gun Acquisitions'. *Journal of Urban Health*, Vol. 79, No. 1, pp. 60–69.

—. 2006. 'Effects of Undercover Police Stings of Gun Dealers on the Supply of New Guns to Criminals.' *Injury Prevention*, Vol. 12, No. 4, pp. 225–30.

Wintemute, Garen. 2007. 'Gun Shows Across a Multistate American Gun Market: Observational Evidence of the Effects of Regulatory Policies.' *Injury Prevention*, Vol. 13, No. 3, pp. 150–56.

—, Philip Cook, and M.A. Wright. 2005. 'Risk Factors Among Handgun Retailers for Frequent and Disproportionate Sales of Guns Used in Violent and Firearm Related Crimes.' *Injury Prevention*, Vol. 11, No. 6, pp. 357–363.

WOLA (Washington Office on Latin America). 2006. *Youth Gangs in Central America: Issues in Human Rights, Effective Policing, and Prevention*. WOLA Special Report. Washington, DC: WOLA. November.

WHO (World Health Organization). 2007a. 'Armed Violence Prevention Programme (AVPP) Programme Document and Project Brief.' <http://www.who.int/violence_injury_prevention/violence/activities/armed_violence/en/index.html>

—. 2007b. *Third Milestones of a Global Campaign for Violence Prevention Report: Scaling Up*. Geneva: WHO.

ACKNOWLEDGEMENTS

Principal authors

Jennifer M. Hazen and Chris Stevenson

Contributor

Emperatriz Crespín

INDEX

A

AAGs *see* anti-aircraft guns
adults, violence risk factors 252
Afghanistan
  MANPADS
    attacks on aircraft 13
    destruction programmes 101
    diversion 119, 120, 125
  non-state actors, light weapons
    holdings 32
  surplus weapons transferred to 79,
    81
  violent incidents 232–3
Africa, firearm homicides and suicides
    219
age
  see also youth
  violence risk factors 251–3, 258
AGS-17 grenade launcher 24
aircraft
  MANPADS attacks 12, 13
  use for diversions 115–16
AKM rifles, diversion to Colombia 113
Albania
  ammunition
    diversion 52
    stockpiles 91, 93
  MANPADS, destruction programmes
    101
  surplus weapons, destruction
    programmes 97
alcohol, and violence 222, 264, 275
Alcotan-100 rocket launcher 25
Algeria, non-state actors, light weapons
    holdings 32
al-Qaeda, guided light weapons
    holdings 33
Al-Qassam rockets, Gaza 15
ammunition
  calibre compatibility 45–6
  diversion 45, 52
    Albania 52
    Brazil 45, 46, 52
    Israel 52
    Kenya 51, 52
    Peru 52
    Uganda 51
  measurement of 89, 90–1
  military requirements 89–94
  security risk coding 50
  surplus 89–94
  tons 90

Angola
  MANPADS attacks on aircraft 13
  non-state actors, light weapons
    holdings 32
  surplus weapons, destruction
    programmes 97
anti-aircraft guns (AAGs), countries
  producing 34–5
anti-materiel rifles
  countries producing 34–5
  prices 22
  types 22–3
anti-personnel landmines (APLs),
  destruction programmes 94
anti-tank guided weapons (ATGWs)
  countries producing 34–5
  held by non-state armed groups
    32–3
  production and values 28–30, 31
  stockpiles 19–20
  types 18–20
anti-tank weapons, unguided rocket
  launchers 25–6
APLs *see* anti-personnel landmines
Argentina
  end-user certificates 128
  light weapons production 34
  surplus weapons 84, 85
Armed Forces Revolutionary Council
  (AFRC) (Sierra Leone), guided light
  weapons holdings 33
Armed Islamic Group (GIA) (Algeria),
  guided light weapons holdings 32
armed violence
  see also violence
  common factors 219–22
  data collection 216–17, 222, 237
  definition 246, 277
  dynamics 231
  firearms interventions 278–9
  global burden 218
  interventions 226–7, 235–6, 275–6,
    278–9, 295–8
    El Salvador 281, 288–95
    United States 280–8
  prevention 223, 227
  public health approach 211–12,
    223–8, 236–40
  regional distribution 218–19
  risk factors 262–3, 282
  school shootings 265–6
  as social phenomenon 236–7
  urban areas 221–2, 257, 291
Arms Transfer Profiling Indicator
  System (ATPIS) 129

Arms-free Municipalities Project (AFMP)
  (El Salvador) 292–5
'Army of the Pure': Lashkar-e-Tayyiba
  (LeT) (Pakistan), guided light
  weapons holdings 33
Asia-Pacific, firearm homicides and
  suicides 219
AT4 rocket launcher 25
ATGWs *see* anti-tank guided weapons
Australia
  civilian weapons, theft of 63, 65
  light weapons production 34
  theft
    of M-72 LAW rocket launchers
      49, 51, 52
    of civilian weapons 63, 65
    from gun shops 64
Austria
  end-user certification 164–5, 171–3
  light weapons production 34
automatic grenade launchers 24–5

B

Barrett M82 anti-materiel rifle 22
Basque Homeland and Freedom (ETA),
  guided light weapons holdings 33
Bazooka 25
behaviour problems, risk factors 254
Belarus
  light weapons production 34
  MANPADS, destruction programmes
    101
  surplus weapons, destruction
    programmes 79, 97
Belgium
  end-user certification 165, 171–3
  light weapons production 34
Biting the Bullet project 128, 142
Blue Lantern end-use monitoring
  programme (United States) 129, 137,
    170
Bolide High Velocity Missile 17
Bolivia
  MANPADS, destruction programmes
    101, 102
  surplus weapons 84
Bosnia and Herzegovina
  ammunition, stockpiles 91, 93
  diversion of arms from 122
  MANPADS, destruction programmes
    101
  surplus weapons
    destruction programmes 97

inted in the United States
Baker & Taylor Publisher Services